Building Websites with ExpressionEngine 1.6

A clear, concise, and practical guide to creating a professional ExpressionEngine website

Leonard Murphy

BIRMINGHAM - MUMBAI

Building Websites with ExpressionEngine 1.6

Copyright © 2008 Packt Publishing

All rights reserved. No part of this book may be reproduced, stored in a retrieval system, or transmitted in any form or by any means, without the prior written permission of the publisher, except in the case of brief quotations embedded in critical articles or reviews.

Every effort has been made in the preparation of this book to ensure the accuracy of the information presented. However, the information contained in this book is sold without warranty, either express or implied. Neither the author, Packt Publishing, nor its dealers or distributors will be held liable for any damages caused or alleged to be caused directly or indirectly by this book.

Packt Publishing has endeavored to provide trademark information about all the companies and products mentioned in this book by the appropriate use of capitals. However, Packt Publishing cannot guarantee the accuracy of this information.

First published: July 2008

Production Reference: 1220708

Published by Packt Publishing Ltd.
32 Lincoln Road
Olton
Birmingham, B27 6PA, UK.

ISBN 978-1-847193-79-7

www.packtpub.com

Cover Image by Phil Hodges (digitalhodges@hotmail.com)

Credits

Author
Leonard Murphy

Reviewer
Mark Bowen

Senior Acquisition Editor
Douglas Paterson

Development Editor
Swapna Verlekar

Technical Editor
Mithun Sehgal

Editorial Team Leader
Mithil Kulkarni

Project Manager
Abhijeet Deobhakta

Project Coordinator
Lata Basantani

Indexer
Rekha Nair

Proofreader
Angie Butcher

Production Coordinator
Nilesh Mohite
Shantanu Zagade

Cover Work
Shantanu Zagade

About the Author

Leonard Murphy has been building websites since 1997. He was one of the earliest adopters of ExpressionEngine when it was first released in 2004, and wrote a series of tutorials to help other new users see what ExpressionEngine had to offer.

Leonard started his career in the UK, graduating from UW Aberystwyth with a Software Engineering degree. In 2004, he moved to the United States, and is currently the Lead Application Engineer for Summit Credit Union (a non-profit financial institution headquartered in Madison, Wisconsin). He also provides consulting and technical support for small business websites.

> I would like to thank my wife, Megan, for her ongoing encouragement and support. I would like to acknowledge my friends who haven't seen me much over the last year: Gina, Isabelle and Jordan, Courtney, Riley and Rosella, and Tina and Eric. Finally, I would also like to thank the people I work with, most notably, Kathy, Sara, Erika, and Vicki.

About the Reviewer

Mark Bowen is a web developer, musician, graphic designer, electronics engineer, and helicopter pilot amongst holding many other talents, and is currently living in Birmingham in the United Kingdom. He is an avid Apple Macintosh user and has been so for well over 15 years now.

Mark studied Performing Arts in college and ended up getting a job at the college as a Music Technician. It was during this time that he gained his City & Guilds 224 in Electronics Servicing, so he is qualified to take a TV apart, put it back together again, leave bits out, and still charge for it!

Now working as a Senior Producer for the second largest independent commercial production house in the UK, Mark has made well over 30,000 adverts-/jingles-/music-based projects in the almost 8 years that he has been working there.

Mark has been developing with Adobe Flash, and was asked to review the Advanced PHP for Flash book by Friends Of Ed due to the work he did on a Flash-based chat application.

After Flash, Mark took up learning HTML/CSS, and now codes sites entirely by hand without the use of any WYSIWYG editors.

Nowadays Mark's preferred tool of choice for creating internet sites is the ExpressionEngine CMS platform as he states, "It is a designers dream come true" due to its very nature of keeping code and content completely separate from each other. Mark is an avid reader of the ExpressionEngine forums, and can usually be found there each day, answering questions wherever and whenever he can.

He is currently in the process of setting up an aviation-based photography website with his wife Sarah (who is also a helicopter pilot—Flight Instructor). It will host and sell the most professional images relating to aviation in the world.

This came about due to Mark being the sole designer for the largest military helicopter magazine in the world, and through his links with that, he now has access to the best aviation photographers in the business. Keep an eye out on the ExpressionEngine forums for when the site launches!

Table of Contents

Preface	**1**
Chapter 1: Introduction to ExpressionEngine	**7**
Why Use a Content Management System?	7
How Does ExpressionEngine Fit In?	8
What Can ExpressionEngine Do?	9
How Does ExpressionEngine Measure Up?	10
Who Is This Book Intended For?	10
Who Is This Book Not Intended For?	11
What Can You Expect From This Book?	11
Further Reading and Resources	12
Chapter 2: Getting Installed	**15**
What Do We Need to Get Started?	15
Download the ExpressionEngine Files	16
Upload the ExpressionEngine Files	17
Install ExpressionEngine	20
Logging into the Control Panel	25
Creating User-Friendly URLs	26
Hiding the index.php in ExpressionEngine URLs	27
Renaming index.php in ExpressionEngine URLs	29
Summary	32
Chapter 3: Start Posting	**33**
Toast for Sale!	33
Inside the Control Panel	34
Templates and URLs	36
Working with Multiple Templates	42
Creating Our First Entry	44
Viewing Our First Entry	51
Make Our Weblog Pretty Using CSS	56

Table of Contents

Creating and Linking to a Styling Template	56
Styling Colors and Fonts	59
Moving Our Elements Around	63
Exercises	**67**
Summary	**68**

Chapter 4: Creating an Easy to Maintain Website — 69

Creating a New Weblog	**70**
Creating Custom Fields	**71**
Creating Our Own Field Group for Our Weblog	72
Customizing the Fields of Our Field Group	73
Associating Our Fields with Our Weblog	79
Creating the First Draft of Our Home Page	**81**
Creating the Template for Our Conventional Website	**83**
Writng an About Us Page	**91**
Customizing Our URLs	**92**
Installing the Pages Module	92
Define Short URLs for Individual Weblog Entries	93
Define a 404 Page Not Found	**94**
Writing a Menu for Our Website	**97**
Exercises	**103**
Summary	**105**

Chapter 5: Create an Advanced Weblog — 107

Create a New Weblog	**107**
Customize Our Weblog Fields	**109**
Publish Our First Products	**113**
Create the Template for Our Product Showcase	**117**
Create Our Single-Entry Page	**123**
Allowing Comments on Our Weblog Entries	**125**
Preventing Comment Spam	126
Creating a Form Where Visitors Can Submit Comments	131
Moderating Comments in the Control Panel	135
Allowing Visitors to Preview Comments Before Submitting	136
Improving Our 404 Page Not Found Capabilities	**138**
Using Variables	**139**
Exercises	**144**
Summary	**144**

Chapter 6: Members — 145

Setting Up Links for Member Functions on Our Menu	**145**
Registering As a New Member	**149**
The Member Profile	**151**

The Member List	**156**
Global Member Preferences	**159**
Introduction to Member Groups	**162**
Configuring Our Member Groups	**164**
Configuring Options Outside of the Control Panel	165
Configuring Options within Our Control Panel	167
Create a Member	**170**
Log in As Editor Phil	**172**
Creating a Member-Only Section	**175**
Making Content Visible to Members Only	176
Making an Entire Template Accessible to Members Only	180
Changing Content Based on Member Group	182
The Stand-Alone Entry Form (SAEF)	**185**
Create the Stand-Alone Entry Form	185
Modify the CSS for Our Stand-Alone Entry Form	192
The Mailing List Module	**196**
Creating a Mailing List	197
Allow Members to Register for a Mailing List	199
Sending Emails	200
Exercises	**201**
Summary	**201**
Chapter 7: Creating a Calendar	**203**
Create an Events Calendar Weblog	**203**
Create the Weblog	204
Create Custom Fields for Our Calendar	205
Associate the Custom Field Group with the Calendar	207
Post Example Events to Our Calendar	207
Create the Calendar Template	**212**
Create a Blank Calendar Template	212
Create a Blank Calendar	213
Formatting the Calendar with CSS	218
Create the Calendar CSS Template	219
Add Styles to Our Calendar CSS	220
Create a Separate Template for Our Calendar Events	**227**
Displaying Events on Our Calendar	**230**
Styling the Events on Our Calendar	232
Displaying Upcoming Events Underneath Our Calendar	**236**
Going Further with Our Calendar	**238**
Handling Different Event Types	238
Displaying Fields Other Than the Title on Our Calendar	238

[iii]

Exercises	**241**
Summary	**241**
Chapter 8: Creating a Photo Gallery	**243**
Install the Photo Gallery Module	**244**
Setting Up Our Photo Gallery	**244**
Define the Basic Settings	245
Create Categories	249
Upload Our First Photos	**250**
View Our Photo Gallery	**252**
Changing the Design of Our Photo Gallery	**257**
Create the Single-Entry Page Layout	257
Create Our Template Outline	257
Create the Headings in Our Template	260
Display Our Photograph	261
Display Information About Our Photograph	263
Display Comments on Our Photograph	265
Create the Category Page Layout	269
Create the Main Index Page	276
Backup the Existing Index Template	276
Create the Main Page for Our Photo Gallery	278
Advanced Photo Gallery Features	**283**
Batch Uploads	283
Image Editing	285
Put a Watermark on Our Images	286
Custom Fields	288
Creating a Photo Gallery without the Photo Gallery Module	**291**
Exercises	**291**
Summary	**292**
Chapter 9: Other Modules and Functionality	**293**
ExpressionEngine Add-Ons	**294**
Finding and Managing Add-Ons	294
Modules	294
Plug-Ins	295
Extensions	296
The Discussion Forum	296
Setting up the Discussion Forum	296
What Does the Discussion Forum Do?	300
Customizing the Discussion Forum	301
Customizing a Discussion Forum for Our Toast Website	303
The Simple Commerce Module	305
Setting Up the Simple Commerce Module	305
Customizing Simple Commerce for Our Toast Website	307
Testing the Simple Commerce Module	310

The Wiki Module	310
Setting up the Wiki	311
How Does the Wiki Work?	313
Customizing the Wiki	315
More ExpressionEngine Features	**317**
Adding Search Functionality to Our Site	317
How to Add Search Box to Our Site	317
Customizing the Search Functionality	319
Using Status Groups in Our Weblogs	321
Create a Custom Status Group	322
Display a Queue of Entries That Have a Certain Status	323
Using Categories to Create Our Site Structure	325
Creating Our Category Groups	325
Displaying Our Categories with Our Entries	328
Creating Our Category Browsing Page	329
Display All Our Categories	330
Using Related Entries	331
Creating a Related Entry	332
Reverse Related Entries	334
Backups and Restores	**335**
To Backup an ExpressionEngine-Powered Site	335
To Restore an ExpressionEngine-Powered Site	338
Upgrading ExpressionEngine	**340**
Summary	**342**
Appendix A: Installing XAMPP	**343**
Installing XAMPP	**344**
Download XAMPP	344
Install XAMPP	345
Using XAMPP	**348**
Allowing .htaccess Files to Be Used	349
XAMPP in Action	349
Setting Up the ExpressionEngine Database	**350**
Appendix B: Solutions to Exercises	**353**
Chapter 3	**353**
Exercise 1	353
Exercise 2	354
Exercise 3	**356**
Chapter 4	**358**
Exercise 1	358
Exercise 2	359
Exercise 3	361
Exercise 4	361

Chapter 5 — 362
- Exercise 2 and 3 — 362
- Exercise 4 — 366
- Exercise 5 — 366

Chapter 6 — 367
- Exercise 1 — 367
- Exercise 2 — 367
- Exercise 3 — 368

Chapter 7 — 368
- Exercise 1 — 368
- Exercise 2 — 369
- Exercise 3 — 369

Chapter 8 — 372
- Exercise 1 — 372
- Exercise 2 — 373

Index — 375

Preface

ExpressionEngine is a content management system that is designed to make it easy to manage engaging, interactive websites for your visitors.

This book provides clear, concise, and practical guidance to take you from the basics of setting up ExpressionEngine to developing the skills you need to create feature-rich, professional ExpressionEngine websites. The book will walk you through the process of setting up a website with ExpressionEngine.

Starting with the installation itself, you will learn how to work inside the ExpressionEngine control panel, how to customize your site, and how to publish and manage content. You will also learn how to set up member-features such as member-only pages and mailing lists, and you will learn how to implement modules that really enhance your site, such as a photo gallery and an events calendar. Throughout the book, there are tips, hints, and best practice recommendations that will get your website working in no time.

What This Book Covers

Chapter 1 introduces you to ExpressionEngine—what it can do and how it compares. It describes who this book is aimed at and describes how this book will help you. Finally, it provides links to other resources that will help you on your ExpressionEngine journey.

In *Chapter 2*, you will learn how to install and configure ExpressionEngine, including removing or renaming the `index.php` file that appears in ExpressionEngine URLs and keeping your ExpressionEngine files secure. At the end of this chapter, ExpressionEngine will be up and running.

Preface

In *Chapter 3*, we take a short tour of the ExpressionEngine control panel and experiment with creating templates, before diving right into the first section of our example website—a News from the President weblog. By the end of the chapter, you will have a completely working weblog, and a great understanding of how you can use HTML and CSS in templates.

In *Chapter 4*, we really start building our site. Clear, step-by-step instructions guide you through creating an attractive multiple-page website of our own design by using only ExpressionEngine templates and weblog entries. We discuss everything you need to build a search-engine and visitor-friendly website, including 404 pages, customized URLs and a stylish menu. By the end of this chapter, adding a new page to our website will be as simple as typing in the text you want and choosing the URL you want it to appear on.

In *Chapter 5*, we take our knowledge of weblogs and templates one step further by building a product showcase. Visitors can browse the toast we have for sale, view detailed information on individual products, and leave feedback in the form of comments that other visitors can see. We'll talk about securing the comment entry system to avoid comment spam, and we talk about making your templates easier to manage by using variables.

In *Chapter 6*, we really dive deep into the member functionality of ExpressionEngine. We talk about creating member-only areas on our website, and creating cool mailing lists for our members to sign up for. We also walk through the process of creating new member groups, and we create a special member group with locked-down control panel access that can be used for people who want to update the website.

In *Chapter 7*, we apply our skills to creating an events calendar. At the end of the chapter, you will have a stylish calendar that you can add new events to at the click of a button. Although there is a lot of code required to generate a calendar and make it look pretty, we walk through it slowly, patiently explaining everything we're doing. So you not only have a calendar, but you have a comprehensive understanding of how it works, and you can make your own adjustments in confidence.

In *Chapter 8*, we take a thorough look at the Photo Gallery module. We cover everything from installing the Photo Gallery module to designing the photo gallery so it is an integral part of our website. We show you how easy it is to upload new photos, edit those photos, create thumbnails, add descriptions, and make them instantly available for the world to browse and comment upon.

By *Chapter 9*, you have the core-skills needed to tackle any project in ExpressionEngine. This final chapter takes you on a whirlwind tour of many advanced modules and functionality that ExpressionEngine has to offer and is packed with hints, tips, and recommendations. We discuss the discussion forum, create a wiki, integrate PayPal into our product showcase, and talk through status groups, categories, related entries.

We also cover how to safely back up your site, and how to upgrade ExpressionEngine to take advantage of the latest and greatest features.

Appendix A talks you through installing XAMPP, which puts PHP, MySQL, and Apache on your own computer so that you can experiment and test ExpressionEngine without a web server.

Appendix B gives you the solutions to exercises that are found throughout the book.

What You Need for This Book

No prior knowledge of Expression Engine is expected, and the book does not require any detailed knowledge of programming or web development. Any IT-confident individual will be able to use the book to produce an impressive website. However, the knowledge of HTML and the basic idea of what CSS is and how it relates to HTML is required.

Who is This Book For

This book is ideal for new users of ExpressionEngine who have some HTML experience. The book is targeted at people who are responsible for creating and managing a site with ExpressionEngine. It is suitable for web developers, designers, webmasters, content editors, and marketing professionals who want to develop a fully featured web presence in a simple and straightforward process.

Conventions

In this book, you will find a number of styles of text that distinguish between different kinds of information. Here are some examples of these styles, and an explanation of their meaning.

Code words in text are shown as follows: "Your hosting server must have `mod_rewrite` enabled (see Appendix A for doing this in XAMPP).".

Preface

A block of code will be set as follows:

```
#content h3{
  color: #F0E68C;
  font-family: Arial, Helvetica, sans-serif;
  font-weight: bold;
     margin-bottom: 0px;
}
```

When we wish to draw your attention to a particular part of a code block, the relevant lines or items will be made bold:

```
#content h3{
  color: #F0E68C;
  font-family: Arial, Helvetica, sans-serif;
  font-weight: bold;
     margin-bottom: 0px;
}
```

New terms and **important words** are introduced in a bold-type font. Words that you see on the screen, in menus or dialog boxes for example, appear in our text like this: "Go to the **Templates** tab, select the **news** template group, and click **New Template** to create a new template called **post_entry**. Create an empty template and click **Submit**.".

 Warnings or important notes appear in a box like this.

Reader Feedback

Feedback from our readers is always welcome. Let us know what you think about this book, what you liked or may have disliked. Reader feedback is important for us to develop titles that you really get the most out of.

To send us general feedback, simply drop an email to feedback@packtpub.com, making sure to mention the book title in the subject of your message.

If there is a book that you need and would like to see us publish, please send us a note in the **SUGGEST A TITLE** form on www.packtpub.com or email to suggest@packtpub.com.

If there is a topic that you have expertise in and you are interested in either writing or contributing to a book, see our author guide on www.packtpub.com/authors.

Customer Support

Now that you are the proud owner of a Packt book, we have a number of things to help you to get the most from your purchase.

Downloading the Example Code and Images for the Book

Visit http://www.packtpub.com/files/code/3797_Code.zip to directly download the example code. You can download the images by visiting http://www.packtpub.com/files/code/3797_Graphics.zip.

The downloadable files contain instructions on how to use them.

Errata

Although we have taken every care to ensure the accuracy of our contents, mistakes do happen. If you find a mistake in one of our books—maybe a mistake in text or code—we would be grateful if you would report this to us. By doing this you can save other readers from frustration, and help to improve subsequent versions of this book. If you find any errata, report them by visiting http://www.packtpub.com/support, selecting your book, clicking on the **let us know** link, and entering the details of your errata. Once your errata are verified, your submission will be accepted and the errata added to the list of existing errata. The existing errata can be viewed by selecting your title from http://www.packtpub.com/support.

Piracy

Piracy of copyright material on the Internet is an ongoing problem across all media. At Packt, we take the protection of our copyright and licenses very seriously. If you come across any illegal copies of our works in any form on the Internet, please provide the location address or the website name immediately, so we can pursue a remedy.

Please contact us at copyright@packtpub.com with a link to the suspected pirated material.

We appreciate your help in protecting our authors, and our ability to bring you valuable content.

Questions

You can contact us at questions@packtpub.com if you are having a problem with some aspect of the book, and we will do our best to address it.

1
Introduction to ExpressionEngine

ExpressionEngine is a content management system that is designed to manage websites. This chapter will briefly review what ExpressionEngine is and what it can do for you.

Why Use a Content Management System?

For a small website, using HTML files is perfectly feasible. To update the website, you simply update the files. It's easy if you know what you are doing.

In many cases, the person who created the website is not the one who makes updates to the site. With the content and the HTML code for the website intermingled in the same file, it is difficult to update the content without understanding the code. The harder it is to update, the less the site is updated.

A good content management system takes this problem and neatly solves it. It makes it easier to update the website without any knowledge of HTML. The person who creates the website does not have to be the person who updates it. And because it is easier to update, the site changes more frequently, visitors come back more frequently, and the site becomes popular.

A content management system also turns your website from a one-way flow of information (you write the content, the visitors read it) to a more conversational website. Not only are visitors reading the content you wrote, but they can add their own comments into the mix. Your site becomes dynamic, changing even when you aren't doing anything.

To illustrate the difference between a static and a dynamic website, consider a newspaper website. If the site had the same articles every day, you would stop visiting. Why would you read an article you've already read? To keep visitors coming back, it pays to keep the content of your website dynamic. If there is always something new to read, there is more incentive for your visitors to keep coming back.

How Does ExpressionEngine Fit In?

ExpressionEngine makes it easy to separate out the HTML code from the content of your website. Once the design of your website is built, you can add new content to the website simply by filling in a web form. It's easy enough that anyone can learn to do it.

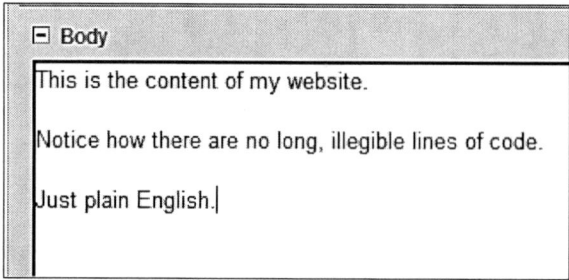

Your HTML code exists in **templates**. However, instead of having paragraphs of content inside these templates like you would in most HTML files, your content is stored elsewhere (in a database) and retrieved dynamically.

With ExpressionEngine, it is possible to have no HTML tags in the content and no content in the templates—a true separation of content and code.

What Can ExpressionEngine Do?

Although ExpressionEngine makes it easy for the HTML-illiterate to update a website, that alone would not be worth the $99.95+ price tag.

ExpressionEngine not only allows us to separate out the code, but makes it easy to implement very advanced features, which are more often associated with large social-networking websites, like Facebook or MySpace. Visitors can leave comments, or join your site as fully-fledged members. You can set up RSS feeds, a photo gallery, a mailing list, a calendar, a wiki, or a discussion forum, and you can sell items through PayPal.

	Entry Title	Comments	Date	Filename	Status	
	Toast in the Mountains	(0) View	03/18/08 01:16 pm	winter1.jpg	Open	☐
	Stop Sign	(0) View	02/26/08 08:52 am	winter3.jpg	Open	☐
	Winter Field	(0) View	02/24/08 05:17 pm	winter2.jpg	Open	☐
	Snowman	(0) View	02/06/07 08:59 am	winter4.jpg	Open	☐

ExpressionEngine also comes packed with industry-leading features to keep your website secure and spam-free amid all the activity. You can force people to register as members before they can submit comments to your site; you can personally review every member application before approving; or you can allow non-members to submit data if they type in a **captcha** correctly. (A captcha is an image of letters that a person must correctly type in order to submit data; it ensures that it is not an automated **spambot** that is submitting the comment or member application.)

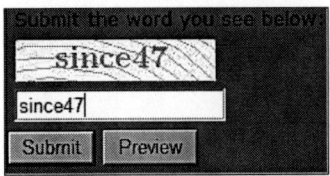

Further, you can prevent people from submitting the same comment twice, restrict how much data a person can request from your website in a certain timeframe (to prevent denial of service attacks), blacklist certain words so that they cannot be used in comments, and blacklist URLs or IP addresses of spammers that you don't want accessing your site.

How Does ExpressionEngine Measure Up?

ExpressionEngine is not open-source. So why would you choose to pay for ExpressionEngine when you could use a free, open-source alternative?

It depends on your goals. ExpressionEngine is not open-source, but the code is certainly available if you want to look at how it works. While the core code is controlled centrally by **EllisLab**, the community can and does contribute their own set of modules, plug-ins, and other add-ons.

ExpressionEngine is not free, but is very reasonably priced for the features (especially for a non-profit or non-commercial license). The fee, in part, goes to support future development as well as software support via the forums. The response times in the support forums are very good, and for a business, it's reassuring to know that there is paid support staff—you are not just relying on a random member of the community to answer your question (though often, if a member of the community can answer your question first, they will).

ExpressionEngine is not for everyone. If you have never developed a website before and are less than familiar with HTML, you will find it more difficult to master ExpressionEngine There are very few pre-built templates for ExpressionEngine, and those that do exist will still require knowledge of HTML in order to customize.

To get the most out of ExpressionEngine, a background in developing websites is a huge advantage. If you know some HTML and CSS, ExpressionEngine is an extremely flexible tool allowing you to integrate ExpressionEngine tags into your own HTML/CSS designs. The end result is a site that looks entirely like something you have created, but has all the features of ExpressionEngine built right in. For this reason, ExpressionEngine is very popular with website designers who already work with HTML and CSS and want to continue to do so.

Who is This Book Intended For?

If any of the following sound familiar, this book is for you:

- You've used HTML to build websites before, and you are comfortable editing HTML by hand.
- You have at least a basic idea of what CSS is and how it relates to HTML. CSS is a large, complex subject, and though this book tries to explain the CSS it uses, this is not an introductory guide to CSS.

- You have never used ExpressionEngine or another content management system before. This book is a tutorial book, designed for new users of ExpressionEngine, and will walk you through step-by-step for everything you need to do.
- You want to build an interactive, feature-packed website. This book is geared towards using ExpressionEngine on a website (not as a blogging tool).
- You want to get started using ExpressionEngine as fast as possible, and you don't have time for lots of reading. This book takes a very hands-on approach, and will get you using ExpressionEngine as fast as possible.

Who is This Book Not Intended For?

This book is not intended for use in the following situations. Although it may have some uses in the following situations, it is not written with these goals in mind:

- You have never developed a HTML web page before, but you want your own blog. (A blogging service might be more appropriate.)
- You want to create a full-featured blog, including trackbacks, RSS feeds, server pinging, emoticons, and moblogs. While ExpressionEngine supports such features, this book focuses more on creating a website rather than a traditional blog.
- You want to see advanced CSS and HTML, with AJAX and all sorts of other fancy technology. The HTML and CSS in this book is designed to be as simple as possible without being plain.
- You have extensive experience in ExpressionEngine, but want to learn advanced tips and tricks. This book is intended as an introduction for new users to ExpressionEngine. That said, experienced users may find new ideas, especially in the later chapters of this book.
- You want a definitive guide to ExpressionEngine. As a printed book, it is almost a given that ExpressionEngine will have changed since this book was written. This book is meant more as a springboard into your own exploration of what ExpressionEngine can do, and does not attempt to cover every available feature.

What Can You Expect From This Book?

Learning ExpressionEngine is a hands-on activity. In the forums on the ExpressionEngine website, you will see lots of references to the *lightbulb moment*. This is the moment when it dawns on you just how ExpressionEngine works, opening up your imagination to all the possibilities that ExpressionEngine has to offer.

Introduction to ExpressionEngine

The fastest (and the only) way to your *lightbulb moment* is by using ExpressionEngine. Working through these tutorials on your own installation, particularly the first few chapters, will give you a practical understanding of the terminology ExpressionEngine uses, and will help to bring you to your own *lightbulb moment*.

Each chapter has step-by-step instructions, not a mouse-click is missed. This makes it very easy to follow along and understand everything that we're doing and why we're doing it.

However, as a result, each chapter is not comprehensive—it does not tell you all the possibilities that could be. There are always multiple ways to the same solution, and often the best way will vary depending on the individual site. One template and template group structure might work great for a website that sells toast, but not so well on a political analysis website.

The aim of each chapter is to equip you with the basic training you need to venture out into the documentation or the forums, and feel confident asking for help and experimenting with different ideas.

Throughout this book, we use the example of building a website that sells toast online. The website is fairly basic; it is a small business which sells sliced bread that has been browned by exposure to dry heat. Although a ridiculous premise, it serves the purpose of demonstrating the various features of ExpressionEngine.

Further Reading and Resources

While reading this book, you may want further information on a particular feature. Some of the most important resources will be:

- `http://www.expressionengine.com/docs/` — the ExpressionEngine documentation is very comprehensive, and it should be your first port of call when you want to learn more about a feature or tag.

> The ExpressionEngine documentation is always for the latest version. If there is any discrepancy between what you are seeing and what the documentation says, be sure that you are running the latest version of ExpressionEngine.

- `http://expressionengine.com/forums` — if you have a question or need support on any aspect of ExpressionEngine, this is the place to visit. Staffed by paid support representatives of EllisLab, as well as thousands of active members of the ExpressionEngine community, the support provided in these forums is phenomenal.

> To get the best results from the ExpressionEngine forums, always search the forums first in case your question has already been answered. When posting a question, include as much detail as possible regarding what you are trying to achieve — include your template code and/or a link to your website if possible.

- `http://expressionengine.com/showcase/` — the ExpressionEngine showcase shows you the huge variety of sites that have been built using ExpressionEngine, and is a great place to get inspired.
- `http://expressionengine.com/wiki/Special:Categories` — the ExpressionEngine wiki allows ExpressionEngine users to swap tips and tricks outside of the forums.
- `http://www.boyink.com/splaat/weblog/category/building-an-expressionengine-site/` — Michael Boyink has produced a very comprehensive set of online tutorials for building a business website in ExpressionEngine (also available in a printed book) as well as building a church website.
- `http://www.solspace.com/` — SolSpace is one of the biggest third-party developers of ExpressionEngine modules and plug-ins.

Last but not the least, you can download the code and images required to follow along in this book from `http://www.packtpub.com/files/code/3797_Code.zip` and `http://www.packtpub.com/files/code/3797_Graphics.zip` respectively, and you can view working examples of the code used in this book at `http://www.leonardmurphy.com/book/`.

Let's get started!

2
Getting Installed

The first step is to get ExpressionEngine installed. In this chapter, we will walk through the installation process in a local test environment. However, this chapter can also be used when installing directly onto a live web hosting server.

Following completion of this chapter, we will be able to:

- Install ExpressionEngine
    - Download the files
    - Copy the files to the server
    - Go through the installation utility
- Mask the true location of the ExpressionEngine files by changing where we log into the control panel
- Use `.htaccess` to keep our ExpressionEngine URLs user-friendly (optional)

Throughout this chapter, you will also want to refer to the official installation guide at `http://expressionengine.com/docs/installation/installation.html`. If you encounter any difficulties during installation, seek help at `http://expressionengine.com/forums/` — there is a dedicated forum for installation problems.

What Do We Need to Get Started?

ExpressionEngine has certain minimum requirements that can be found at `http://expressionengine.com/docs/requirements.html`. These include:

- PHP version **4.1** or newer
- MySQL version **3.23.32** or newer (not running in strict mode)
- **10Mb** of free space on your server
- **2Mb** of free space in your database (more will be needed as your site grows)

Getting Installed

If you have not yet purchased ExpressionEngine and are unsure as to whether your hosting provider meets these requirements, there is a **Server Wizard** available at the previous URL that can be uploaded to a host server to verify that ExpressionEngine will work.

Although ExpressionEngine can run on either Windows IIS or Apache, this book will assume the use of Apache. In Appendix A, we walk through how to set up a test Apache and MySQL environment on your computer with XAMPP (or MAMP for Mac users if preferred), including the setup of the MySQL database that ExpressionEngine will use and the enabling of `mod_rewrite`. This allows us to explore the use of ExpressionEngine without having to worry about the nuances between different hosting servers.

[ Installing ExpressionEngine directly to a hosting server is same as installing it in XAMPP or MAMP.]

At this stage, we need to know the following information about the hosting server:

- The MySQL database name
- The MySQL server address
- The MySQL username and password

If you are using XAMPP, this information is established in Appendix A. Otherwise, this information would normally have been provided when you signed up for a hosting service. Contact the support department of your hosting provider if you are unsure.

For the optional section on creating user-friendly URLs, there are additional requirements:

- Your hosting server must run Apache.
- Your hosting server must have `mod_rewrite` enabled (see Appendix A for doing this in XAMPP).

If this is not the case for your server, you can skip this section—ExpressionEngine will still work.

Download the ExpressionEngine Files

The first step in installing ExpressionEngine is to place the ExpressionEngine files on our server. If installing to a web server where an existing website is running, it is recommended to backup the existing website before proceeding.

Chapter 2

1. Once purchased, ExpressionEngine is available as a ZIP file download from the **My Downloads** section of the `www.expressionengine.com` website. Download this ZIP file and then unzip the files.

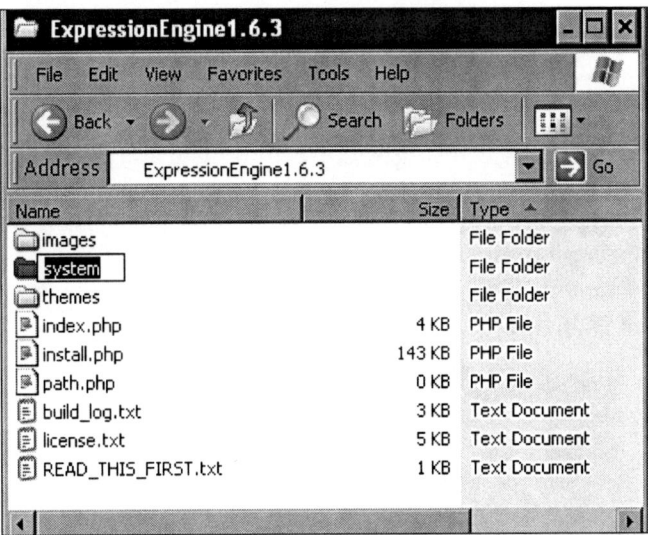

2. Inside the extracted directory is a subdirectory called `system`. As the name suggests, this directory contains the important files needed to run ExpressionEngine. It is therefore strongly recommended to rename this directory to something that is known only to you and is not easily guessed. This will protect our files from being accessed by unauthorized individuals.

 Throughout this book, this directory will still be referred to as `system`. Whenever there is a reference to the word `system`, substitute whatever you have chosen in this step.

Upload the ExpressionEngine Files

We now want to copy all the ExpressionEngine files to our server. The directories and files we want to copy are:

- `images\`
- `system\`
- `themes\`
- `index.php`
- `install.php`
- `path.php`

[17]

Getting Installed

This does not include the following directory and file, which do not need to be uploaded when installing for the first time:

- `system\updates\`
- `system\update.php`

All these files are found in the extracted **ExpressionEnginex.x.x** directory, where **x.x.x** represents the version of ExpressionEngine being installed (e.g. **1.6.4**).

1. If using XAMPP, we can simply copy-and-paste all the files in the extracted ExpressionEnginex.x.x directory to `C:\xampp\htdocs\` (do not copy the ExpressionEnginex.x.x directory itself). If you are using MAMP on a Macintosh, copy-and-paste to `/Applications/MAMP/htdocs/`. If you are using an actual website, upload these files directly to a web hosting server via an FTP program.

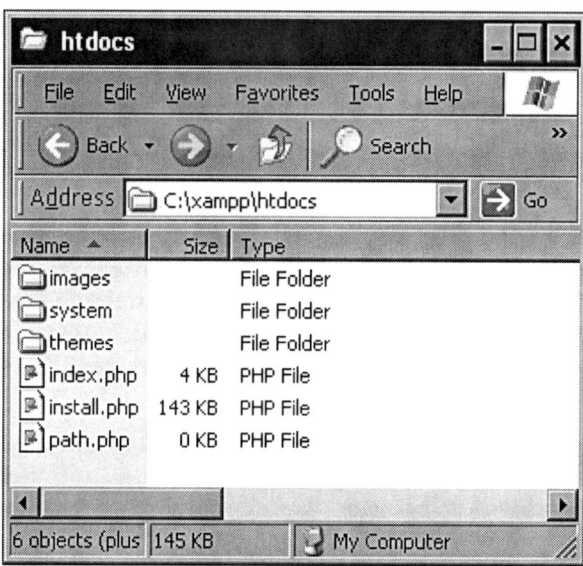

2. If the system\update.php file or the system\updates\ directory has been uploaded, delete them now. (These are for when we need to update ExpressionEngine to the latest release, and pose a slight security risk if left on the server). The system directory should look like the following screenshot:

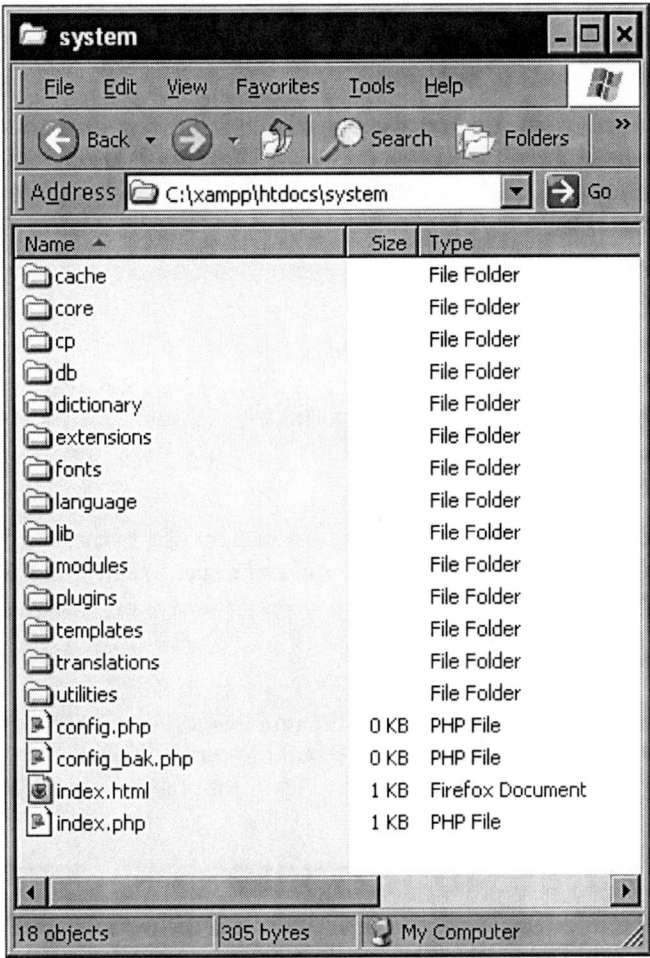

3. Next, we need to change the permissions of certain files.

 There is no need to change any file permissions when using ExpressionEngine with XAMPP or MAMP on a local computer. These steps only apply when installing directly to a web hosting server.

Getting Installed

4. In most FTP clients, right-click on the file to change the permissions. The following files must be set to `666` on a UNIX server, or set as `writeable` on a Windows server. `666` means that the owner, group, and the public can read and write to these files.

    ```
    path.php
    system\config.php
    system\config_bak.php
    ```

    We also need to set the permissions on the following directories to `777` on a UNIX server, or set as `writeable` on a Windows server. `777` means that the owner, group, and the public can read, write, and execute the files in these directories.

    ```
    images\avatars\uploads\
    images\captchas\
    images\member_photos\
    images\pm_attachments\
    images\signature_attachments\
    images\uploads\
    system\cache\
    ```

5. The ExpressionEngine website offers a variety of site themes that can also be downloaded and installed. We will not make use of these themes in this book but they are available at `http://expressionengine.com/templates/themes/category/site_themes/`.

[If you are interested in using a different theme, you may want to upload the files to your site before you install ExpressionEngine.]

Install ExpressionEngine

Now that the ExpressionEngine files are in place and the permissions have been set, we are ready to install ExpressionEngine. This is done entirely in the web browser.

1. First, navigate to the `install.php` file (`http://localhost/install.php` or `http://www.example.com/install.php`) and click on Click here to begin!.

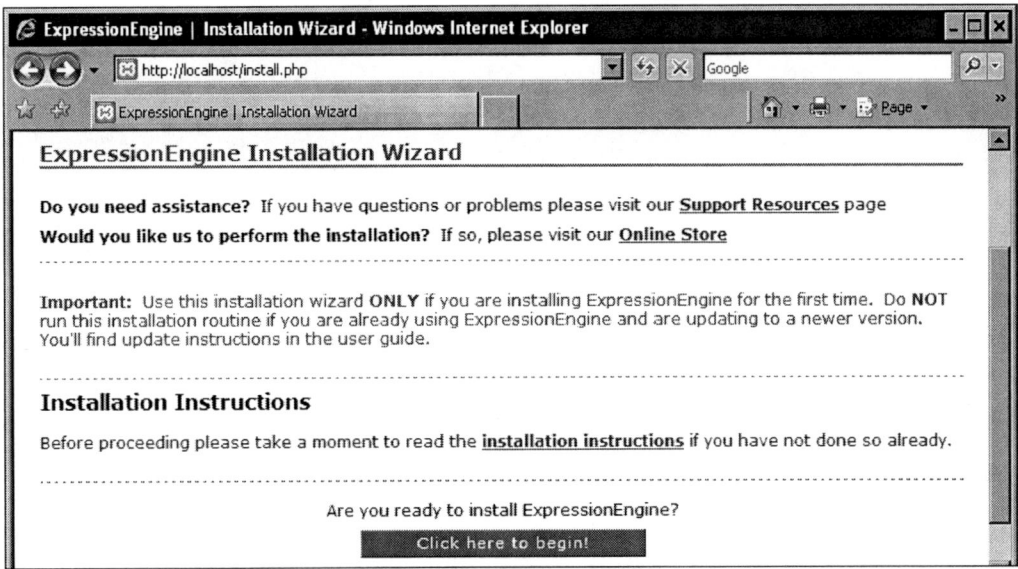

2. On the next page, we will have to agree with the **license Terms and Conditions**, then click **Submit**.

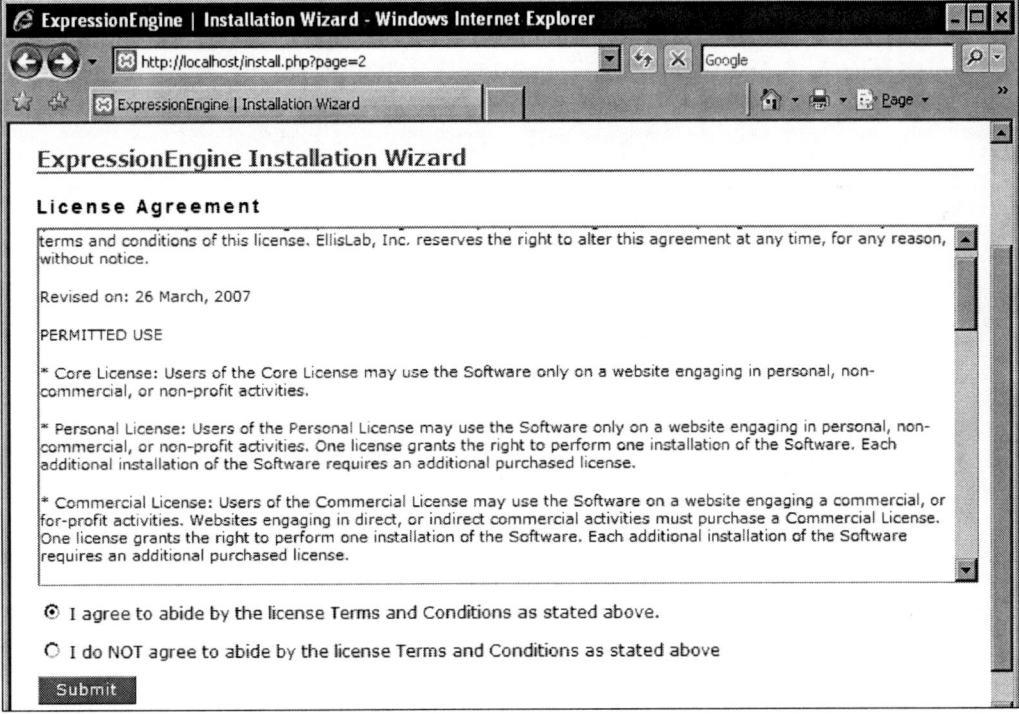

Getting Installed

3. When we downloaded our ExpressionEngine files, we renamed our `system` directory. Type in what you renamed this directory to, so that ExpressionEngine can find the installation files. Then click **Submit**.

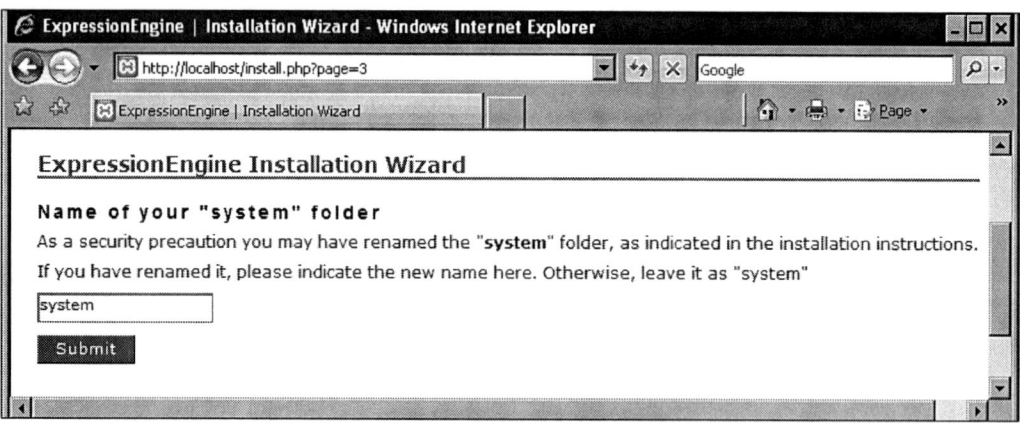

4. We will now be prompted for various settings.
5. The **Server Settings** will prefill many of the fields correctly. The index page of the site is `index.php`. The URL of the site is the domain (`http://localhost/` or `http://www.example.com/`). If you installed in a subdirectory, the URL will include the subdirectory. Enter your email address as the webmaster. If you are on a Windows server, select **Windows** as the **type of server**. If using XAMPP, MAMP or any other Apache server, choose **Unix**. If in doubt, choose **Unix** (more common).

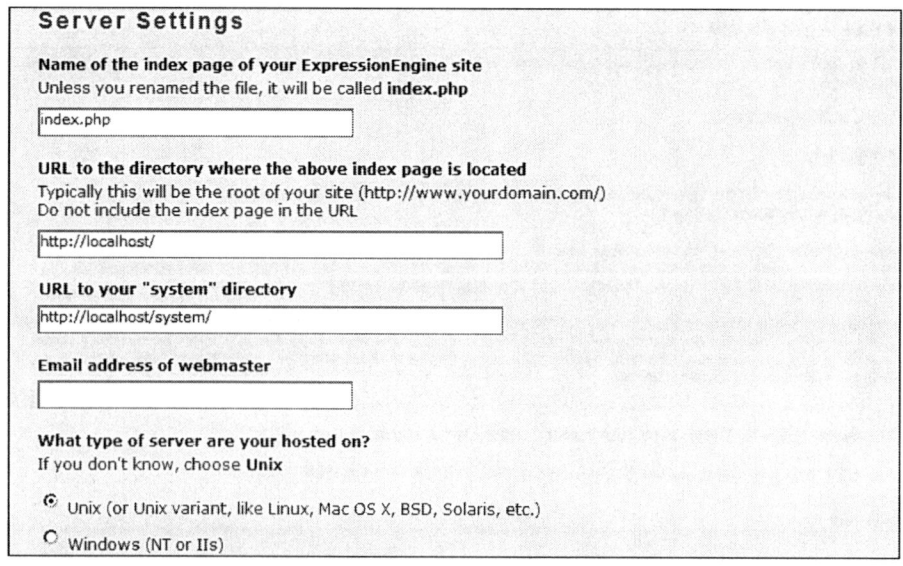

[22]

6. In Appendix A we established the MySQL **Database Settings** for our test environment, which were **localhost** for the **MySQL Server Address**, **eeuser** for the **MySQL Username**, and **ee** for the **MySQL Database Name**. Your hosting provider would have provided the settings for your website. Enter the server address (usually an IP address or `localhost`), username, password, and database name that they provided. You can leave the **Database Prefix** as **exp**, and the **database connection** as **non-persistent**.

```
Database Settings

MySQL Server Address
Usually you will use 'localhost', but your hosting provider may require something else
[ localhost ]

MySQL Username
The username you use to access your MySQL database
[ eeuser ]

MySQL Password
The password you use to access your MySQL database
[ password ]

MySQL Database Name
The name of the database where you want ExpressionEngine installed.
Note: The installation wizard will not create the database for you so you must specify the name of a
database that exists.
[ ee ]

Database Prefix
Use exp unless you need to use a different prefix
[ exp ]

What type of database connection do you prefer?
A non-persistent connection is recommended.

(•) Non-persistent
( ) Persistent
```

7. The **Encryption Settings** can be left as SHA-1, as SHA-1 is the successor to MD5 and is more secure.

8. Choose the username, password, email address, screen name, and site name to **Create your Admin Account** in ExpressionEngine. These can be anything, but *do not* forget the username or password.

9. Choose the appropriate time zone in the **Localization Settings**, and if you downloaded additional themes, you can also **Choose your default template design**.

Getting Installed

10. When ready to proceed, click on **Click Here to Install ExpressionEngine**. A success page with two links should then load—one link will go to the control panel and the other to the ExpressionEngine home page.

11. Follow the link to the ExpressionEngine home page (http://localhost/index.php or www.example.com/index.php) to verify that the main page is a working example website. It should look similar to the following screenshot (though you may have chosen a different theme).

12. Finally, delete the `install.php` file from the root of your website using an FTP program. In most FTP clients, you can right-click on the file and select **Delete**. If you are using XAMPP or MAMP, the file will be located in `C:\xampp\htdocs\install.php` or `/Applications/MAMP/htdocs/install.php` respectively.

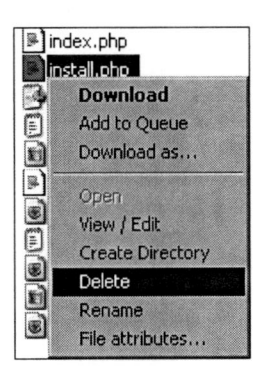

Logging into the Control Panel

We have already taken a step to mask the location of our installation files. This was done by renaming the system directory. Taking this one step further, we can change where we log into the control panel, so that we do not reveal our installation directory when we give others access to the control panel.

1. Copy (do not move) the file `system\utilities\admin.php` to the root of the ExpressionEngine website, where the `path.php` file is.

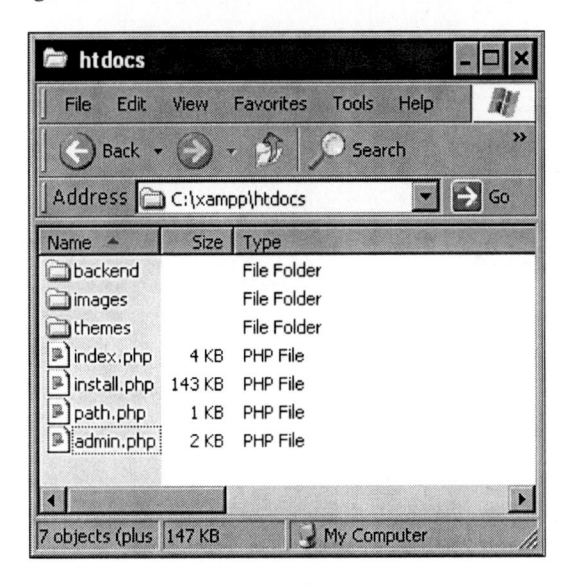

2. Now try logging into the control panel by pointing a browser at `http://localhost/admin.php` or `http://www.example.com/admin.php` and using the username and password chosen during installation.

Creating User-Friendly URLs

Every ExpressionEngine page includes the rather ugly `index.php` in the address, such as `http://localhost/index.php/site/about/` or `http://www.example.com/index.php/site/about/`.

The `http://localhost/index.php` returns the same page as `http://localhost/`, so many people prefer to rename or suppress the `index.php` altogether. It is better to do this before we start developing a site than when we already have links incorporating the `index.php`.

Removing the `index.php` entirely is not an officially supported technique. Not all hosting providers support the use of `.htaccess`, and different servers can require slightly different commands.

Although many people do choose to remove `index.php`, many others prefer to rename it rather than remove it, using a word that fits in with the overall theme of the site. Renaming `index.php` is officially supported and can look just as seamless to your visitors, though to remove the extension still requires the use of `.htaccess`.

Neither removing nor renaming `index.php` is required for ExpressionEngine to function. However, if you choose to do neither, bear in mind that this book does assume that the `index.php` has been removed.

Hiding the index.php in ExpressionEngine URLs

If your hosting provider uses Apache and the server recognizes .htaccess files (that is, has mod_rewrite enabled), we can do this by creating a .htaccess file. In Appendix A we demonstrated how to enable mod_rewrite for our local test environment.

> If following these instructions does not work for your site, there is much more information including alternative methods at http://expressionengine.com/wiki/Remove_index.php_From_URLs/.

1. Open Notepad or any other plain text editor and save the blank file as .htaccess (there are no letters before the period but the period is important; htaccess is the extension).

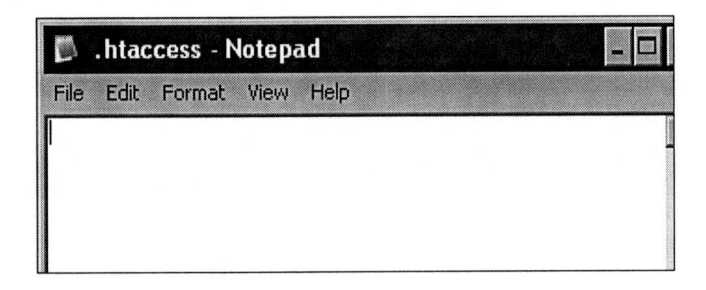

2. In this file, type the following three lines:

   ```
   RewriteEngine on
   RewriteCond $1 !^(images|system|themes|index\.php|admin\.php) [NC]
   RewriteRule ^(.*)$ /index.php/$1 [L]
   ```

> During installation, we renamed the system directory to a different name, so replace system with that name instead.

This essentially says to parse all files as if the index.php file is there, except for the files and directories listed between the brackets in the second line. If there are files or directories beyond those listed, also add them to the list in the second line, each separated with a | character. The path.php does not need to be listed here as it is never accessed directly via a web browser.

This is called the exclude method because we are excluding those files not to be treated as ExpressionEngine files.

Getting Installed

3. Save this file to `C:\xampp\htdocs\.htaccess` if using XAMPP, `/Applications/MAMP/htdocs/` if using MAMP on the Macintosh, or upload `.htaccess` to the root directory of the ExpressionEngine website.

> If using IIS on a Windows Server, the same effect may be achievable by renaming `.htaccess` to `httpd.conf`. The function `ISAPI_Rewrite` must be enabled on the server.

4. Finally, log into the control panel (`http://localhost/admin.php` or `http://www.example.com/admin.php`) and select **Admin | System Preferences | General Configuration**. Now, change the **Name of your site's index page** field from `index.php` to nothing.

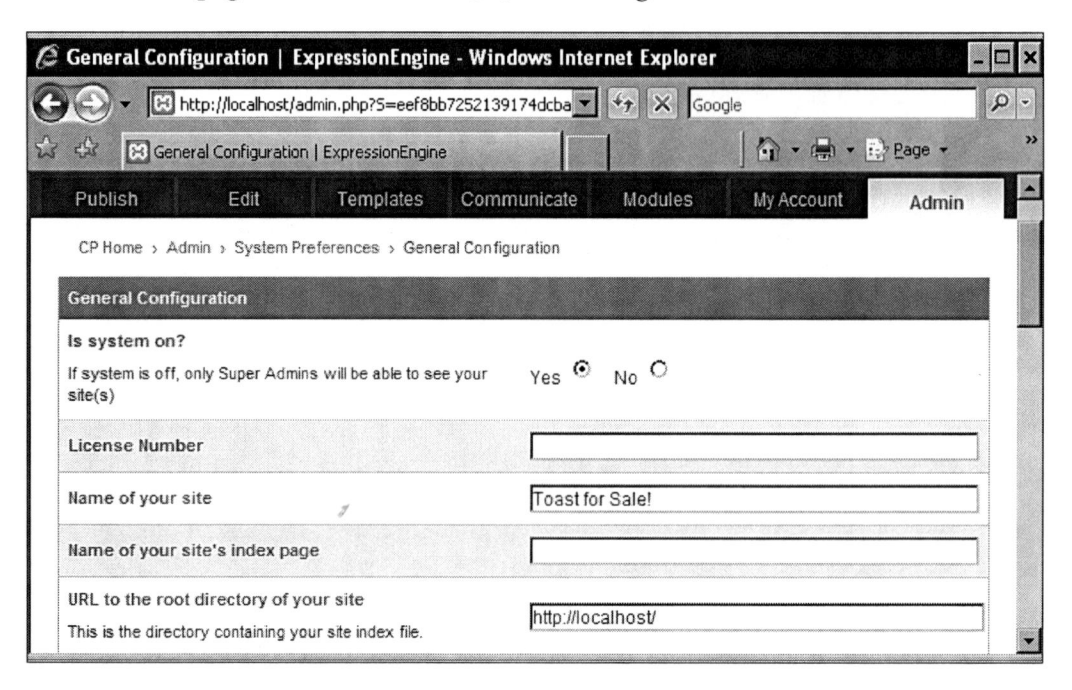

5. Open `http://localhost/site/about/` or `http://www.example.com/site/about/`. If it looks like the following screenshot, the changes were successful. If the changes were not successful, your hosting provider may not support the commands we are using in the `.htaccess` file. In this case, change the **Name of your site's index page** back to `index.php` and delete the `.htaccess` file from your server in order for ExpressionEngine to keep working.

> If you are unable to remove the `index.php` from your URLs, it is also possible to rename it—see the next setion.

Renaming index.php in ExpressionEngine URLs

If you have successfully removed the `index.php` from ExpressionEngine URLs using the previous technique, then you can skip this section.

Whether due to technical limitations or personal preference, renaming the `index.php` is also popular. The easiest way to do it requires keeping the `.php` extension:

1. In the root folder of your server, or in `C:\xampp\htdocs` or `/Applications/MAMP/htdocs/`, rename the file `index.php` to any other name that ends in `.php` (for example, `toast.php`).

Getting Installed

2. Next, log into the control panel (`http://localhost/admin.php` or `http://www.example.com/admin.php`) and select **Admin | System Preferences | General Configuration**. Now, change the **Name of your site's index page** field from `index.php` to the new name. This will ensure that any ExpressionEngine generated links include the new name.

General Configuration	
Is system on? If system is off, only Super Admins will be able to see your site(s)	Yes ⊙ No ○
License Number	
Name of your site	Toast for Sale!
Name of your site's index page	welcome.php
URL to the root directory of your site This is the directory containing your site index file.	http://localhost/

If you wish to remove the `.php` extension entirely, your server must use Apache and have `mod_rewrite` enabled (that is, recognize `.htaccess` files). In Appendix A we demonstrated how to enable `mod_rewrite` for our local test environment.

> If following these instructions does not work for your site, there is more information at `http://expressionengine.com/docs/installation/renaming_index.html`.

3. Follow the previous two steps to rename the `index.php` file to a name without an extension (for example, `welcome`), and set the ExpressionEngine control panel accordingly.

4. Open Notepad or any other plain text editor and save the blank file as `.htaccess` (there are no letters before the period but the period is important; `htaccess` is the extension).

Chapter 2

5. In this file, type the following to parse the files named `welcome` (or whatever you choose) as a PHP file, even though it does not have a PHP extension.

   ```
   DirectoryIndex welcome index.php

   <Files welcome>
   ForceType application/x-httpd-php
   </Files>
   ```

6. Save this file to `C:\xampp\htdocs\.htaccess` or `/Applications/MAMP/htdocs/.htaccess`, or upload `.htaccess` to the root directory of the ExpressionEngine website.

7. Open `http://localhost/welcome/site/about/` or `http://www.example.com/welcome/site/about/`. If you get the same style webpage we received after our initial installation, the changes were successful. If the changes were not successful, you want to make one of the following two changes to your `.htaccess` code:

   ```
   <Files welcome>
   AcceptPathInfo on
   SetOutputFilter PHP
   SetInputFilter PHP
   </Files>
   Or
   <Files welcome>
   SetHandler application/x-httpd-php
   </Files>
   ```

8. If neither of those alternatives works, your hosting provider may not support the commands we are using in the `.htaccess` file. In this case, rename the file on your server so that it once again has a `.php` extension, change the **Name of your site's index page** back to reflect the same name, and delete the `.htaccess` file from your server in order for ExpressionEngine to keep working.

> If you do rename the `index.php` file, bear in mind that this book assumes the `index.php` file has been removed entirely.

[31]

Summary

By now, we have:

- Downloaded ExpressionEngine and unzipped the files
- Uploaded the files to our server
- Run through the installation process in our browser
- Seen the default ExpressionEngine site
- Changed where we log into the control panel
- Logged into the control panel successfully
- Used a `.htaccess` file to remove or rename the `index.php` that otherwise is part of every ExpressionEngine URL

In the next chapter, we will start using ExpressionEngine to create the first pages of a brand new website.

3
Start Posting

By now, we should have ExpressionEngine installed, and we are ready to start creating our website. In this chapter, we are going to start from scratch and use ExpressionEngine to create a single web page that is easy for anyone to update. Following completion of this chapter, we will be able to:

- Create a simple ExpressionEngine template that we can publish to the world
- Create a simple ExpressionEngine weblog that we can use to keep our website content fresh
- Integrate some basic CSS into our ExpressionEngine templates

Toast for Sale!

To demonstrate the power of ExpressionEngine, we are going to use a fictitious business as an example throughout this book, with each chapter building on the next. Our website is in the business of selling toast (heated bread with melted butter) online.

With this example, we will be able to explore many of the nuances of building a complete website with ExpressionEngine. Though unlikely that we would really want to sell toast over the internet, the concepts of our example should be transferable to any website.

In this chapter, we want to introduce the world to our business, so we are going to create a 'News from the President' webpage. This will allow the President of our company to communicate to customers and investors the latest goings-on in his business.

Start Posting

Inside the Control Panel

When you first log into the control panel, there are lots of options. Let us take a quick tour of the control panel.

First, we will need to log into ExpressionEngine. If you are using XAMPP to follow along with this chapter, go to `http://localhost/admin.php` or `http://localhost/system/index.php` to log in.

> Throughout this book, it is assumed that you are using XAMPP with `http://localhost/` addresses. If you are following along on an actual website, substitute `http://localhost/` for your website domain (for example, `http://www.example.com/`).

> In Chapter 2, we discussed moving the login page to the root of our website to mask the location of our system directory. If `http://localhost/admin.php` does not work, refer to Chapter 2.

- The first page we see is the **CP Home**. We can return to this page anytime by selecting **CP Home** from the menu at the top-right of the screen, above the main menu. In the left column, we have **EllisLab News Feed**. Below, we have **Most Recent Weblog Entries** as well as any **Recent Comments** or **trackbacks** visitors may have left. In our case, our site is brand new, so there will be no recent comments or trackbacks, and only **1** recent weblog entry (**Getting Started with ExpressionEngine**). Clicking on the link will take you directly to that entry.

- On the right, there is a **Bulletin Board** (a way for you to pass messages to other members of your control panel), the **Site Statistics** and a **Notepad** (we can write anything here, and it will be available every time we log-in).

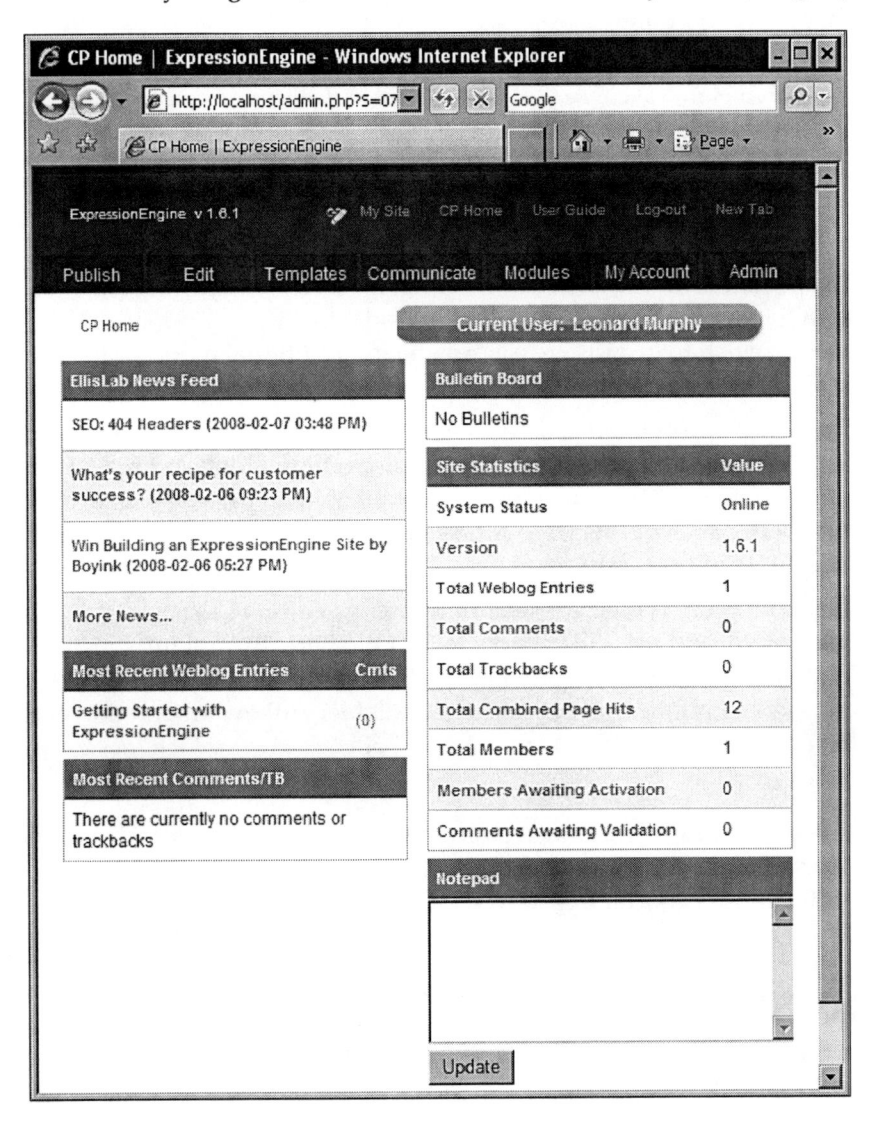

- Across the top is the main menu bar, and at the top-right are links to your website (**My Site**), this page (**CP Home**), the ExpressionEngine user-guide (**User Guide**), and to log-out (**Log-out**). The **Publish** and **Edit** links in the main menu bar are where you can create new entries and edit existing entries. The **Templates** link is where we can create new templates and edit existing templates. We will spend most of our time in these sections.

Start Posting

- The **Communicate** tab is where we can manage bulk-emails to our website members. At this time we do not have any members to email (other than ourselves), but as our site grows larger, this feature can be a useful communication/marketing tool.

> Be careful to avoid sending unsolicited bulk emails (or *spam*) using this feature. In many countries, there are laws governing what can or cannot be done. In the United States, commercial emails must meet very specific guidelines set by the Federal Trade Commission (http://www.ftc.gov/spam/).

- The **Modules** tab is where we can manage all the modules that come with ExpressionEngine, as well as optional third-party modules that we may wish to install. We can download additional modules from http://expressionengine.com/downloads/addons/category/modules/.

- The **My Account** tab is where we can edit our login preferences, including our username and password. We can also edit the look and feel of the control panel home page from this screen, as well as send private messages to other members. Much of this page is irrelevant when we are the only member of the site (as we are right now).

- The **Admin** tab is where most of the configuration of ExpressionEngine takes place, and we will spend a lot of time here. By default, most of the ExpressionEngine settings are already properly set, but feel free to browse and explore all the options that are available. Full documentation on each of the options is available at http://expressionengine.com/docs/cp/admin/index.html.

This concludes our brief tour of ExpressionEngine. We will be returning to these controls many times over the course of this book, but for now we are going to delve into one of the most important parts of the control panel—templates.

Templates and URLs

The basic concept in ExpressionEngine is that of a **template**. Go to any ExpressionEngine-powered website and you will undoubtedly be looking at a template. Templates are what the outside world sees.

At its most basic, a template in ExpressionEngine is a HTML (or CSS or JavaScript) file. If we wanted to, we could use a template exactly like a HTML file, without any problems. We could create an entire website without ever using any other part of ExpressionEngine.

However, we can take templates a lot further than that. By using ExpressionEngine tags inside our templates, we can take advantage of all the features of ExpressionEngine and combine it with all the flexibility that HTML and CSS offers in terms of layout and design. We are not limited to pre-defined 'cookie-cutter' templates that have been carefully adapted to work with ExpressionEngine. This is why ExpressionEngine is very popular with website designers.

On the flip side, this is also why there is such a learning curve with ExpressionEngine. There is no point-and-click interface to change the look and feel of your website; you have to have some experience with HTML to get the most out of it.

Let us take a closer look at templates and how they relate to URLs:

1. If you are not already logged in, log into ExpressionEngine at either `http://localhost/admin.php` or `http://www.example.com/admin.php`.

2. Click on the **Templates** button on the top of the screen.

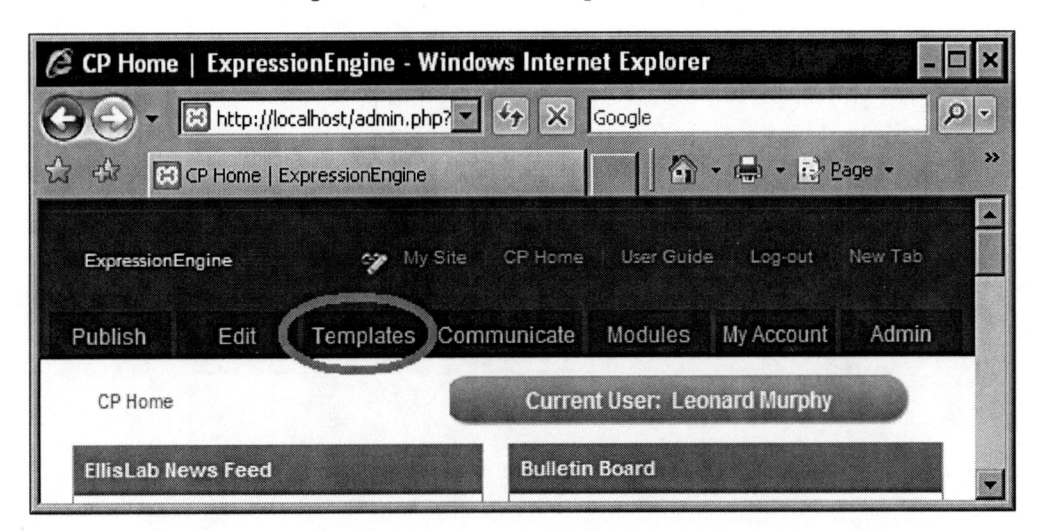

3. Templates are stored in groups. There is no 'right' way to group templates—some sites have all their templates in a single group and other sites have lots of template groups. We are going to create a new template group for each section of our website.

> ExpressionEngine does come pre-installed with two template groups: the `site` template group and the `search` template group. As a new user, it is best not to delete these template groups in case you want to refer to them later.

Start Posting

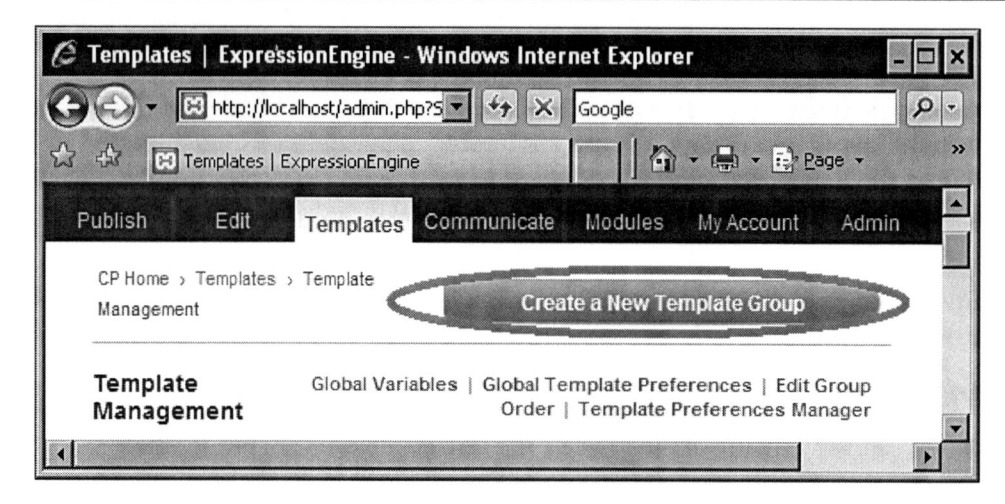

4. In the next screen we can give our template group a name; let us use **toast**. There is an option to **Duplicate an Existing Template Group** which copies all the templates from one template group into our new template group. This can be useful if we are creating one template group that will work very similarly to the one that we already created, but as this is our first template group, we are going to start from scratch.. Checking the box **Make the index template in this group your site's home page?** means that visitors will see the toast website in place of the ExpressionEngine example site. If you are using the XAMPP test server, go ahead and check this box.

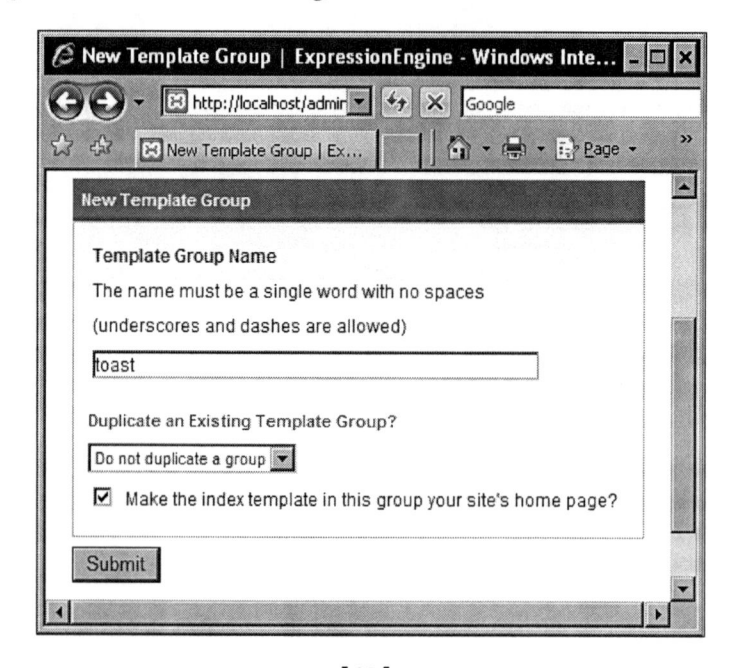

5. Hit **Submit** to create the template group. We will be returned to the **Template Management** screen. A message will appear saying **Template Group Created**, and the new template will appear in the box of groups on the left-hand side.

6. Left-click on the **New Template** group in the **Choose Group** box on the left-hand side. Each template group comes with an initial template, called **index**. Remembering that a template is like an HTML file, a template group is like a directory on our server. The **index** template is the equivalent of the `index.html` file—when a visitor visits our template group, the **index** template is displayed first. For that reason, the **index** template cannot be renamed or deleted. Let us edit the **index** template to see what it does. Click on the word **index**.

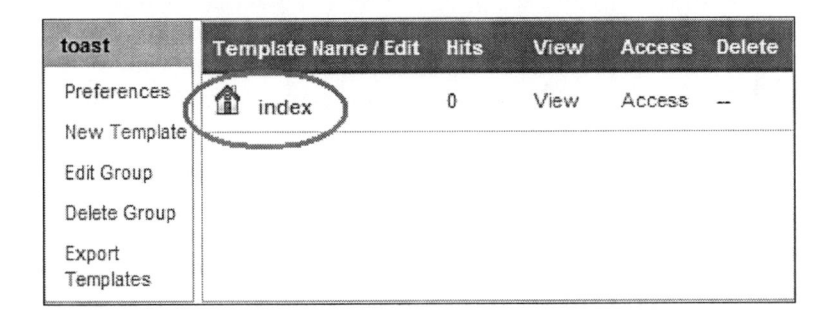

[39]

Start Posting

7. A template is essentially just text (although it usually contains HTML, CSS, or ExpressionEngine code). When we first create a template, there is no text, and therefore all we see is an empty white box. Let us write something in the box to demonstrate how templates are seen by visitors. Type in a sentence and click **Update and Finished**.

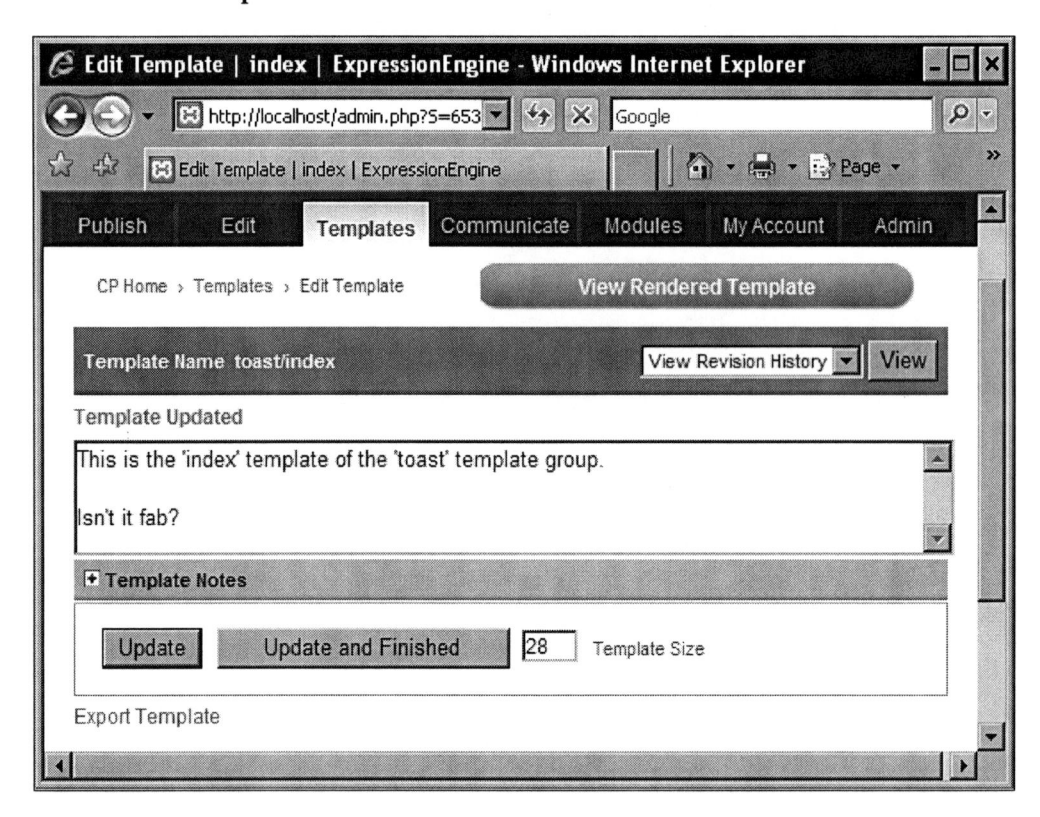

8. Just like HTML files and directories, templates and template groups relate directly to the URL that visitors see. In the URL `http://www.example.com/index.php/toast/index`, the `index.php` is what distinguishes this as an ExpressionEngine page. Then comes the template group name, in our case called **toast**. Finally, we have the template name, in this case **index**.

> In Chapter 2, we discussed removing `index.php` from URLs using an `.htaccess` file. If this was successful, `index.php` would not be a visible part of the URL. Further, because **index** is the default template, it does not have to be explicitly defined. Linking to `http://www.example.com/index.php/toast` would return the same page as `http://www.example.com/index.php/toast/index`.

9. Go to the previous URL (with or without the `index.php` as appropriate, for example, `http://www.example.com/toast/index` or `http://localhost/toast/index`) and the template we just edited should appear.

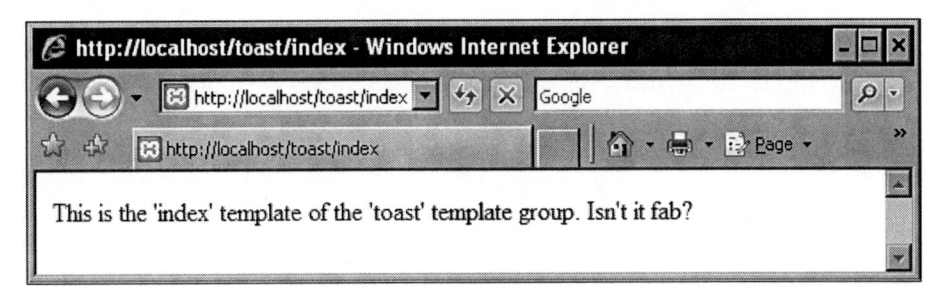

   ![Browser showing http://localhost/toast/index with text: This is the 'index' template of the 'toast' template group. Isn't it fab?]

10. Now try typing the template group without specifying which template to load. The index template is always returned.

    ![Browser showing http://localhost/toast with text: This is the 'index' template of the 'toast' template group. Isn't it fab?]

11. What happens if we do not specify the template group, and just go to our base domain (`http://localhost/` or `http://www.example.com/`)? In this case, the **toast** template of the default template group is returned. The default template group is indicated on the templates screen with an * before the template group name and underneath the list of template groups.

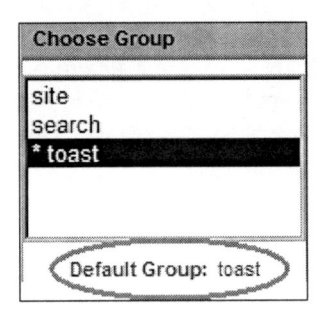

    ![Choose Group list showing: site, search, * toast; Default Group: toast circled]

Start Posting

Working with Multiple Templates

Now that we have created one template, let us create a second template in the **toast** template group so that we can really play around with these URLs.

1. Back on the templates screen in the control panel, select the **toast** template group on the left-hand side, and then select **New Template**.

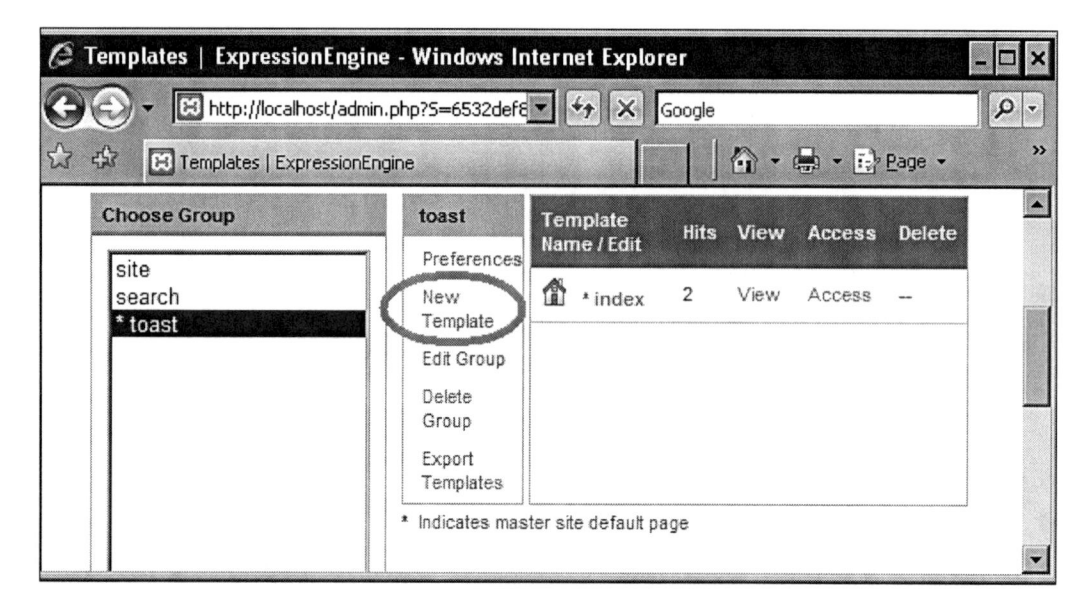

2. Let us call the new template **test**. Leave the **Template Type** as **Web Page**. The **Default Template Data** allows us to choose between starting with a blank template, duplicating an existing template, or using a template from our library. ExpressionEngine does not come with a pre-defined library of templates that we can pick from. This is because templates are the equivalent of HTML files, and the HTML for one website will be very different to the HTML for another website. However, as we build our site, we may find ourselves reusing the same templates repeatedly, so we can build our own template library based on those templates. Right now, we are going to create an empty template. Click **Submit**.

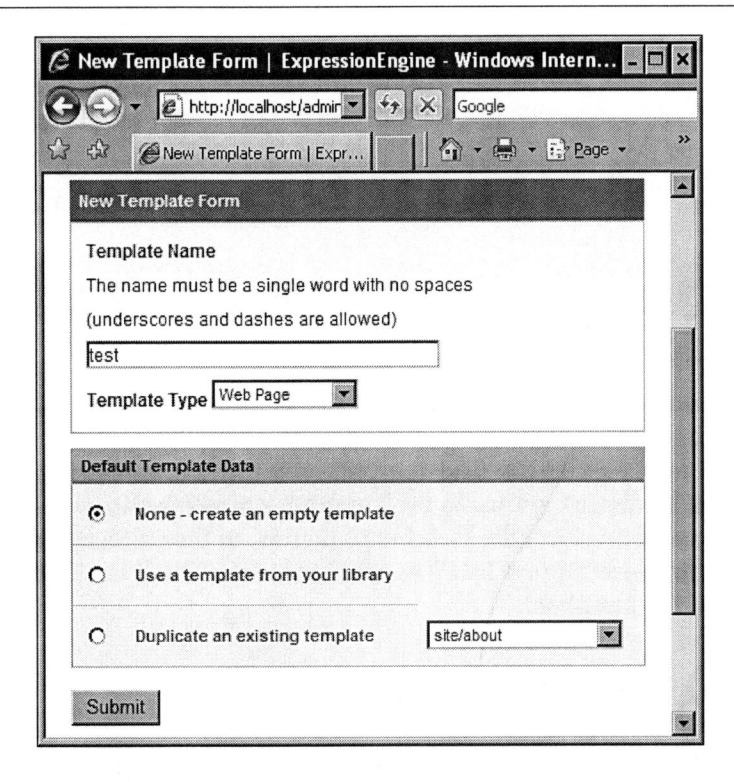

3. Now we need to edit the template so that it is not completely blank. From the **Templates** screen, click on the **New Template** to edit it. Then type in some text (or HTML code), making sure it is different from the previous template we created. Then click **Update and Finished**.

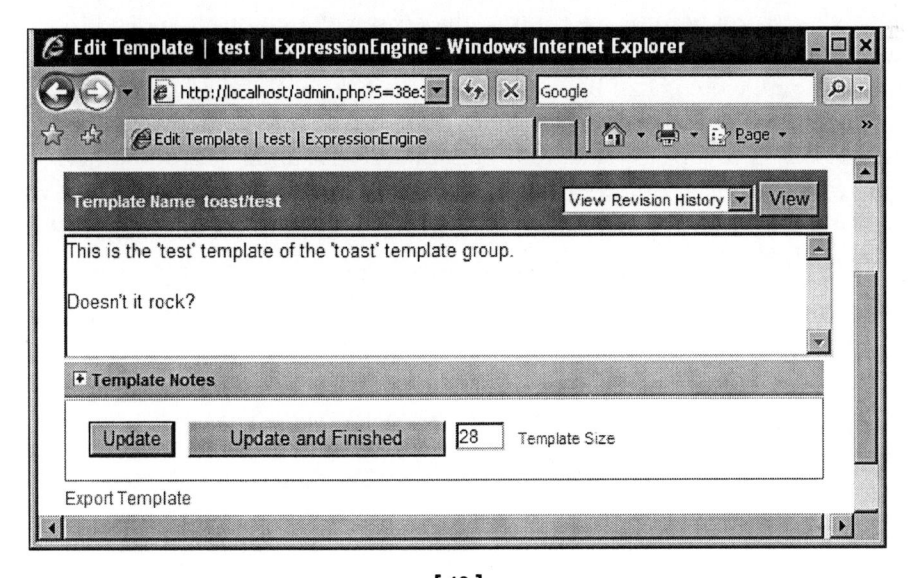

Start Posting

4. Now we can go to `http://localhost/toast/test` (or `http://www.example.com/toast/test`) and see the new template. At `http://localhost/toast`, we can still see the **index** template.

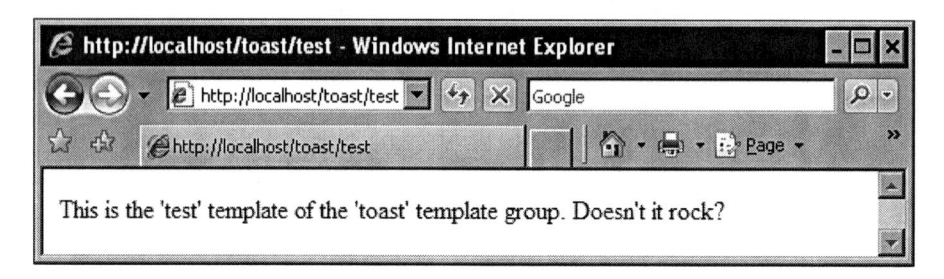

> This is the 'test' template of the 'toast' template group. Doesn't it rock?

5. We will not be using the `test` template any further, so we can go ahead and delete it. To do this, return to the **Templates** screen, select the **toast** template group, and then select the **Delete** option next to the **test** template. We will see a warning telling us **THIS ACTION CANNOT BE UNDONE**. Hit **Delete** to delete the template.

Creating Our First Entry

At this stage, we know that templates are a fundamental concept in ExpressionEngine. Everything the visitor sees on our ExpressionEngine website is going to be in a template. We could, at this stage, use templates to create an entire website. However, the beauty of ExpressionEngine is that we do not have to.

One of the most important concepts after a template is that of a **weblog**. Many people new to ExpressionEngine confuse the term weblog with that of a blog. Not surprising, because the association is intentional. At its most basic, an ExpressionEngine weblog can be used to set up a blog with dated entries in descending chronological order. However, there are so many other uses for a weblog that it is more appropriate to think of it as a dynamic data container. Anything that changes regularly (that is, the text of our website) should be a weblog, and anything that stays the same (that is, the HTML formatting of our website) should be a template.

In this section, we are going to create a basic weblog to demonstrate the concept.

> Although we use the term **weblog** in this book, many people prefer to use a more generic term, such as section. It is entirely possible to change weblog to section throughout ExpressionEngine. To do this, go to **Admin | System Preferences | General Configuration | Section Designation Word**.

Chapter 3

1. In the menu bar at the top of any control panel screen, select **Admin**.

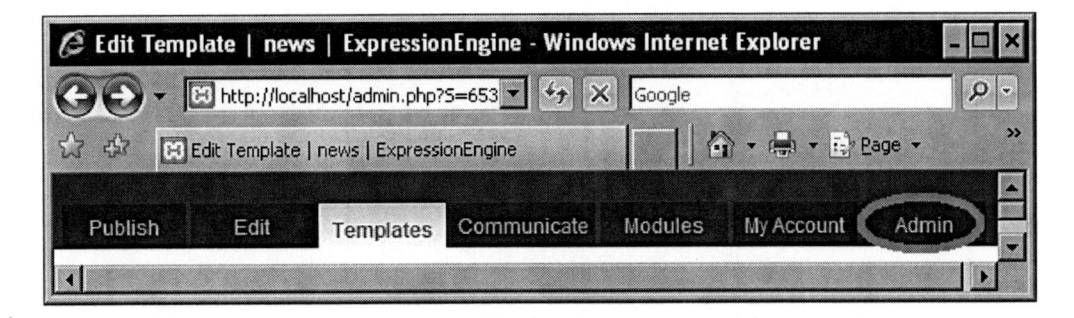

2. On the left-hand side, select **Weblog Administration**.

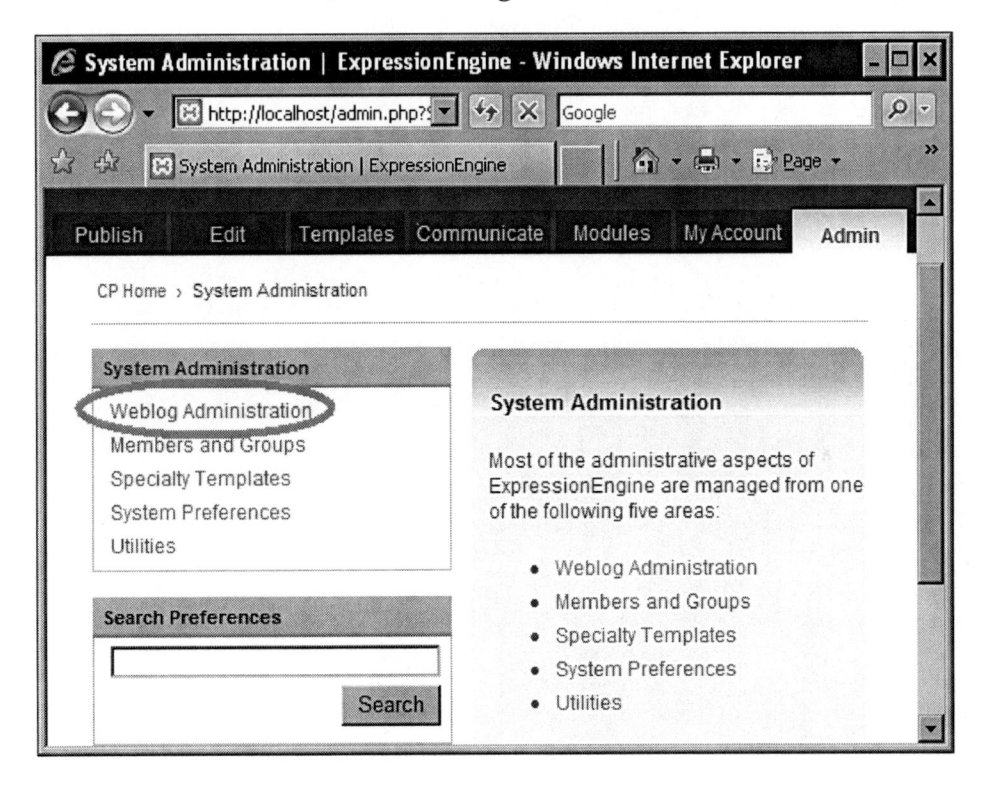

Start Posting

3. Now, select **Weblog Management** in the center of the screen.

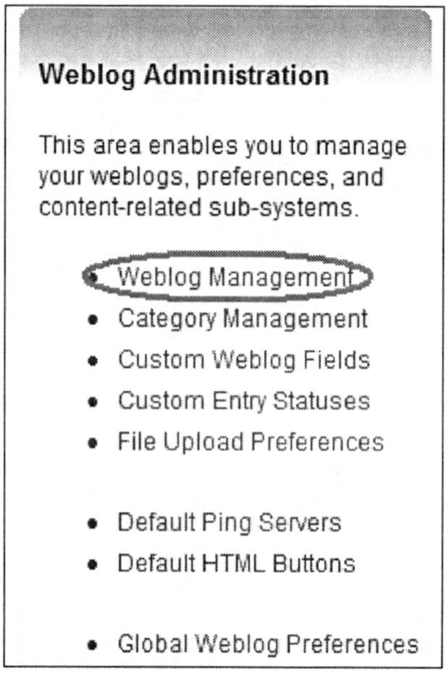

Weblog Administration

This area enables you to manage your weblogs, preferences, and content-related sub-systems.

- Weblog Management
- Category Management
- Custom Weblog Fields
- Custom Entry Statuses
- File Upload Preferences

- Default Ping Servers
- Default HTML Buttons

- Global Weblog Preferences

4. On the next screen, we have a list of all our weblogs. ExpressionEngine comes with one weblog out of the box, called **Default Site Weblog**, but we will create our own from scratch. At the top-right, select **Create a New Weblog**.

![Weblog Management screen showing the Create a New Weblog button highlighted]

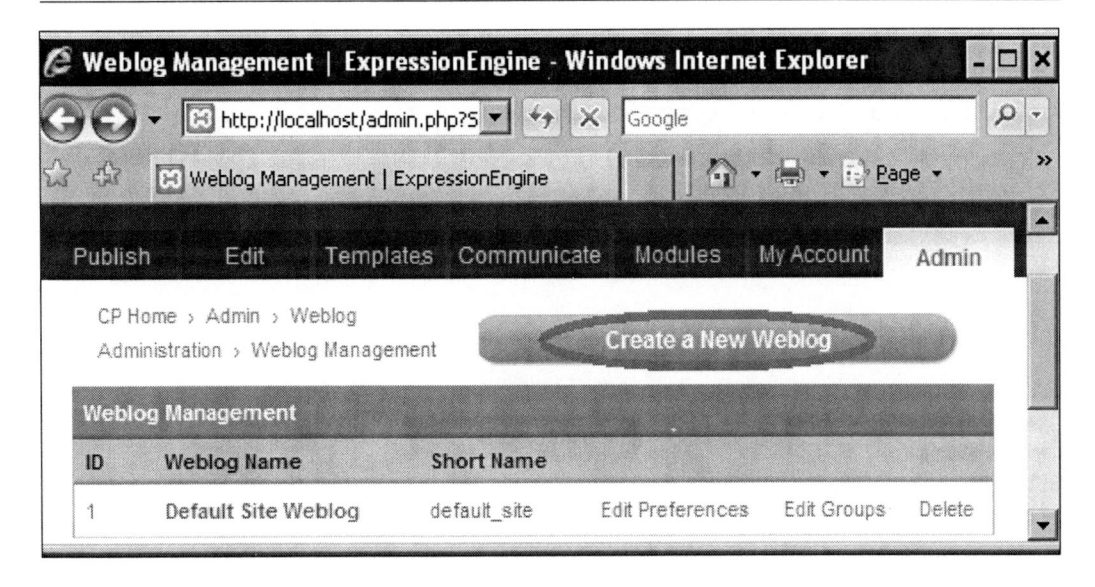

5. On the next screen, we have some more options. Many of these options are designed to save time when creating multiple weblogs.

- The **Full Weblog Name** should describe the dynamic data that we will be storing in this weblog. For this tutorial, we will use **Toast News**.
- The **Short Name** is the name that we will use in our templates to use the weblog data. We usually want to aim for a nice balance between easy-to-type and easy-to-remember. A good rule is to use the same name for both the short and the full names. For this example, we will use **toastnews**.
- We do not want to **Duplicate existing weblog's preferences**.

Start Posting

- Select **Edit Group Preferences**, and select a **Category Group** of **Default Category Group**, a **Status Group** of **Default Status Group**, and a **Field Group** of **toastwebsite**.
- We also do not want to **Create New Templates For This Weblog**.

Create a New Weblog	
* Full Weblog Name	Toast News
* Short Name single word, no spaces	toastnews
Duplicate existing weblog's preferences	Do Not Duplicate
Edit Group Preferences	● Yes ○ No

Edit Group Preferences	
Category Group	None **Default Category Group**
Status Group	Default Status Group
Field Group	toastwebsite

Create New Templates For This Weblog?	
● No	
○ Use one of the default themes ☐ Include RSS Templates	Default
○ Duplicate an existing template group	news
* New Template Group Name Field is required if you are creating a new group single word, no spaces	

[48]

6. Click **Submit,** and we will see our new weblog in the list of existing weblogs.

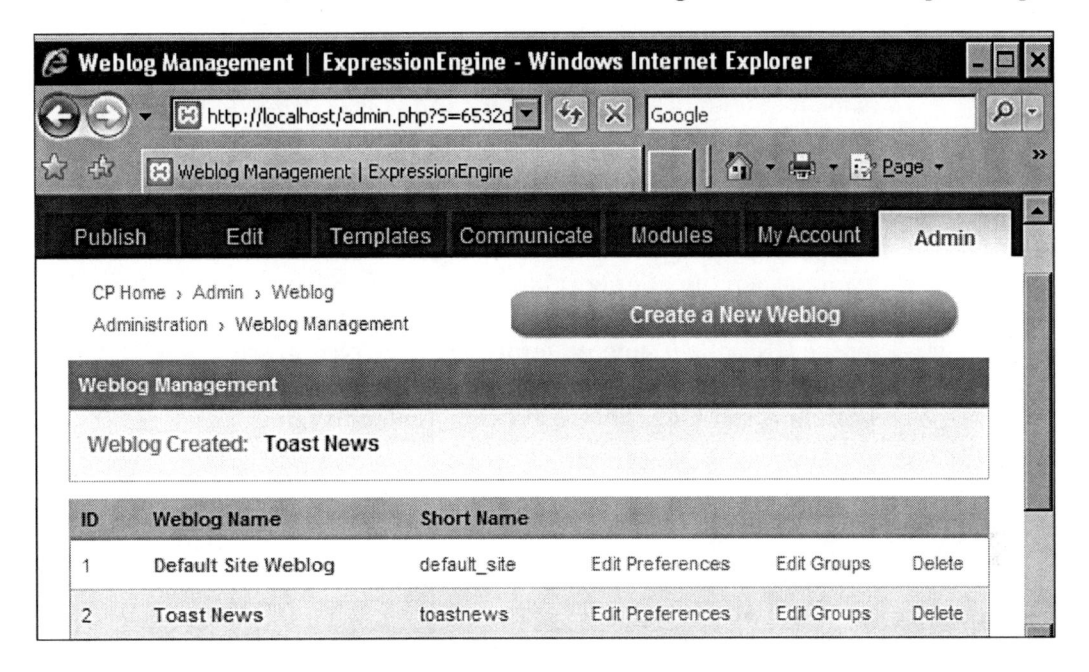

7. Now that we have a weblog (or dynamic data container), we need to create some dynamic data. Select **Publish** on the left of the top menu bar (first red circle in the next screenshot). If a drop-down appears with **Toast News** when you hover over the **Publish** button (second red circle in the next screenshot), you can click to directly publish to that weblog. Otherwise, you will be brought to a screen where you can select the weblog (third red circle below). Select **Toast News**.

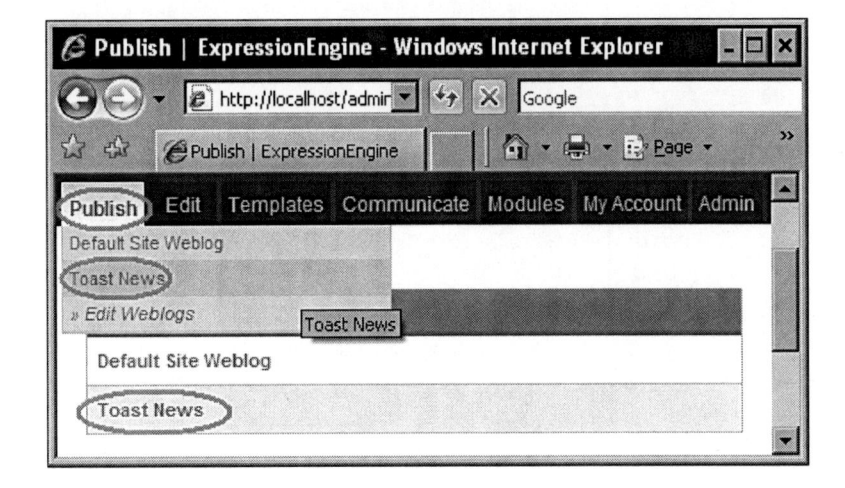

Start Posting

8. This screen has a lot of options, and can be a little overwhelming.

   - First, our new entry needs a **Title**. This title will appear on our website (unless you choose not to display it), so we want to give it a name that both describes the entry and grabs our readers' attention. As this is our first entry, we are going to give it the title of **Exciting First Entry**.
   - The **URL Title** is a little more involved. Every entry we post is given its own page, and this is the URL to get to that page. We therefore want to keep the title short but still understandable. It cannot contain spaces (though underscores or dashes are acceptable). A suggestion for the URL title is entered for us when we type in the title field. We are not required to keep this suggestion, but for our purposes we will. Therefore, our **URL Title** is **exciting_first_entry**.

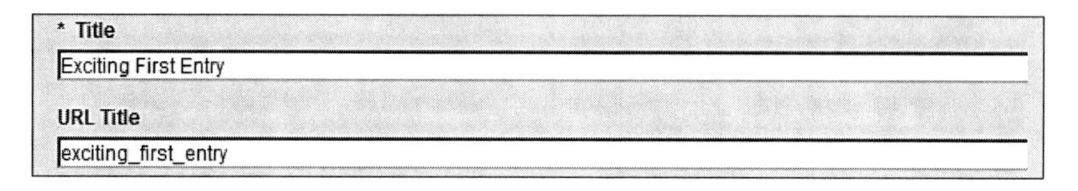

   ```
   * Title
   Exciting First Entry

   URL Title
   exciting_first_entry
   ```

   - Further down, there are three collapsible sections called **Summary**, **Body**, and **Extended text**. Only the **Body** section is expanded by default. Go ahead and expand the **Summary** section, then write some text in both the **Summary** and the **Body** fields.

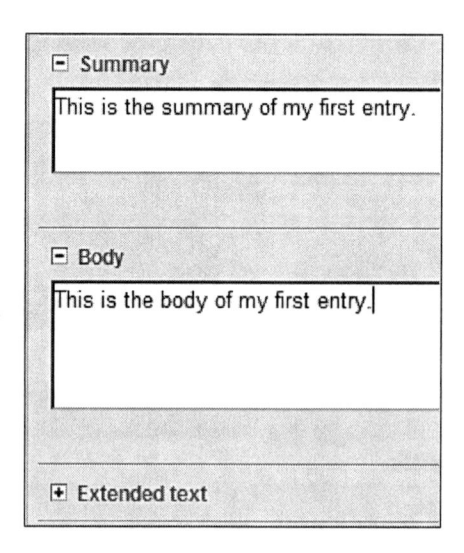

   ```
   ⊟ Summary
   This is the summary of my first entry.


   ⊟ Body
   This is the body of my first entry.



   ⊞ Extended text
   ```

- Ignore the plethora of other options and click **Submit** on the right hand side. We can see a message saying that the entry has been submitted.

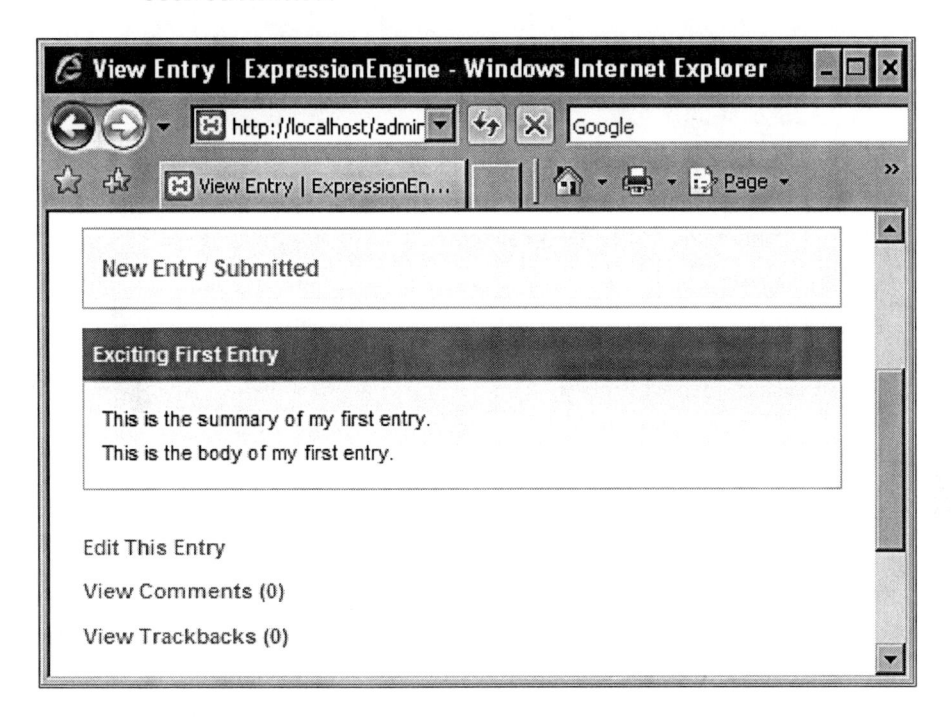

Viewing Our First Entry

Now one question remains: where do we have to go to see our entry? The answer is that our entry is not yet on our website. That is because the entry does not appear in a template and everything on an ExpressionEngine website must go into a template before it can be viewed. Follow these instructions to point a template to our new weblog.

1. Click on **Templates** in the menu bar. Select **Create a New Template Group**, and call the **New Template Group** to be **news**. Leave all the other options at their default and click **Submit**.

Start Posting

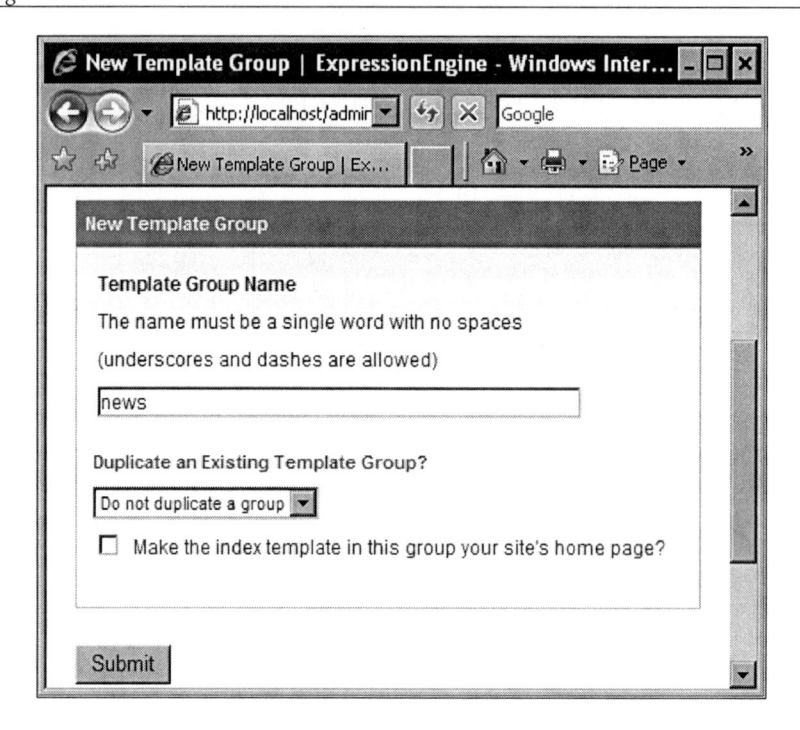

2. Select the **news** template group, and then click on the **index** template to edit it.
3. To include a weblog in a template, we use a **tag**. A tag is a unique ExpressionEngine piece of code that is used in templates to include extra functionality. In this case, we want to include a weblog, so we need a weblog tag. A tag has two parts: variables and parameters. **Parameters** are always part of the opening tag whereas **variables** are used between the opening tag and the closing tag. In the **news/index** template we will add in the weblog tag as well as some standard HTML code.

```
<!DOCTYPE html PUBLIC "-//W3C//DTD XHTML 1.0 Strict//EN"
"http://www.w3.org/TR/xhtml1/DTD/xhtml1-strict.dtd">
<html xmlns="http://www.w3.org/1999/xhtml">
  <head>
    <title>News from the President</title>
    <meta http-equiv="content-type" content="text/html;
                                    charset=UTF-8" />
  </head>
  <body>
    <h1>Toast for Sale!</h1>
    <h2>News from the President</h2>
    {exp:weblog:entries weblog="toastnews"}
```

```
    <h3>{title}</h3>
    {summary}
    {body}
    {extended}
  {/exp:weblog:entries}
 </body>
</html>
```

> The indentation helps to demarcate related sections and therefore make the code more readable, but is certainly not required.

4. Click **Update and Finished** to save our updates.

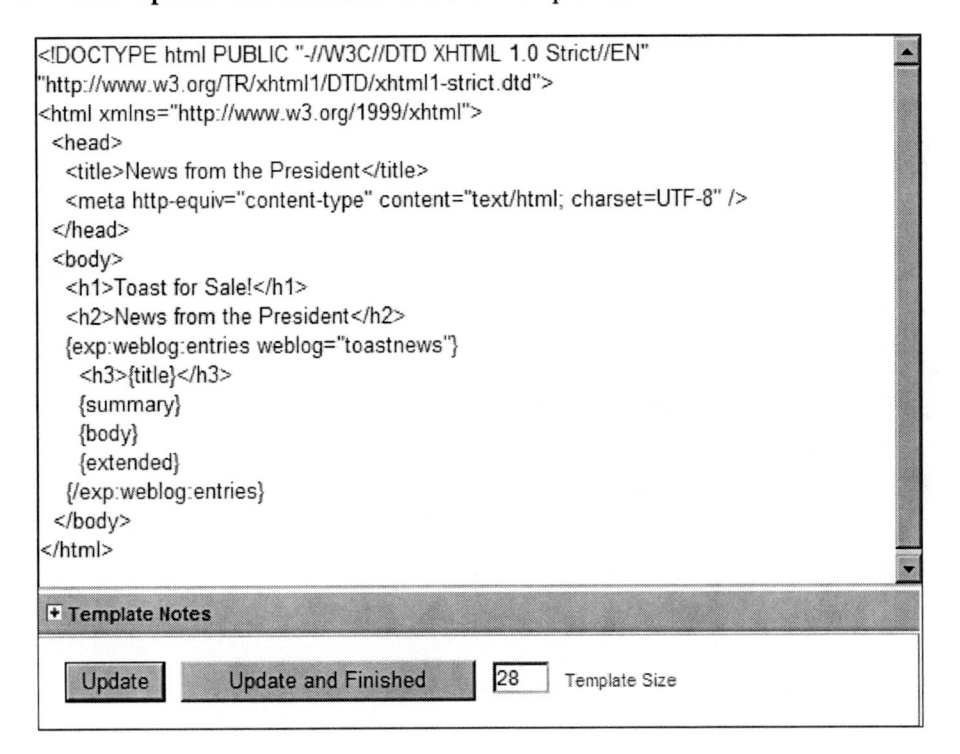

```
<!DOCTYPE html PUBLIC "-//W3C//DTD XHTML 1.0 Strict//EN"
"http://www.w3.org/TR/xhtml1/DTD/xhtml1-strict.dtd">
<html xmlns="http://www.w3.org/1999/xhtml">
 <head>
  <title>News from the President</title>
  <meta http-equiv="content-type" content="text/html; charset=UTF-8" />
 </head>
 <body>
  <h1>Toast for Sale!</h1>
  <h2>News from the President</h2>
  {exp:weblog:entries weblog="toastnews"}
    <h3>{title}</h3>
    {summary}
    {body}
    {extended}
  {/exp:weblog:entries}
 </body>
</html>
```

> The difference between **Update** and **Update and Finished** is that **Update** will keep you in the template editing screen so that you can continue to make further edits, whereas **Update and Finished** returns you to the main templates screen.

Start Posting

5. Now view the news template at `http://localhost/news` or `www.example.com/news` to see how it looks. It should look like the following screenshot. Notice how the {title} has been changed to reflect the actual title of our entry (and so has {summary} and {body}).

6. What happens if we post two entries? Let us try it and see! Back in the control panel, select **Publish | Toast News** and write a second entry with a different title, URL title, and so forth. Hit **Submit**, and then visit `http://localhost/news` or `http://www.example.com/news` to see what happens. It should look like as follows:

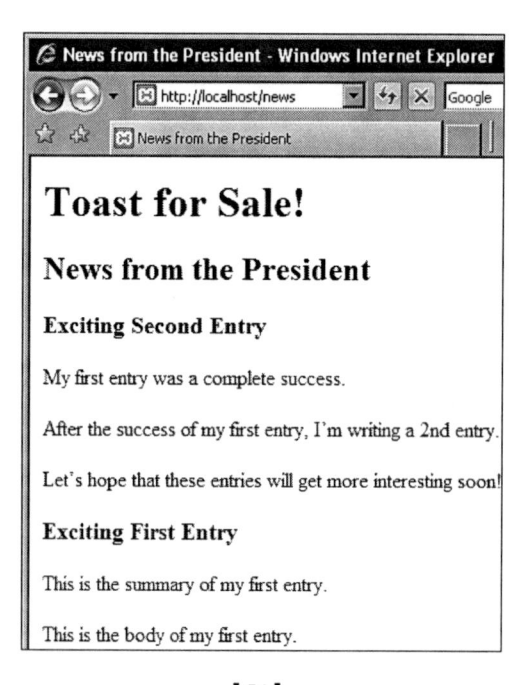

7. For our final enhancement, let us edit the template to include variables for the author name and the date of the entry. To do this, add the highlighted code as shown next:

```
<body>
  <h1>Toast for Sale!</h1>
  <h2>News from the President</h2>
  {exp:weblog:entries weblog="toastnews"}
    <h3>{title}</h3>
    {summary}
    {body}
    {extended}
    <p class="footnote">Written by {author} on {entry_date
                                     format="%F %j%S"}</p>
  {/exp:weblog:entries}
</body>
```

- {author} is a variable that returns the name of the person who was logged in when the entry was created.
- {entry_date} is a variable that displays the date that the entry was written on. format is a parameter of the entry_date variable that is used to specify how the date should be formatted.
- %F is the month of the year spelled out; %j is the day of the month; and %S is the suffix (for example, nd or th). So %F %j%S is rendered as 'February 7th'. For a complete list of date formats, visit http://expressionengine.com/docs/templates/date_variable_formatting.html.

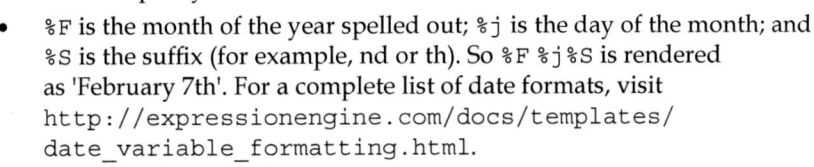

8. Revisit http://localhost/news or http://www.example.com/news, and you can now see the author name underneath both entries.

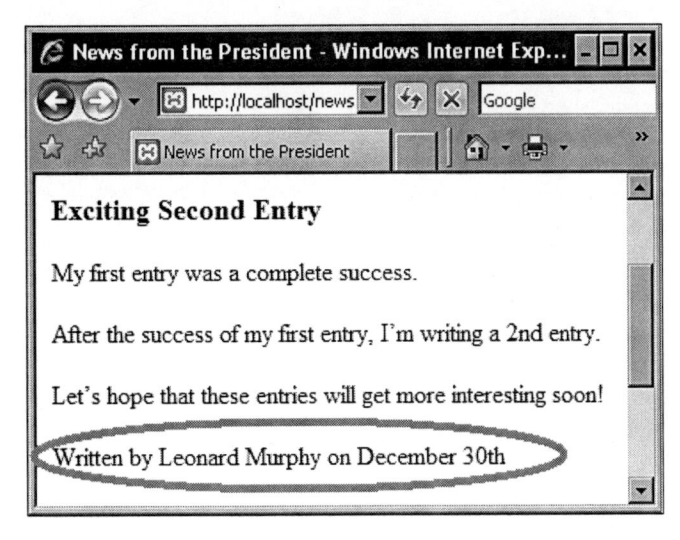

Start Posting

Make Our Weblog Pretty Using CSS

Our weblog, whilst functional, is not exactly the prettiest on the web. We will spruce it up with some more HTML and CSS. This section will not introduce any new ExpressionEngine features but will demonstrate how to incorporate standard CSS into our templates. An understanding of HTML and CSS will be invaluable as we develop our ExpressionEngine site.

> Please note that this book can only demonstrate the basics of using HTML with CSS in an ExpressionEngine website. There are lots of books and websites dedicated to CSS that will teach far more than can be possibly covered here.
>
> If you are already familiar with using HTML and CSS, then you will only need to go through the first section (*Creating and Linking to a Styling Template*) to create the CSS template and link to it from the HTML template.

Creating and Linking to a Styling Template

As with a more conventional HTML/CSS website, our CSS code will be separated out from our HTML code, and placed in its own template (or file). This requires creating a new CSS template and modifying our existing template to identify the main styling elements, as well as to link to the CSS template.

1. First, let us go back into our news template and add the following code (highlighted). The trick with writing HTML with CSS is to identify the main sections of the HTML code using the `<div>` tag.

```
<body>
  <div id="header">
    <h1>Toast for Sale!</h1>
    <h2>News from the President</h2>
  </div>
  <div id="content">
    {exp:weblog:entries weblog="toastnews"}
      <h3>{title}</h3>
      <div class="contentinner">
        {summary}
        {body}
```

```
        {extended}
      </div>
      <p class="footnote">Written by {author} on {entry_date
                                   format="%F %j%S"}</p>
    {/exp:weblog:entries}
  </div>
</body>
```

> Here we have identified three sections using the `<div>` tag. We have encapsulated our website title in a `header` section. We have wrapped up all of our ExpressionEngine entries into a `content` section. Finally, we have created a `contentinner` section that contains just the text for each ExpressionEngine entry, but does not include the title. Also note that `footnote` is a section.
>
> What is the difference between an `id` and a `class` in our `<div>` tags? A section defined with an `id` only appears once on a page. In our case, the `header` only appears once, so we can use the `id`. A section defined with a `class` may appear multiple times. As the `contentinner` section will appear on the page for each entry present there, we have used a `class` for this section.

2. Next, we want to create a CSS template that tells us what to do with these sections. To do this, go back to the main **Templates** page, select the **toast** template group, and then select **New Template**.

toast	Template Name / Edit	Hits	View	Access	Delete
Preferences	🏠 * index	11	View	Access	--
New Template					
Edit Group					
Delete Group					
Export Templates					

Start Posting

3. Call the new template **toast_css**. Under **Template Type** select **CSS Stylesheet** instead of **Web Page**. Leave the **Default Template Data** as **None – create an empty template** and hit **Submit**.

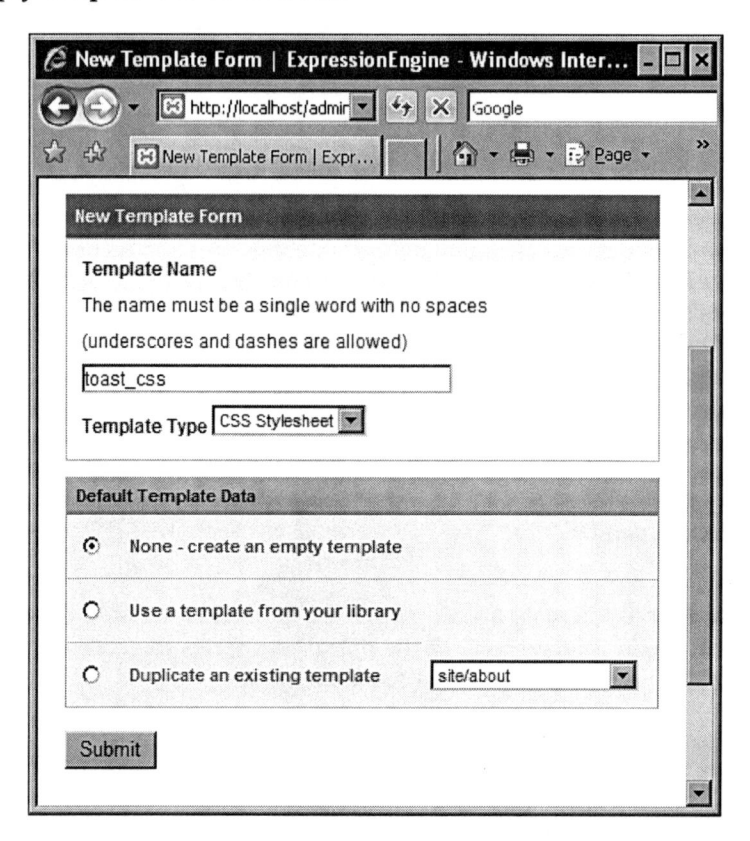

4. Before we start editing our new CSS template, we must be sure to tell the HTML template about it. Select to edit the **index** template in the **news** template group.

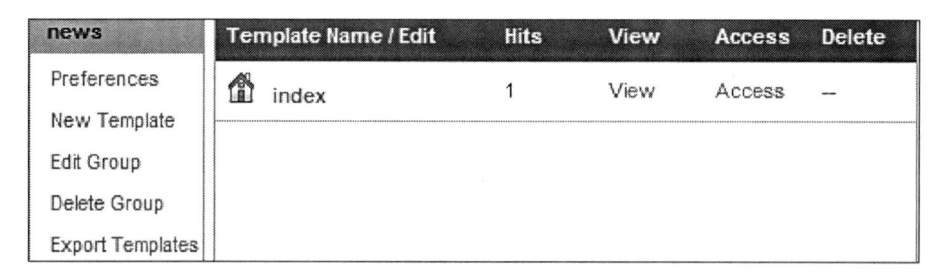

Chapter 3

5. Insert the following highlighted commands between the `<head>` and `</head>` tags to tell the HTML template where the CSS template is.

   ```
   <head>
     <title>News from the President</title>
     <link rel='stylesheet' type='text/css' media='all'
                       href='{path=toast/toast_css}' />
     <style type='text/css' media='screen'>@import
               "{path=toast/toast_css}";</style>
     <meta http-equiv="content-type" content="text/html;
                                       charset=UTF-8" />
   </head>
   ```

Styling Colors and Fonts

We now have a blank CSS template, `toast_css`. We are now going to start editing our CSS template, defining the various elements we use in our `news` template, and defining the background colors and fonts we want to use.

> If you already know how to use CSS, this section can be skipped in favor of your own CSS design.

1. We will define the four sections we used earlier (`header`, `content`, `contentinner`, and `footnote`). Note that because `contentinner` and `footnote` were defined as `class`, they are preceded by a period. The `header` and the `content` sections are preceded with `#` as they were identified in the HTML with `id`.

> As well as identifying the four sections that are unique to us, we have defined some HTML elements within those sections as well. For example, we have an h1 and an h2 style within our `header` div; so we have defined the corresponding elements in our CSS template.

```
body{
  background: #8B4513;
}
#header{
  background-color: #DEB887;
}
#header h1{
  color: black;
}
#header h2{
  color: #8B4513;
```

```
}
#content{
}
#content h3{
  color: #F0E68C;
}
#content p{
}
.contentinner{
  background: #DEB887;
}
.footnote{
  color: #F0E68C;
}
```

2. Click **Update** and view your news template in a browser (`http://localhost/news` or `http://www.example.com/news`). It will look like the following screenshot. Essentially, all we have done is color in some of our CSS elements. By doing this, we can better see the structure of our page. For example, the tan (`#DEB887`) box shows us where our `contentinner` section is.

> If you do not see anything as colorful as the following screenshot, it is usually a sign that the HTML template is not referencing the CSS template correctly (see the previous step), or that the **Template Type** of **toast_css** was not set as **CSS Stylesheet** when it was first created. If this is the case, delete the **toast_css** template and follow the steps to create it again, this time selecting **CSS Stylesheet** instead of **Web Page**.

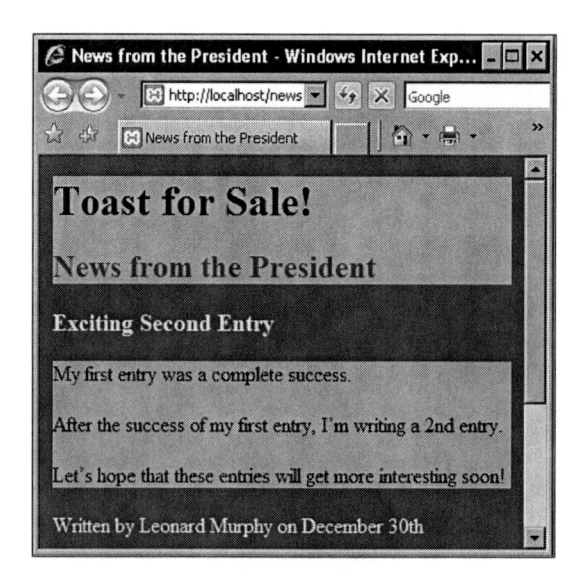

3. Next, we are going to change some of the fonts. Make the following highlighted changes to the code:

```css
body{
    background: #8B4513;
    font-family: Verdana, "Trebuchet MS", Arial, Helvetica,
                                                sans-serif;
}

#header h1{
    color: black;
    font-family: Arial, Helvetica, sans-serif;
    font-size: 300%;
    font-weight: bold;
    text-align: left;
}

#header h2{
    color: #8B4513;
    font-family: Arial, Helvetica, sans-serif;
    font-size: 200%;
    font-weight: bold;
    text-align: left;
}

#content{
    font-size: 80%;
}

#content h3{
    color: #F0E68C;
    font-family: Arial, Helvetica, sans-serif;
    font-weight: bold;
}

.footnote{
    color: #F0E68C;
    font-size: 75%;
}
```

> Instead of reprinting the entire template, we are showing only the elements that are changing, with the changes highlighted.

4. Click **Update**, and now view the template in the browser (`http://localhost/news` or `http://www.example.com/news`). The `font` tag in the `body` section means that all the text on our page will be Verdana. We then placed `font` tags in our `h1`, `h2`, and `h3` headings which will override the `body` font tag and make our headings Arial. If the computer or device viewing the page does not have the first font in the list, then the next is tried and so on. If the device does not have any of the listed fonts, then any sans-serif font that the device does have is used. We have also changed the size of our fonts, making our `h1`, `h2`, and `h3` headings bigger, and in bold, and reducing the size of our `footnote` element.

> Note that where one CSS element is inside another (such as where `content` is inside `body`), any properties assigned to the parent element also apply to the child elements. As `content` is inside `body`, we do not have to specify the font for the `content` separately. However, if we do specify the font in both places, then it is the child element that overrides the parent element. (This is where the **cascading** of Cascading Style Sheets comes in).
>
> Also note that as `content` has a font-size of 80% and `footnote` has a font-size of 75% and `footnote` is inside `content`, footnote has an actual font-size of 75% of 80% (that is, 60%).

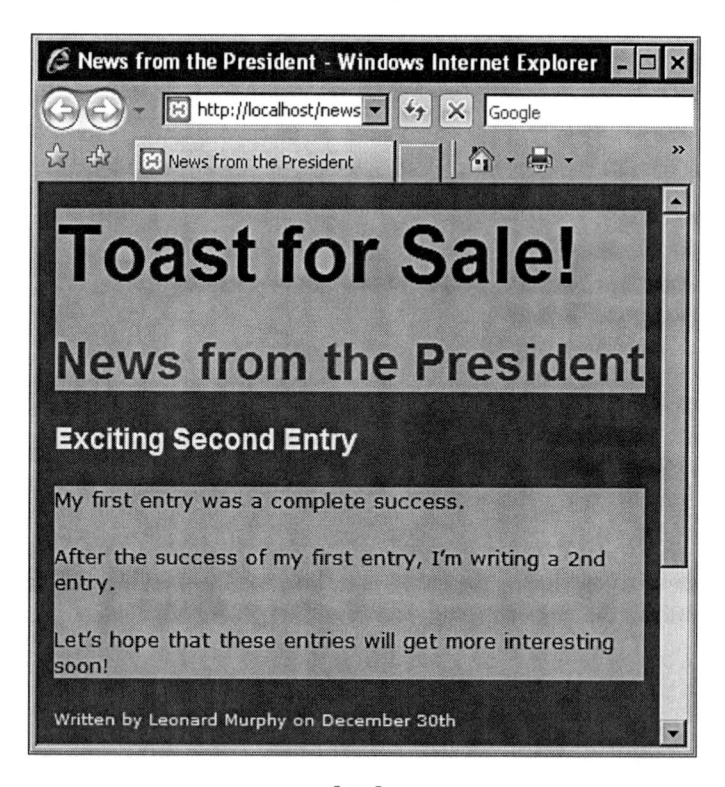

Moving Our Elements Around

We have now used CSS to alter the colors and fonts on our page. However, the page still reads from top to bottom. Ahead of us, we have the challenge of moving our elements around to provide a more natural flow. We will also put our logo in as part of the heading.

> CSS positioning can be challenging for newcomers. As this book focuses principally on ExpressionEngine, we cannot delve too much into the ins and outs of CSS.

1. First, we are going to change where some elements will appear on the page. We are going to add a margin to our entire page. To do this, we use `margin: 5% auto`. The `5%` provides a buffer on the top side (to prevent the header from touching the top edge of the browser). The `auto` results in centering the entire page (`auto` means that the left and right margins are being calculated automatically depending on the width of the page in the browser). We can then set our page width to be `770px`. By doing this, it ensures that our website will be rendered on a screen resolution of 800x600 without any horizontal scrolling. We then change the width of our `content` section so that it only takes up the left 70% of the page. This will give us the room to put a menu on the right hand side at a later stage. We will also add a margin around all our paragraphs in the `content` section—the 1% means that there will be less space between paragraphs than there otherwise would be. Finally, we are putting a border around our `contentinner` section to make it look more interesting and right-aligning our `footnote`.

```
body{
    background: #8B4513;
    font-family: Verdana, "Trebuchet MS", Arial, Helvetica, sans-
                                                           serif;
    margin: 5% auto;
    width: 770px;
}
#content{
    font-size: 80%;
    width: 70%;
    float: left;
}
#content p{
    margin: 1%;
}
.contentinner{
    background: #DEB887;
```

Start Posting

```
  border: 2px dotted #FFEFD5;
}
.footnote{
  color: #F0E68C;
  font-size: 75%;
  text-align: right;
}
```

> In addition to being able to change the **margin** of any element, we can also alter the **padding**. The difference is that a margin is applied outside the box (and so creates space between the box and other elements). The padding is applied to the inside of the box, so the box does not move but there is more space between the edge of the box and the contents of the box.

2. Click **Update** again, and visit `http://localhost/news` or `http://www.example.com/news` to see the changes.

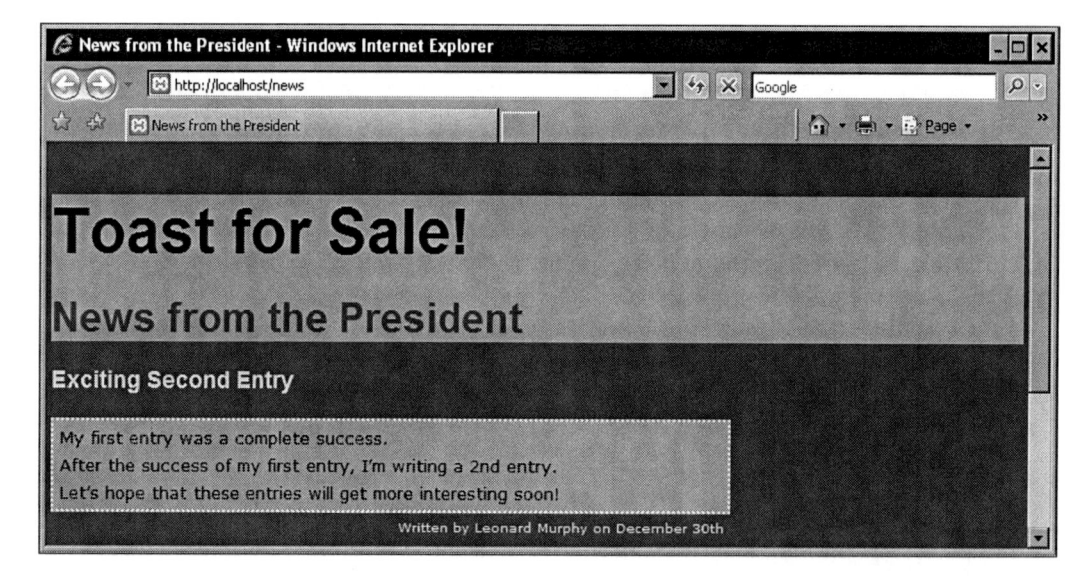

3. We are getting close to being done. One element that our site is missing that most normal sites would have is a logo. Luckily, our toast website does have a logo that we can now use. First, copy `square.png` to your website `images` directory via FTP (`C:\xampp\htdocs\images\` if you are using XAMPP, or `/Applications/MAMP/htdocs/images/` if you are using MAMP on a Macintosh).

> The file `square.png` can be downloaded from the Packtpub website at http://www.packtpub.com/support.
>
> When uploading new files to your website, you must place them in an existing subdirectory, or you must add the new file or directory to your `.htaccess` file (if you are using a `.htaccess` file to remove `index.php` as outlined in Chapter 2).

4. Once the logo is uploaded, we will make the following adjustments to our CSS. The following is the entire CSS template that we should now have. We are going to make the `header` have a background image of our logo. Our image has a `height` of `151` pixels, so we can set the height of the `header` section to match. Our image also has a `width` of `201` pixels, so we are going to offset the `h1` and `h2` margins by more than this so that the `h1` and `h2` headings do not overlap. Be sure to change the URL of the file to match the actual URL.

```css
body{
   background: #8B4513;
   font-family: Verdana, "Trebuchet MS", Arial, Helvetica,
                                                sans-serif;
   margin: 5% auto;
   width:770px;
}
#header{
   background: url('{site_url}images/square.png') no-repeat top
                                                        left;
   background-color: #DEB887;
   height: 151px;
   margin-bottom: 30px;
}
#header h1{
   color: black;
   font-family: Arial, Helvetica, sans-serif;
   font-size: 300%;
   font-weight: bold;
   text-align: left;
   margin-top: 25px;
   margin-left: 225px;
}
#header h2{
   color: #8B4513;
   font-family: Arial, Helvetica, sans-serif;
```

Start Posting

```
      font-size: 200%;
      font-weight: bold;
      text-align: left;
    margin-left: 225px;
}
#content{
    font-size: 80%;
    width: 70%;
    float: left;
}
#content h3{
    color: #F0E68C;
    font-family: Arial, Helvetica, sans-serif;
    font-weight: bold;
}
#content p{
    margin: 1%;
}
.contentinner{
    background: #DEB887;
    border: 2px dotted #FFEFD5;
}
.footnote{
    color: #F0E68C;
    font-size: 75%;
    text-align: right;
}
```

> {site_url} is an ExpressionEngine variable that, when the CSS is loaded by a browser, will be converted into the actual URL of your site (in this case, http://localhost/ or http://www.example.com/). By using this variable, we can avoid hard-coding the URL name of the website in our CSS file.

5. Going back to our page after making these updates, we can see that our website is looking a lot more visually appealing. You may have noted, however, that the website may not exactly look like the following screenshot. This is because different browsers and different operating systems and different screen resolutions can all make a difference on how the final product looks. The key is not to try and make it look identical on all platforms, but to make it usable on all platforms.

> If everything appears to match with the folowing screenshot, except the background color of the heading is not a light-tan, be sure that in the `#header`, the `background` line comes before the `background-color` line. Otherwise, the `background` line takes precedence over the `background-color` declaration.

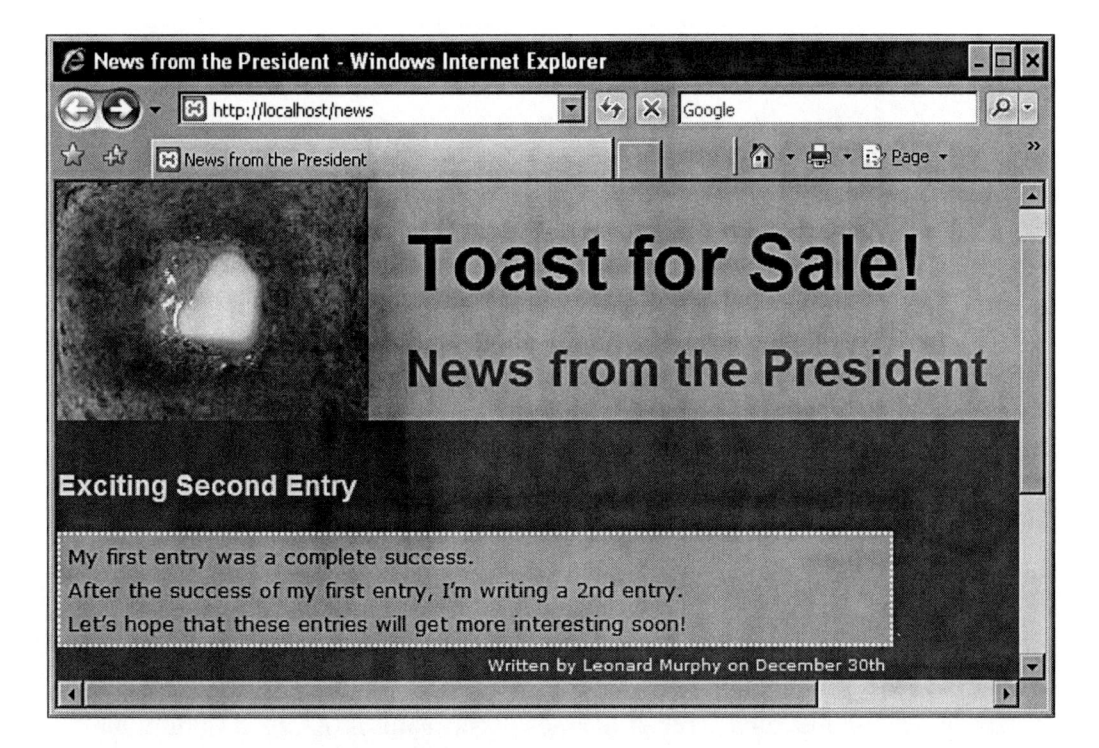

Exercises

1. By now we should be pretty familiar with posting entries in ExpressionEngine. To be sure, try posting a third entry to our weblog.

2. In this chapter, we created a weblog for the President of our fictitious company to post his latest news. Try creating a completely separate weblog in a separate template, where we can post the latest changes and newest additions to our rapidly growing website. (You can use the same **toast_css** template that we already created).

3. The only way to really get to grips with CSS is to experiment through trial and error. Try removing or changing a line in our CSS template, saving it, and then seeing what changes on our website. The following changes are a good start:

- Have a go at changing the color scheme of the **toast_css** without touching the **news** template. Instead of our shades of cream and brown, try creating your own color combo. A list of color names and their corresponding HTML codes is available at `http://www.w3schools.com/css/css_colornames.asp`. Additionally, `http://en.wikipedia.org/wiki/Web_colors` has good information.
- As part of our design, we deliberately left space for a menu on the right-hand side. If we decided that we didn't want to have a menu after all, what line of code could we change to fill the space?
- Try playing around with the photo on the website. I chose a photo of 201x151 pixels. If you upload a photo of a different size, what lines of code would you have to change?

> To find out the size of a photo in Windows, you can open the image in Paint, and then select **Image | Attributes** to see what the height and width are.

Summary

We have now demonstrated some of the most basic features of ExpressionEngine, including templates, weblogs, and tags. To summarize, tags go in templates to point to weblogs.

Everything you do in ExpressionEngine must eventually be viewable in a template. To create a new weblog, you first create the weblog, and then place tags into a template that will pull the weblog data into the browser.

Templates map directly to URLs that visitors can see. Within templates, you can write standard HTML and CSS. The stronger your HTML skills, the better your site will look.

In the next chapter, we will use ExpressionEngine to create what appears to visitors to be a conventional website, but with the added benefit that anyone can make editorial changes without ever seeing (or inadvertently deleting) HTML code.

4
Creating an Easy to Maintain Website

By now, we have already used ExpressionEngine to create our first weblog. While ExpressionEngine makes it easy to create and maintain a weblog on the internet, it is just as easy to create and maintain a more conventional website. In this chapter we will:

- Create a new weblog (or section) that will hold the text of our website pages
- Add customized fields to our weblog
- Create a template that will be used for our conventional website pages
- Create the first few pages of our new website using our new weblog and template
- Create a menu to navigate between these pages
- Create a 404 page for visitors who may otherwise get lost on our site

Note that this chapter will require the **Pages** module, included with the ExpressionEngine Personal or Commercial installations but not available in the free ExpressionEngine Core.

The Pages module allows us to use one template and one weblog for all the conventional pages on our website. Each posting to the weblog corresponds to a different page on our website.

Creating a New Weblog

Whenever we take on a new task in ExpressionEngine, we usually start with creating a new weblog. A weblog can be thought of as a dynamic data container, and most tasks in ExpressionEngine are going to involve some form of dynamic data. In this case, our dynamic data will be the text of our website pages.

Now let's look at how to create a new weblog:

1. Log into the control panel (http://localhost/admin.php or http://www.example.com/admin.php) and select **Admin** from the top menu.
2. Select **Weblog Administration** on the left-hand side and then select **Weblog Management**.
3. Select **Create a New Weblog**.

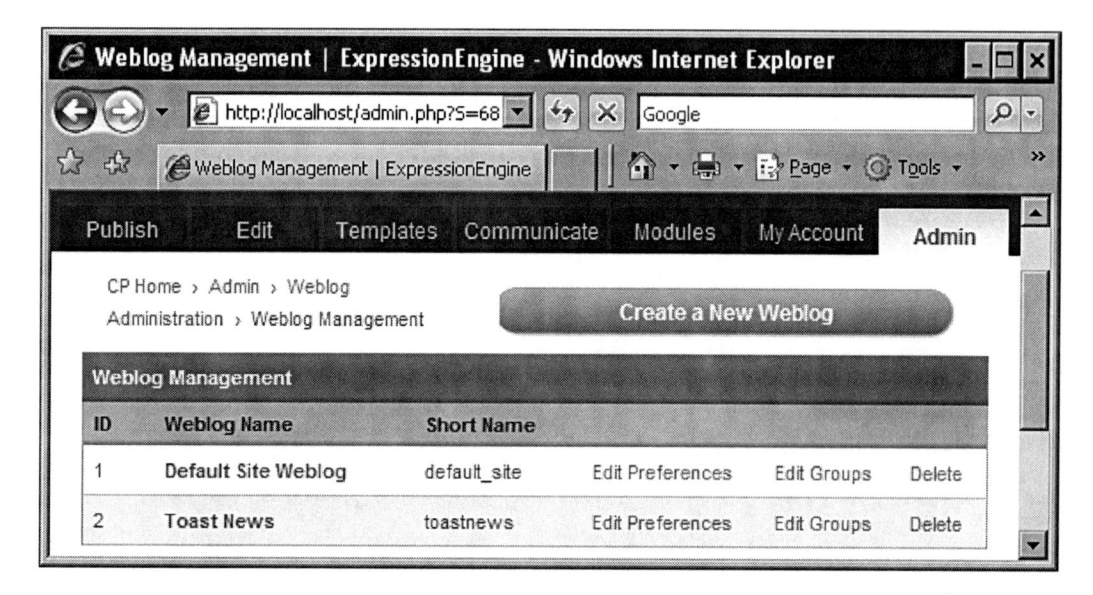

4. Now we need to choose a **Full Weblog Name** and a **Short Name**. Rather imaginatively, let us use **Toast Website** and **toastwebsite** respectively. Leave the rest of the options set as their defaults—do not duplicate an existing weblog's preferences; do not edit the group preferences; and do not create new templates for the weblog. We will do all of this later.

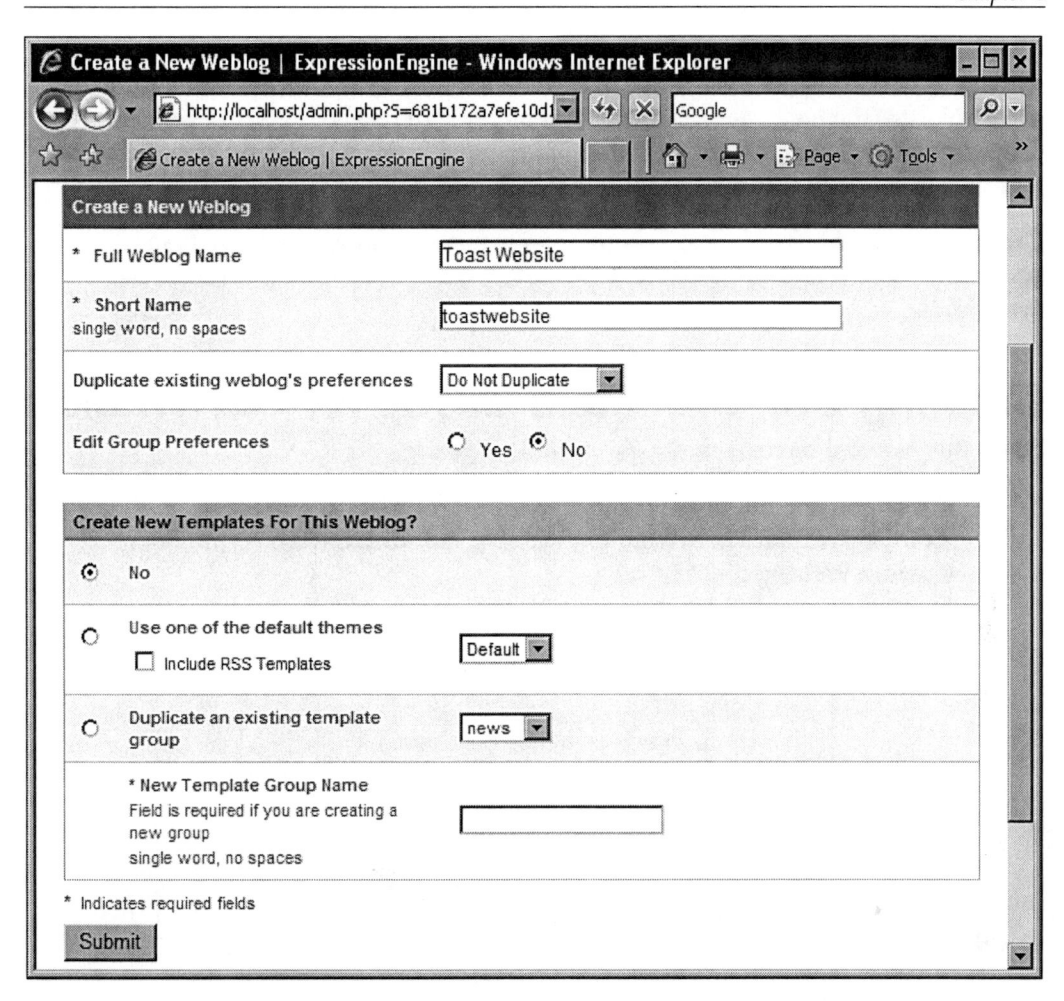

That's it! Our weblog has been created.

Creating Custom Fields

In the last chapter, we chose to use the Default Field Group for our Toast News weblog. These fields are the Summary, Body, and Extended text fields. One of the features that makes ExpressionEngine so flexible is that we do not have to use these fields at all, but can create our own fields customized to how we are going to use them.

Creating customized fields can be useful in any weblog. For example, if you have a weblog to post book reviews, you can have fields for the author, the ISBN number, a link to order the book, as well as the text of your review. You could even use a drop-down list (1 star, 2 stars, or 3 stars) to rate the book, using conditionals in your template to render a different graphic for each rating.

Certainly, a typical conventional website page has a lot more going on than a summary, a body, and extended text. To reflect this, we are going to create our own fields.

Creating Our Own Field Group for Our Weblog

To do this, we first have to create our own field group.

1. While you are still in the control panel, select **Admin | Weblog Administration**. Then, from the **Weblog Administration** menu, select **Custom Weblog Fields**.

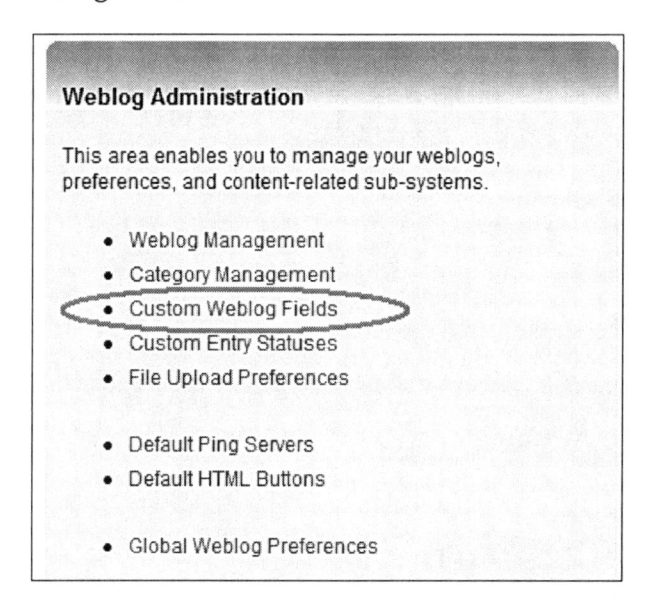

2. Here, you can see that the only custom field group we have is the **Default Field Group**. Select **Create a New Weblog Field Group**.

Chapter 4

> We do not want to edit the **Default Field Group** at this time as we already have a weblog (**Toast News**) using this field group. Editing or deleting fields that are already in use by a weblog may cause the data in those fields to be deleted or to no longer display on your website.

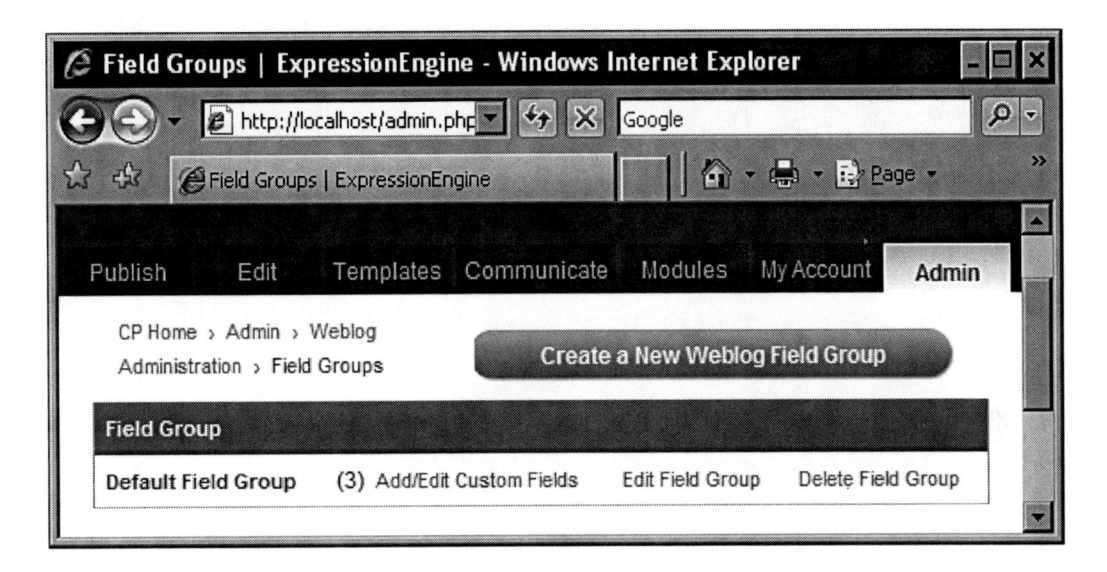

3. Next, we get prompted for a group field name. We are going to use **toastwebsite** so that we will remember which weblog these fields are associated with. Type this in and select **Submit**.

We have now created our new field group. However, it will be fairly useless until we create the fields within the group.

Customizing the Fields of Our Field Group

Now we have a field group and so we need to create our own fields. We will still keep our fields pretty generic, so that they will apply to the multiple pages. Therefore, we will use an introduction, a heading, text, a subheading, and more text.

Creating an Easy to Maintain Website

1. Still in the **Field Groups** screen, select **Add/Edit Custom Fields** for our field group.

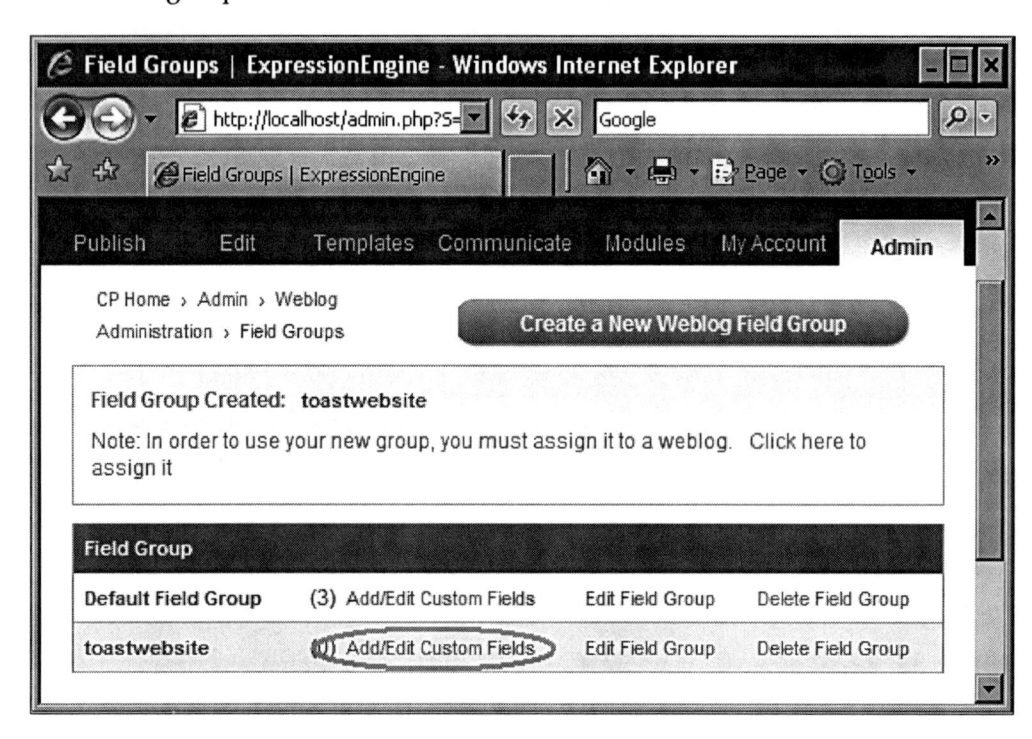

2. We are now presented with a screen showing us that we have no custom fields. Click the button that says **Create a New Custom Field**.

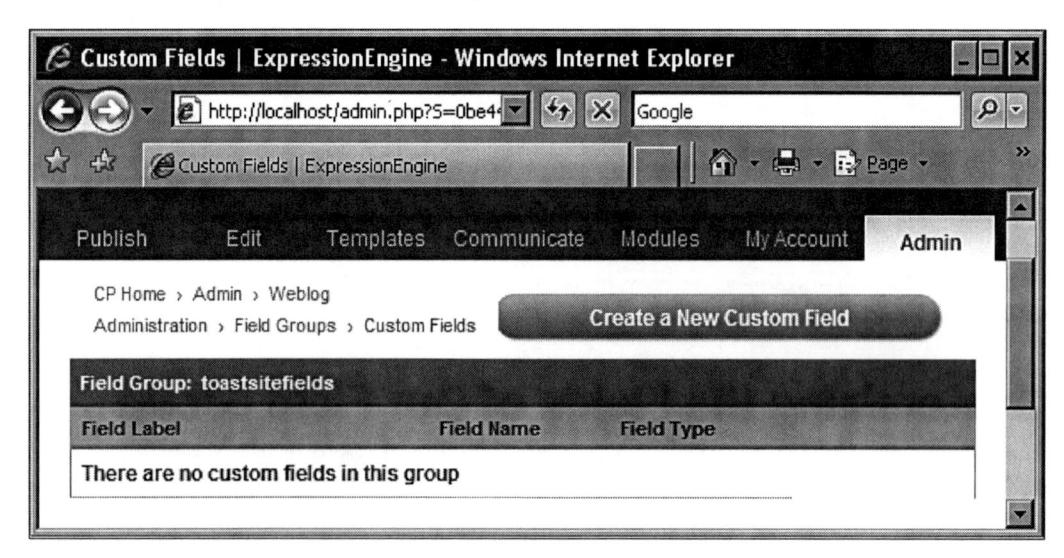

3. Our first field is going to be called **toastwebsite_introduction**. Why such a long name? Field names have to be unique across all field groups. In case we ever want a second field group with an introduction field, we are going to precede the field names with the name of the field group. The **Field Label** is the name that people see on the **Publish** page, and we will leave this as **Introduction**. We will also type in a short blurb into the **Field Instructions** telling users (who may not be as technically knowledgeable as us) what should be entered into this field.

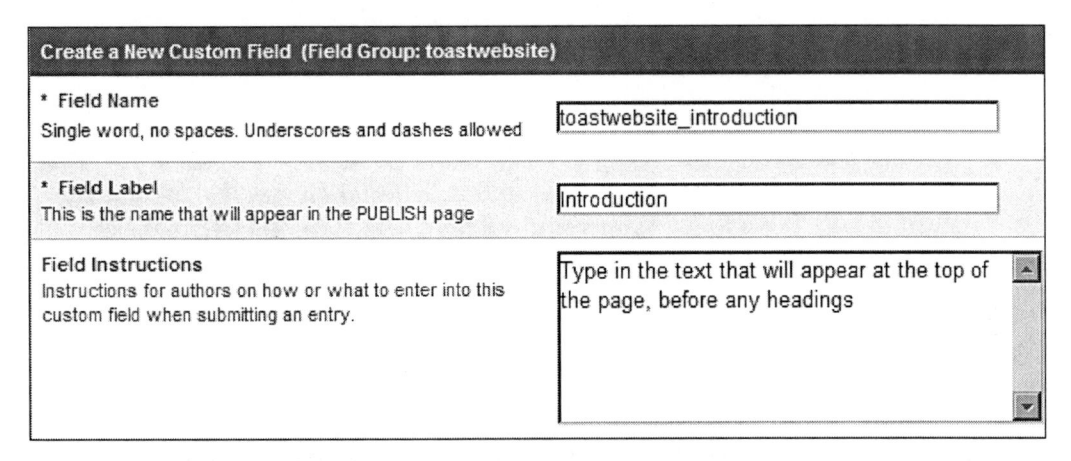

Create a New Custom Field (Field Group: toastwebsite)	
* **Field Name** Single word, no spaces. Underscores and dashes allowed	toastwebsite_introduction
* **Field Label** This is the name that will appear in the PUBLISH page	Introduction
Field Instructions Instructions for authors on how or what to enter into this custom field when submitting an entry.	Type in the text that will appear at the top of the page, before any headings

4. Further down on the same form, select a **Field Type** of **Textarea** and leave it as having **6 Textarea Rows**. **Textarea** is a text box that allows unlimited characters (just like the **Summary**, **Body**, and **Extended text** fields used in the **Toast News** publish page). Leave the **Display Formatting Menu** option checked, and leave the **Default Formatting** of this field as Auto <br />.

> For most custom fields, a default text formatting of None is appropriate. This means that no formatting is applied to the data in the field. Whatever we submit in our field will be treated as one continuous block of text. For a single line or paragraph of text, this means that we can handle all our formatting in our template.
>
> For fields where there might be multiple paragraphs of text, an alternative is Auto <br />, which inserts a line break (<br />) after every line in our entry.
>
> The xhtml option goes one step further, and wraps every paragraph in <p> and </p> paragraph tags. This is okay when we are planning to write one or more paragraphs in our entry, but often conflicts with the HTML in our template, creating extra unwanted white space.

Creating an Easy to Maintain Website

Field Type

[Textarea ▼]

[6] Textarea Rows

Default Text Formatting for This Field [Auto
 ▼]

◉ Display Formatting Menu
○ Hide Formatting Menu

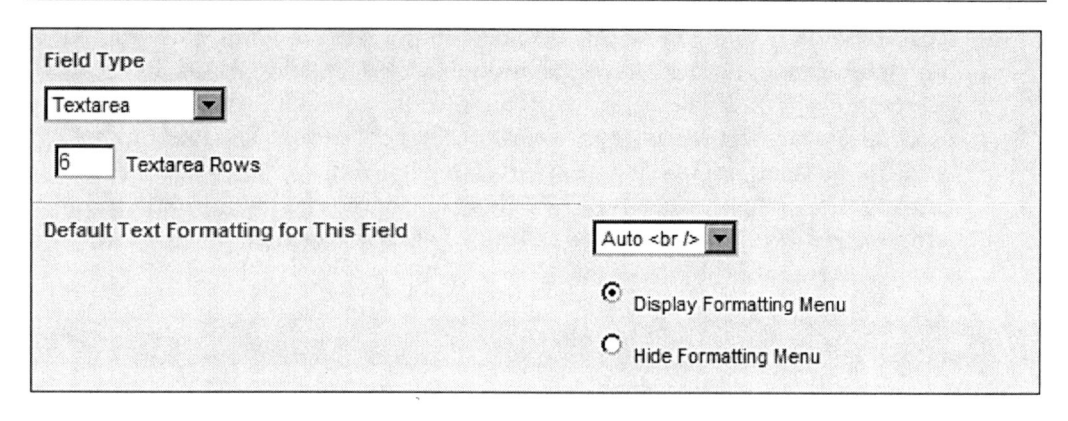

5. The last few settings are going to be the same for most of our fields. The **Text Direction** will be **Left to Right** (this option is for languages that are written right to left). We will leave the **required field** set to **No**. We will make the **field searchable**, and we will **Show this field by default**. We will not alter the **Field Display Order**; this can be used to insert a new field between existing fields, and only affects the display order of the fields on the **Publish** page. It has nothing to do with the display order of the fields on our website.

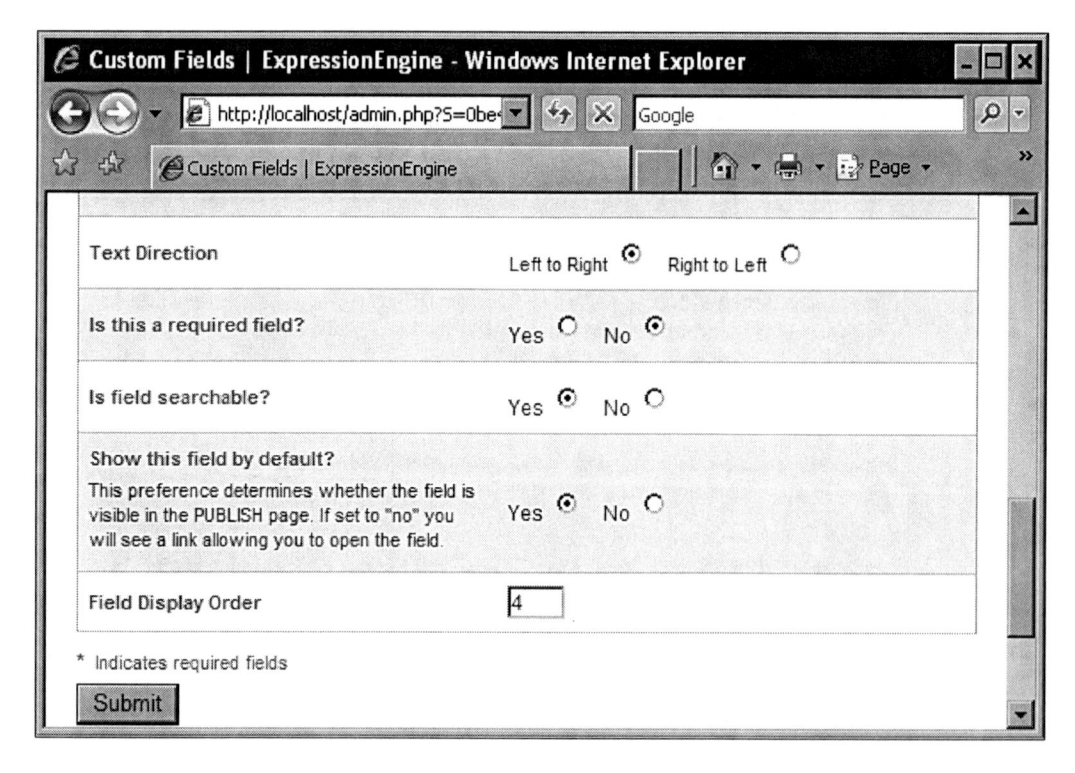

Text Direction — Left to Right ◉ Right to Left ○

Is this a required field? — Yes ○ No ◉

Is field searchable? — Yes ◉ No ○

Show this field by default?
This preference determines whether the field is visible in the PUBLISH page. If set to "no" you will see a link allowing you to open the field.
Yes ◉ No ○

Field Display Order — [4]

* Indicates required fields

[Submit]

[76]

6. Once we are happy with all the settings, hit **Submit**. We are returned to the **Custom Fields** page and can now see our new field listed.

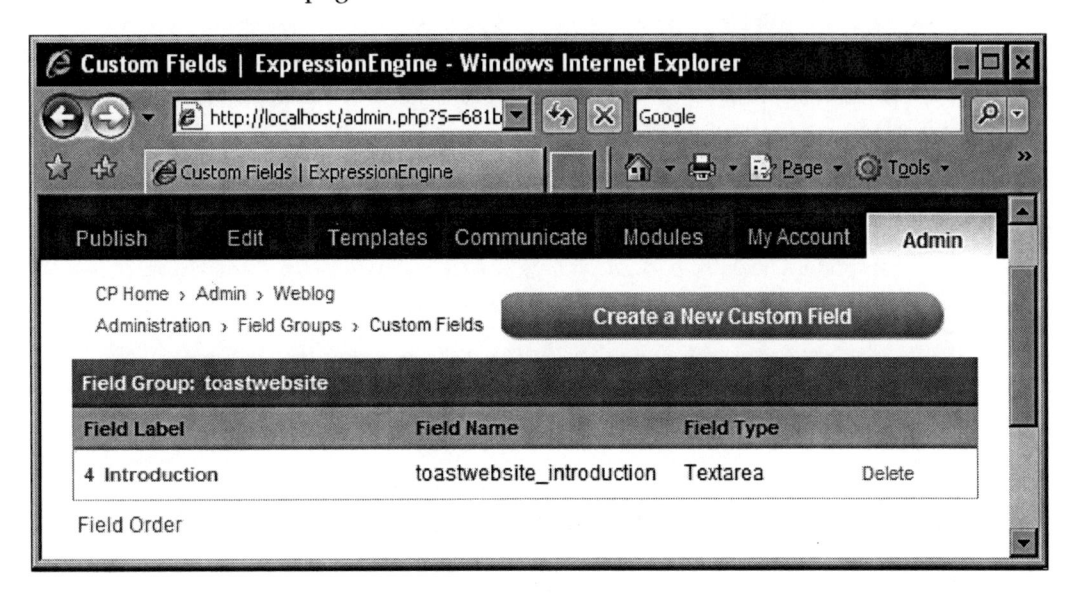

![Custom Fields screenshot showing Field Group: toastwebsite with Introduction field, toastwebsite_introduction, Textarea]

7. One field is not enough though. Our next field is going to be a heading field. This will allow non-technical users who are publishing content to put headings into their text without having to worry about the HTML required to format them. Once again, click the button that says **Create a New Custom Field**.

8. We are going to call the field as **toastwebsite_heading1**, and give it a **Field Label** of **Heading 1**. We will also add some rudimentary **Field Instructions**.

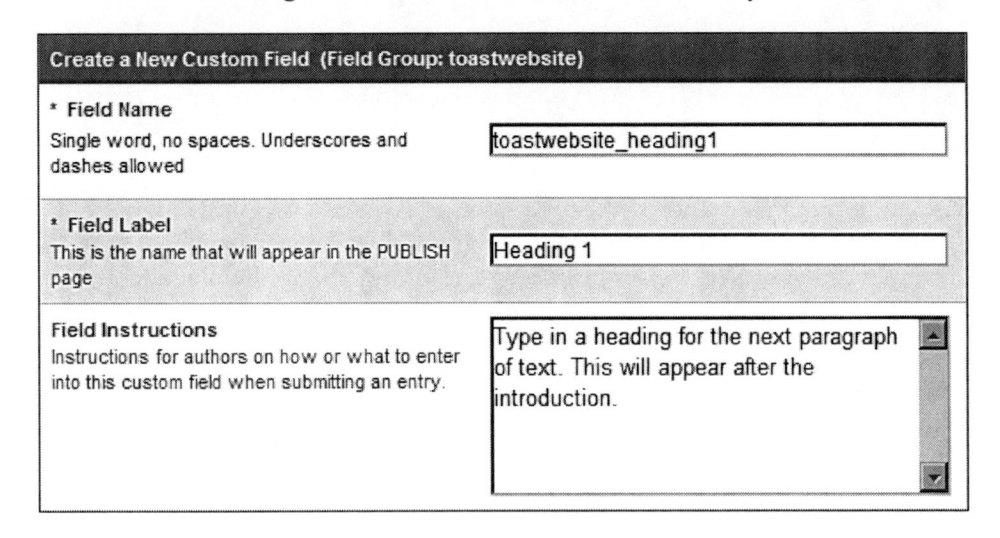

![Create a New Custom Field form screenshot with Field Name toastwebsite_heading1, Field Label Heading 1, and Field Instructions "Type in a heading for the next paragraph of text. This will appear after the introduction."]

Creating an Easy to Maintain Website

9. Because a heading should not be too long, we are going to make this field a **Text Input** instead of a **Textarea**. A **Text Input** is like a **Textarea**, except that only one line of text can be entered and there is a set character limit. The default **128** character limit should be sufficient.

10. This time, we will change the **Default Text Formatting** to be **None**, and we will **Hide Formatting Menu**.

> Because our heading is already going to be formatted within heading tags and will only be one line long, we will take care of the formatting in the template. The extra paragraph tags generated by the `<br />` or `xhtml` options will only create weird extra space before and after the heading.
>
> Hiding the formatting menu means that the option to switch back to `xhtml` or `<br />` is not displayed on the publish screen where someone might accidentally select it.

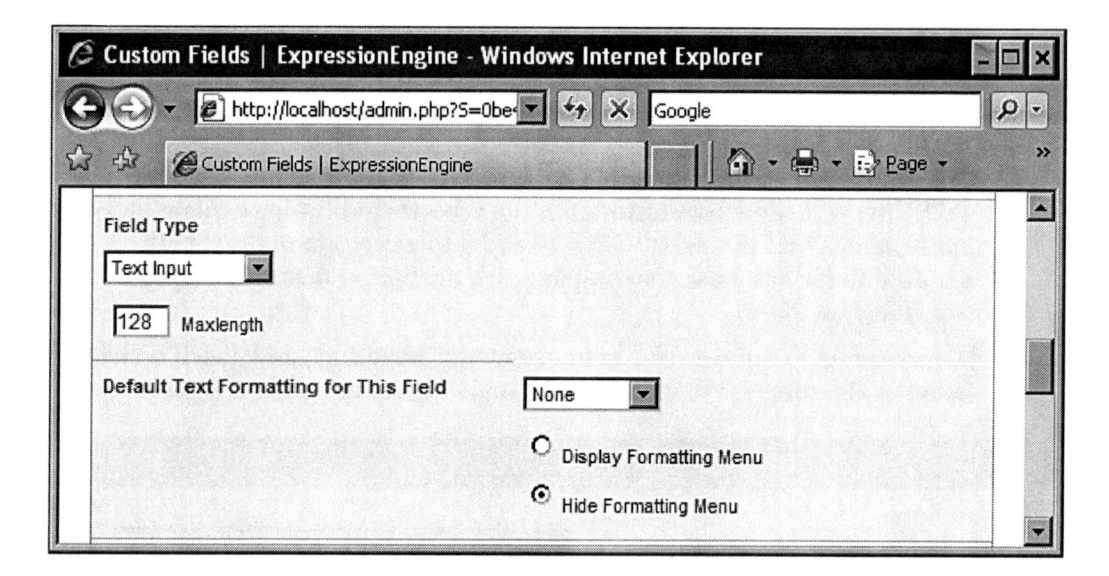

11. The rest of the options will be the same as last time, except that the **Field Display Order** number will be different (and as we discussed last time, the **Field Display Order** does not change anything about how our site looks). Once ready, click **Submit** and we can now see two fields in our **Custom Fields** list.

Chapter 4

Field Group: toastwebsite			
Field Label	**Field Name**	**Field Type**	
4 Introduction	toastwebsite_introduction	Textarea	Delete
5 Heading 1	toastwebsite_heading1	Text Input	Delete

12. The rest of the fields we are going to create are either like the **Introduction Textarea** or the **Heading 1 Text input** that we have already created. Go ahead and create the following fields on your own:

Field Name	Field Label	Field Type
toastwebsite_text1	Text 1	Textarea
toastwebsite_heading2	Heading 2	Text Input
toastwebsite_text2	Text 2	Textarea

We should now have at least five fields to use for our website. This is more flexible than the default **Summary**, **Body**, and **Extended text** fields. Of course, we could always create more if we saw a need arising.

Field Group: toastwebsite			
Field Label	**Field Name**	**Field Type**	
4 Introduction	toastwebsite_introduction	Textarea	Delete
5 Heading 1	toastwebsite_heading1	Text Input	Delete
6 Text 1	toastwebsite_text1	Textarea	Delete
7 Heading 2	toastwebsite_heading2	Text Input	Delete
8 Text 2	toastwebsite_text2	Textarea	Delete

Associating Our Fields with Our Weblog

If you were to now go to the Publish page and attempt to publish to our Toast Website weblog, you may be surprised to see that the Summary, Body, and Extended text fields are still showing and not our customized fields. This is because our customized fields need to be associated with our weblog.

Creating an Easy to Maintain Website

1. To do this, first select **Admin | Weblog Administration | Weblog Management**. Select **Edit Groups** for our **Toast Website**.

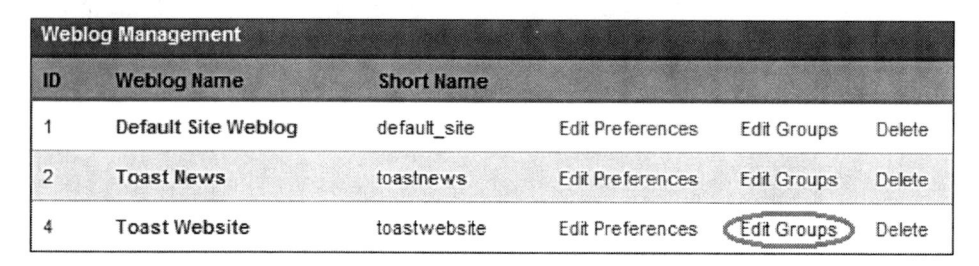

Weblog Management						
ID	Weblog Name	Short Name			
1	Default Site Weblog	default_site	Edit Preferences	Edit Groups	Delete
2	Toast News	toastnews	Edit Preferences	Edit Groups	Delete
4	Toast Website	toastwebsite	Edit Preferences	Edit Groups	Delete

2. Under **Status Group**, select **Default Status Group**, and under **Field Group**, select **toastwebsite**. Then select **Update**.

> The **Default Status Group** allows us to mark an entry as either **open** or **closed**. Without this option, only Super Admin members can publish open entries to a weblog.

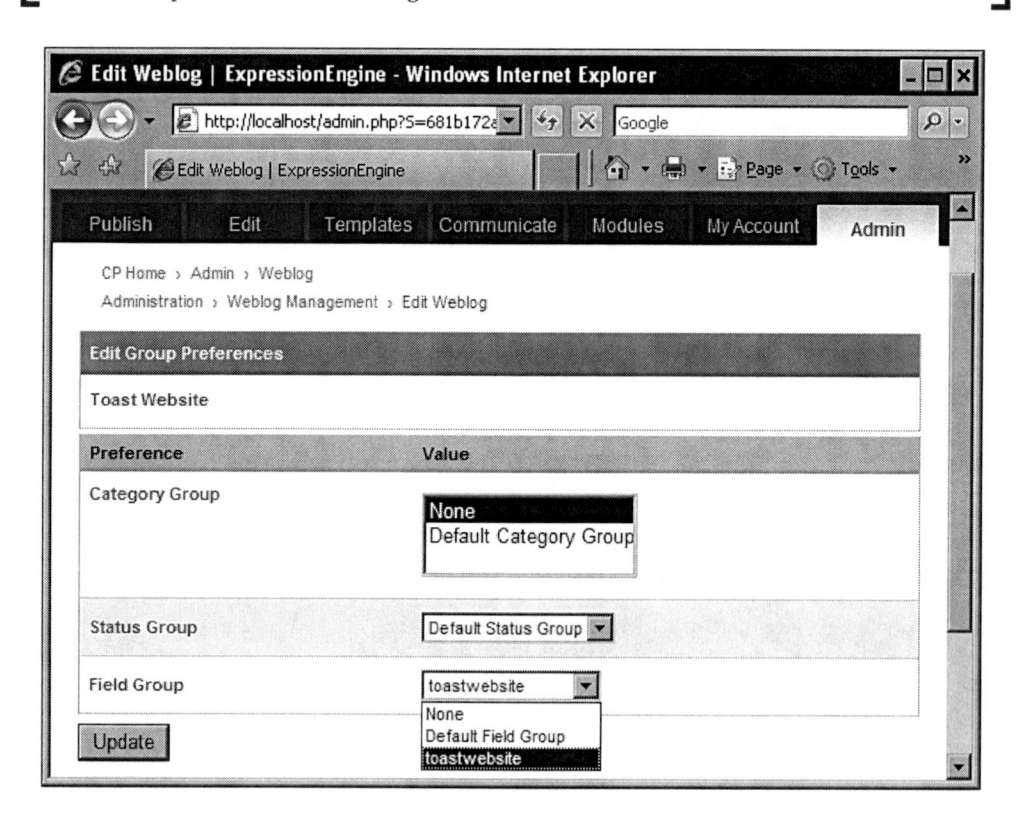

That's it. We are now ready to create the first draft of our home page.

[80]

Creating the First Draft of Our Home Page

Before we start creating a template for our home page, we first need to publish a first draft of our home page.

1. In the control panel, click on **Publish** and then select the **Toast Website** weblog.
2. We can see that the **Publish** page looks different than it did for the **Toast News** weblog. We still have a **Title** and a **URL Title**, but instead of the **Summary**, **Body**, and **Extended text**, we can now see our customized fields. Type in a first draft of the home page; we are going to use a **Title** of **Welcome** (which will default with a **URL Title** of **welcome**).

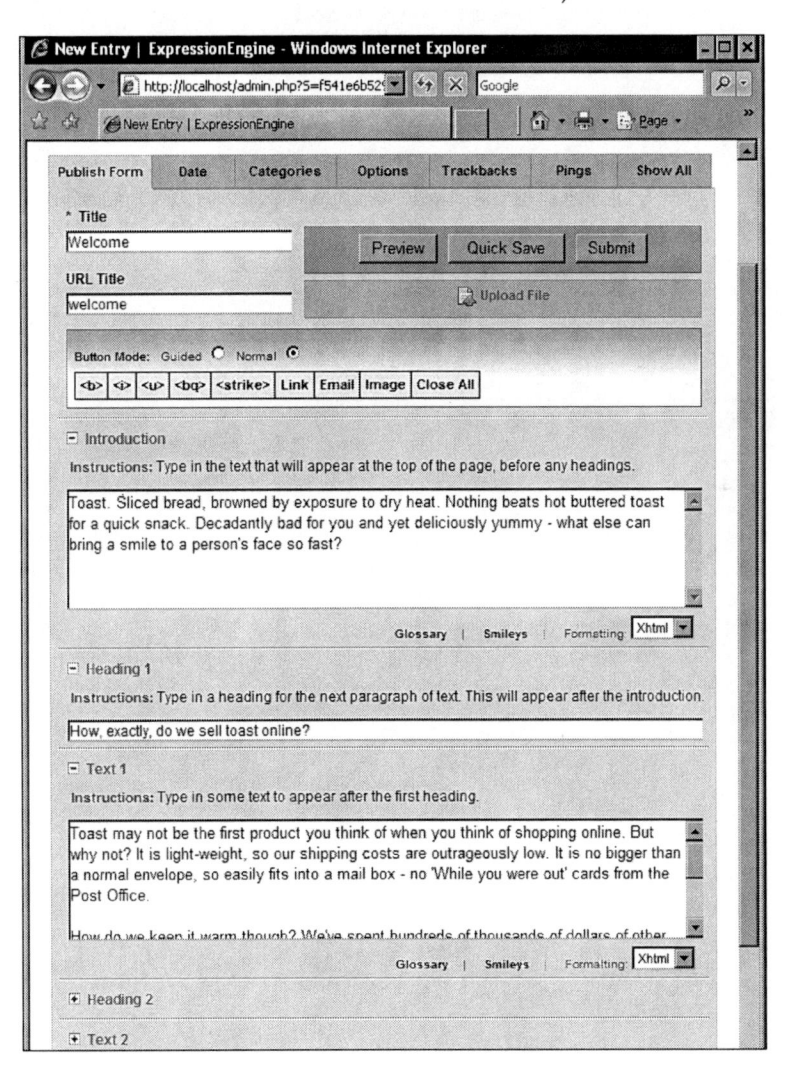

Creating an Easy to Maintain Website

> Notice how our text boxes are followed by a couple of options (**Glossary**, **Smileys**, and **Formatting**) and our headings are not. This is because we hid the formatting options for our headings while setting up the customized fields.

3. By default, ExpressionEngine will always show the most recent post to a weblog first. As this is our home page post, we want this post to appear by default, not the newest one. To do this, we are going to mark the entry as **sticky**. To do this, select **Options** from the menu above the fields and then check the box **Make Entry Sticky**.

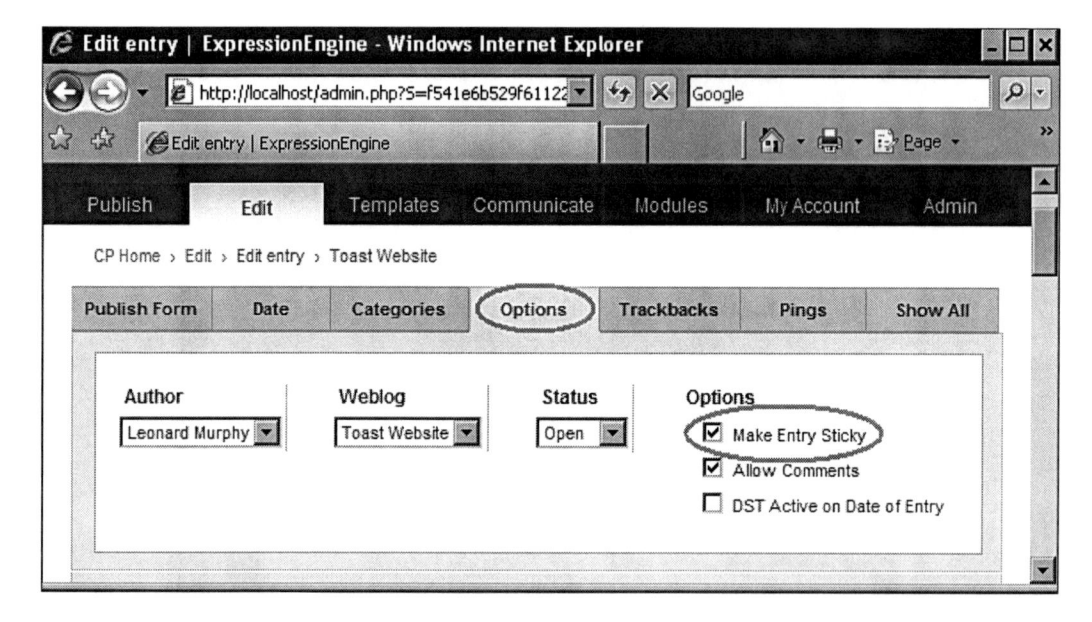

4. Hit **Submit** to save your entry.

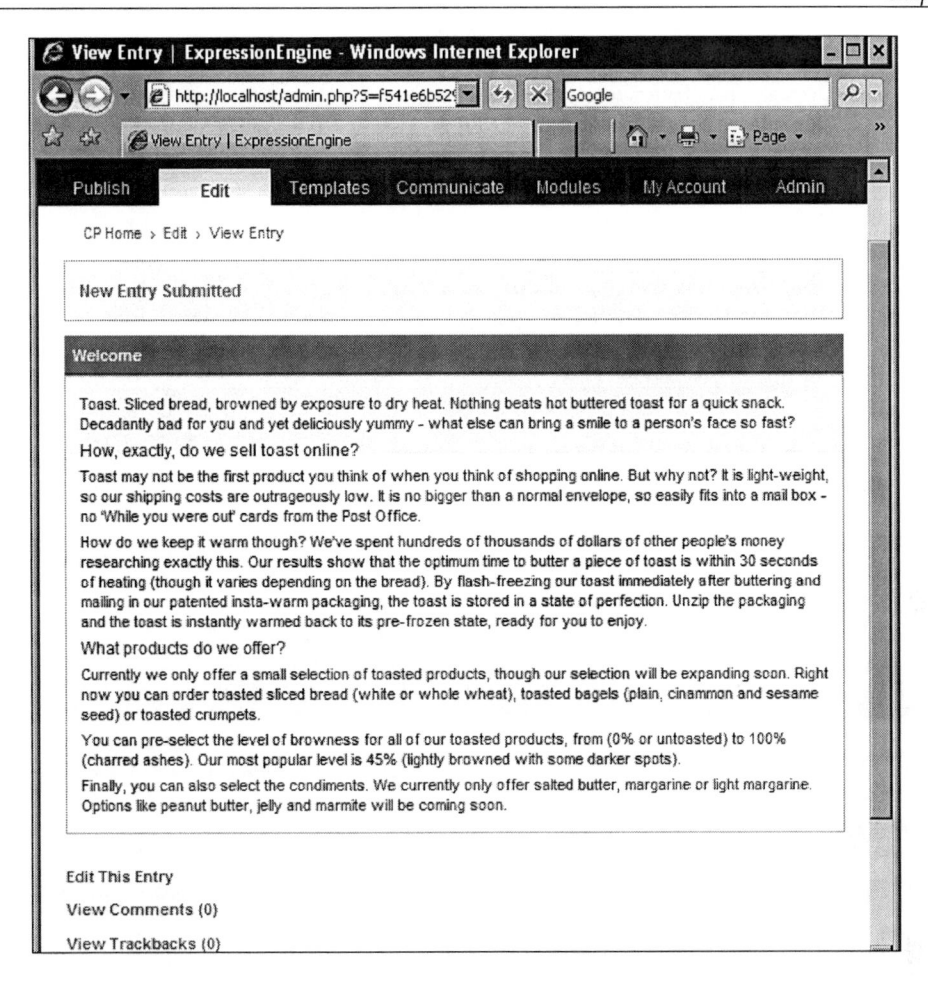

At this stage, we have written our home page but it's not yet visible on our website. Why is this so? This is because, as we saw in Chapter 3, everything on our ExpressionEngine powered website has to be in a template.

Creating the Template for Our Conventional Website

One nice feature of using ExpressionEngine to power a website in this way is that we need a minimum number of templates, regardless of how many entries are in our weblog. For this example we are going to display all our conventional site pages through a single template. As the first page on our website will be a conventional page, we are going to use the **index** template of our **toast** template group as our template.

Creating an Easy to Maintain Website

> Remember from Chapter 3 that every template group has an **index** template. This is the template that is returned if a visitor visits a URL like `http://www.example.com/templategroup` but does not specify which template in the template group they wish to see.
>
> As our **toast** template group is also the default group for our entire site (indicated by an * next to the template group name), this means that the **index** template of our **toast** template group is also the template that is returned if a visitor goes to the root of our website and does not specify a `template group` at all (for example, if they visit `http://www.example.com/`).

1. In the control panel, click on **Templates** and then select the **index** template of the **toast** template group.

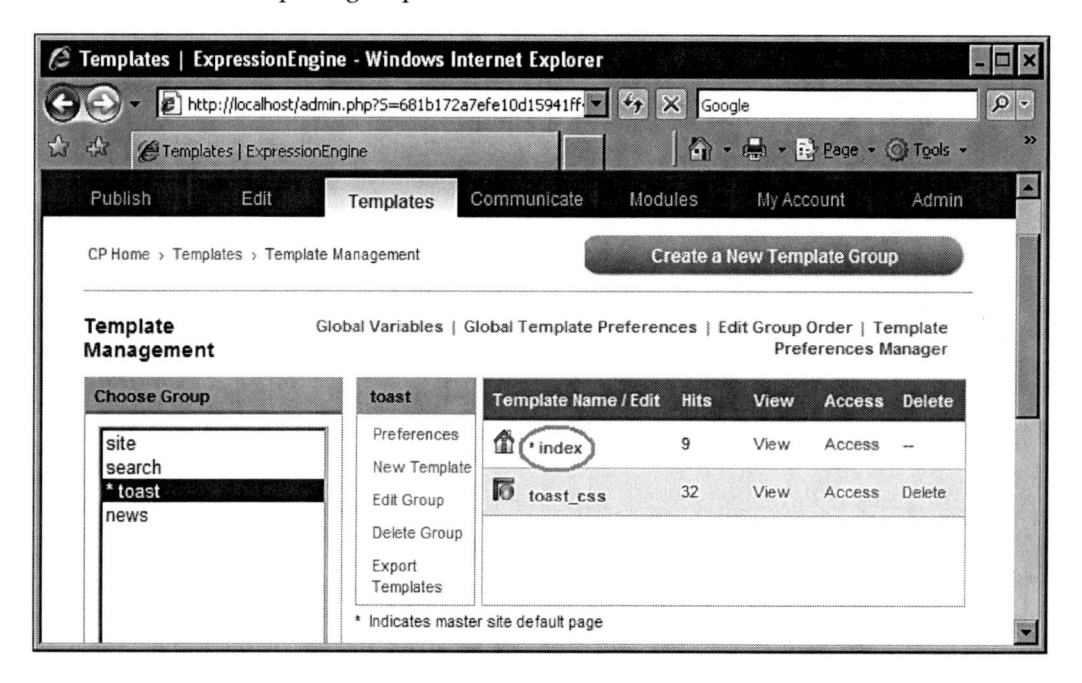

2. For the sake of simplicity, we are going to copy the `news/index` template into the `toast/index` template and modify it, rather than starting from scratch. The `news/index` template is outlined as follows:

   ```
   <!DOCTYPE html PUBLIC "-//W3C//DTD XHTML 1.0 Strict//EN"
   "http://www.w3.org/TR/xhtml1/DTD/xhtml1-strict.dtd">
   <html xmlns="http://www.w3.org/1999/xhtml">
   ```

```
<head>
  <title>News from the President</title>
  <link rel='stylesheet' type='text/css' media='all'
                    href='{path=toast/toast_css}' />
  <style type='text/css' media='screen'>@import
            "{path=toast/toast_css}";</style>
  <meta http-equiv="content-type" content="text/html;
                                    charset=UTF-8" />
</head>
<body>
  <div id="header">
    <h1>Toast for Sale!</h1>
    <h2>News from the President</h2>
  </div>
  <div id="content">
    {exp:weblog:entries weblog="toastnews"}
      <h3>{title}</h3>
      <div class="contentinner">
        {summary}
        {body}
        {extended}
      </div>
      <p class="footnote">Written by {author} on {entry_date
                                    format="%F %j%S"}</p>
    {/exp:weblog:entries}
  </div>
</body>
</html>
```

3. The first modification we are going to make is to change the weblog that the template points to. Rather than using `toastnews`, we are going to use `toastwebsite` (this is the short name of the Toast Website weblog). Change `{exp:weblog:entries weblog="toastnews"}` to `{exp:weblog:entries weblog="toastwebsite"}`.

4. Next, we are going to change the title of the page, currently `<h2>News from the President</h2>`, to be the title of our entry. Change it to:

   `<h2>{exp:weblog:entries weblog="toastwebsite" limit="1" disable="categories|custom_fields|member_data|pagination|trackbacks"}{title}{/exp:weblog:entries}</h2>`

Creating an Easy to Maintain Website

> Note the use of the `disable` parameter. This is optional. Whenever we use the `exp:weblog:entries` tag, a lot of information is requested from our database. This can increase the time it takes to display the page.
>
> As, in this case, we only want to display the title of the weblog, we can use the `disable` parameter to not request other data from the database at all. In this case, we are disabling everything we can (categories, custom fields, member data, pagination, and trackbacks).

5. Click **Update** now and visit `http://localhost/` or `http://www.example.com/`. You will see that our template is looking rather bare. Under **Toast for Sale!** we can see **Welcome**, which is our weblog title, but that's it.

6. Right now we have the title in two places (which is why we can see two **Welcome** headings in the previous screenshot). To change this, let us change `<h3>{title}</h3>` to reference our Heading 1 (using the field name we defined when we created the custom field):

    `<h3>{toastwebsite_heading1}</h3>`

7. So where is our content? Well, our template is still referencing the {summary}, {body}, and {extended} fields that we are not using for this weblog. In our Toast News weblog, we placed all three fields inside one <div class="contentinner"> box. However, we want to have our text in different boxes with headings in between, so we are going to change the content section to reflect this. To clarify what we have so far, the entire <body> section of our template is reproduced as follows:

```
<body>
  <div id="header">
    <h1>Toast for Sale!</h1>
    <h2>{exp:weblog:entries weblog="toastwebsite" limit="1" disabl
    e="categories|custom_fields|member_data|pagination|trackbacks"
                        }{title}{/exp:weblog:entries}</h2>
  </div>
  <div id="content">
    {exp:weblog:entries weblog="toastwebsite"}
      <div class="contentinner">{toastwebsite_introduction}</div>
      <h3>{toastwebsite_heading1}</h3>
      <div class="contentinner">{toastwebsite_text1}</div>
      <h3>{toastwebsite_heading2}</h3>
      <div class="contentinner">{toastwebsite_text2}</div>
```

Creating an Easy to Maintain Website

```
            <p class="footnote">Written by {author} on {entry_date
                                    format="%F %j%S"}</p>
        {/exp:weblog:entries}
    </div>
</body>
```

8. Each weblog posting corresponds to one page, and we only want to display one entry on each page. To limit this, we add a `limit` parameter to the `exp:weblog:entries` tag to limit the number of entries per page. Combined with our earlier setting of our home page posting as sticky, this means that whenever a person visits the index page of our website, they will only see the home page.

   ```
   {exp:weblog:entries weblog="toastsite" limit="1"}
   ```

9. We are starting to look more like a real website. However, you may have noticed that it still says **News from the President** in the title bar at the top of the window. As we are going to have multiple pages using this template, we do not want every page to have the same title. So, we will use the `exp:weblog:entries` tag to pull in the actual `{title}` from the weblog entry in the same way that we do for the `<h2>` title. Change `<title>News from the President</title>` to the following line:

   ```
   <title>Toast for Sale: {exp:weblog:entries weblog="toastwebsite"
   limit="1" disable="categories|custom_fields|member_data|pagination
   |trackbacks"}{title}{/exp:weblog:entries}</title>
   ```

   Toast for Sale: Welcome -
   `http://localhost/`

10. Finally, what happens if we were to leave one or more of our customized fields blank? A line like `<h3>{toastwebsite_heading1}</h3>` would be rendered in HTML as `<h3></h3>`, resulting in a blank space where the heading would normally be. To fix this, we can use a conditional `if` statement in the format `{if fieldname}<h3>{fieldname}</h3>{/if}`. This means that the entire line, including the `<h3>` tags, will only display if there is data in the field.

> To clarify our progress so far, our entire template, including this addition, is shown next.

```
<!DOCTYPE html PUBLIC "-//W3C//DTD XHTML 1.0 Strict//EN"
"http://www.w3.org/TR/xhtml1/DTD/xhtml1-strict.dtd">
<html xmlns="http://www.w3.org/1999/xhtml">
  <head>
    <title>Toast for Sale: {exp:weblog:entries
    weblog="toastwebsite" limit="1"
    disable="categories|custom_fields|member_data|
    pagination|trackbacks"}{title}{/exp:weblog:entries}</title>
```

```
        <link rel='stylesheet' type='text/css' media='all'
                    href='{path=toast/toast_css}' />
        <style type='text/css' media='screen'>@import
              "{path=toast/toast_css}";</style>
        <meta http-equiv="content-type" content="text/html;
                                    charset=UTF-8" />
    </head>
    <body>
      <div id="header">
        <h1>Toast for Sale!</h1>
        <h2>{exp:weblog:entries weblog="toastwebsite" limit="1"
        disable="categories|custom_fields|member_data|pagination|
              trackbacks"}{title}{/exp:weblog:entries}</h2>
      </div>
      <div id="content">
        {exp:weblog:entries weblog="toastwebsite" limit="1"}
         {if toastwebsite_introduction}
            <div
            class="contentinner">{toastwebsite_introduction}</div>
         {/if}
         {if toastwebsite_heading1}
            <h3>{toastwebsite_heading1}</h3>
         {/if}
         {if toastwebsite_text1}
            <div class="contentinner">{toastwebsite_text1}</div>
         {/if}
         {if toastwebsite_heading2}
            <h3>{toastwebsite_heading2}</h3>
         {/if}
         {if toastwebsite_text2}
            <div class="contentinner">{toastwebsite_text2}</div>
         {/if}
            <p class="footnote">Written by {author} on {entry_date
            format="%F %j%S"}</p>
         {/exp:weblog:entries}
      </div>
    </body>
</html>
```

Writng an About Us Page

So far, we have created a new weblog, customized its fields, posted to the new weblog, and created a template to display our weblog posts. However, we have not yet demonstrated how to manage multiple pages. To do this, we first need to create a new page—this time to tell the story of our company.

In the control panel, select **Publish**. Then select the **Toast Website** weblog, and create a new entry for an About Us page. We will use a **Title** of **About Us** and a **URL Title** of **about**. Unlike when we wrote the home page, we will not make this entry sticky. (If we did, it would cause this page to display on our home page). When you are ready, click **Submit**.

> The **URL Title** determines the final URL where the entry will be located. In most cases, the default URL title is fine. In this case, having a URL of http://localhost/about/ or http://www.example.com/about/ is arguably better than http://localhost/about_us/.

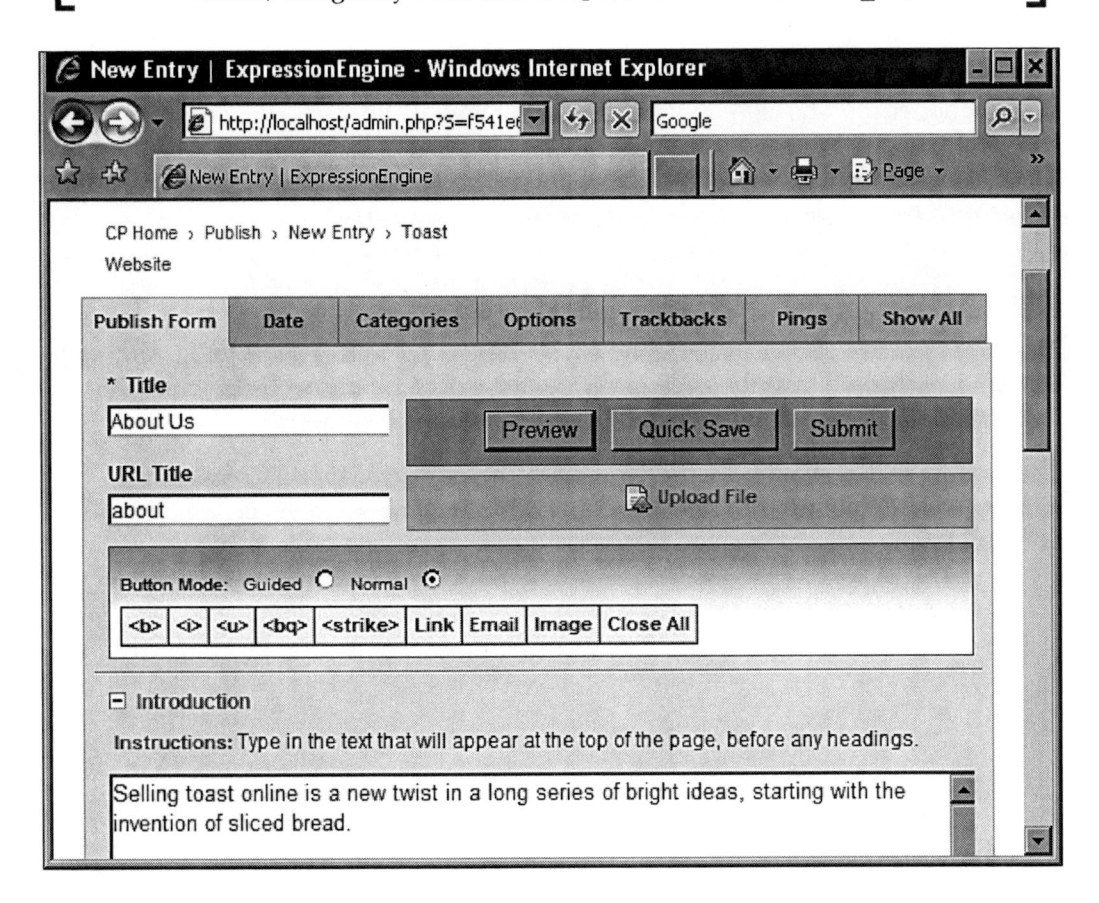

[91]

Now we have two pages. Where do we go to see our About Us page? Only if our toast template group is the default site template group and if our template is the index template of the group, then we can go to our URL Title to see the page (in this case, `http://localhost/about` or `http://www.example.com/about`). However, if our toast template group is not the default template group, the URL is `http://localhost/toast/about` or `http://localhost/toast/index/about/`. To get around the restriction of having to use the index template of the default site template group, we need the **Pages** module.

Customizing Our URLs

By default, URLs in ExpressionEngine are made up with the template group, the template name, and then the URL Title of the entry (that is, `http://localhost/template_group/template/entry_url_title`). There are exceptions to this. For example, when we are using the default template group, we do not have to specify the template group in the URL. However, it still means that most ExpressionEngine URLs appear to be two levels deep.

There is a way to override this default setting so we can instead choose the specific URL for our entry. This way, even if the **Toast** template group is not our default template group or we are not using the index template of that template group for our **Toast Website** weblog, we can still have the entries to our weblog appear at the root of our website (that is, `http://localhost/entry_url_title`).

Installing the Pages Module

The **Pages** module allows us to define any weblog entry with a short URL. Although this can be achieved by only using one template group for our website, using the Pages module allows us more flexibility and is not quite as limiting.

The module comes standard with ExpressionEngine Personal and Commercial editions—we do not need to download any additional files. However, we do need to install it.

In the control panel, select **Modules**. We will be presented with a long list of modules, some of which will show as installed (such as the **Weblog** module that we have already been using in our templates to display our weblog entries). Find the **Pages** module and select **Install** on the right-hand side.

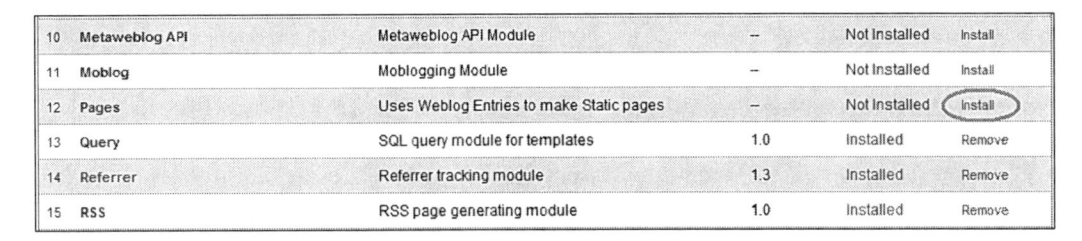

10	Metaweblog API	Metaweblog API Module	--	Not Installed	Install
11	Moblog	Moblogging Module	--	Not Installed	Install
12	Pages	Uses Weblog Entries to make Static pages	--	Not Installed	Install
13	Query	SQL query module for templates	1.0	Installed	Remove
14	Referrer	Referrer tracking module	1.3	Installed	Remove
15	RSS	RSS page generating module	1.0	Installed	Remove

You should now see a message that says **Module Installed: Pages** at the top of the screen.

Define Short URLs for Individual Weblog Entries

Next, we need to define the short URL for our weblog entries.

1. To use the Pages module to set a short URL for a weblog entry, we have to edit the corresponding weblog entry. First, click on **Edit** in the top menu bar.
2. Select the **About Us** entry from the **toastwebsite** weblog.
3. In the top menu, there is a new option, **Pages**. Select that.

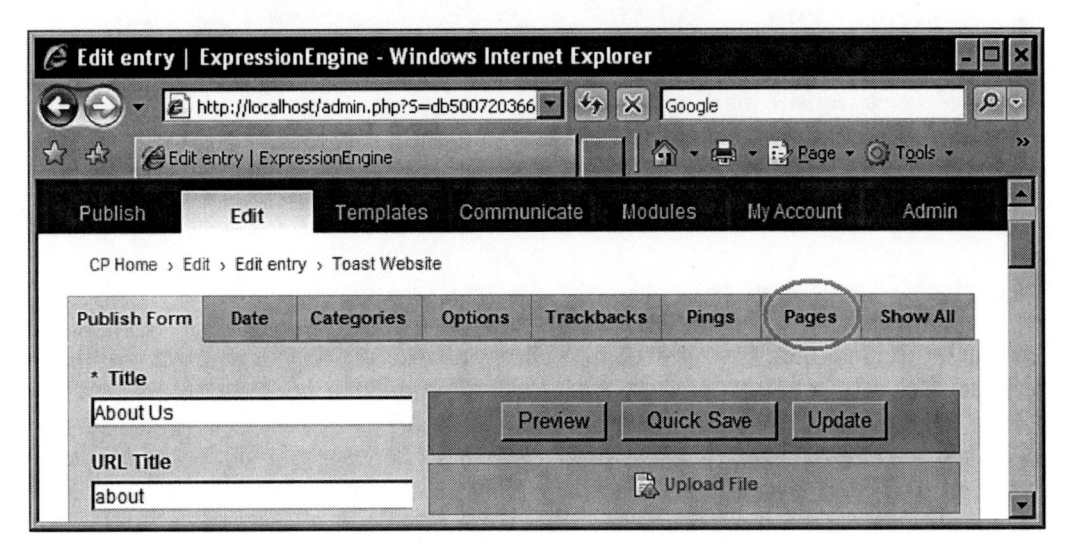

4. In the **Pages URL**, we want to type **/about**. This means that this page can be accessed via the URL `http://localhost/about` or `http://www.example.com/about`. We can also choose a **Pages URL** of **/about.html**, or even **/company/information**, and the URLs `http://www.example.com/about.html` or `http://www.example.com/company/information` would work equally as well.

5. For the **Template**, select **toast/index**. This means that the above URL will return this weblog entry using this template. This is important because ExpressionEngine usually uses the URL to determine which template to use. By using any URL, we have to explicitly specify the template we want used for the page to be rendered correctly. Click **Update**.

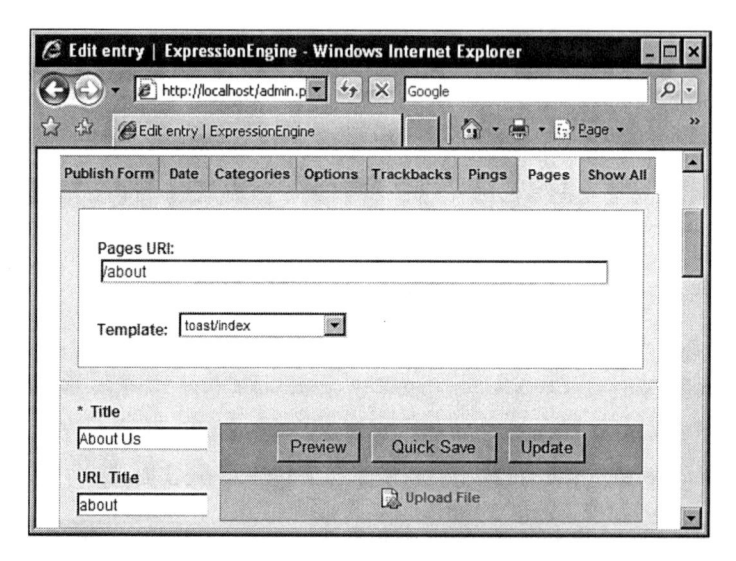

We now have a website that anyone can maintain. Instead of having to manipulate templates and template code when you want to make a change to a page, all you have to do is login, click on **Edit**, edit the text, and Click **Update**. No coding knowledge required!

Define a 404 Page Not Found

One of the challenges of ExpressionEngine is that, because we are not dealing with physical files, it is not always clear to ExpressionEngine if a page being requested is a valid page or not. Try visiting `http://localhost/ihatetoast` or `http://www.example.com/ihatetoast`; ExpressionEngine does not recognize `ihatetoast`, and so returns the index page of the default template group. This is terrible for search engines as it can make our website look like it has thousands of pages all with the same content. To combat this, we can define our own 404 page.

> In some situations, defining a 404 page can cause existing URLs on your ExpressionEngine site to stop working. If you have URLs on your site that do not include the template group name and do not use the Pages module, those pages will be returned 404. To work around this, either use the Pages module to maintain your existing URL structure or do not turn on the 404 functionality.

1. First, we need to create a template for our 404 page. Go to **Templates**, select the **Toast** template group, and then select **New Template**. Call the new template as **404**. The **Template Type** will be **Web Page**, and we will create an empty template. Click **Submit**.

2. Let us now take the base template for our conventional website, copy-and-paste it into our new `toast/404` template group, and modify the content so that it appears as a 404 page:

```
<!DOCTYPE html PUBLIC "-//W3C//DTD XHTML 1.0 Strict//EN"
"http://www.w3.org/TR/xhtml1/DTD/xhtml1-strict.dtd">
<html xmlns="http://www.w3.org/1999/xhtml">
  <head>
    <title>Toast for Sale: Page not Found</title>
    <link rel='stylesheet' type='text/css' media='all'
                  href='{path=toast/toast_css}' />
    <style type='text/css' media='screen'>@import
              "{path=toast/toast_css}";</style>
    <meta http-equiv="content-type" content="text/html;
                                  charset=UTF-8" />
  </head>
  <body>
    <div id="header">
      <h1>Toast for Sale!</h1>
      <h2>Page not Found (404)</h2>
    </div>
    <div id="content">
      <h3>We're Sorry</h3>
      <div class="contentinner"><p>The page you were looking for
      does not exist. There may be a spelling mistake in the
      URL in the address bar, or we may have removed this page
      inadvertently. Please use the menu on the right to visit a
                              page that does exist.</p></div>
    </div>
  </body>
</html>
```

Creating an Easy to Maintain Website

3. Once we have a 404 page we like the look of, we can define this page to appear when a page is not found. Select **Templates** from the top menu, and then select **Global Template Preferences** (located above the list of templates).

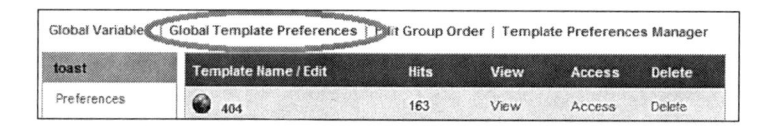

4. Under the **404 Page**, select **toast/404** as the template to display. While we are in this menu, we can also select **Yes** to **Save Template Revisions** and set the **Maximum Number of Revisions to Keep** to **10**. This is not an equivalent to regular backups, but it does provide an extra failsafe if we accidentally ruin an existing template and want to quickly return to an earlier version. Click **Update**.

> To restore a template to an earlier version, on every Template editing screen, there is a drop-down box named **View Revision History**. After changing and saving a template, we can select a previous version (up to 10) and Click **View**. This will open a new window with the template as it appeared at that time. We can then copy either the entire template or just parts of it into our existing template.

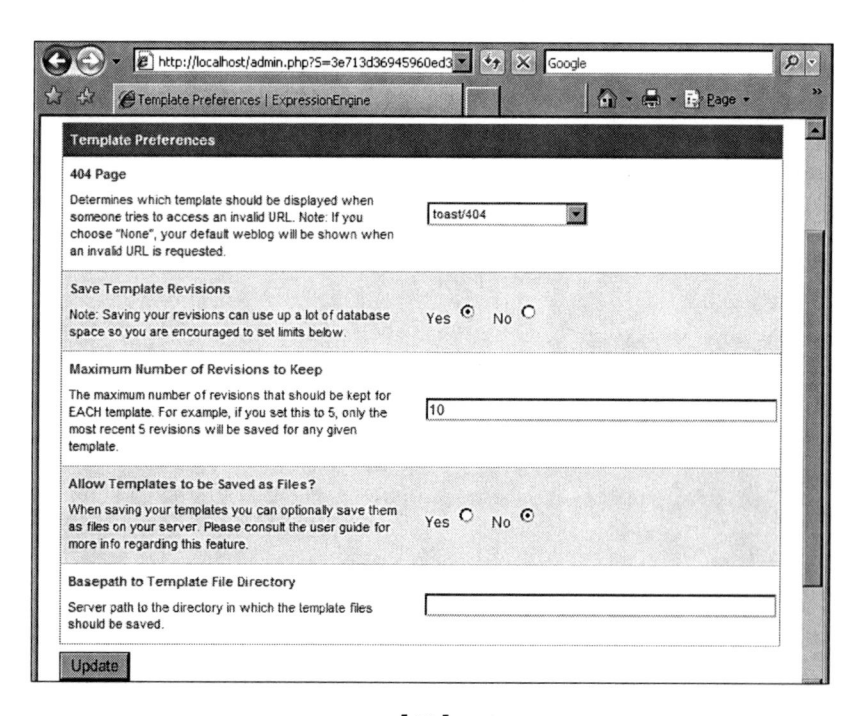

[96]

Now, when we visit `http://localhost/ihatetoast` or `http://www.example.com/ihatetoast`, we are returned with a valid 404 page.

Writing a Menu for Our Website

Now we have multiple pages so it is only appropriate that we create a menu to link them together. So far, we have seen that each template is equivalent to a page of our website. We are now going to break with that trend and create our menu in a new template which will then be embedded into several of our existing templates.

1. First, we need to create a template for our menu. Go to **Templates**, select the **Toast** template group, and then select **New Template**.

Creating an Easy to Maintain Website

2. We are going to call our new template **.menu**. The preceding period marks the template as a hidden sub-template. This means that the template can be embedded into other templates, but if you try and visit the template URL directly (for example, `http://localhost/.menu` or `http://www.example.com/.menu`), it will not work. The **Template Type** will be **Web Page**, and we will create an empty template. Click **Submit**.

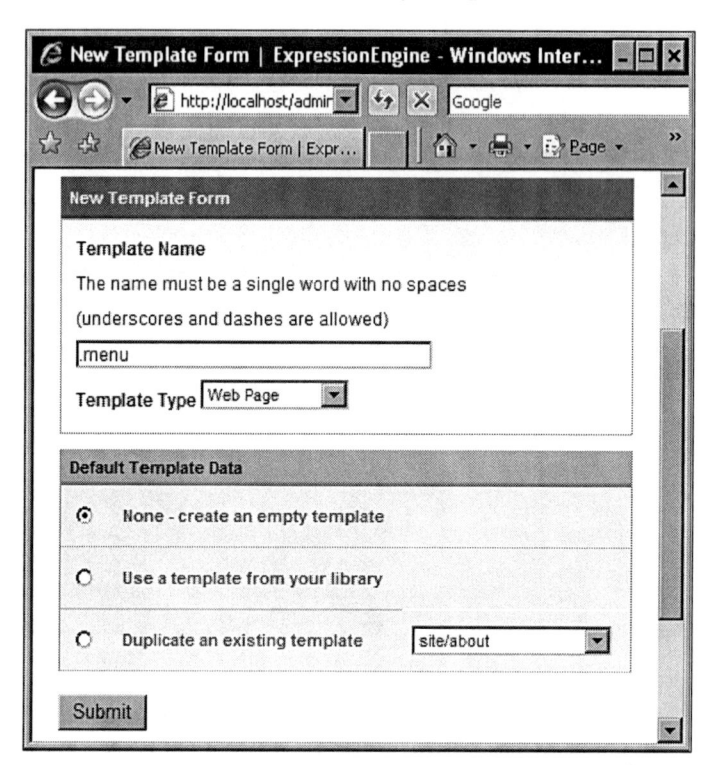

3. A menu is essentially a list, so we will use the `<ul>` HTML tags (for an unordered list). Edit your new template and type in the following:

```
<h4>Menu</h4>
<ul>
  <li>
    <a href="{site_url}" title="Welcome page ">Welcome</a>
      <div>Introduction to our business</div>
  </li>
  <li>
    <a href="{site_url}about" title="About our company ">More
                                    About our Company</a>
      <div>Is online toast the best thing since sliced bread? We
                                    think so</div>
  </li>
  <li>
```

[98]

```
          <a href="{site_url}news" title="News from the President">News
                                              from the President</a>
          <div>The latest news our President deems worthy of
                                                      sharing</div>
    </li>
</ul>
```

> Notice how we use `{site_url}` instead of typing out our actual website. As this menu may appear on any page of our site, it would be difficult to write out relative links. When the page is displayed in a browser, ExpressionEngine will automatically substitute the right URL.

4. Next, we want to embed the menu in each of our templates. To do this, add the following code after the closing `</div>` of the `<div id="content">` section.

```
      {/exp:weblog:entries}
    </div>
    <div id="menu">
      {embed="toast/.menu"}
    </div>
  </body>
</html>
```

> The `{embed}` tag is used to insert the entire contents of another template into this template. You can embed any template into any other, but be careful not to create an infinite loop.
>
> Why are we putting the `<div id="menu">` here and not in the menu template? It really does not matter, but doing it here will allow us to add items to the menu that may be unique to a certain section of the website.

5. Initially, our **Menu** does not look all that impressive. That is because we need to write the CSS to style it. Edit the `toast_css` template.

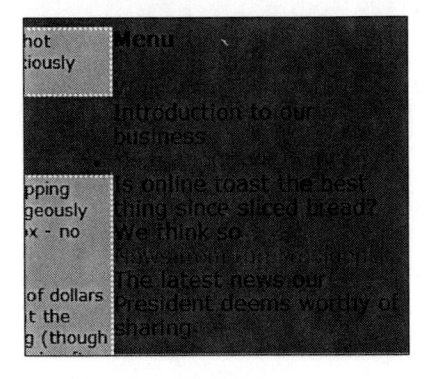

Creating an Easy to Maintain Website

6. There are four styles associated with the `<div id="menu">`: the `#menu` itself, the heading inside the menu `#menu h4`, the unordered list `#menu ul`, and the unordered list items `#menu ul li`. First and foremost, let us position the menu on the page a little better:

```css
#menu{
   width: 25%;
   float: right;
   margin-top: 50px;
   border: 2px dotted #FFEFD5;
   background: #DEB887;
   font-size: 70%;
}

#menu h4{
}

#menu ul{
   list-style: none;
}

#menu ul li{
}
```

> This sets the menu to only take up 25% (instead of the full 30%) of the right-hand side of the page. We use padding to create a small amount of space between the top of the menu and the text. We put a border around our menu and change the background color in the same way we did for the `#contentinner` section.
>
> The `list-style: none;` is what removes the bullet marks from our unordered list. While a menu is a list, we do not necessarily want to present it as such.

Menu

Welcome
Introduction to our business
More About our Company
Is online toast the best thing since sliced bread? We think so
News from the President
The latest news our President deems worthy of sharing

7. Now we are going to change some of the fonts and colors. First, we have our links. Links are styled in CSS using the style a. The style a:hover applies whenever we hover our mouse over a link, and a:visited is applied whenever we have visited the page that is being linked to. We can use a to apply to all links in a template, or we can use a within other CSS elements so that the styling only applies to links in our menu (for example). The following applies to all links on a page. We are going to have unvisited links be red and bold. Visited links will be brown. If we hold our mouse over a link, we will see a border above and below the link in question.

```
a{
  color: red;
  text-decoration: none;
  font-weight: bold;
}
a:hover{
  border-top: 1px solid #FFEFD5;
  border-bottom: 1px solid #FFEFD5;
}
a:visited{
  color: #A52A2A;
}
```

8. Although we removed the bullet mark from our unordered list, we can see that the space where the bullet mark used to be is left intact. To remove this, we can shift our list items to the left using a negative margin-left property.

```
#menu{
  width: 25%;
  float: right;
  margin-top: 50px;
  border: 2px dotted #FFEFD5;
```

Creating an Easy to Maintain Website

```
    background: #DEB887;
    font-size: 70%;
}
#menu h4{
}
#menu ul{
    list-style: none;
}
#menu ul li{
    margin-left: -25px;
    padding-left: -25px;
    margin-bottom: 5px;
}
```

9. Finally, let us make our **Menu** title more interesting. We will use a `border-bottom` to create an underline, and then create a gap after the heading and before any text using the `margin` property.

```
#menu h4{
    border-bottom: 1px solid #FFEFD5;
    margin: 10px;
}
```

[Screenshot of the "Toast for Sale!" welcome webpage in Internet Explorer, showing the header with a toast image, introductory text about toast, a section titled "How, exactly, do we sell toast online?", and a Menu sidebar with Welcome, More About our Company, and News from the President entries.]

Our menu is complete!

Exercises

1. Having two pages on a website is great, but having three pages is even better. Try creating a 'Promotions' page, where the latest promotions can be added.

2. In this chapter, we used a weblog to store and retrieve the text of our website, thereby saving us from having to edit HTML in our templates when we want to make a simple change to a page. We also have a template for our menu, so now let us try the same technique so that the menu items come from a weblog instead of being typed out in a template.

    - The first step will be to create a weblog dedicated to the menu.

Creating an Easy to Maintain Website

- The next step will be to create the custom fields for a menu. The basic fields are likely to be:

Field Name	Field Label	Field Type
`toastmenu_link`	Link URL	Text Input (999 chars)
`toastmenu_description`	Description	Text Input (999 chars)

- We will then want to publish our links into the weblog (we do not need to use the Pages module because we will never want to access a menu item individually).
- Finally, we will want to modify our menu template to bring in the links from the weblog using the `{exp:weblog:entries}` tag.

> As we want to pull the same menu items on different pages, we will have to use the `dynamic="off"` parameter in our weblog tag. Normally a weblog looks to the URL title to determine which entry to display—as the menu can display on any page, `dynamic` switches off this feature, forcing ExpressionEngine to display all weblog entries, regardless of the page.

3. Let us practice more CSS. Add the following code to the bottom of each template to create a footer. Now try styling the footer.

```
    <div id="footer">
        <p>This site was written by Leonard Murphy</p>
    </div>
  </body>
</html>
```

4. In this chapter we created a side-menu. Not everyone wants a side-menu. The below code is very similar to the code we used to create the side menu, except without the descriptions. Add this code to your templates inside the `<div id="header">` tags, just after the `<h2>` heading. Now try and create the CSS that will format this into a menu running across the top of the page instead.

> The magic piece of CSS is `display:inline;`—this causes a bulleted list item to display on the same line as the previous bullet.

```
<div id="topmenu">
  <ul>
    <li>
      <a href="{site_url}" title="Welcome">Welcome</a>
    </li>
    <li>
      <a href="{site_url}about" title="About">About</a>
    </li>
    <li>
      <a href="{site_url}news" title="News">News</a>
    </li>
  </ul>
</div>
```

Summary

In this chapter:

- We reinforced how to create weblogs, post entries, and create and edit templates.
- We used customized fields to tailor our Publishing screen to the needs of the weblog.
- We expanded our use of parameters, using the `limit` parameter to limit the number of weblog entries on a template and the `disable` parameter to reduce the amount of unnecessary data being retrieved from the database.
- We installed and used the Pages module to create pages for our new website.
- We created a menu in a separate template that we could embed into any of our other templates.
- We expanded our CSS template to style our menu.
- We created a 404 page for when a valid ExpressionEngine page does not exist.

In the next chapter, we will use ExpressionEngine to really get in-depth with our weblogs, and create a showcase of the various toasty products we offer.

5
Create an Advanced Weblog

So far we have used ExpressionEngine in two very different ways. We have created a basic weblog for the President's news and created an entire website. With both of these we can edit the existing text on the page or post new content without seeing a HTML tag at all. In this chapter, we are going to create a more advanced weblog that we will use to showcase our products. This weblog will:

- Use customized fields tailored to the products we are selling
- Allow us to browse multiple products and then drill-down to get more information on specific products
- Use comments to allow visitors to submit reviews of the products they have tried

From what we learned in the last chapter, we should now be familiar with the process of creating a weblog, creating customized fields, associating the fields with our weblog, posting our first entry, and creating a template. We will follow that same process in this chapter.

Create a New Weblog

As we have previously seen, a weblog is really a dynamic data container. In this chapter, the data we want to contain are the products we are selling.

1. Log into the control panel (http://localhost/admin.php if you are using XAMPP, otherwise http://www.example.com/admin.php) and select **Admin** from the top menu. Select **Weblog Administration** on the left-hand side, and then select **Weblog Management**. Now select **Create a New Weblog**.

Create an Advanced Weblog

The **Create a New Weblog** page looks like the following:

2. The **Full Name** for our weblog will be **Toast Products**, and the **Short Name** will be **toastproducts**. Leave the rest of the options set as their defaults—do not duplicate an existing weblog's preferences; do not edit the group preferences; and do not create new templates for the weblog. We will do all of this later. Click **Submit**.

Our weblog has now been created!

Customize Our Weblog Fields

As discussed in the previous chapter, one of the big benefits of using ExpressionEngine is the ability to customize our fields. This allows us to really tailor the fields we are using with the application we are using them for.

In our case, we are creating a weblog to showcase our toast products. We are going to have two text-based fields: a summary and a description. The summary will be displayed on our browsing pages so that visitors can briefly see what distinguishes each product. The description will be displayed on our individual product pages, and will allow us to go more in depth in describing the product.

As we are selling products, we will also want a photo of the product, so we will have a field for the photo file name. Finally, because toast is a food-based product, we are going to have fields for all our nutritional information (for example, calories, fat, carbohydrates, and protein).

1. Still in the control panel, select **Admin**. Select **Weblog Administration** from the left-hand side, and then select **Custom Weblog Fields** from the menu in the center. Now select **Create a New Weblog Field Group**.

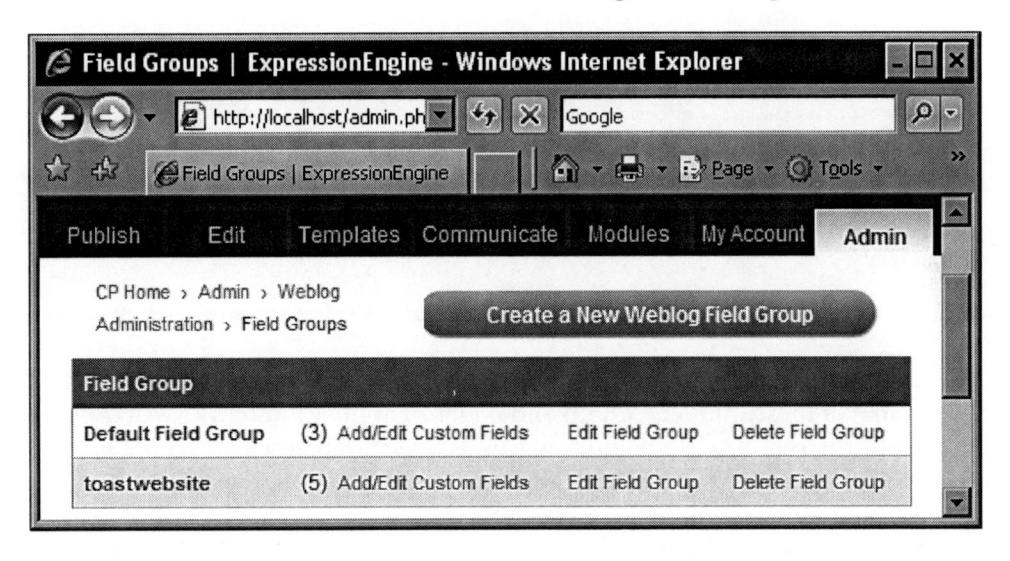

2. We are going to use a **Field Group Name** of **toastproducts**, as this field group will only be suitable for our toastproducts weblog. Click **Submit**.

Create an Advanced Weblog

3. You will see a message about assigning the field group to a weblog in order to use it. We will do this after we create the custom fields inside the field group. Select **Add/Edit Custom Fields** for our **toastproducts** field group, and then select **Create a New Custom Field**.

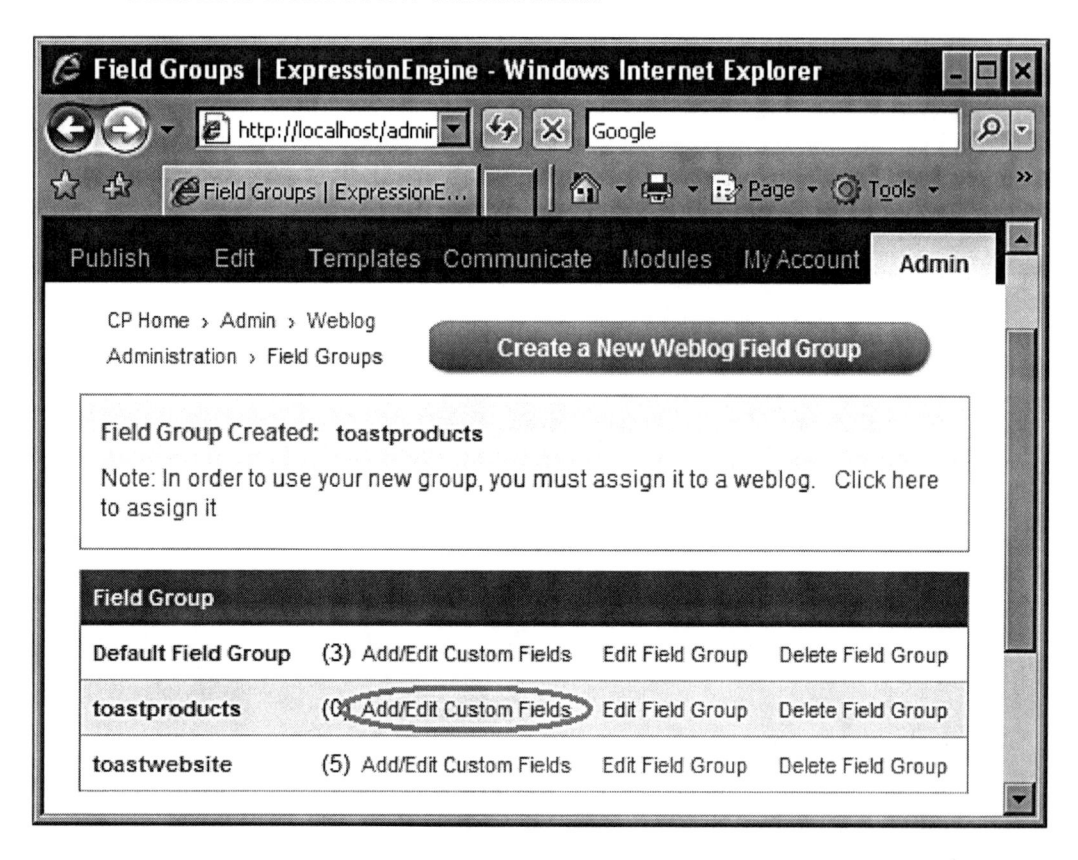

4. The first field we are going to create is the Photo field. We will give it a **Field Name** of **toastproducts_photo** and a **Field Label** of **Photo**. We will leave the **Field Instructions** blank for now (these would only appear on the Publish page). The **Field Type** will be **Text Input**. The **Maxlength** can be left at **128**. We will set the **Default Text Formatting** to be **None**, and we will select to **Hide Formatting Menu**. We will leave the field as not searchable and not required. **The Field Display Order** can be left as the default.

Create a New Custom Field (Field Group: toastproducts)	
* Field Name Single word, no spaces. Underscores and dashes allowed	toastproducts_photo
* Field Label This is the name that will appear in the PUBLISH page	Photo
Field Instructions Instructions for authors on how or what to enter into this custom field when submitting an entry.	
Field Type Text Input 128 Maxlength	
Default Text Formatting for This Field	None ○ Display Formatting Menu ⊙ Hide Formatting Menu
Text Direction	Left to Right ⊙ Right to Left ○
Is this a required field?	Yes ○ No ⊙
Is field searchable?	Yes ○ No ⊙
Show this field by default? This preference determines whether the field is visible in the PUBLISH page. If set to "no" you will see a link allowing you to open the field.	Yes ⊙ No ○
Field Display Order	9

5. Click **Submit**.

Create an Advanced Weblog

6. The following table contains the rest of the custom fields we are going to create. Go ahead and create the following fields in the same way as outlined in Chapter 4. Remember that the **Textarea** fields should have a default text formatting of `Auto <br />`, should not display the formatting menu, and should be searchable. The Text Input fields should have a default text formatting of `None`, should not display the formatting menu, and do not need to be searchable.

Field Name	Field Label	Field Type	Text Formatting	Formatting Menu
toastproducts_photo	Photo	Text Input	None	Hide
toastproducts_thumbnail	Thumbnail	Text Input	None	Hide
toastproducts_summary	Summary	Textarea	Auto 	Display
toastproducts_description	Description	Textarea	Auto 	Display
toastproducts_calories	Calories	Text Input	None	Hide
toastproducts_fat	Fat	Text Input	None	Hide
toastproducts_sodium	Sodium	Text Input	None	Hide
toastproducts_carbs	Carbs	Text Input	None	Hide
toastproducts_fiber	Fiber	Text Input	None	Hide
toastproducts_sugars	Sugars	Text Input	None	Hide
toastproducts_protein	Protein	Text Input	None	Hide

Field Label	Field Name	Field Type	
9 Photo	toastproducts_photo	Text Input	Delete
10 Thumbnail	toastproducts_thumbnail	Text Input	Delete
11 Summary	toastproducts_summary	Textarea	Delete
12 Description	toastproducts_description	Textarea	Delete
13 Calories	toastproducts_calories	Text Input	Delete
14 Fat	toastproducts_fat	Text Input	Delete
15 Sodium	toastproducts_sodium	Text Input	Delete
16 Carbs	toastproducts_carbs	Text Input	Delete
17 Fiber	toastproducts_fiber	Text Input	Delete
18 Sugars	toastproducts_sugars	Text Input	Delete
19 Protein	toastproducts_protein	Text Input	Delete

7. Now we have the custom fields; we will associate the field group with the weblog. Select **Admin | Weblog Administration | Weblog Management**. Now select **Edit Groups** for the **Toast Products** weblog.

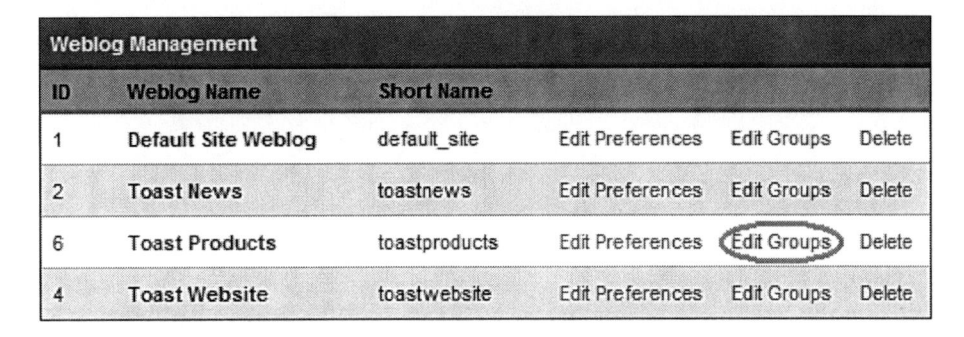

Weblog Management					
ID	Weblog Name	Short Name			
1	Default Site Weblog	default_site	Edit Preferences	Edit Groups	Delete
2	Toast News	toastnews	Edit Preferences	Edit Groups	Delete
6	Toast Products	toastproducts	Edit Preferences	Edit Groups	Delete
4	Toast Website	toastwebsite	Edit Preferences	Edit Groups	Delete

8. Under **Status Group** select **Default Status Group**, and under **Field Group** select **toastproducts**. Click **Update**.

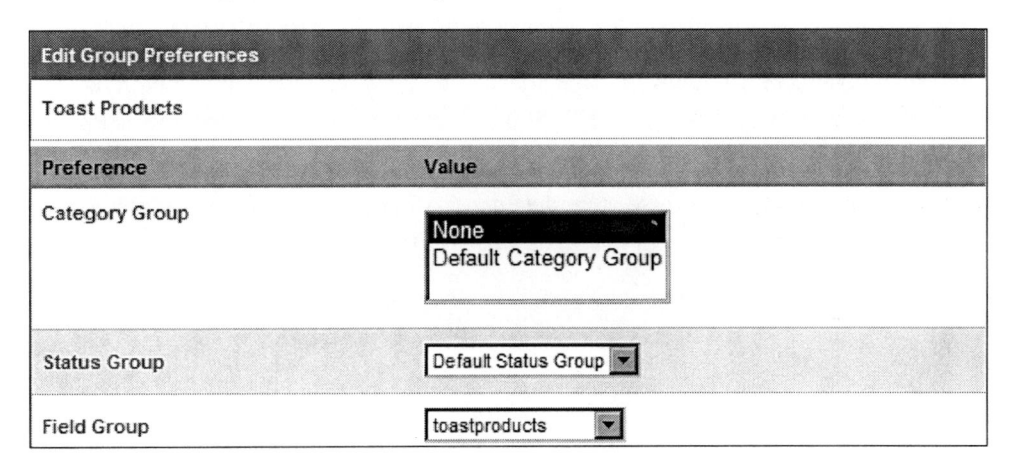

Edit Group Preferences	
Toast Products	
Preference	Value
Category Group	None / Default Category Group
Status Group	Default Status Group
Field Group	toastproducts

That's it! Our custom fields have been created and associated with our weblog.

Publish Our First Products

We have a weblog created and the fields customized. The next step is to publish some example entries so that we have entries to work with when we start formatting the weblog in a template.

> The images used in this chapter are available for download from
> http://www.packtpub.com/files/code/3797_Graphics.zip.

Create an Advanced Weblog

1. Select **Publish | Toast Products**. Our first product is going to be titled **Toasted Plain Bagel** with a URL Title of **toasted_plain_bagel**.

2. Next to the **Title** and **URL Title** fields, you will see an option to **Upload File**. Click this.

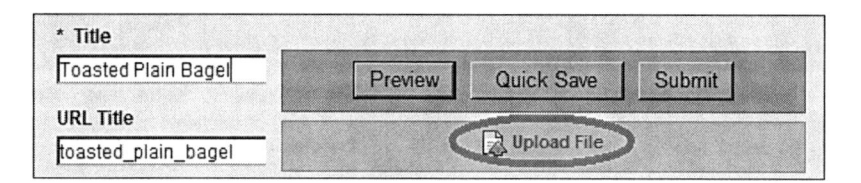

3. Browse to the `toasted_plain_bagel.jpg` file that comes with this book, leave the destination directory as **Main Upload Directory**, and click **Upload**.

> This will upload the file to your `images/upload` directory (for example, `http://localhost/images/uploads/` or `http://www.example.com/images/uploads/`). This is a nice way for people to upload images without needing to use a separate FTP tool, especially if the person posting entries does not have FTP access. However, there are limitations on the size of the file(s) that can be uploaded (controlled by the `php.ini` file that not all web hosting providers provide access to). You can edit the location of the main upload directory, restrict what kinds of files can be uploaded, or create other destination directories in **Admin | Weblog Administration | File Upload Preferences**.

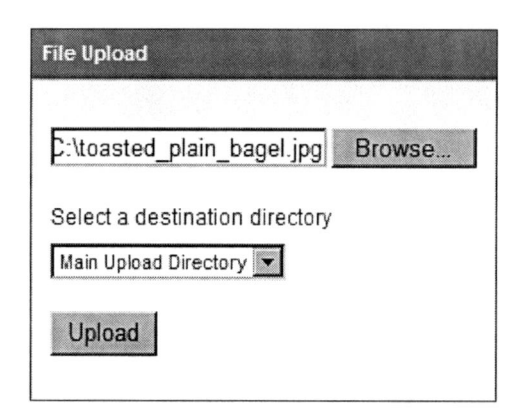

[114]

Chapter 5

4. Select **Resize Image** and we will be able to create a thumbnail of the image we just uploaded. Change the **Width** and **Height** to **100** pixels, leave the box **Constrain Proportions** checked, select **Create a separate copy**, and click the button **Resize Image**.

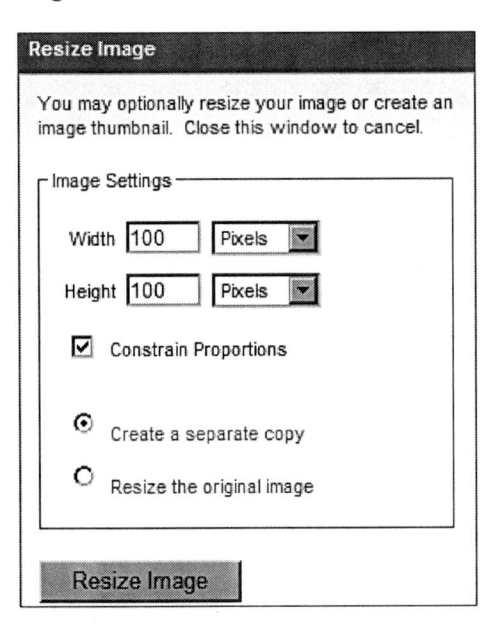

5. Next we are going to place a link to the file in one of our customized fields. In this case, we want to choose a **File Type** of **URL Only** and an **Image Location** of **Thumbnail**. Click **Place Image and Close Window**.

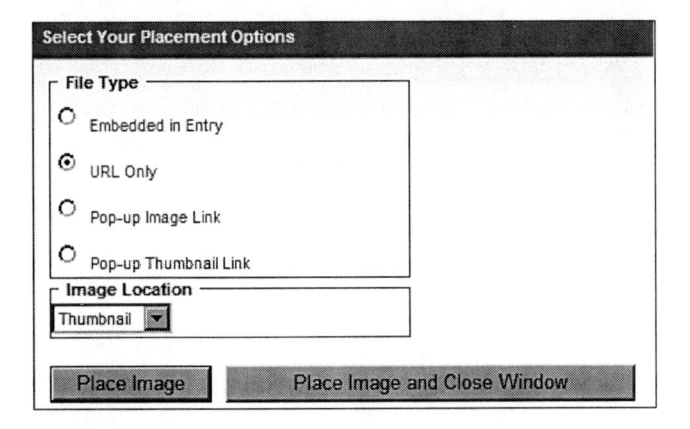

6. This will place the following text in our thumbnail field: `{filedir_1}toasted_plain_bagel_thumb.jpg`. The `{filedir_1}` is a variable that refers to our main upload directory.

[115]

Create an Advanced Weblog

7. In our Photo field, add `{filedir_1}toasted_plain_bagel.jpg`. This is the same code as in the thumbnail field, except without `_thumb` at the end of the filename—this links to our original photo.

8. For the rest of the fields, feel free to make up some text and nutrition information. Click **Submit**.

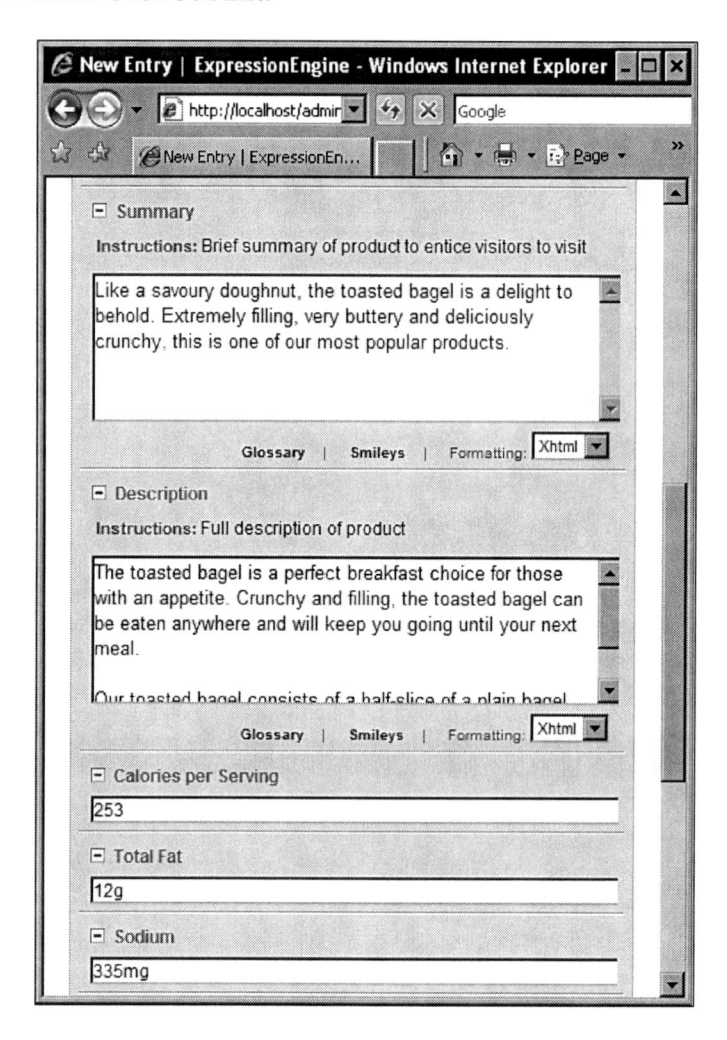

9. Repeat all these steps for a second entry called **Whole Wheat Toast**, uploading the `whole_wheat_toast.jpg` image file, and creating a thumbnail version as well. Again, please make up whatever text you like for the body of the entry.

We now have our first products written up, but before we can see this information on our website, we will need to create the template to showcase our products.

Create the Template for Our Product Showcase

Our first weblog, Toast News, displayed multiple entries on a single page using a single template. Our second weblog, Toast Website, displays a single entry on a single page using a single template. With our Toast Products weblog, we will want to display our entries both ways—a single page with multiple entries that a visitor can browse through, and a single page with a single entry where visitors can get more detail about a specific product and read reviews.

There are two ways to accomplish this. We can use one template for both the multiple-entry page and the single-entry page, using conditional statements to distinguish between them. Alternatively, we can create two templates—one for the multiple-entry page and one for the single-entry page.

For the purposes of this example, we are going to use one template. The advantage is that all our products information is in a single template. Additionally, the URLs for each entry will be more logical; the multiple-entry page will be at `http://www.example.com/products/`, and our single-entry page will be at `http://www.example.com/products/whole_wheat_toast/`.

The downside of using one template for both multiple- and single-entry pages is that the template can get complicated and confusing. We can use two separate templates and use the `permalink` tag on our multiple-entry template to point to the separate single-entry template. This does mean our URLs will work differently. For example, if our single-entry template is called `browse` and is in the `products` template group, the URL for the single-entry template will be `http://www.example.com/products/browse/whole_wheat_toast/`.

To distinguish between the multiple and single-entry pages in our template, it is important to know that ExpressionEngine divides up each URL into segments. So, `http://www.example.com/products/toasted_plain_bagel/` has two segments. `Products` is segment 1 and `toasted_plain_bagel` is segment 2. If the URL does not have a segment 2, then we know we can show our multiple-entry page, otherwise we can show the individual product page (in this case, our toasted plain bagel).

1. First, let us create our new template group. Click on **Templates**, select **Create a New Template Group**, call the new template group **products**, and click **Submit**. **Do not duplicate a group** and do not **Make the index template in this group your site's home page**. (We still want the toast template group to be the site's home page).

> We are creating a new group for our product showcase so that our URLs remain shorter. Creating a new template in our toast template group (for example, products) would mean all our URLs would be similar to `http://www.example.com/toast/products/toasted_plain_bagel`. By using the index template of the products template group, the same URL is shortened to `http://www.example.com/products/toasted_plain_bagel`.

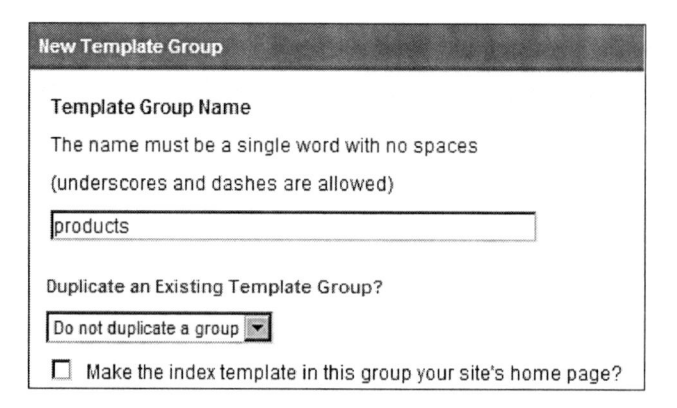

New Template Group

Template Group Name

The name must be a single word with no spaces
(underscores and dashes are allowed)

    products

Duplicate an Existing Template Group?

    Do not duplicate a group

☐ Make the index template in this group your site's home page?

2. Let us get the basics of the template defined. Edit the `index` template of the new `products` template group and type in the following. This will result in a page with our header, menu, and footer but no content. It is similar to all our other templates.

```
<!DOCTYPE html PUBLIC "-//W3C//DTD XHTML 1.0 Strict//EN"
"http://www.w3.org/TR/xhtml1/DTD/xhtml1-strict.dtd">
<html xmlns="http://www.w3.org/1999/xhtml">
  <head>
    <title>Toast for Sale</title>
    <link rel='stylesheet' type='text/css' media='all'
                      href='{path=toast/toast_css}' />
    <style type='text/css' media='screen'>@import
              "{path=toast/toast_css}";</style>
    <meta http-equiv="content-type" content="text/html;
                                    charset=UTF-8" />
  </head>
  <body>
    <div id="header">
      <h1>Toast for Sale!</h1>
      <h2>Our Selection</h2>
    </div>
    <div id="content">
    </div>
    <div id="menu">
      {embed=toast/.menu}
```

```
      </div>
   </body>
</html>
```

3. The first place we are going to use our conditional statement is in the `<title>` of the page. Replace the existing title with the following code. If there is a `segment_2` in the URL, we know we are on a single-entry page, and will display the title of that entry. Otherwise, we will display a generic title because we are on the multiple-entry page.

```
<head>
  {if segment_2}
     <title>Toast for Sale: {exp:weblog:entries
     weblog="toastproducts" limit="1"
     disable="categories|custom_fields|member_data|pagination|
            trackbacks"}{title}{/exp:weblog:entries}</title>
  {if:else}
    <title>Toast for Sale: Products</title>
  {/if}

<link rel='stylesheet' type='text/css' media='all'
href='{path=toast/toast_css}' />
```

4. We want to use a similar technique to change the `<h2>` page subtitle, depending on whether we are on an individual page or the browsing page. Replace the existing code in the `<div id="header">` tag with the following:

```
<div id="header">
   <h1>Toast for Sale!</h1>
   {if segment_2}
      {exp:weblog:entries weblog="toastproducts" limit="1" disable=
      "categories|custom_fields|member_data|pagination|trackbacks"}
         <h2>{title}</h2>
      {/exp:weblog:entries}
   {if:else}
      <h2>Our Selection</h2>
   {/if}
</div>
```

5. Next, we are going to write the code to display all the products, as long as there is no `segment_2` in our URL. We will write the code for the single entry pages in the next section. In the `content` section, type:

```
<div id="content">
   {if segment_2==''}
      {exp:weblog:entries weblog="toastproducts"}
         <h3><a href="{title_permalink="products"}">{title}</a></h3>
      {/exp:weblog:entries}
   {/if}
</div>
```

> The permalink tag generates a HTML `<a href>` link to the URL for that specific entry. A permalink is so called because it is a permanent link to that entry. For example, `http://www.example.com/products` may display different products in different orders at different times, but the permalink `http://www.example.com/products/toasted_plain_bagel` will always be a link to the Toasted Plain Bagel entry.
>
> The permalink tag includes one parameter, which is the template to use to display the entry. In our case, the `index` template is the default template of the `products` template group, so we only need to specify the `products` template group. If you are using a different template for your individual product entries, this is where you would need to specify the template that you are using, for example, `title_permalink="products/browse"}`.

6. If we now visit `http://localhost/products/` or `http://www.example.com/products/`, we can see the titles for the weblog entries we have already submitted. Notice that they link to individual pages, such as `http://localhost/products/toasted_plain_bagel/`. This also uses the `products` template group.

7. Finally, we are going to add the content of our entry. As we are still working on the multiple-entry page, we are only going to display the summary and the thumbnail of the product. We are going to create a new class, `innerbox`, to help format our product showcase.

```
{if segment_2==''}
  {exp:weblog:entries weblog="toastproducts"}
    <h3><a href="{title_permalink="products"}">{title}</a></h3>
    <div class="contentinner">
      <div class="innerbox">
        <a href="{title_permalink="products"}"><img
        src="{toastproducts_thumbnail}" alt="{title}" /></a>
        {toastproducts_summary}
      </div>
    </div>
  {/exp:weblog:entries}
{/if}
```

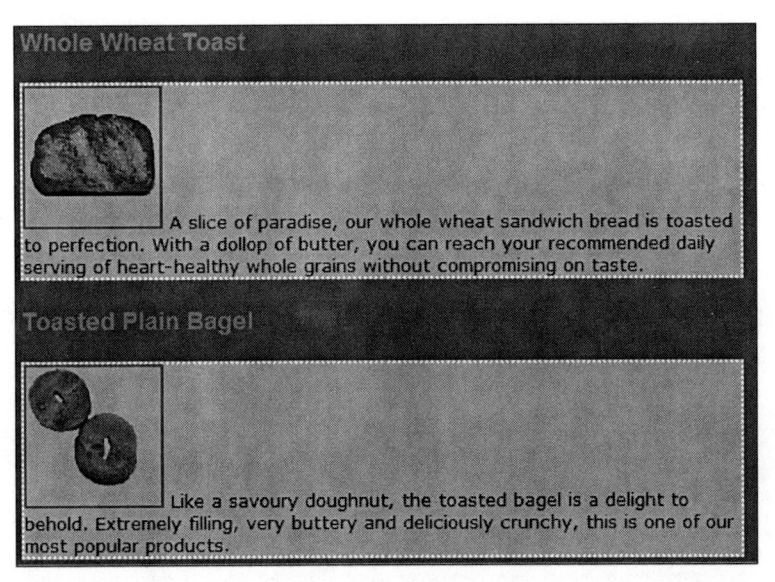

8. Let us make some brief additions to the `toast_css` template to present this showcase a little better. The `#content h3 a` and `#content h3 a:visited` will color our headings (which are hyperlinks) so they are not red like our other links. (Dark red on dark brown does not make for good visibility.) The `float` command in the `.innerbox img` allows our text and our image to sit alongside each other (rather than having the text following the image). The margin and padding ensures that our elements have some space between them (that is, the image and the text do not touch, and the image does not touch the edges of our box). The `overflow: auto;` forces the box the image is in to stretch to encompass the image. Without this, floating the image to the left would result in it overflowing the boundaries of the box.

```
#content h3 a{
  color: #F0E68C;
}
```

```css
#content h3 a:visited{
  color: #F0E68C;
}
.contentinner{
  background: #DEB887;
  border: 2px dotted #FFEFD5;
  overflow: auto;
  width: 100%;
}
.innerbox{
  margin: 5%;
}
.innerbox img{
  float: left;
  padding-right: 5%;
  border: 0px;
}
```

This is it! Our **Products** page is complete, allowing us to browse all our products and click on the one that interests us. Next, we have to create the individual product pages.

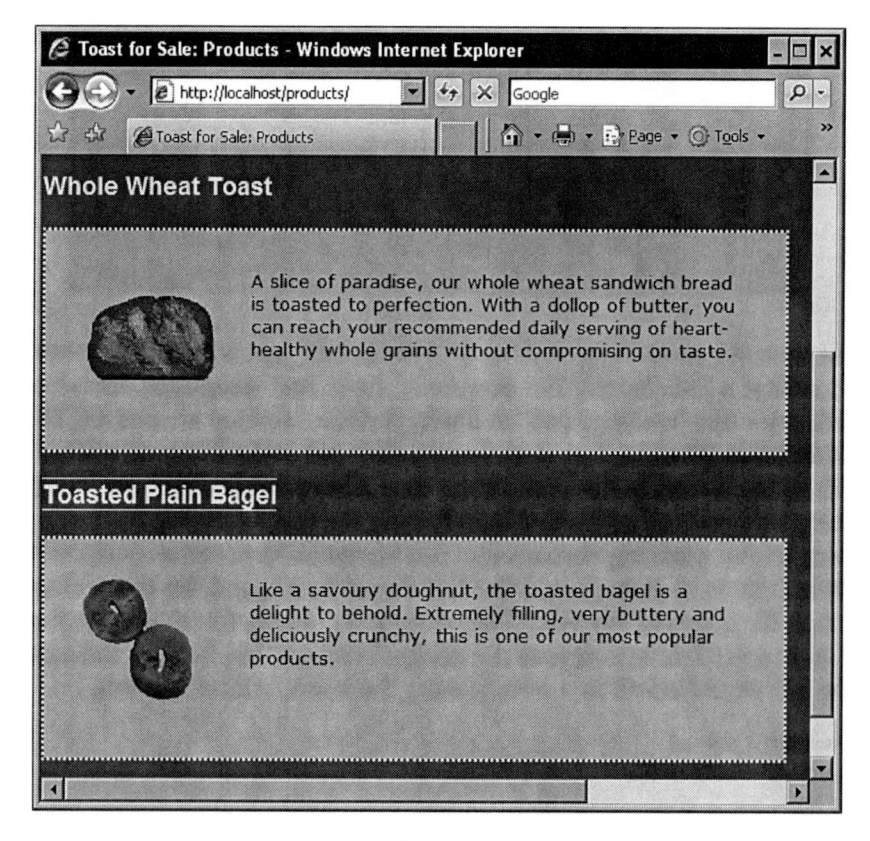

Create Our Single-Entry Page

As we said before, we are also going to use the `products/index` template for our individual entry pages.

1. Edit the `index` template in the `products` template group, and add the following code in the `<div id="content">` section. This code is very similar to the code for our browsing page, except that we are using the full size photo. (As we do not limit the height and width of the photos, we will have to be sure when we upload new photos that they are appropriately sized for the Web.) Also, instead of displaying the summary, we are only displaying the description. The reason for this is to reduce duplicate content on the site—visitors will have already read the summary when they were browsing for products, so they do not need to read the same exact text again here.

```
<div id="content">
  {if segment_2==''}
    [Code omitted]
  {/if}
  {if segment_2}
    {exp:weblog:entries weblog="toastproducts" limit="1"}
      <h3>{title}</h3>
      <div class="contentinner">
        <div class="innerbox">
          <img src="{toastproducts_photo}" alt="{title}" />
          {toastproducts_description}
        </div>
      </div>
    {/exp:weblog:entries}
  {/if}
</div>
```

> Remember that only the bolded code needs to be inserted, the unbolded code should already exist.

2. Next up, we are going to add the nutrition information to the template. We'll put this in a separate `contentinner` box and use the standard HTML element `strong` to emphasize the headings.

```
          <img src="{toastproducts_photo}" alt="{title}" />
            {toastproducts_description}
        </div>
      </div>
      <h3>Nutritional Information</h3>
      <div class="contentinner">
```

```
            <p><strong>Calories per Serving:
            </strong>{toastproducts_calories}</p>
            <p><strong>Total Fat: </strong>{toastproducts_fat}</p>
            <p><strong>Sodium: </strong>{toastproducts_sodium}</p>
            <p><strong>Total Carbohydrate:
            </strong>{toastproducts_carbs}</p>
            <p><strong>Dietary Fiber:
            </strong>{toastproducts_fiber}</p>
            <p><strong>Sugars: </strong>{toastproducts_sugars}</p>
            <p><strong>Protein: </strong>{toastproducts_protein}</p>
        </div>
    {/exp:weblog:entries}
  {/if}
</div>
```

Toasted Plain Bagel

The toasted bagel is a perfect breakfast choice for those with an appetite. Crunchy and filling, the toasted bagel can be eaten anywhere and will keep you going until your next meal.

Our toasted bagel consists of a half-slice of a plain bagel with one tablespoon of salted butter spread on top. For best taste, eat shortly after opening.

Nutritional Information

Calories per Serving: 253
Total Fat: 12g
Sodium: 335mg
Total Carbohydrate: 30g
Dietary Fiber: 1g
Sugars: 3g
Protein: 6g

3. Next, we want to link back to the main product browsing screen. We will do this in the `footnote` class that we previously defined in Chapter 3. We will also use the `{site_url}` variable, which will translate to the URL where ExpressionEngine is installed.

```
        <p><strong>Protein: </strong>{toastproducts_protein}</p>
      </div>
      <p class="footnote"><a href="{site_url}products" title="Back
                    to Products">Go back to all products</a></p>
    {/exp:weblog:entries}
  {/if}
</div>
```

4. Finally, because we have added links to our footnote class, we need to add to our `toast/toast_css` template in order to format our links appropriately:

```
.footnote a{
  color: #F0E68C;
}
.footnote a:visited{
  color: #F0E68C;
}
```

We now have a Products page that displays all our products and allows us to click on individual products to see a bigger photograph and more detailed information. The next step is to add some user interactivity; in our case, we are going to allow visitors to leave comments or reviews on our products.

Allowing Comments on Our Weblog Entries

Comments are one of the easiest ways for visitors to interact with your site. They are also an easy way to attract spammers, who will be glad to leave hundreds of comments linking to websites of dubious quality. Luckily, ExpressionEngine includes features designed to prevent abuse. So first, we are going to review our options:

Preventing Comment Spam

1. Comment preferences are set on a per-weblog basis. This allows you to choose different preferences for different parts of your website. Go to **Admin | Weblog Administration | Weblog Management**. Select **Edit Preferences** for the **Toast Products** weblog.

Weblog Management					
ID	Weblog Name	Short Name			
1	Default Site Weblog	default_site	Edit Preferences	Edit Groups	Delete
2	Toast News	toastnews	Edit Preferences	Edit Groups	Delete
6	Toast Products	toastproducts	Edit Preferences	Edit Groups	Delete
4	Toast Website	toastwebsite	Edit Preferences	Edit Groups	Delete

2. On the left are all the aspects of the weblog that you can fine-tune, and in the main screen are the preferences themselves. The **General Weblog Preferences** were set when we created the weblog, and include the weblog name and short name. We will not change these.

3. Click on **Path Settings**. The path settings are the URLs that are unique to this weblog. ExpressionEngine does not know which template will be used for a weblog, but we can specify which templates are being used here. Our **Weblog URL** is http://localhost/products/ (or http://www.example.com/products/) and our **Comment Page URL** will be the same. None of the other URLs apply to this weblog. Click on **Update**.

4. The **Administrative Preferences** and **Weblog Posting Preferences** set up defaults for each entry. For example, if we know the weblog does not have comments or trackbacks, we can disable them by default by selecting No to the respective options. In our case, we can select **No** to the trackbacks question. Or if we are doing a weblog that will involve lots of example HTML code, we can **Convert HTML into character entities**, meaning that any HTML entered as part of an entry will display on screen as-is and not be interpreted by the browser. Click on **Update**.

Chapter 5

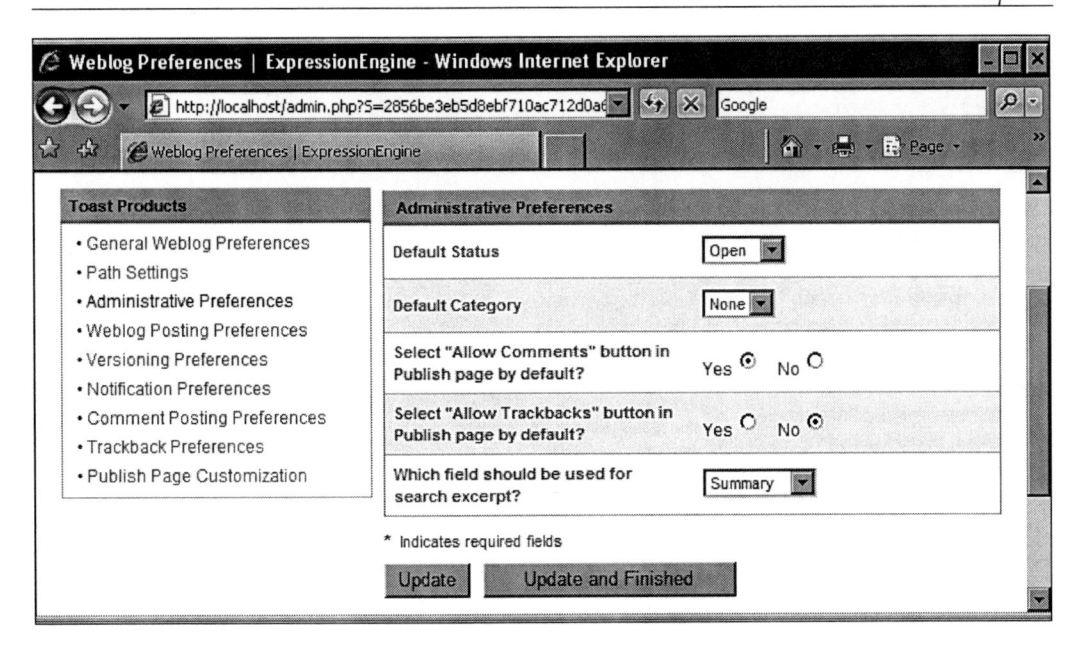

5. Now click on **Versioning Preferences**. **Versioning Preferences** is very useful to set. By **Enabling Entry Versioning** and by saying **Yes** to **Save Revisions During Quicksave**, you can keep old versions of a weblog entry saved. This is useful in a weblog, such as Products, since it provides a quick undo feature for edits being made erroneously. Enabling this option creates a new Revisions Tab in your weblog and Publish and Edit pages where you can load previous revisions. Click **Update** to save the changes.

> This option is not a substitute for doing a full database backup at regular intervals.

Create an Advanced Weblog

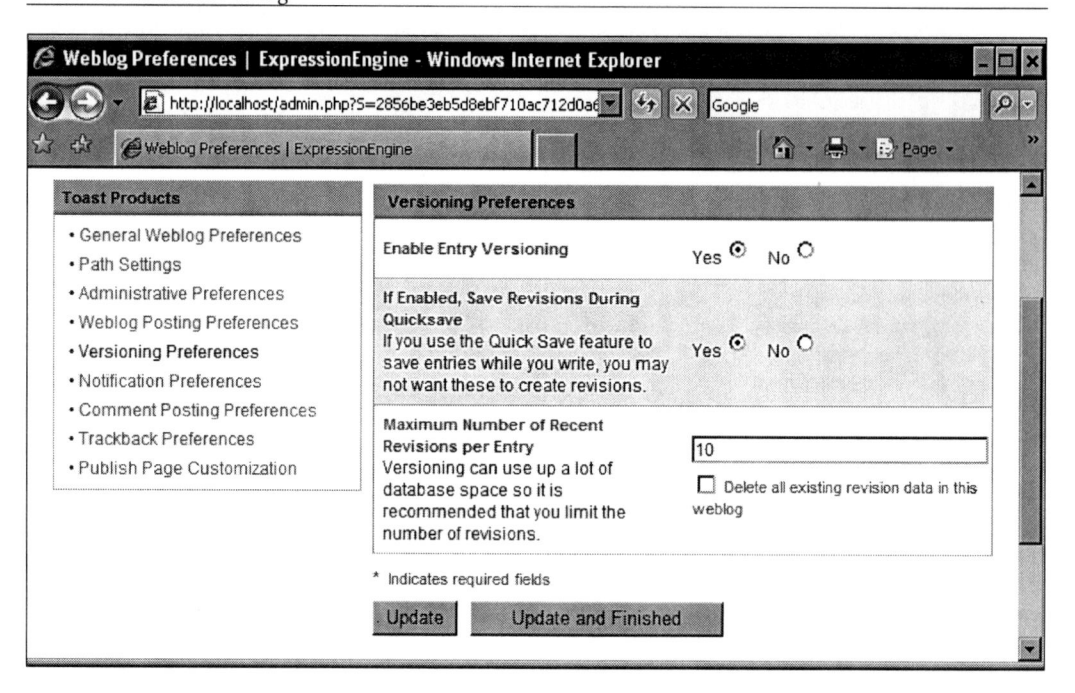

6. Select **Notification Preferences**. The **Notification Preferences** allows us to set up individuals to receive emails whenever a new weblog entry is posted or whenever a new comment is received. This is useful if you require a moderator to approve all comments.

7. Select **Comment Posting Preferences**. The **Comment Posting Preferences** is where we can lock down or open up who can post comments and how many hoops they have to jump through. In our case, we are going to **Allow comments in this weblog**, and we are not going to **Require membership in order to post comments**. As we are not requiring membership, we are going to **Require email address to post comments** and **Enable Captcha for Comment Posting**. A **captcha** is an image of letters. The person submitting the comment must type in the letters from the image. This prevents automated software programs from submitting hundreds of comments (but will also make your site more difficult for visually-impaired visitors using screen-readers).

> Although the default captcha functionality is not very accessible for those using screen-readers, Purple Dogfish has created an alternative Accessible Captcha extension, available at `http://www.purple-dogfish.co.uk/free-stuff/accessible-captcha`. This extension changes the captcha graphics to user-definable questions and answers. The example they give is a question that asks `2+2 is equal to?`. A human could easily answer `4`, but an automated spam program would not be able to do so.

Comment Posting Preferences	
Allow comments in this weblog?	Yes ● No ○
Require membership in order to post comments?	Yes ○ No ●
Enable Captcha for Comment Posting? A captcha is an image containing a security code that users have to submit. Please consult the user guide for more info.	Yes ● No ○
Require email address to post comments?	Yes ● No ○

8. Continuing with the **Comment Posting Preferences**, we are also going to **Moderate Comments**. This means that the newly posted comments are not immediately visible on your site, but require a moderator (such as yourself) to read the comment and approve it. This is important since we are allowing any visitors to post a comment.

9. We are not going to set a **Maximum number of characters allowed in comments**, we will not have **Comment Expiration,** and as we are moderating all comments, we are not going to set a **Comment Re-submission Time Interval**. For the **Comment Text Formatting**, we are going to use **xhtml** but **Allow only safe HTML**. This means that formatting HTML such as `<b>` and `<i>` will work but more complex HTML will be rendered in plain text rather than being interpreted by a browser. We will also not **Allow image URLs in comments**, and we will not **Automatically turn URLs and email addresses into links**. Click **Update**.

Moderate Comments? If set to yes, comments will not be visible until a moderator approves them.	Yes ⊙ No ○
Maximum number of characters allowed in comments	0
Comment Re-submission Time Interval The number of seconds that must pass before a user can submit another comment. Leave blank or set to zero for no limit.	0
Comment Expiration The number of days after an entry is posted during which to allow comments. Enter 0 (zero) for no expiration.	0 ☐ Update all existing comments with this expiration setting?
Comment Text Formatting	xhtml
Comment HTML Formatting	Allow only safe HTML
Allow image URLs in comments?	Yes ○ No ⊙
Automatically turn URLs and email addresses into links?	Yes ○ No ⊙

10. The **Trackback Preferences** section is for trackbacks (a way for bloggers to receive notification when someone else links to their weblog entry). We will not allow trackbacks in this weblog as this is not a traditional blog.

11. The **Publish Page Customization** allows us to customize whatever options are visible on the Publish page. For example, if we do not allow trackbacks, we can switch off the Trackback Form. This section is very useful to simplify the Publish page. Go ahead and experiment, looking to see what is different about the Publish page each time.

We have now set our comment preferences and we are ready to begin allowing comment submissions.

> More information on all of these preferences can be found in the ExpressionEngine documentation at `http://expressionengine.com/docs/cp/admin/weblog_administration/weblog_edit_preferences.html`.

Creating a Form Where Visitors Can Submit Comments

The first step in accepting comments is creating a form where visitors can write and submit their comments. Comments have to be tied to a specific weblog entry, and therefore the comment form can only appear on pages with a single weblog entry. We are going to add our comment form to the `products/index` template, within the conditional statement `{if segment_2}`.

1. Open the `index` template in the `products` template group for editing and type in the following code. The entire `content` section so far is reproduced below with the new code highlighted. This code displays the comments that other people have submitted. We will title the section **Reviews** and put each comment in their own `contentinner` box with a footnote for who posted the review.

```
<div id="content">
  {if segment_2==''}
    {exp:weblog:entries weblog="toastproducts"}
      <h3><a href="{title_permalink="products"}">{title}</a></h3>
      <div class="contentinner">
        <div class="innerbox">
          <a href="{title_permalink="products"}"><img
            src="{toastproducts_thumbnail}" alt="{title}" /></a>
          {toastproducts_summary}
        </div>
      </div>
    {/exp:weblog:entries}
  {/if}
  {if segment_2}
    {exp:weblog:entries weblog="toastproducts" limit="1"}
      <h3>{title}</h3>
      <div class="contentinner">
        <div class="innerbox">
          <img src="{toastproducts_photo}" alt="{title}" />
            {toastproducts_description}
        </div>
      </div>
      <h3>Nutritional Information</h3>
      <div class="contentinner">
        <p><strong>Calories per Serving:
        </strong>{toastproducts_calories}</p>
        <p><strong>Total Fat: </strong>{toastproducts_fat}</p>
        <p><strong>Sodium: </strong>{toastproducts_sodium}</p>
```

Create an Advanced Weblog

```
            <p><strong>Total Carbohydrate:
            </strong>{toastproducts_carbs}</p>
            <p><strong>Dietary Fiber:
            </strong>{toastproducts_fiber}</p>
            <p><strong>Sugars: </strong>{toastproducts_sugars}</p>
            <p><strong>Protein: </strong>{toastproducts_protein}</p>
        </div>
            <p class="footnote"><a href="{site_url}products" title="Back
                    to Products">Go back to all products</a></p>
    {/exp:weblog:entries}
    <h3>Reviews</h3>
    {exp:comment:entries}
        {if comments}
            <div class="contentinner">
                {comment}
            </div>
            <p class="footnote">Posted by {name} on {comment_date
            format='%m/%d'} at {comment_date format='%h:%i %A'}</p>
        {/if}
    {/exp:comment:entries}
  {/if}
</div>
```

2. Next, we are going to add the code to create a comment form. We will add this after the {/exp:weblog:entries} tag. First, we will create the fields for the visitors name and email address. As we already have the name and email address of any member who is logged in, we are only going to ask for this information if the visitor is logged out.

```
    {/exp:comment:entries}
    <h3>Post a Review</h3>
    {exp:comment:form}
        {if logged_out}
            <p>
                Name:<br />
                <input type="text" name="name" value="{name}" size="50" />
            </p>
            <p>
                Email:<br />
                <input type="text" name="email" value="{email}" size="50"
                                                                        />
            </p>
        {/if}
        <p>
            <textarea name="comment" cols="50"
```

[132]

```
              rows="12">{comment}</textarea>
        </p>
        {if logged_out}
          <p><input type="checkbox" name="save_info" value="yes"
              {save_info} /> Remember my personal information</p>
        {/if}
        <p><input type="checkbox" name="notify_me" value="yes"
            {notify_me} /> Notify me of follow-up comments?</p>
        {if captcha}
          <p>Submit the word you see below:</p>
          <p>
            {captcha}
            <br />
            <input type="text" name="captcha" value="" size="20"
                      maxlength="20" style="width:140px;" />
          </p>
        {/if}
        <input type="submit" name="submit" value="Submit" />
        <input type="submit" name="preview" value="Preview" />
    {/exp:comment:form}
  {/if}
</div>
```

> You can also add fields for a visitor's location or website. Use the same format as the `email` field in the previous code, but replace the word `email` with either `location` or `url`.

3. Let us now try posting our first comment. Go to http://localhost/products/ or http://www.example.com/products/, select a product such as the Toasted Plain Bagel, and fill in all the fields. Notice how the captcha works—we must type in the words from the image in order to submit our comment. Each time we refresh the page, a different image with a different word is shown. Once we have filled in all the fields, we will click **Submit**.

> If you are using a `localhost` environment, posting comments can be more difficult than when using an installation on a real website. If you are unable to post comments in the `localhost` environment, try changing the setting **Require IP Address and User Agent for Login** to **No**. This setting can be found in the control panel under **Admin | System Preferences | Security and Session Preferences**.

If a visitor selects to **Remember my Personal Information**, then the next time the visitor comes across a comment form, they will find all their personal information (name, email address, location, and URL) pre-filled.

> Note that if we are logged in when we visit this page (for example, if we were previously logged into the control panel), then we will not see the fields for the name or email, and we will not see the captcha. This is not an error. It is a design feature as we already know the names and email addresses of our members.
>
> To see the form as someone who is not logged in, go to the control panel and select **Log-out** from the top-right-hand corner, then visit this page.

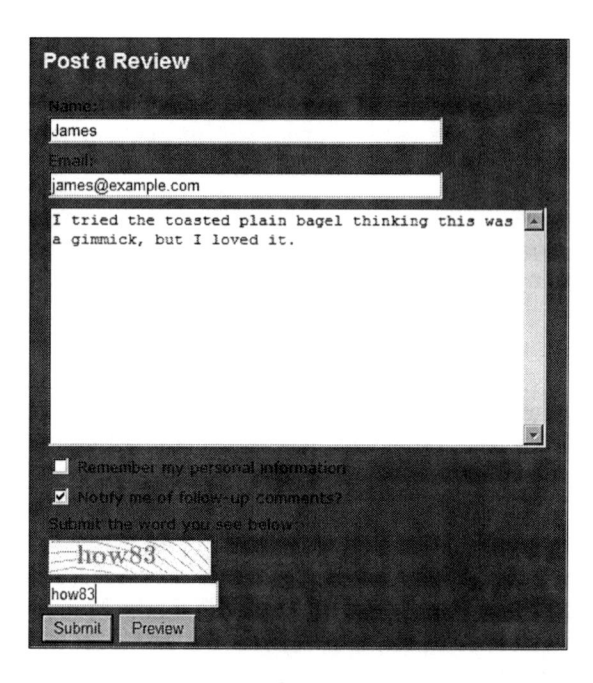

[Screenshot: Post a Review form with Name "James", Email "james@example.com", comment "I tried the toasted plain bagel thinking this was a gimmick, but I loved it.", captcha "how83", Submit and Preview buttons]

4. In the comment preferences option earlier, we selected to have all comments viewed by a moderator before they appear on our website. A message to that effect appears. The page will then auto-refresh back to the page with the comment form.

> Note that if you are logged in as the administrator, your comment may by-pass the moderation step. Certain member groups can be set up so that their comments are not subject to moderation. The Super Admin group is set like this by default.

[Screenshot: Thank You! Your comment will be reviewed by a moderator for approval. Click here if you are not redirected automatically]

Moderating Comments in the Control Panel

We have now submitted our first comment(s), but they are not yet visible on our website because they have not yet been approved by a moderator. Let us do that now.

1. Log into the control panel at http://localhost/admin.php (or http://www.example.com/admin.php) or select **CP Home** from the top-right of any screen in the ExpressionEngine control panel.

2. On the home page of the control panel (the first screen you see after we log in), there is a **Site Statistics** section. The last statistic will say, at a glance, if there are any comments awaiting moderation.

Site Statistics	Value
System Status	Online
Version	1.6.2
Total Weblog Entries	15
Total Comments	1
Total Trackbacks	0
Total Combined Page Hits	1194
Total Members	1
Members Awaiting Activation	0
* Comments Awaiting Validation	3

3. Click on the hyperlinked **Comments Awaiting Validation** and we will be taken straight to the comments needing validation. Notice how the **Status** of these comments is **Closed**.

Comment	Author	Email	Date	IP:	Status	Action
I tried the toasted plain...	James	james@example.com	2008-01-30 09:39 PM	127.0.0.1	Closed	

4. The first column is a link to the entire comment. Click this link to read the comment in its entirety. You can also add to or edit any part of the comment at this stage.

Create an Advanced Weblog

5. Once you are satisfied with the comment, we can change the status of the comment to **Open**, thus making it visible on our site. Check the box to the right-hand side for each comment you wish to approve and then select **Open Selected** from the drop-down menu underneath the **Action** column. Click **Submit** and you will see the Status changed to **Open**.

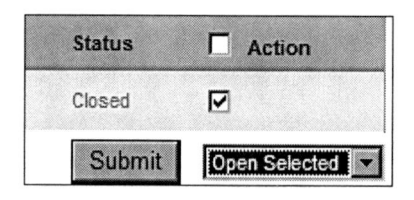

> If the comment is not suitable for approving, you can use **Delete Selected** to remove the comment(s) from ExpressionEngine.

6. Back on our Products page, we will now be able to see the comment in all its glory.

Allowing Visitors to Preview Comments Before Submitting

One final aspect of comments that we have not yet covered is the ability to preview the comment before publishing. You may have noticed the **Preview** button on the comment form that does not yet work.

1. First, modify the `products/index` template to include the following code after the `<h3>` heading Reviews and before the `{exp:comment:entries}` tag. Notice how this is almost exactly the same as the code inside the `{exp:comment:entries}` tag. This is to make sure that the look and feel of the previewed comment is identical to how it would look if it were an actual comment.

   ```
   <h3>Reviews</h3>
   {exp:comment:preview}
     <div class="contentinner">
       {comment}
   ```

```
        </div>
        <p class="footnote">Being Previewed by {name} on {comment_date
                format='%m/%d'} at {comment_date format='%h:%i %A'}</p>
{/exp:comment:preview}
{exp:comment:entries}
    {if comments}
```

2. Finally, we want to add the following `preview` parameter to the `{exp:comment:form}` tag. This parameter tells the form which template to load if the preview button is clicked.

    `{exp:comment:form` **`preview="products/index"`** `}`

3. Now go to the **Products** page, type in a comment, and hit **Preview** instead of **Submit**. We can see that the comment appears and looks exactly as if we had submitted it, except that instead of **Posted by** in the footnote, it says **Being Previewed by**. We can keep editing the text and hitting **Preview** as often as we like.

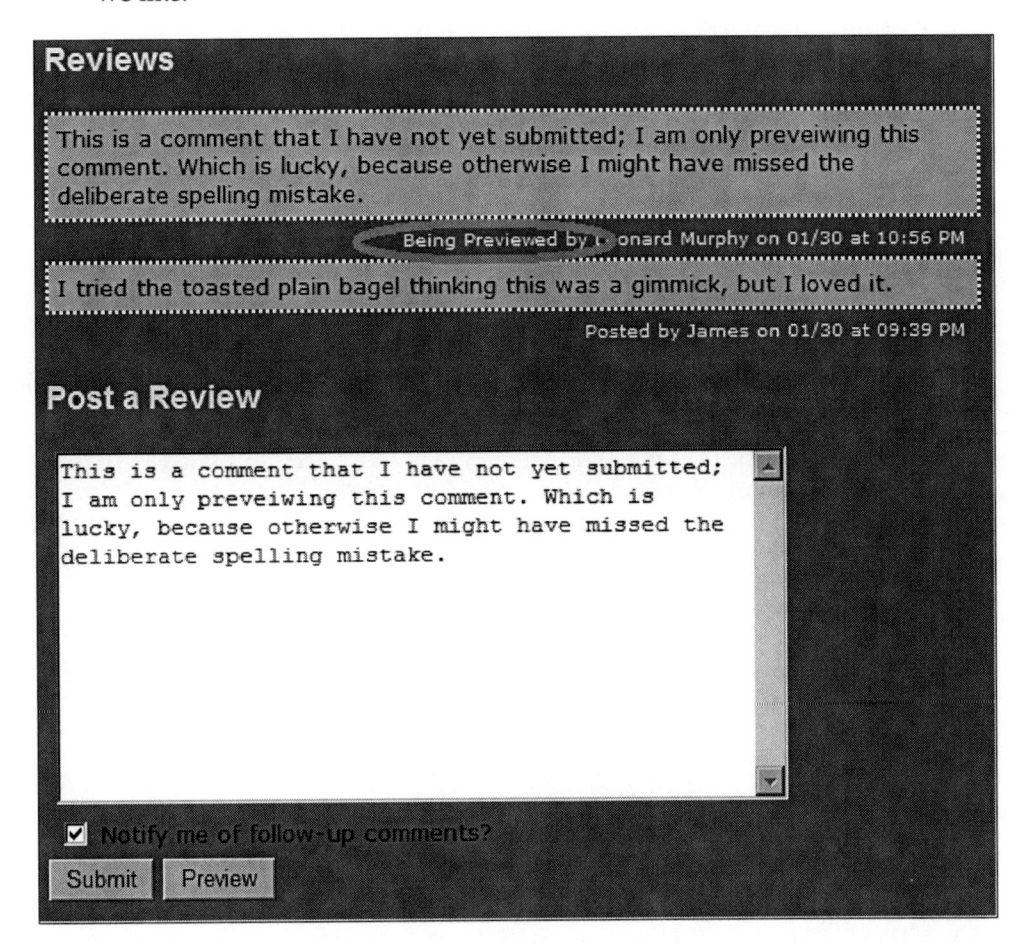

[137]

Improving Our 404 Page Not Found Capabilities

In our last chapter, we created a 404 Page Not Found template that appears when we type in a non-existent URL (such as `http://localhost/ihatetoast` or `http://www.example.com/ihatetoast`) Now that we are using single-entry pages there is a new flaw. When we go to a second layer URL that does not exist (such as `http://localhost/products/ihatetoast` or `http://www.example.com/products/ihatehotast`), we see an actual page with content instead of our 404 template. This can be both confusing to visitors (who mistype a URL) and to search engine robots that will see hundreds of URLs for your site (all with the same duplicate content).

We can alter this default behavior so that instead of our most recent entry being displayed, our 404 page is displayed.

1. To do this, we need to edit the `index` template of the `products` template group. Insert the following code:

    ```
    {if segment_2}
      {exp:weblog:entries weblog="toastproducts" limit="1"
                                          require_entry="yes"}
        {if no_results}
          {redirect="404"}
        {/if}
        <h3>{title}</h3>
    ```

2. Click **Update** and now visit `http://localhost/products/ihatetoast` or `http://www.example.com/products/ihatetoast`. We can see that our 404 template is now returned.

3. To make this work for the `index` template in our `news` template group (which is not a single-entry page), we have to add the following code.

    ```
    <div id="content">
      {if segment_2}
        {exp:weblog:entries weblog="toastnews" limit="1"
                                          require_entry="yes"}
          {if no_results}
            {redirect="404"}
          {/if}
        {/exp:weblog:entries}
      {/if}
      {exp:weblog:entries weblog="toastnews"}
        <h3>{title}</h3>
    ```

This solution has two parts. If there is a segment 2 (segment 1 is the `products` or `news` part of the URL, and segment 2 is the `ihatetoast`), the `require_entry` parameter means that if `ihatetoast` is not a valid entry, display nothing (rather than displaying the most recent entries). The `redirect` tag then redirects visitors to the 404 template if there are no results.

> Note that in order to use the `redirect` tag, it must be embedded within a `{if no_results}` conditional tag, which in turn must be within the `exp:weblog:entries` tag on a single-entry page. For multiple-entry pages (such as our news weblog), we put the `exp:weblog:entries` tag inside an `if segment_2` conditional statement, as there should never be a `segment_2` for a multiple-entry page.

Using Variables

One feature of ExpressionEngine that we have not yet taken advantage of is user-defined variables.

User-defined variables can be defined at the top of a template, and identify a string that may be used throughout the template but is unique to that template. Then, if we later decide that we want to change that string, we only have to change the variable at the top of the template, rather than searching through every line of the template for the string.

For example, most templates are related to a specific weblog. Our `products` template group is related to the `toastproducts` weblog. Throughout our `products` template group, we reference the `toastproducts` weblog. If we wanted to change the name of the `toastproducts` weblog or use the products template group as a base for a new template group, all we would have to do is change the variable at the top of the template.

Variables worth having, no matter how you are using ExpressionEngine, include:

- `my_weblog` — the weblog the template references the most.
- `my_template_group` — the template group the template is in.
- `my_site_wide_templates` — if we have a template group for all our sub-templates (such as `.menu`, `.footer`, our CSS), this variable can reference where that template group is.

Create an Advanced Weblog

Let us now change our `products` template group to use variables where possible:

1. At the top of the `products/index` template, type the following:

   ```
   {assign_variable:my_weblog="toastproducts"}
   {assign_variable:my_template_group="products"}
   {assign_variable:my_site_wide_templates="toast"}

   <!DOCTYPE html PUBLIC "-//W3C//DTD XHTML 1.0 Strict//EN"
   ```

2. Next, find every instance of `toastproducts` within the template and change the code to be `{my_weblog}` instead. There should be four places where this change can be made, for example:

   ```
   {exp:weblog:entries weblog="{my_weblog}" limit="1"
                                   require_entry="yes"}
   ```

3. Replace every instance of `products` with `{my_template_group}`. There should be four places where this change can be made, for example:

   ```
   <p class="footnote"><a href="{site_url}{my_template_group}"
         title="Back to Products">Go back to all products</a></p>
   ```

4. Replace every instance of `toast` with `{my_site_wide_templates}`. There are three places where this change can be made (the two links to the CSS stylesheet and the code that embeds the `.menu` template):

   ```
   <link rel='stylesheet' type='text/css' media='all'
       href='{path={my_site_wide_templates}/toast_css}' />
   ```

The `products/index` template, complete with the variable changes, follows:

```
{assign_variable:my_weblog="toastproducts"}
{assign_variable:my_template_group="products"}
{assign_variable:my_site_wide_templates="toast"}

<!DOCTYPE html PUBLIC "-//W3C//DTD XHTML 1.0 Strict//EN"
"http://www.w3.org/TR/xhtml1/DTD/xhtml1-strict.dtd">
<html xmlns="http://www.w3.org/1999/xhtml">
  <head>
    {if segment_2}
      <title>Toast for Sale: {exp:weblog:entries weblog="{my_weblog}"
        limit="1" disable="categories|custom_fields|member_data|
        pagination|trackbacks"}{title}{/exp:weblog:entries}
                                        </title>
    {if:else}
      <title>Toast for Sale: Products</title>
    {/if}
    <link rel='stylesheet' type='text/css' media='all'
      href='{path={my_site_wide_templates}/toast_css}' />
```

[140]

```
    <style type='text/css' media='screen'>@import
     "{path={my_site_wide_templates}/toast_css}";
                                         </style>
    <meta http-equiv="content-type" content="text/html; charset=UTF-
                                                                8" />
</head>
<body>
   <div id="header">
     <h1>Toast for Sale!</h1>
     {if segment_2}
        {exp:weblog:entries weblog="{my_weblog}" limit="1"
        disable="categories|custom_fields|member_data|
                          pagination|trackbacks"}
          <h2>{title}</h2>
        {/exp:weblog:entries}
     {if:else}
        <h2>Our Selection</h2>
     {/if}
   </div>
   <div id="content">
     {if segment_2==''}
        {exp:weblog:entries weblog="{my_weblog}"}
          <h3><a href="{title_permalink="{my_template_group}"}">
                                           {title}</a></h3>
          <div class="contentinner">
            <div class="innerbox">
              <a href="{title_permalink="{my_template_group}"}"><img
                src="{toastproducts_thumbnail}" alt="{title}" /></a>
              {toastproducts_summary}
            </div>
          </div>
        {/exp:weblog:entries}
     {/if}
     {if segment_2}
        {exp:weblog:entries weblog="{my_weblog}" limit="1"
                                   require_entry="yes"}
          {if no_results}
             {redirect="404"}
          {/if}
          <h3>{title}</h3>
          <div class="contentinner">
            <div class="innerbox">
              <img src="{toastproducts_photo}" alt="{title}" />
                {toastproducts_description}
```

```
            </div>
          </div>
          <h3>Nutritional Information</h3>
          <div class="contentinner">
            <p><strong>Calories per Serving:
            </strong>{toastproducts_calories}</p>
            <p><strong>Total Fat: </strong>{toastproducts_fat}</p>
            <p><strong>Sodium: </strong>{toastproducts_sodium}</p>
            <p><strong>Total Carbohydrate:
            </strong>{toastproducts_carbs}</p>
            <p><strong>Dietary Fiber:
            </strong>{toastproducts_fiber}</p>
            <p><strong>Sugars: </strong>{toastproducts_sugars}</p>
            <p><strong>Protein: </strong>{toastproducts_protein}</p>
          </div>
          <p class="footnote"><a href="{site_url}{my_template_group}"
              title="Back to Products">Go back to all products</a></p>
{/exp:weblog:entries}
<h3>Reviews</h3>
{exp:comment:preview}
          <div class="contentinner">
            {comment}
          </div>
          <p class="footnote">Being Previewed by {name} on
          {comment_date format='%m/%d'} at {comment_date
                              format='%h:%i %A'}</p>
{/exp:comment:preview}
{exp:comment:entries}
    {if comments}
          <div class="contentinner">
            {comment}
          </div>
          <p class="footnote">Posted by {name} on {comment_date
          format='%m/%d'} at {comment_date format='%h:%i %A'}</p>
    {/if}
{/exp:comment:entries}
<h3>Post a Review</h3>
{exp:comment:form preview="{my_template_group}/index"}
    {if logged_out}
        <p>
          Name:<br />
          <input type="text" name="name" value="{name}" size="50"
                                                                   />
```

```
            </p>
            <p>
              Email:<br />
              <input type="text" name="email" value="{email}"
                                              size="50" />
            </p>
          {/if}
          <p>
            <textarea name="comment" cols="50"
                rows="12">{comment}</textarea>
          </p>
          {if logged_out}
            <p><input type="checkbox" name="save_info" value="yes"
                {save_info} /> Remember my personal information</p>
          {/if}
          <p><input type="checkbox" name="notify_me" value="yes"
              {notify_me} /> Notify me of follow-up comments?</p>
          {if captcha}
            <p>Submit the word you see below:</p>
            <p>
              {captcha}
              <br />
              <input type="text" name="captcha" value="" size="20"
                          maxlength="20" style="width:140px;" />
            </p>
          {/if}
          <input type="submit" name="submit" value="Submit" />
          <input type="submit" name="preview" value="Preview" />
        {/exp:comment:form}
      {/if}
    </div>
    <div id="menu">
      {embed={my_site_wide_templates}/.menu}
    </div>
  </body>
</html>
```

Exercises

1. In this chapter, we created a new products section for our toast website. Add the URL for this section to our main menu.
2. In our first chapter on creating weblogs, we created a Toast News weblog. The template for this weblog is a multiple-entry page—it displays multiple entries on a single page. Adapt this weblog so that the multiple-entry page only shows the {summary} field from each entry. Create single-entry pages that you can click on to view the rest of an individual entry.
3. Following on from Exercise 1, further enhance the single-entry pages of the News from the President weblog, so that avid readers can leave comments or questions for the President.
4. Set the comments on the News for the President weblog so that after 30 days no more comments are accepted.
5. Try modifying the Publish Page Preferences for the Toast News weblog so that only a minimum of options are available to change.
6. Now that we are using variables, update all our existing templates to use variables too. After each update, be sure to visit the page and make sure it is still working as expected.

Summary

In this chapter:

- We reinforced how to create weblogs and create customized weblog fields.
- We used the Upload File feature of the Publish page to upload image files to our server and create thumbnails.
- Using a single template, we allowed our visitors to peruse all our entries on one page, with the ability to click on an entry and see more detailed information (including nutrition information and comments).
- We created a comment form that can be used by both members and non-members to leave comments.
- We modified our comment preferences so that we required captchas and required all comments to be moderated before being posted.
- We have enhanced our 404 functionality so that when accessing a made-up template or entry name a 404 page is returned instead of valid content.
- We have used variables to greatly expand the portability of our code.

In the next chapter, we will use ExpressionEngine to really examine the member system, including member registration, logging in and logging out, member privileges, and member management.

6
Members

We have now used ExpressionEngine to build a fairly functional but fictional website for our online toast-selling business. This far, however, we are the only ones who can log into ExpressionEngine and the only ones who have been making any changes. To make our website complete, we are going to explore the **member** functionality of ExpressionEngine.

In this chapter, we will:

- Allow members of the public to register themselves for our site, and allow them to log in and out
- Create a **members only** area of our website to give our members an incentive to join
- Create an Editors member group, whose members will be able to access the control panel to publish and edit entries, but will not be able to edit template code or change administrative options
- Set up a Stand-Alone Entry Form, which allows us to post to a weblog without even logging into the control panel
- Create a mailing list that visitors can sign up for

Before we get started managing members, we will first walk through the basics of registration and logging in as if we were a new member.

Setting Up Links for Member Functions on Our Menu

The membership functionality in ExpressionEngine is very rich, so rather than having to design our own membership templates from scratch, ExpressionEngine comes with a pre-built membership module that we can take advantage of.

Members

For example, to login to the website without ending up in the control panel, visitors can visit `http://localhost/member/login` (or `http://www.example.com/member/login` if you are not using a local development environment). This URL works without any setup whatsoever. The membership module is installed by default.

To make our website member-friendly, we will first add these pre-defined URLs to our menu, so they can be accessed by anyone visiting our website. We will set up links for non-members to either register or log in. For members who are logged in, we will set up links to logout, as well as to the member control panel (not the same as the administrator control panel that we have been using this far).

1. Log into the control panel at `http://localhost/admin.php` or `http://www.example.com/admin.php`. Select **Templates**, and then select the `toast` template group. Edit the `.menu` template.

2. Add the following code to the end of the `.menu` template. Rather than incorporating the membership menu items as part of the existing menu, we are going to include them as a submenu underneath the existing menu.

```
<h4>Members</h4>
<ul>
  <li>
    <a href="{path=member/login}" title="Log into our toast
                                        website">Login</a>
    <div>Log into our toast website to access the member-only
                                                       areas</div>
  </li>
  <li>
    <a href="{path=member/forgot_password}" title="Forgot
                      Password?">Forgot Password?</a>
    <div>Get a password reminder</div>
  </li>
  <li>
    <a href="{path=member/register}" title="Register as a new
                                        member">Register</a>
    <div>Not yet a member? Sign-up today!</a>
  </li>
  <li>
    <a href="{path=member/profile}" title="Member
                          profile">Profile</a>
    <div>View or edit your member profile</div>
  </li>
  <li>
    <a href="{path=member/memberlist}" title="Member list">Member
                                                         list</a>
    <div>See everyone who has signed up</div>
```

[146]

Chapter 6

```
    </li>
    <li>
      <a href="{path=logout}" title="Log out of our toast
                                     website">Logout</a>
      <div>Log out of our toast website</div>
    </li>
  </ul>
```

3. Click **Update**, and now visit any page of the website that has the menu included. We can now see all the member options underneath the main menu options.

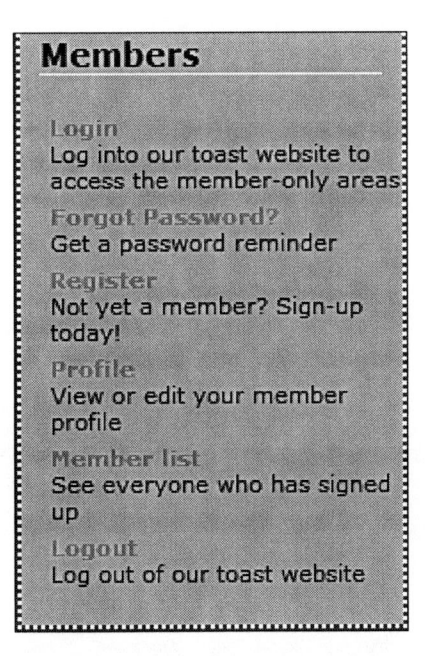

   Members

   Login
   Log into our toast website to access the member-only areas

   Forgot Password?
   Get a password reminder

   Register
   Not yet a member? Sign-up today!

   Profile
   View or edit your member profile

   Member list
   See everyone who has signed up

   Logout
   Log out of our toast website

4. The only downside to the current setup is that if a visitor is logged in and clicks the **Register** option, they will get an error message saying that they are already registered and logged in. Likewise, if we are not logged in, the logout option is perhaps unnecessary. Let us add some conditionals to the menu items, so that only the relevant options display depending on the visitors' current status. Edit the .menu code as follows:

```
<ul>
  {if logged_out}
    <li>
      <a href="{path=member/login}" title="Log into our toast
                                          website">Login</a>
      <div>Log into our toast website to access the member-only
                                                     areas</div>
```

[147]

Members

```
      </li>
      <li>
        <a href="{path=member/forgot_password}" title="Forgot
                      Password?">Forgot Password?</a>
        <div>Get a password reminder</div>
      </li>
      <li>
        <a href="{path=member/register}" title="Register as a new
                                  member">Register</a>
        <div>Not yet a member? Sign-up today!</div>
      </li>
  {/if}
  {if logged_in}
      <li>
        <a href="{path=member/profile}" title="Member
                            profile">Profile</a>
        <div>View or edit your member profile</div>
      </li>
      <li>
        <a href="{path=member/memberlist}" title="Member
                                list">Member list</a>
        <div>See everyone who has signed up</div>
      </li>
      <li>
        <a href="{path=logout}" title="Log out of our toast
                                website">Logout</a>
        <div>Log out of our toast website</div>
      </li>
  {/if}
</ul>
```

Now, if a visitor turns up and is not logged in, they only see the options that are appropriate to them.

Registering As a New Member

We are now going to walk through the steps of registering as a new member. This experience will be invaluable later as we change our membership preferences to suit our own needs.

1. Go to `http://localhost` or `http://www.example.com` as appropriate. If already logged in, select **Logout** from the menu. Then select **Register**.
2. We are presented with a standard **Member Registration** screen, complete with a generic **Terms of Service**. Fill in the screen with settings different than the administrator login that we have been using up to this point. Check the box to agree to the terms of service.

> There can only be one username per email address. This means we cannot use the same email address for this member as we did for our administrator member. At this stage, we also cannot register with a fake email address, because the default configuration requires membership to be activated by clicking on a link in an email.

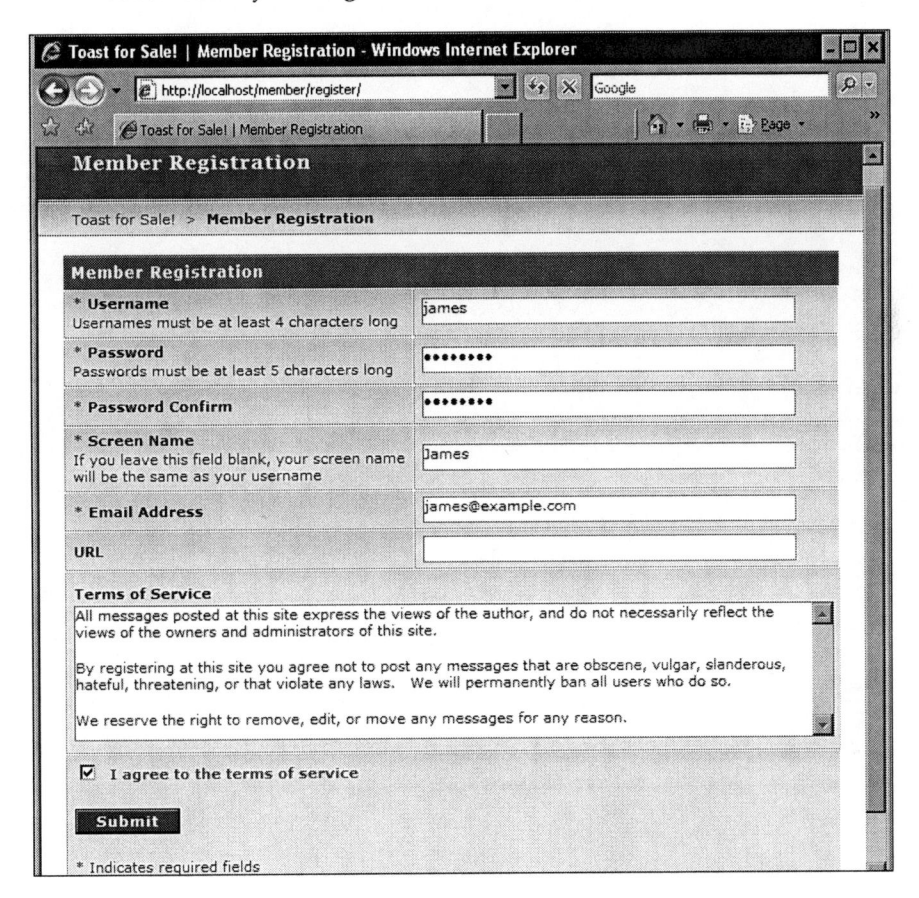

Members

3. Click **Submit**, and as long as there were no errors with the information provided, we are presented with a **Registration Complete** screen. Click on the link **Toast for Sale!** and we should be returned to our website.

4. If you are using XAMPP and the localhost environment, you will not get an email—that is to be expected. On a Mac with MAMP you may get an email, and certainly when using a live website server we will get an email that contains an activation code that we must click on to activate our membership.

5. After we click on the link, we are returned to our website with an account activation message:

> **Thank You!**
>
> Your account has been activated.
>
> You may now log in and begin using it.
>
> Toast for Sale!

We are now registered as a new member.

The Member Profile

Now that we have walked through registering as a new member let us explore the member profile. This section can be followed by either using the login information for the new member or the login information that we have been using to access the control panel.

1. Go to `http://localhost` or `http://www.example.com`. If not already logged in, select **Login** from the menu and log in.

> If you ever forget your password, you can click on the **Forgot your Password** link from either the main menu or the login page. You will be prompted to enter your email address. An email is then sent with a link that, when clicked on, will cause another email to be sent with a new password. If you are using a localhost environment where emails do not work, be sure not to forget your password!

Members

2. Click on the **Profile** link from the menu and we are brought to a screen with our account statistics: our email address, when we became a member, when we last visited the website, how many weblog entries we've posted, and how many comments we've made.

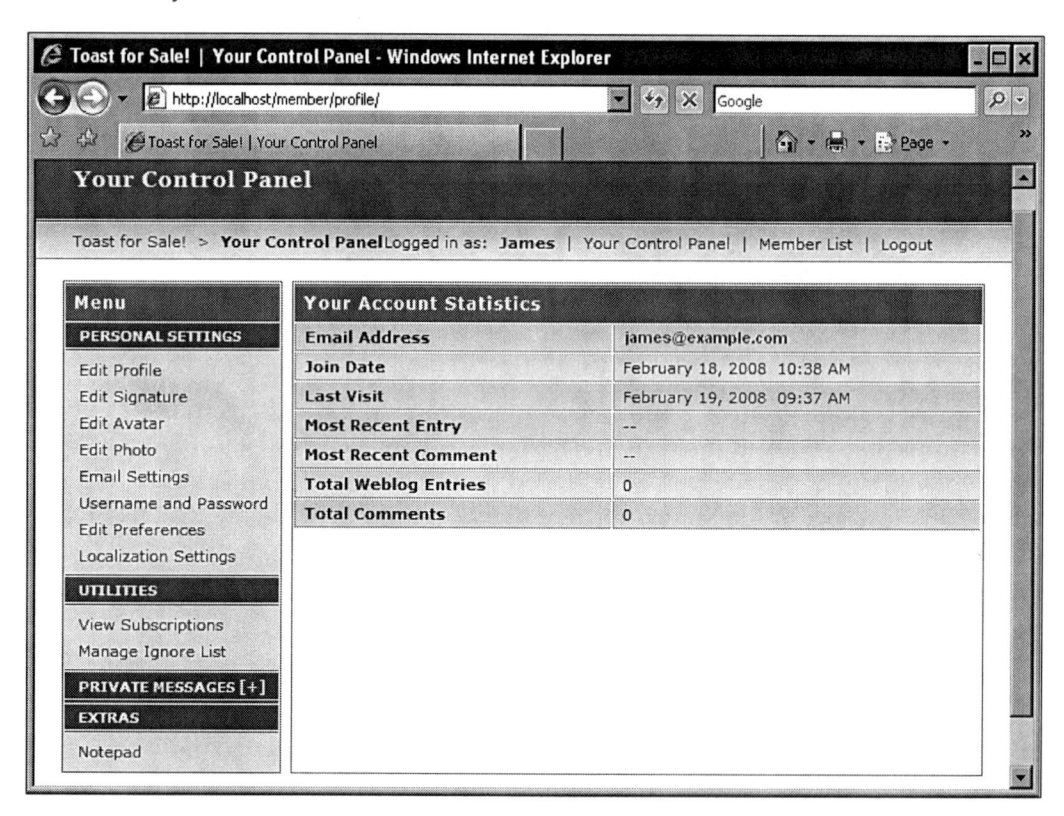

3. Down the left-hand side are a set of links that allow us to modify and personalize our website settings. Under **Edit Profile**, we can change what other members see about us. Go ahead and fill it in.

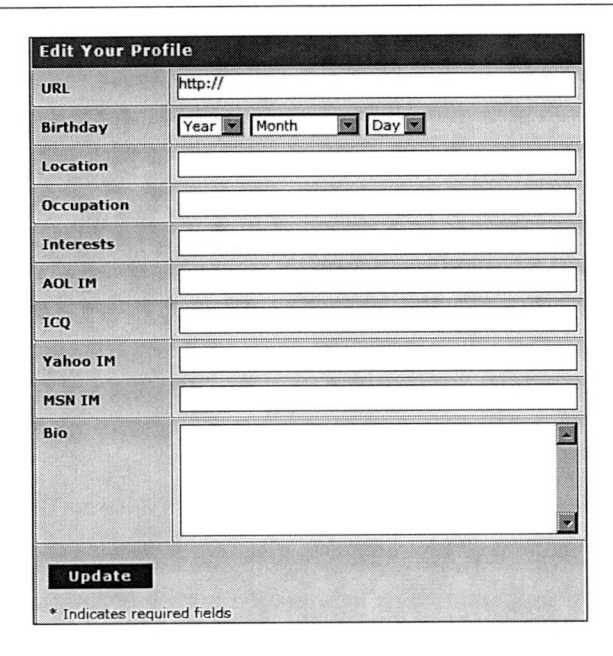

4. **Edit Signature** and **Edit Avatar** are more associated with the forum module. (A module that is not a part of the default ExpressionEngine installation but can be purchased separately.) These options allow a member to have a signature appear underneath every forum post, or an avatar to appear alongside every forum post. With **Edit Photo** we can also associate a member photo that other members can see when they visit our profile (although this option is not enabled by default).

5. Select **Email Settings** from the left-hand side. This allows members to fine-tune what notification emails they receive from our site. By default, ExpressionEngine allows members to email other members—this can be turned off on this page. We can also change our email address on this page.

Members

6. **Username and Password** allows us to change how we login and what other members see as our name. By default, ExpressionEngine allows members to message privately to other members. **Edit Preferences** allows us to turn off that functionality, as well as whether our signature or avatar is used when we make forum posts.

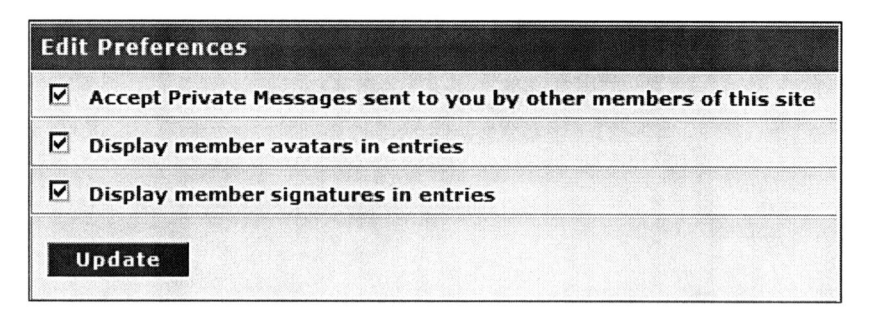

7. The **Localization Settings** allow a member to specify their **Time Zone**, their **Time Formatting** (US or European), and their **Language** (if we have language packs installed). By default, when a comment or entry is posted, the time shown is the time on the server where the website is hosted. (The server time zone was chosen during the installation.) However, by selecting a different time zone, the member can see times in their local time zone. For example, if the server time zone is set to Central Time (UTC-6) and we post a comment at 3.03 pm Central Time, then a non-member visiting would see the comment as posted at 3.03 pm. However, if a member in London with a time zone set to UTC visits, they would see the comment as posted at 9.03 pm.

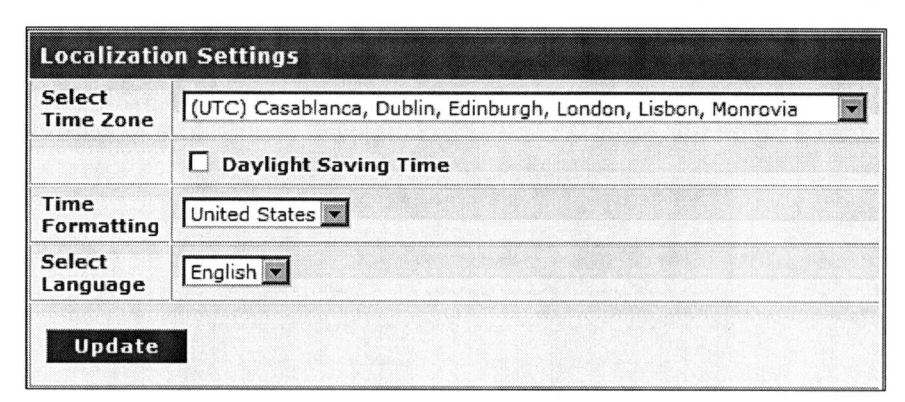

[154]

8. If a member has posted comments and selected to be notified of follow-up comments, then they are considered subscribed to that weblog post. The **Subscription Manager** shows which posts a member is subscribed to and allows them to unsubscribe if desired.

Subscription Manager		
Title	Type	☐ Unsubscribe
Exciting First Entry	Comment	☐
Toasted Plain Bagel	Comment	☐
Whole Wheat Toast	Comment	☐
		Unsubscribe

9. The **Ignore list** allows members to ignore other members. As a result, any forum posts made by them will not display. The **Private Messages** section allows members to message each other entirely within our site. The **Notepad** is really a scratch pad—any text typed into the notepad will be there next time the member logs in.

The member profile section of ExpressionEngine is very feature rich, allowing a lot of functionality and configurability for our members right out of the box. Members can control how much email they receive, what other members can see about them, and how other members can interact with them.

Members

The Member List

The final option in our main menu is the member list.

1. Go to `http://localhost` or `http://www.example.com` and select **Member List**. Here, we are provided with a list of all our active members. If there are lots of members, we can use filters or searches to find the person we are looking for.

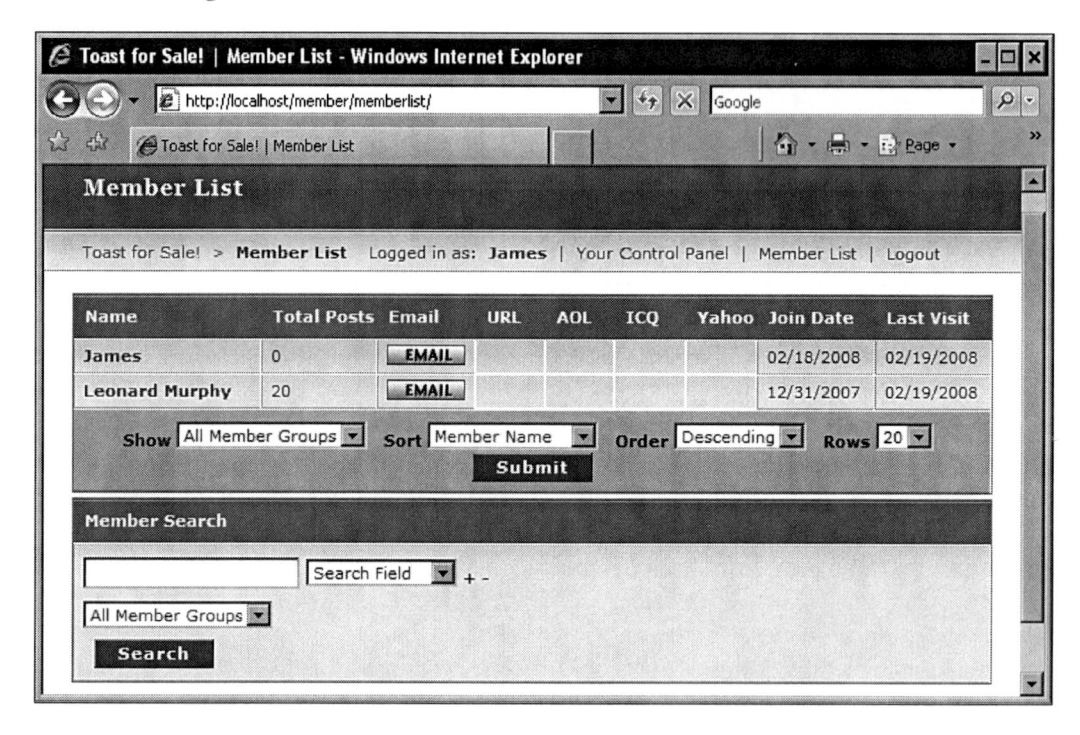

2. Click on an individual member and we can see the member profile, including any information we have personalized from our Profile page.

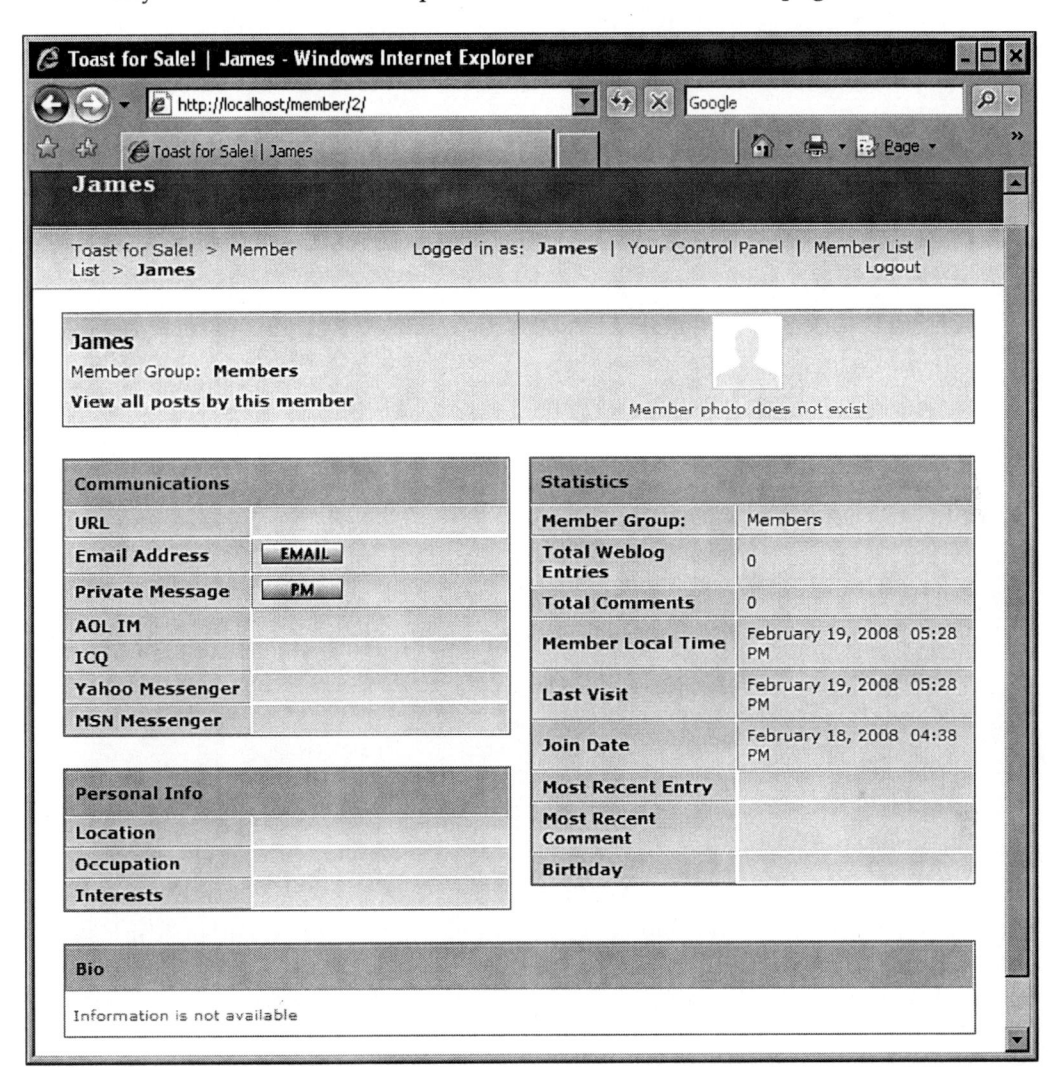

![Screenshot of member profile page for James, showing Communications, Personal Info, Statistics, and Bio sections. URL is http://localhost/member/2/. Member Group: Members. Statistics include Total Weblog Entries: 0, Total Comments: 0, Member Local Time: February 19, 2008 05:28 PM, Last Visit: February 19, 2008 05:28 PM, Join Date: February 18, 2008 04:38 PM. Bio: Information is not available.]

Members

3. Notice how the member's **Email Address** is not publicly displayed. Click on the **EMAIL** button and we are brought to a form that we must fill in to send an email.

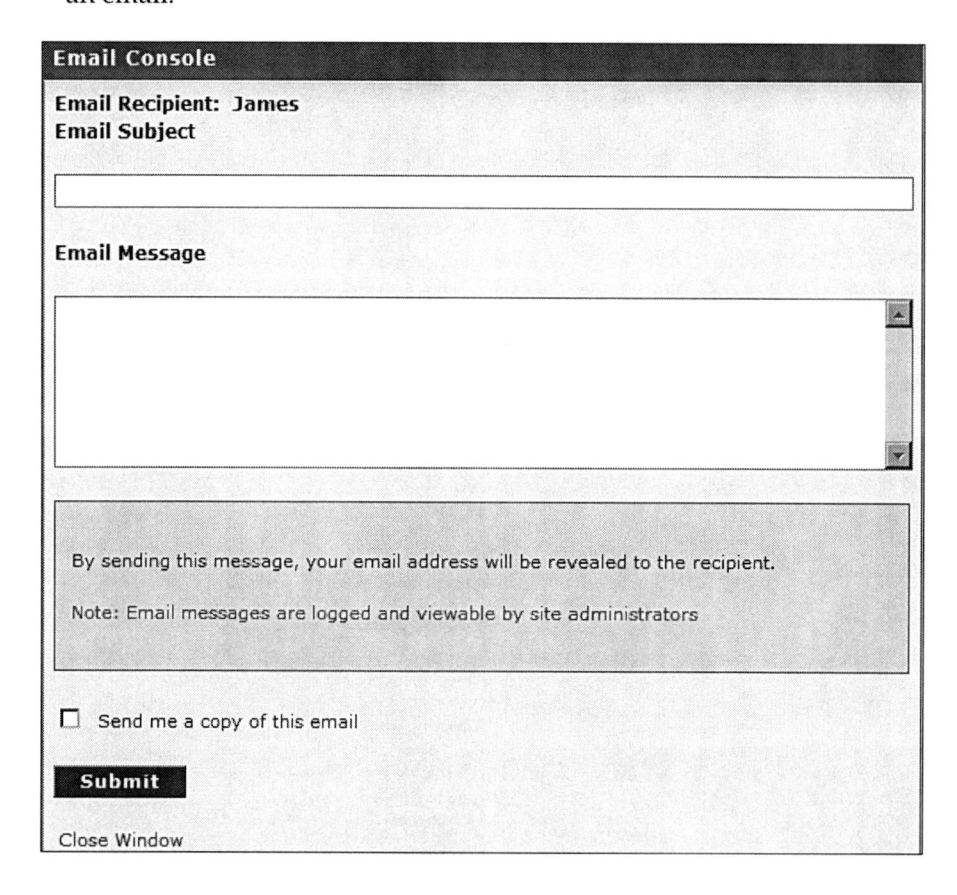

```
Email Console
Email Recipient: James
Email Subject

[                                                                    ]

Email Message

[                                                                    ]
[                                                                    ]
[                                                                    ]

By sending this message, your email address will be revealed to the recipient.

Note: Email messages are logged and viewable by site administrators

☐ Send me a copy of this email

[ Submit ]

Close Window
```

With all this functionality, it is very easy to build a website that members can use as a springboard to interact with other like-minded people. We can also control which functionality is available to members in the global member preferences.

> Although ExpressionEngine can be used to create a community-driven website, you cannot use ExpressionEngine to build a social networking site in the style of Facebook, Blogger, or MySpace (where each member has their own blog that they can customize). ExpressionEngine does not have the functionality to automatically set up blogs (you would have to set up each blog, including the templates). Further, ExpressionEngine's license specifically states that you cannot use the software as the basis of a hosted weblogging service, or to provide hosting services to others. Read more at http://expressionengine.com/knowledge_base/article/myspace_blogservice/.

Global Member Preferences

Now that we have experienced registering and setting up our member profile as a member, we are better placed to understand all the options we can set for our members on a global level.

1. We now need to log into the control panel (`http://localhost/admin.php` or `http://www.example.com/admin.php`) with our administrator login.
2. Select **Admin** from the top menu and then select **Members and Groups**. Now select **Membership Preferences**.
3. Here, we can control many of the options controlling members. On the first screen, we can require all members to be approved by an administrator instead of allowing members to self-activate via email. Alternatively, we could not require approval at all, but could instead use the captcha system (a captcha is an image of letters that a person must correctly type in order to submit data, such as a comment, thus preventing spammers from submitting hundreds of comments). We can also control whether members have to agree to our terms of service (if not, the terms of service are still displayed), and whether they can set their own localization (we might want to turn this off if all our members live in the same area). Finally, we can change the **Profile Triggering Word**. If we wanted to call our members clients, we could do this and then all our URLs would have client instead of member (for example, `http://www.example.com/client/register`).

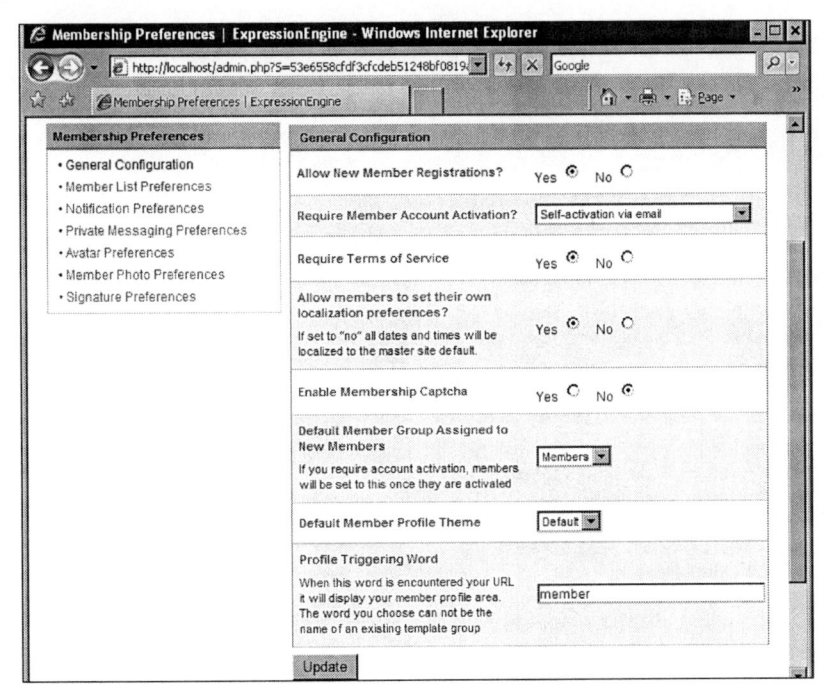

Members

4. The **Member List Preferences** allows us to change the default sort and order of our member list page.

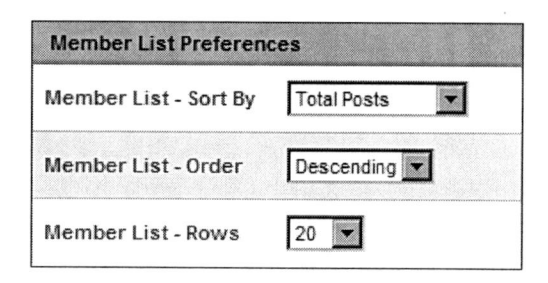

Member List Preferences	
Member List - Sort By	Total Posts
Member List - Order	Descending
Member List - Rows	20

5. The **Notification Preferences** allows us to receive emails whenever a new member registers for our site.

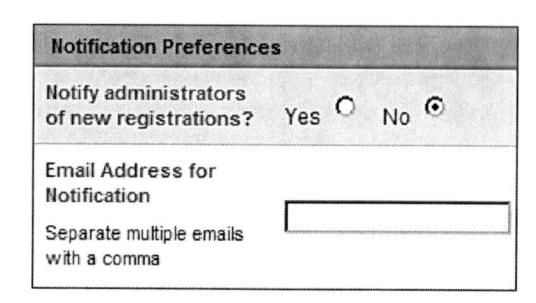

Notification Preferences	
Notify administrators of new registrations?	Yes ○ No ⊙
Email Address for Notification (Separate multiple emails with a comma)	

6. The **Private Messaging Preferences** allows us to restrict the number of characters or the size of attachments for private messages.

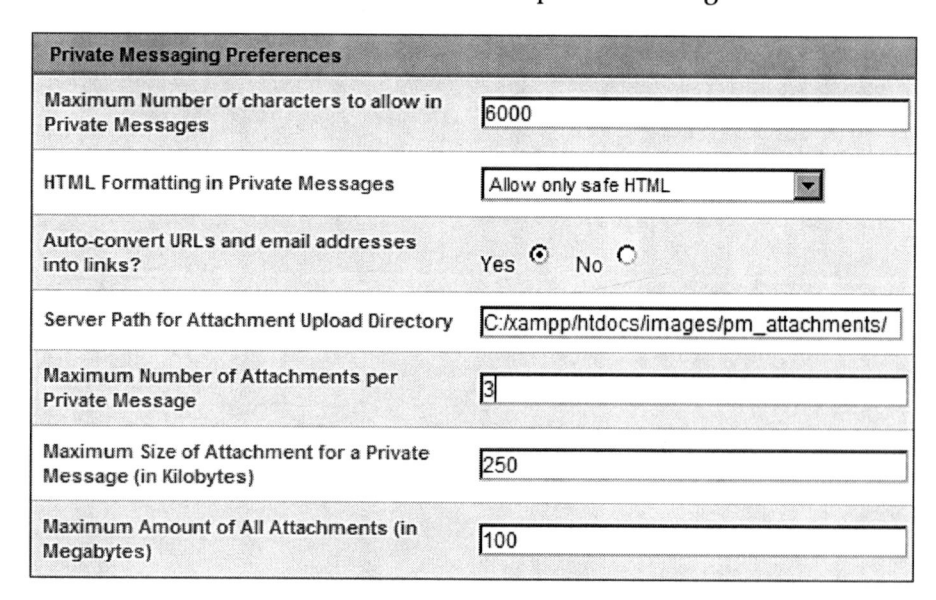

Private Messaging Preferences	
Maximum Number of characters to allow in Private Messages	6000
HTML Formatting in Private Messages	Allow only safe HTML
Auto-convert URLs and email addresses into links?	Yes ⊙ No ○
Server Path for Attachment Upload Directory	C:/xampp/htdocs/images/pm_attachments/
Maximum Number of Attachments per Private Message	3
Maximum Size of Attachment for a Private Message (in Kilobytes)	250
Maximum Amount of All Attachments (in Megabytes)	100

[160]

7. The **Avatar Preferences** allows us to control whether avatars are enabled and whether members can upload their own images. For our site, as we do not have the forum module, we are going to disable Avatars. Click **Update** and our changes should be saved.

Avatar Preferences	
Enable Avatars	Yes ○ No ⦿
Allow members to upload their own avatars?	Yes ○ No ⦿
URL to Avatar Folder	http://localhost/images/avatars/
Server Path to Avatar Folder Note: Must be a full server path, NOT a URL. Folder permissions must be set to 777.	C:/xampp/htdocs/images/avatars//
Avatar Maximum Width	100
Avatar Maximum Height	100
Avatar Maximum Size (in Kilobytes)	50

8. The **Avatar Preferences** and **Member Photo Preferences** allow us to control whether avatars or member photos are enabled, and whether members can upload their own images. For our site, as we do not have the forum module, we are going to disable Avatars but **Enable Member Photos**. Click **Update** and our changes should be saved.

Member Photo Preferences	
Enable Member Photos	Yes ⦿ No ○
URL to Photos Folder	http://localhost/images/member_photos/
Server Path to Photo Folder Note: Must be a full server path, NOT a URL. Folder permissions must be set to 777.	C:/xampp/htdocs/images/member_photos/
Photo Maximum Width	100
Photo Maximum Height	100
Photo Maximum Size (in Kilobytes)	50

Update

Members

9. Finally, the **Signature Preferences** are allowed by default, but we are going to turn them off for our site. Say **No** to **Allow Users to have Signatures**, and click **Update**.

Signature Preferences	
Allow Users to have Signatures?	Yes ○ No ⊙
Maximum number of characters per signature	500
Allow image hot linking in signatures?	Yes ○ No ⊙
Allow users to upload an image in their signature?	Yes ○ No ⊙
URL to Signature Image Upload Folder	http://localhost/images/signature_attachments/
Server path to Signature Image Upload Folder Note: Must be a full server path, NOT a URL. Folder permissions must be set to 777.	C:/xampp/htdocs/images/signature_attachments//
Maximum Width of Signature Image	480
Maximum Height of Signature Image	80
Maximum Size (in Kilobytes) of Signature Image	30

Now that we have made these modifications, we can return to our Profile page (`http://localhost/member/profile` or `http://www.example.com/member/profile`) and select **Edit Avatar** (for example). We will then see a message saying Avatars are currently disabled.

Introduction to Member Groups

So far, the options we have looked at impact all members. Members are categorized into groups, and it is also possible to allow members in different groups to have different permissions (note that a member can only be in one group at a time).

By default, there are five member groups. All of these can be renamed, deleted, or modified by us. The most important member group for us is the **Super Admins** member group. The login we have been using to do all our work so far is considered a Super Admin. Super Admins can do everything and cannot be restricted. Pretty much, the only options we have are to rename the Super Admin group and to exclude members of the Super Admin group from the member list.

The **Members** group is the next most important. This is the group that approved members are put into by default. They can do most tasks, but cannot log into the control panel. The **Pending** members group is for members who have registered but have either not activated their membership via email (if we allow self-activation by email) or have not yet been approved by an administrator (if we require all members to be approved in this way). If we do allow self-activation by email, it is a good idea to review the members of this group periodically and remove any old member registrations.

Members in the **Banned** member group cannot see our ExpressionEngine website at all, and the **Guests** member group is used for members who are not logged in.

Right now, let us create a new member group called Editors. We want this group to be able to log into the control panel and publish or edit entries. We do not want them touching our templates, setting administrative preferences, or administering members.

1. The first step is to create the member group. Log into the control panel as a Super Admin, go to the **Admin** page, select **Members and Groups**, and then select **Member Groups**.
2. For simplicity, we are going to base our new member group on the Members member group. Underneath the member group listing is the option **Create a new group based on an existing one**. Select the **Members** group from the drop-down box and click **Submit**.

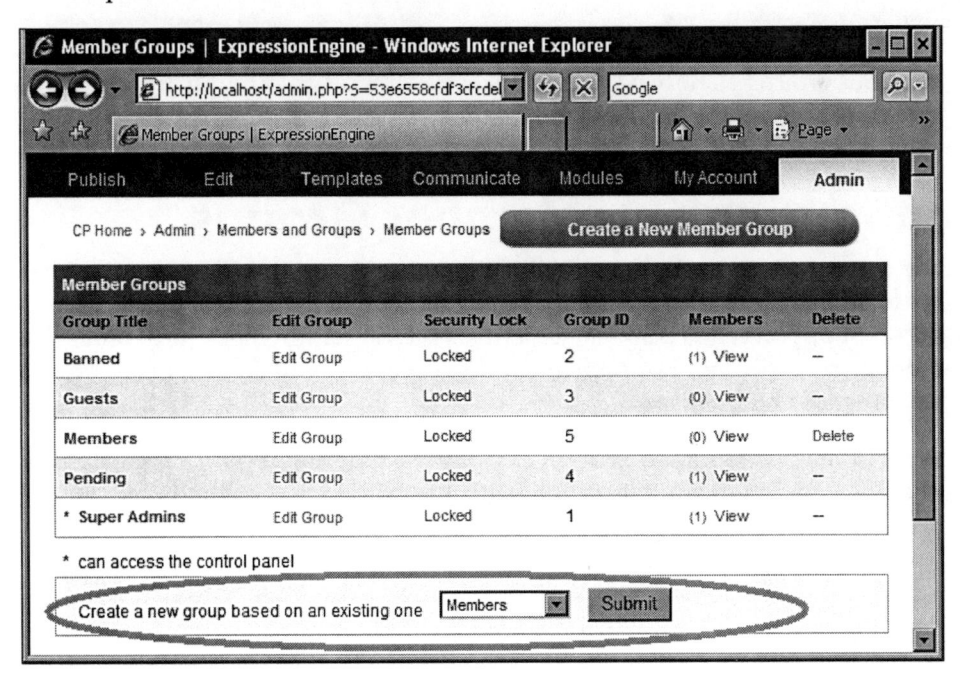

3. We are brought to a new screen where we can give the new group a name of **Editors**. Optionally, we can type in a **Description**. Click **Submit**.

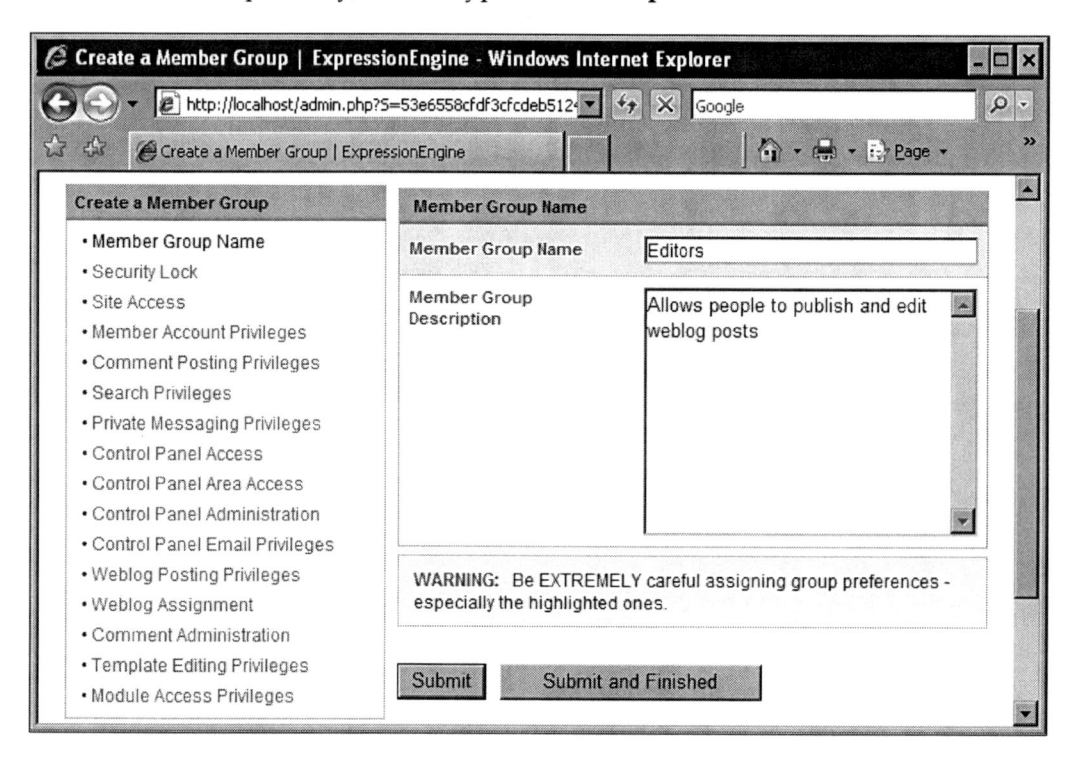

Our member group has now been created. We will now go through and configure the options shown on the left-hand side.

Configuring Our Member Groups

There are two parts to the options within a member group. The first set of options applies to all members who are using the site outside of the control panel. The second set of options controls what a member can do within the control panel. For most members, we would not even allow them access to our control panel, so this second set would be irrelevant.

Throughout the configuration process any options that might pose a security risk or we otherwise might not want to assign freely are bolded and colored red.

Configuring Options Outside of the Control Panel

1. Starting down the left-hand side menu, our first option is **Security Lock**. We haven't done so, but we can allow groups other than Super Admins to administer members. For example, we might want an admin member group that can set up new members and moderate comments but who cannot change our website content. If we had done this, we could exclude our Editors group so that admins cannot assign members to this group—only Super Admins such as us can. We will therefore leave this group **Locked**.

   Member Group Security Lock

   Enable Group Security Lock

   When a group is locked, only a Super Admin can assign a member to that group. If you allow other users to administrate member accounts, it is highly recommended that you ONLY unlock groups you want them to be able to assign other users to.

   Locked ●
   Unlocked ○

   [Update] [Update and Finished]

2. Our next option is **Site Access**. We will likely want to give our editors access to see our site when it is offline, so set both options to **Yes** and click **Update**.

> Within **Admin | System Preferences | General Configuration**, we can choose whether our system is on or not. We might choose to turn it off if we are doing updates and don't want members of the public to stumble across an incomplete site while our updating is in progress.

Members

3. The next option, **Member Account Privileges**, is set just fine as it is. If we wanted one 'editor' login to be used for multiple people, we may wish to restrict the editors' ability to email other members and be emailed.

Member Account Privileges		
Can view public profiles	Yes ●	No ○
Can email other members via the profile email console	Yes ●	No ○
Include Members in PUBLISH page multi-author list?	Yes ○	No ●
Include Members in Site's Member List?	Yes ●	No ○
Allow Members in Site's Mailing Lists and Related Abilities? (i.e. Group Available in Communicate section)	Yes ●	No ○
Can delete own account - deletes all posts, entries, and comments as well	Yes ○	No ●
Email Address of Delete Notification Recipient(s)		

[Update] [Update and Finished]

4. **Comment Posting Privileges** would allow us to prevent members of this group from submitting comments, or allow us to exclude these members from comment moderation. We will allow our editors to post comments, and we will exclude them from comment moderation (after all, we trust them with editing our website content). Click **Update** after making these changes.

Comment Posting Privileges		
Can submit comments	Yes ●	No ○
Exclude member from comment moderation	Yes ●	No ○

[Update] [Update and Finished]

5. **Search Privileges** and **Private Messaging Privileges** allow us to control whether this member group can search our site or send private messages (including how many they can send and whether they can add attachments or send bulletins). We will not make any changes to these screens.

We are now done with configuring what our member group can do outside of the control panel. Let us now configure what they can do within the control panel.

Configuring Options within Our Control Panel

The rest of the options down the left-hand side allow us to fine-tune what members in our member group can do inside the control panel. We want to allow our editors to publish and edit content, but they should not be able to modify templates, administer members. or change administrative settings.

1. Under **Control Panel Access**, we do want to allow our editors access to the control panel. If this is set to **No**, a member in this group who attempts to login at http://localhost/admin.php or http://www.example.com/admin.php will not be able to do so. Click on **Update** after making the change.

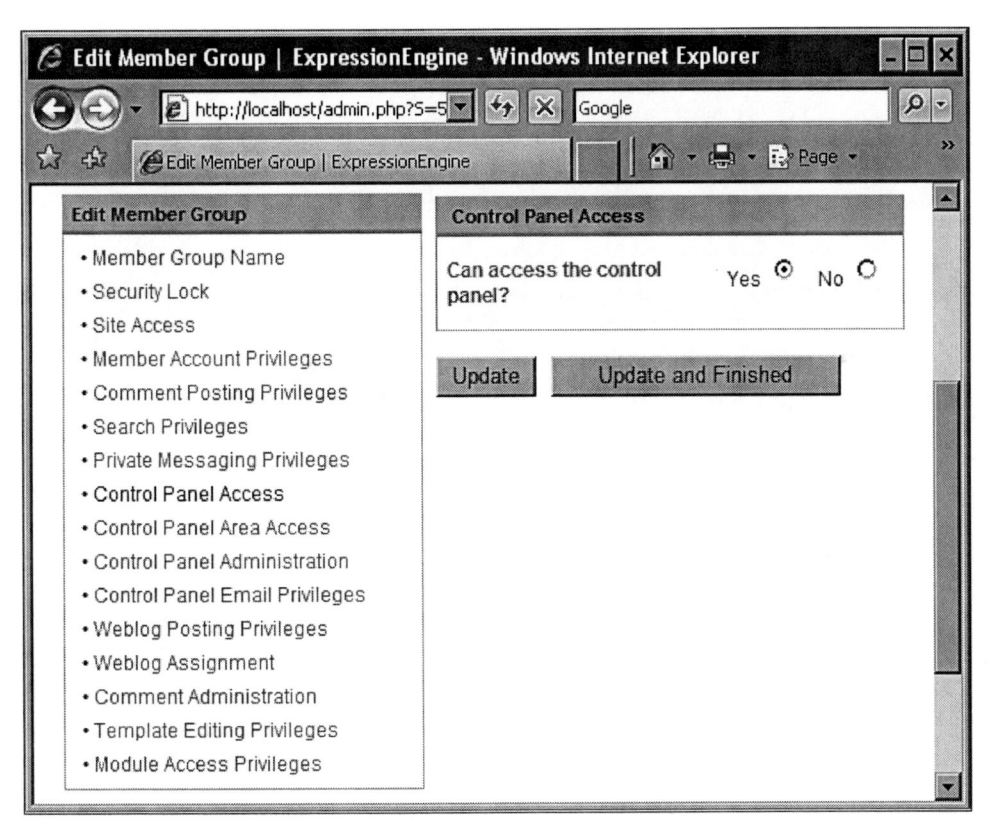

Members

2. **Control Panel Area Access** allows us to control which of the menus (along the top of the control panel) are available to our editors. We want them to be able to access our **PUBLISH page** and our **EDIT page** but none of the others. Click **Update**.

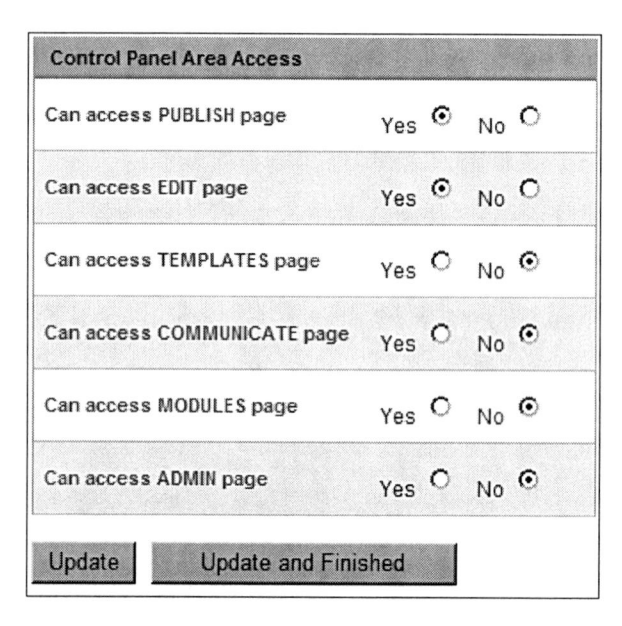

Control Panel Area Access		
Can access PUBLISH page	Yes ●	No ○
Can access EDIT page	Yes ●	No ○
Can access TEMPLATES page	Yes ○	No ●
Can access COMMUNICATE page	Yes ○	No ●
Can access MODULES page	Yes ○	No ●
Can access ADMIN page	Yes ○	No ●

[Update] [Update and Finished]

3. **Control Panel Administration** allows us to more finely tune which areas of admin they can administer. As we are not allowing our editors to access the Admin page, we can bypass this.

4. **Control Panel Email Privileges** allows us to more finely tune what our editors can do within the Communicate page. This page typically allows us to send emails to either all members of a member group or all members signed up for a mailing list. As we do not allow our editors to access the Communicate page, we can bypass this.

5. The **Weblog Posting Privileges** allows us to decide what editors can do while posting weblogs (for example, if they can delete entries or edit other people's entries). We are going to allow our editors to do everything except edit, add, and delete categories (as we are not using categories). Click **Update** after making this change.

[168]

Weblog Posting Privileges		
Can view weblog entries authored by others	Yes ⊙	No ○
Can delete their own weblog entries	Yes ⊙	No ○
Can edit entries authored by others	Yes ⊙	No ○
Can delete weblog entries authored by others	Yes ⊙	No ○
Can change the author name when posting weblog entries	Yes ⊙	No ○
Can edit and add new categories	Yes ○	No ⊙
Can delete categories	Yes ○	No ⊙

[Update] [Update and Finished]

6. The **Weblog Assignment** allows us to edit which weblogs the editors can publish and edit. For example, we may not want our editors to be able to publish to our **Toast News** weblog. For now, we are going to allow our editors to edit everything except the **Default Site Weblog** (which was created when we installed ExpressionEngine). Click **Update** after making this change.

Weblog Assignment		
Can post and edit entries in: Default Site Weblog	Yes ○	No ⊙
Can post and edit entries in: Toast News	Yes ⊙	No ○
Can post and edit entries in: Toast Products	Yes ⊙	No ○
Can post and edit entries in: Toast Website	Yes ⊙	No ○

7. **Comment Administration** allows us to configure whether editors can moderate, edit, or delete comments for themselves or anyone else. We will say **Yes** to all options here. Click **Update** after doing so.

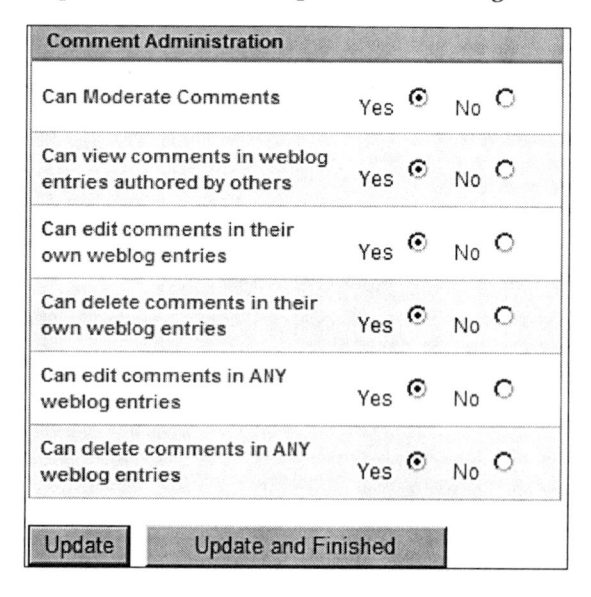

Comment Administration		
Can Moderate Comments	Yes ●	No ○
Can view comments in weblog entries authored by others	Yes ●	No ○
Can edit comments in their own weblog entries	Yes ●	No ○
Can delete comments in their own weblog entries	Yes ●	No ○
Can edit comments in ANY weblog entries	Yes ●	No ○
Can delete comments in ANY weblog entries	Yes ●	No ○

[Update] [Update and Finished]

8. **Template Editing Privileges** allows us to control which templates our editors can edit. However, we are not giving our editors access to the Templates page at all, so we can bypass this.
9. **Module Access Privileges** is set up in the same way. We are not giving our editors access to the Modules screen, so we do not need to fine-tune which modules they have access to.

We are now done creating our Editors member group, and all our changes have been updated. Let us now see how to log into the control panel as an editor and what it looks like.

Create a Member

Earlier in this chapter, we walked through how to register ourselves as a new member. Thankfully, as Super Admins, we can bypass this process and also create new members directly in the control panel. Let us now create our first editor member.

1. In the control panel, select **Admin | Members and Groups**, and then select **Register a New Member** (the top menu item).
2. Fill in the **Username**, **Password**, **Screen Name**, and **Email Address** for our new member. Be sure to select the **Editors** member group, and then click **Submit**.

> Remember that only one email address can be used per member. Registering a member through the control panel bypasses the activation email, so go ahead and use an invalid email address if necessary.

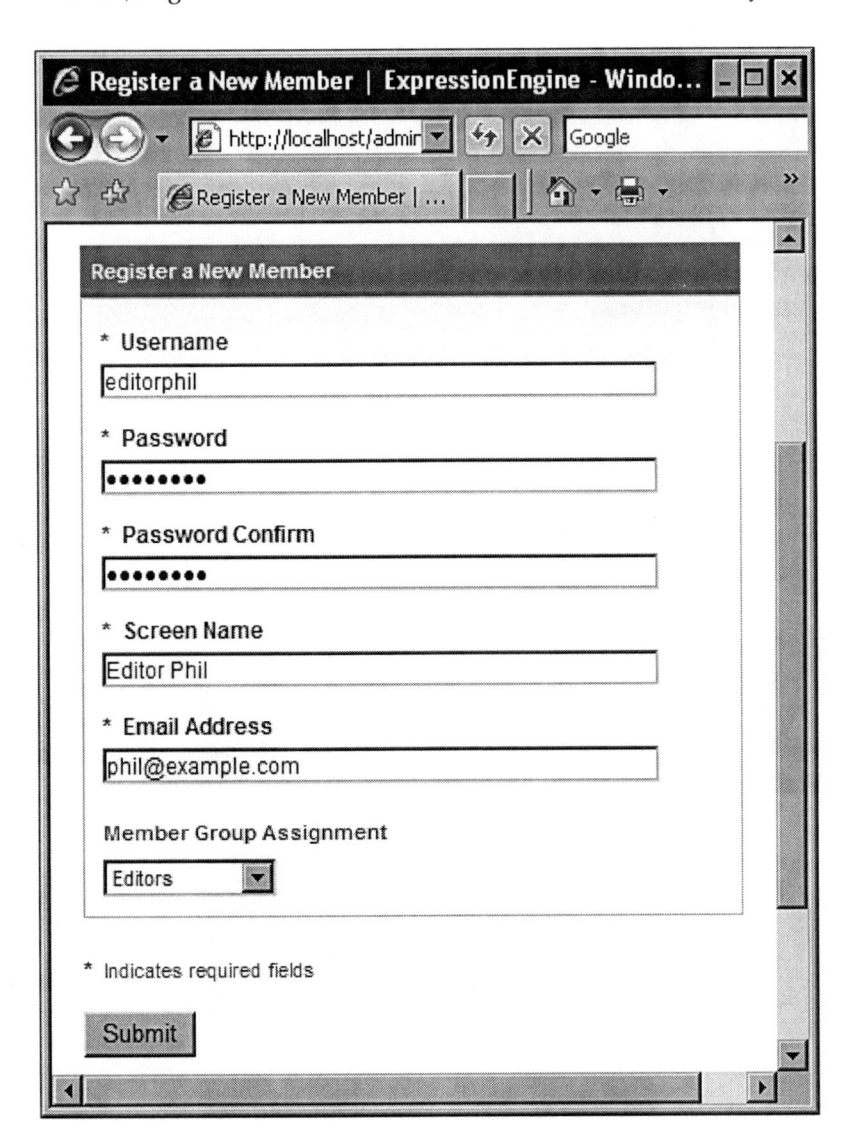

Register a New Member

* **Username**

    editorphil

* **Password**

    ••••••••

* **Password Confirm**

    ••••••••

* **Screen Name**

    Editor Phil

* **Email Address**

    phil@example.com

Member Group Assignment

Editors

* Indicates required fields

Submit

Members

3. We will be returned to a list of members in the Editors member group (right now **Editor Phil** is our first and the only editor). Do not close out of this listing just yet though.

Log in As Editor Phil

Another advantage of being a Super Admin is that we can log in as any other member without having to know that members password. This allows us to see our website as they see it—very helpful when developing new features or troubleshooting reported issues.

1. From the **View Members** screen that we are in, click on the **editorphil** hyperlink.

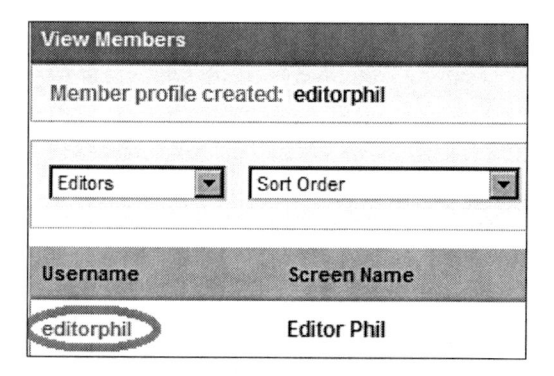

2. From the menu on the left-hand side of Editor Phil's member account, select **Member Administration**, and then click **Login as Member**.

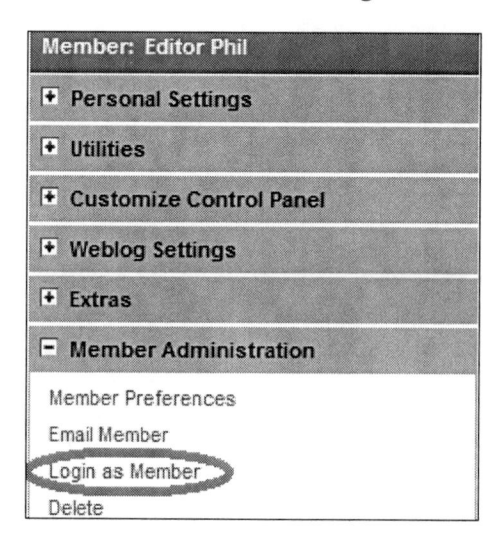

[172]

3. Here, we can choose which page of our website we want to log into as **Editor Phil**. Although we want to log into the control panel, we are going to type in the actual page we want to log into (`http://localhost/admin.php` or `http://www.example.com/admin.php`), rather than selecting the **Control Panel** option.

> The reason for this is that the default control panel page is set as `http://localhost/system/index.php`. In Chapter 2, we changed this to be the `admin.php` page we are currently using.

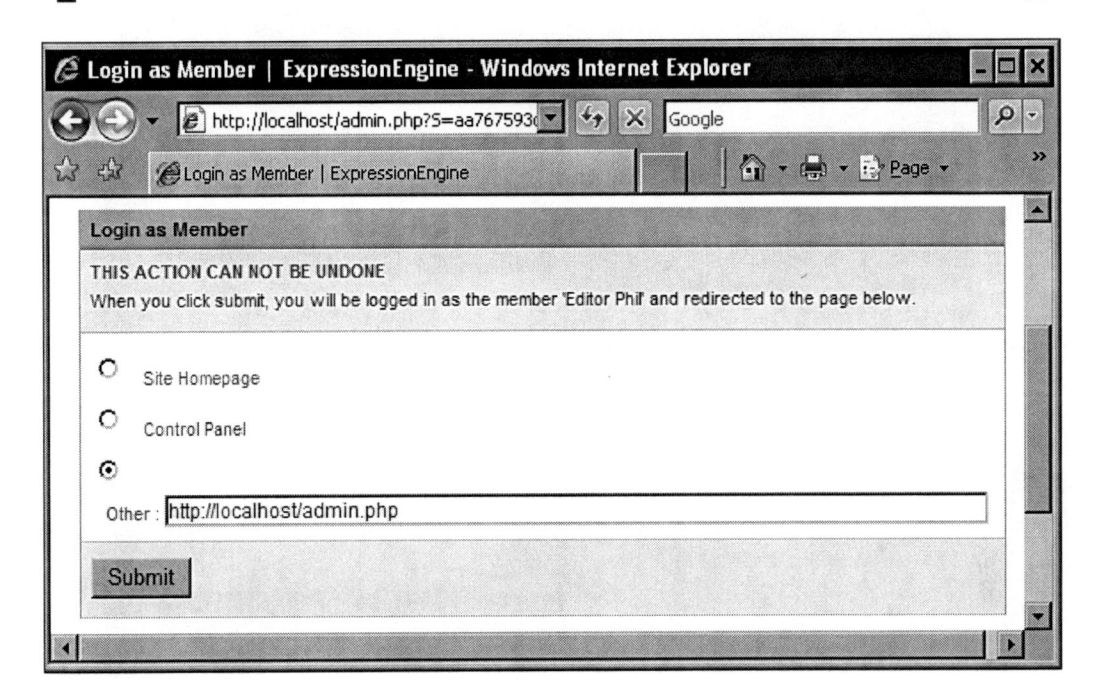

Members

4. We are now automatically logged in as **Editor Phil**. Although it looks like the control panel we have been working in so far, notice that there are far fewer tabs along the top. Essentially all Editor Phil can do is publish new entries and edit existing entries.

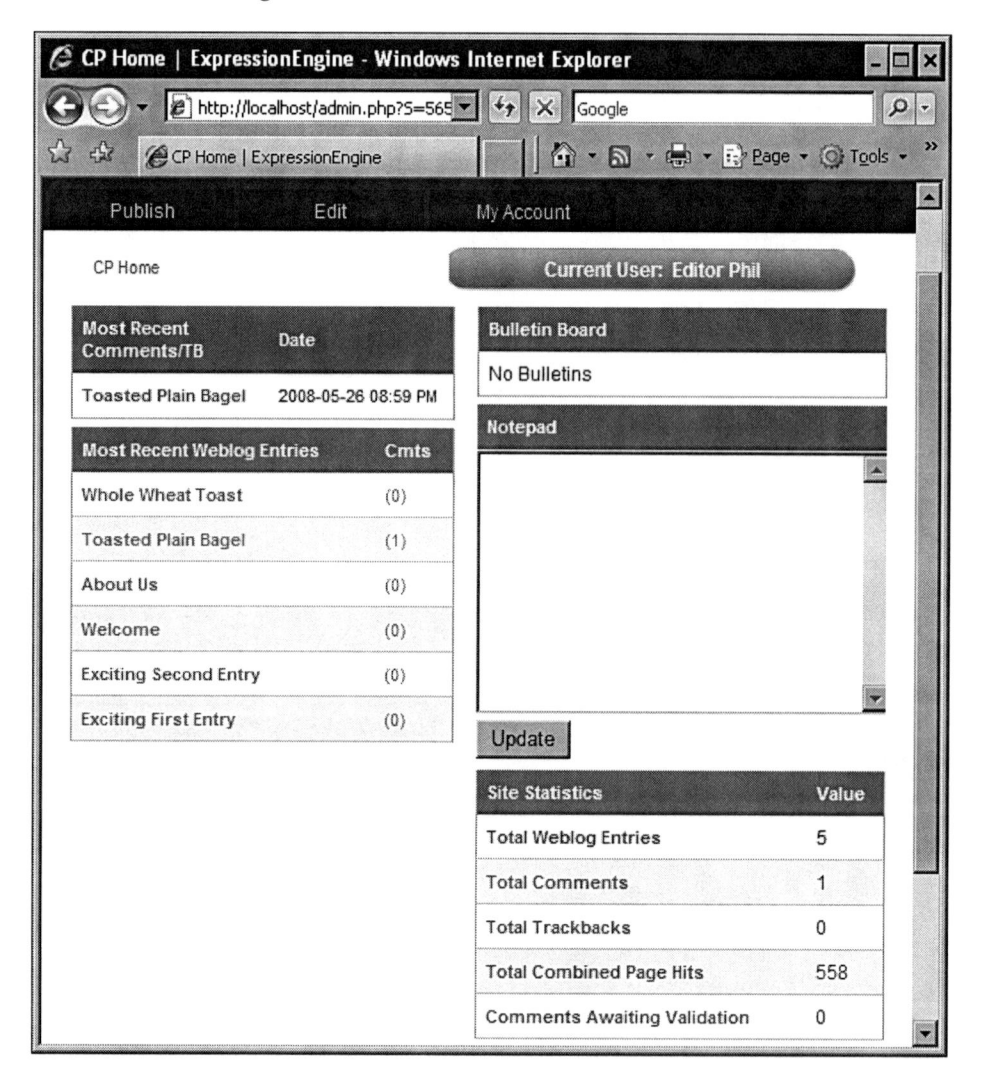

5. Click on **Publish** and another noticeable difference is that the Default Site Weblog is not an option—it is as if the weblog does not even exist.

6. Try publishing to one of the weblogs, such as **Toast News**, and then visiting the website (`http://localhost/news` or `http://www.example.com/news`) to see how the new post looks. Notice that the author is listed as **Editor Phil** (our screen name).

[174]

> If the new entry does not appear on the website, it may be that there is no status group assigned to the weblog and therefore any entries not published by a Super Admin have a status of **closed**.
>
> To fix this, log in as Super Admin, go to **Admin | Weblog Administration | Weblog Management**, and select **Edit Groups** for the corresponding weblog. Change the **Status Group** from **None** to **Default Status Group**.
>
> Now, go back to the weblog entry that is not displaying and select **Options**. Change the **Status** from **Closed** to **Open**.

New Editor

Editor Phil will be responsible for maintaining the content of our website, including keeping those hotly anticipated promotions up to date.

Editor Phil was made up in the last hour and has been editing website content for almost all that time.

Written by Editor Phil on February 20th

ExpressionEngine has many options that allow us to decide how much access members can have to the control panel—we could set up a member group for the President so that he or she can publish his or her own Toast News weblog entry without ever seeing the rest of the control panel. At the other end of the scale, we could set up a member group that can do pretty much everything we can, except publish to the President's weblog.

What we have not demonstrated so far is how to serve different content to different members on our main site.

Creating a Member-Only Section

So far we have discussed the options available to us in the control panel when setting up member groups. For members with control panel access, our options were very comprehensive—we could disable entire tabs (like the **Admin** tab), or disable individual items within a tab. For members without control panel access, there is a lot less that we can control—why is this?

From the standpoint of a member of the public joining our site, it is entirely up to us how attractive we make membership of our site, because any member-only features have to be specifically coded that way in our templates. We can do this by using a few conditional tags.

Members

To demonstrate this, we are going to make our **Promotions** page a member-only page.

> The Promotions page was created as part of an exercise at the end of Chapter 4 (Creating an Easy to Maintain Website) — we can use any page of our website as an example.

Making Content Visible to Members Only

The first step in creating a member-only area is to make sure that content does not appear unless a member is logged in. As our Promotions page is not a template in itself, but is part of the `toast/index` template that several other pages of our conventional website use, we have to use conditional statements to achieve the desired effect.

1. If you have not already created the Promotions page, post a new entry to the Toast Website weblog (select **Publish | Toast Website**). Select the **Pages** tab and use a **Pages URI** of **/promotions** and a template of **toast/index**. The URL for this page will then be `http://localhost/promotions` or `http://www.example.com/promotions`.

2. Verify what the **URL Title** of the page that we wish to make accessible to members only is. Go to **Edit** and select the **Promotions** weblog entry (it is part of the **toastwebsite** weblog). Doing this, we can clearly see that the **URL Title** is **promotions**.

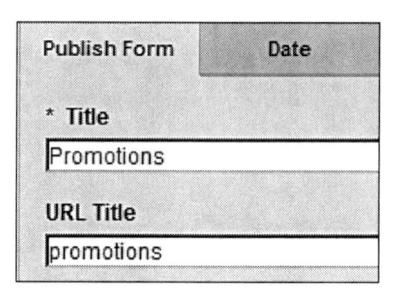

Publish Form	Date
* Title	
Promotions	
URL Title	
promotions	

3. Now, go to **Templates** and edit the `index` template of the `toast` template group.

4. Insert the following conditional statement after the `<div id="content">` line. This conditional statement is determining whether the visitor is currently logged in, and if not, whether the page being displayed is the Promotions page. Only if the member is either logged in or logged out and the page is not the Promotions page, will the content will be displayed.

```
<div id="content">
  {exp:weblog:entries weblog="toastwebsite" limit="1"}
    {if (logged_out AND url_title!="promotions") OR logged_in}
      {if toastwebsite_introduction}
        <div class="contentinner"> {toastwebsite
                         _introduction}</div>
      {/if}
      {if toastwebsite_heading1}
        <h3>{toastwebsite_heading1}</h3>
      {/if}
      {if toastwebsite_text1}
        <div class="contentinner">{toastwebsite_text1}</div>
      {/if}
      {if toastwebsite_heading2}
        <h3>{toastwebsite_heading2}</h3>
      {/if}
      {if toastwebsite_text2}
        <div class="contentinner">{toastwebsite_text2}</div>
      {/if}
      <p class="footnote">Written by {author} on {entry_date
                         format="%F %j%S"}</p>
    {/if}
  {/exp:weblog:entries}
</div>
```

5. Click **Update** and now log out of the control panel (link in the upper right-hand corner of the screen).

6. Visit `http://localhost/promotions` or `http://www.example.com/promotions` and we can see that the page looks blank where there was content earlier.

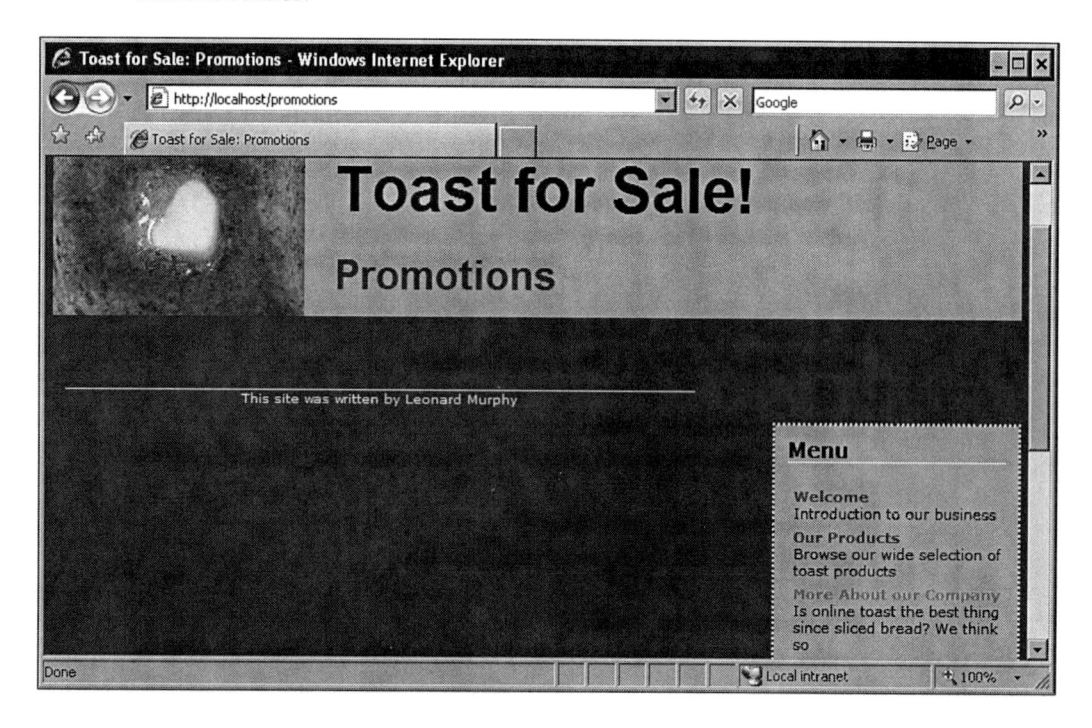

7. Rather than not displaying any information at all, let us update the `toast/index` template so that if a logged out member visits our Promotions page, they at least see a message encouraging them to log-in. Go back and edit our `toast/index` template and add the following code:

```
            <p class="footnote">Written by {author} on {entry_date
                                            format="%F %j%S"}</p>
   {if:else}
      <h3>Members Only</h3>
      <div class="contentinner"><p>Please log in to see our latest
            promotions. Not a member? Register today!</p></div>
   {/if}
  {/exp:weblog:entries}
</div>
```

8. Now when members who are logged out visit `http://localhost/promotions` or `http://www.example.com/promotions`, they see a message advising them to log in.

![Screenshot of Toast for Sale: Promotions page in Internet Explorer showing "Members Only" section with message "Please log in to see our latest promotions. Not a member? Register today!"]

We have now made a specific weblog entry accessible to members only. If we wanted to make multiple weblog entries accessible only to members, the same principals apply. Instead of using the code `{if (logged_out AND url_title!="promotions") OR logged_in}` to restrict only URL Titles of `promotions`, you can use the simpler code `{if logged_in}`, or even a conditional statement based on the member group to display different items for different groups of members. There are many ways a member-only portion of your site can be built.

Making an Entire Template Accessible to Members Only

Another scenario that frequently comes up is that, rather than making a single entry in an existing weblog visible to only members, we want to make an entire weblog accessible only to members. We can do this at the template level. Let us demonstrate this using the Toast News weblog.

1. In the control panel, select **Templates**, and then select **Template Preferences Manager** towards the top-right of the screen.

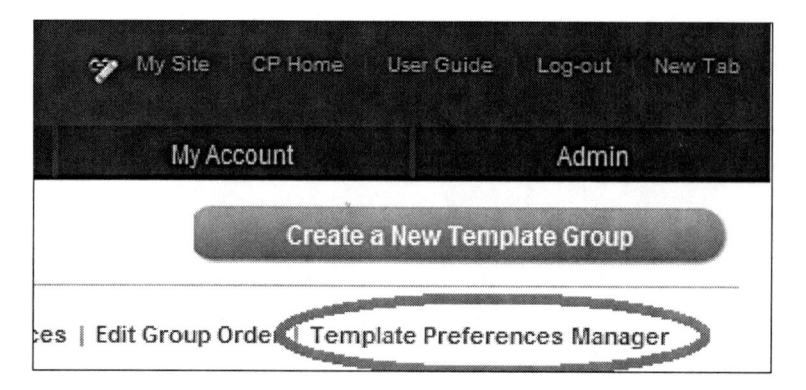

2. Within the **Template Preferences Manager**, first select the **news** template group, and then select the **index** template from the next box that appears.

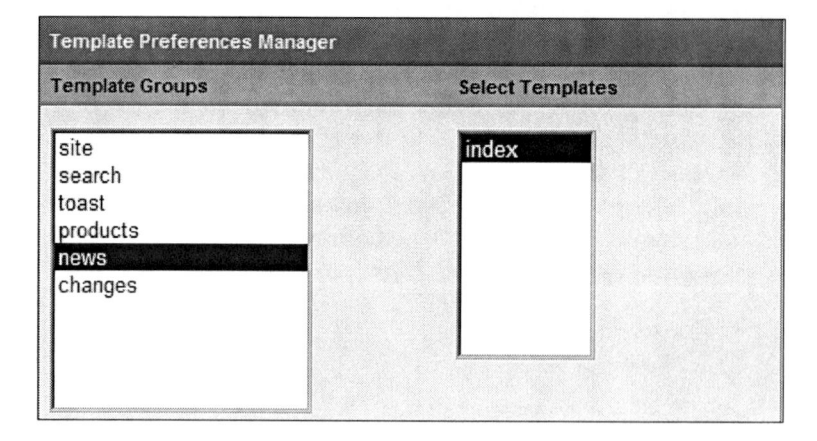

3. In the bottom-half of the page, we can select the member groups we do not want to be able to view this template (**Banned, Guests,** and **Pending**). Finally, we can redirect these members (who do visit this template) to another template. For now, we will choose the **toast/404** template from the drop-down box, though realistically, we would normally want to create a new template for this purpose. Click **Update**.

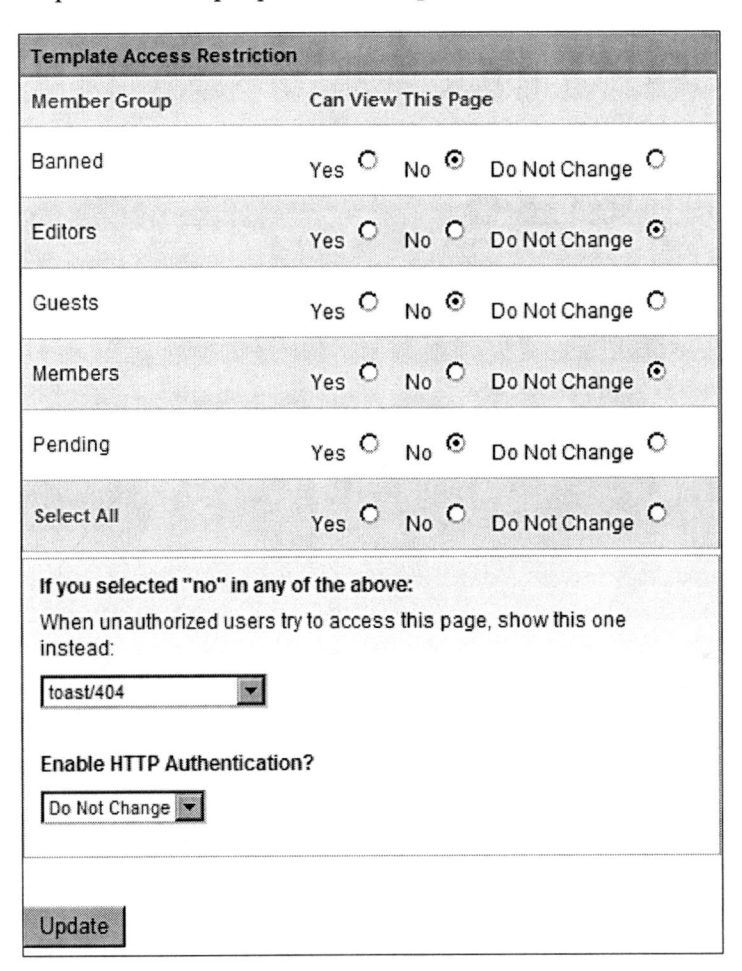

Template Access Restriction	
Member Group	Can View This Page
Banned	Yes ○ No ⦿ Do Not Change ○
Editors	Yes ○ No ○ Do Not Change ⦿
Guests	Yes ○ No ⦿ Do Not Change ○
Members	Yes ○ No ○ Do Not Change ⦿
Pending	Yes ○ No ⦿ Do Not Change ○
Select All	Yes ○ No ○ Do Not Change ○

If you selected "no" in any of the above:
When unauthorized users try to access this page, show this one instead:

[toast/404 ▾]

Enable HTTP Authentication?

[Do Not Change ▾]

[Update]

4. Now log out of the control panel and visit `http://localhost/news` or `http://www.example.com/news`; the **Page Not Found (404)** page will display instead.

We have now demonstrated how we can make entire templates inaccessible to non-members, but how do we make different content appear for different types of members?

Members

Changing Content Based on Member Group

Just as we can have multiple member groups that can all have different permissions in the control panel, we can achieve the same granularity on our main website, showing content to one member group but not another. This time, however, we will not make changes at the template level, but rather within our weblog entry.

1. Each member group has a **Group ID**. If we log into the control panel as a Super Admin user and go to **Admin | Members and Groups | Member Groups**, we can see the **Group ID** assigned to each group. In our case, our **Editors** member group has a **Group ID** of **6**.

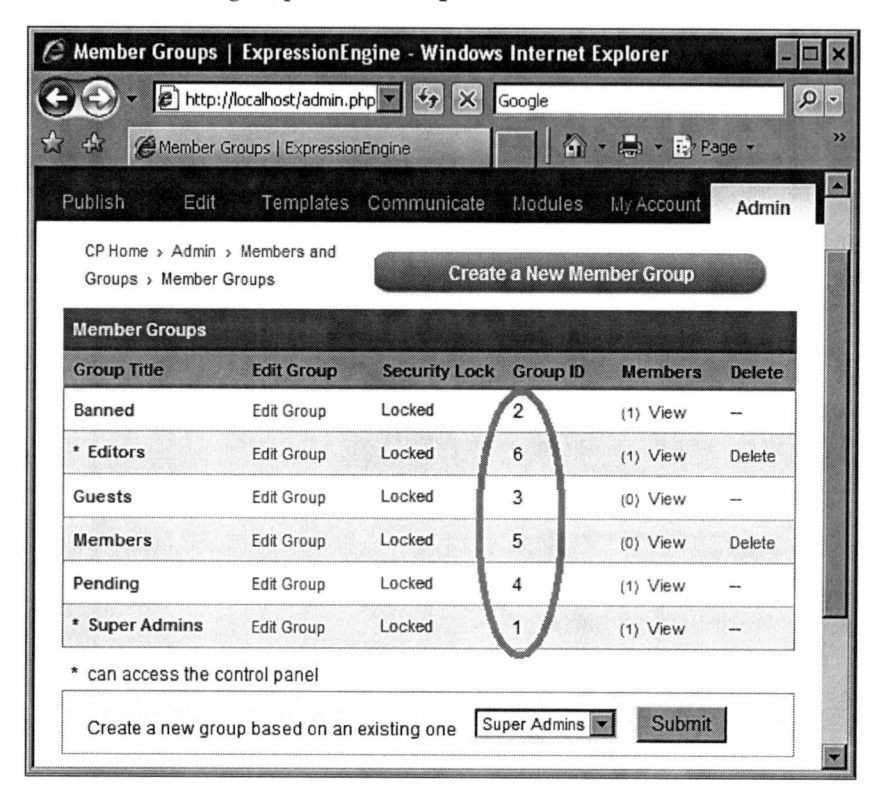

2. Next, edit the **Promotions** entry in the **Toast Website** weblog. (Select **Edit** from the top menu, and then select the **Promotions** weblog entry).

> If we have a lot of weblog entries, we can filter down what we are searching for with the options at the top. For example, we can only show weblog entries for the toastwebsite weblog (only entries in a specific date range), or we can also filter by keyword (in this case **promotion** would be a good keyword).

3. Within the fields of the Promotions weblog entry, we can display different information for different member groups using a conditional statement like {if member_group=='6'} or {if member_group!='6'}. Let us try that now. Replace the existing entry in the Promotions page with the following:

   {if member_group!=6}We currently have no promotions.{/if}{if member_group==6}Editor's Only Promotion - Get 50% off the lowest advertised price of any product on our website{/if}

4. Click **Update**.

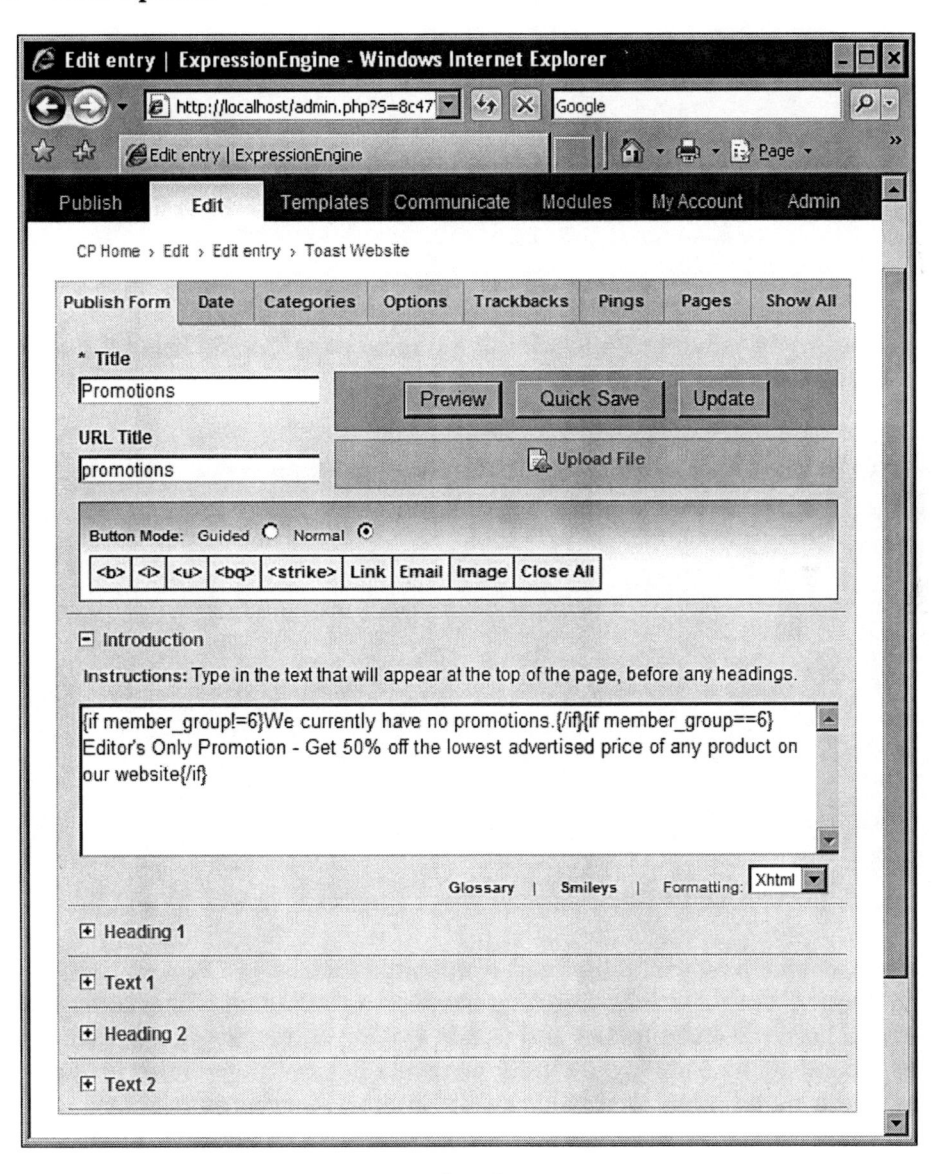

Members

5. Now, visit `http://localhost/promotions` or `http://www.example.com/promotions` while still logged in under our Super Admin membership group and it will look like we have no promotions.

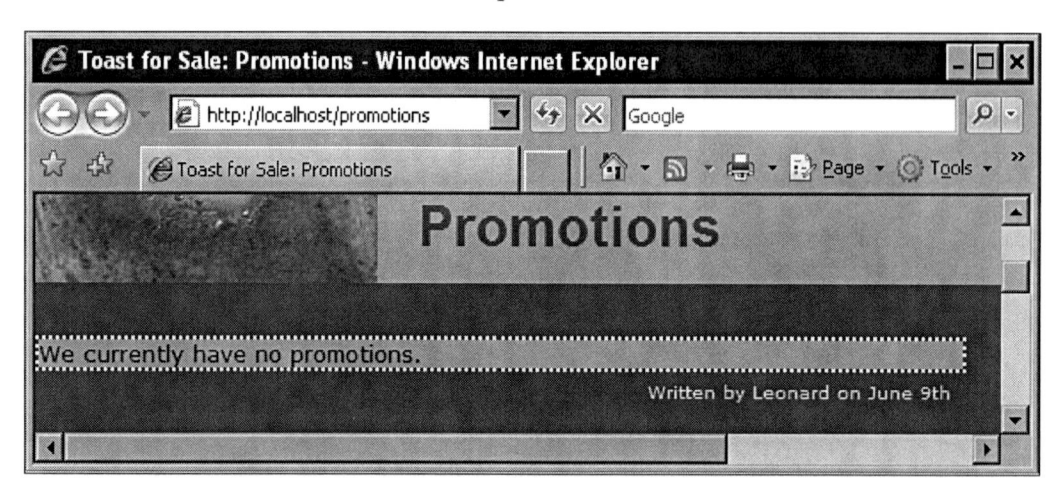

[Screenshot: Toast for Sale: Promotions page showing "We currently have no promotions." Written by Leonard on June 9th]

6. Now log in as Editor Phil and visit the same page. Lo and behold! A fantastic deal awaits us.

[Screenshot: Toast for Sale: Promotions page showing "Editor's Only Promotion - Get 50% off the lowest advertised price of any product on our website" Written by Leonard Murphy on January 6th]

We have now seen how useful the basic commands such as {if logged_in} and {if logged_out} are, when creating member-only content. These commands can be used both within templates and within weblog entries to provide text that only members who are logged in (or members in a certain member group) can see. There are far more commands available as well—read more at http://expressionengine.com/docs/templates/globals/conditionals.html.

[184]

The Stand-Alone Entry Form (SAEF)

Occasionally, we may wish to create a weblog that our members can post to, without giving them access to the control panel at all. The Stand-Alone Entry Form is essentially a recreation of our **Publish** page form, but is an integral part of our main website.

> The code in this section has been adapted from the Stand-Alone Entry Form documentation at http://expressionengine.com/docs/modules/weblog/entry_form.html. For the purposes of this book, not all tags are included. Please refer to the ExpressionEngine website for complete documentation on this feature.

Create the Stand-Alone Entry Form

To demonstrate the Stand-Alone Entry Form, we are going to add the form to our `Toast News` weblog, allowing our Editors member group to post `Toast News` weblog entries without logging into the control panel.

1. Go to the **Templates** tab, select the **news** template group, and click **New Template** to create a new template called **post_entry**. Create an empty template and click **Submit**.

2. We are going to start by creating an empty template modelled after our `news/index` template. Add the following code to the blank template:

```
{assign_variable:my_weblog="toastnews"}
{assign_variable:my_template_group="news"}
{assign_variable:my_site_wide_templates="toast"}
<!DOCTYPE html PUBLIC "-//W3C//DTD XHTML 1.0 Strict//EN"
  "http://www.w3.org/TR/xhtml1/DTD/xhtml1-strict.dtd">
<html xmlns="http://www.w3.org/1999/xhtml">
  <head>
    <title>Post to News from the President</title>
    <link rel='stylesheet' type='text/css' media='all'
                href='{path=toast/toast_css}' />
    <style type='text/css' media='screen'>@import
          "{path=toast/toast_css}";</style>
    <meta http-equiv="content-type" content="text/html;
                                   charset=UTF-8" />
  </head>
```

[185]

Members

```
    <body>
      <div id="header">
        <h1>Toast for Sale!</h1>
        <h2>Post to News from the President</h2>
      </div>
    </body>
</html>
```

3. Next, we are going to add the fields for the Title and the URL Title, as well as the Submit and Preview buttons. We are also going to add in our sidebar menu.

```
    <div id="header">
      <h1>Toast for Sale!</h1>
      <h2>Post to News from the President</h2>
    </div>
    {exp:weblog:entry_form weblog="{my_weblog}"
    return="{my_template_group}/index" preview=
             "{my_template_group}/post_entry"}
      <div id="content">
        <h3>Title</h3>
        <input type="text" name="title" id="title" value="{title}"
            size="50" maxlength="100" onkeyup="liveUrlTitle();" />
        <h3>URL Title</h3>
        <input type="text" name="url_title" id='url_title'
            value="{url_title}" maxlength="75" size="50" />
        <br /><br />
        <input type="submit" name="submit" value="Submit" />
        <input type="submit" name="preview" value="Preview" />
      </div>
      <div id="menu">
        {embed={my_site_wide_templates}/.menu}
      </div>
    {/exp:weblog:entry_form}
  </body>
```

4. We can now visit `http://localhost/news/post_entry/` or `http://www.example.com/news/post_entry/`. Even though we have yet to add all the fields we see on a normal Publish page, our simplified version is a working example. Try typing in a title and hitting **Submit** (the Preview button will not yet work). You should be returned to `http://localhost/news/`, and you should see your new entry at the top of the page. The page that is displayed when selecting **Submit** is defined by the `return` parameter in the `exp:weblog:entry_form` tag.

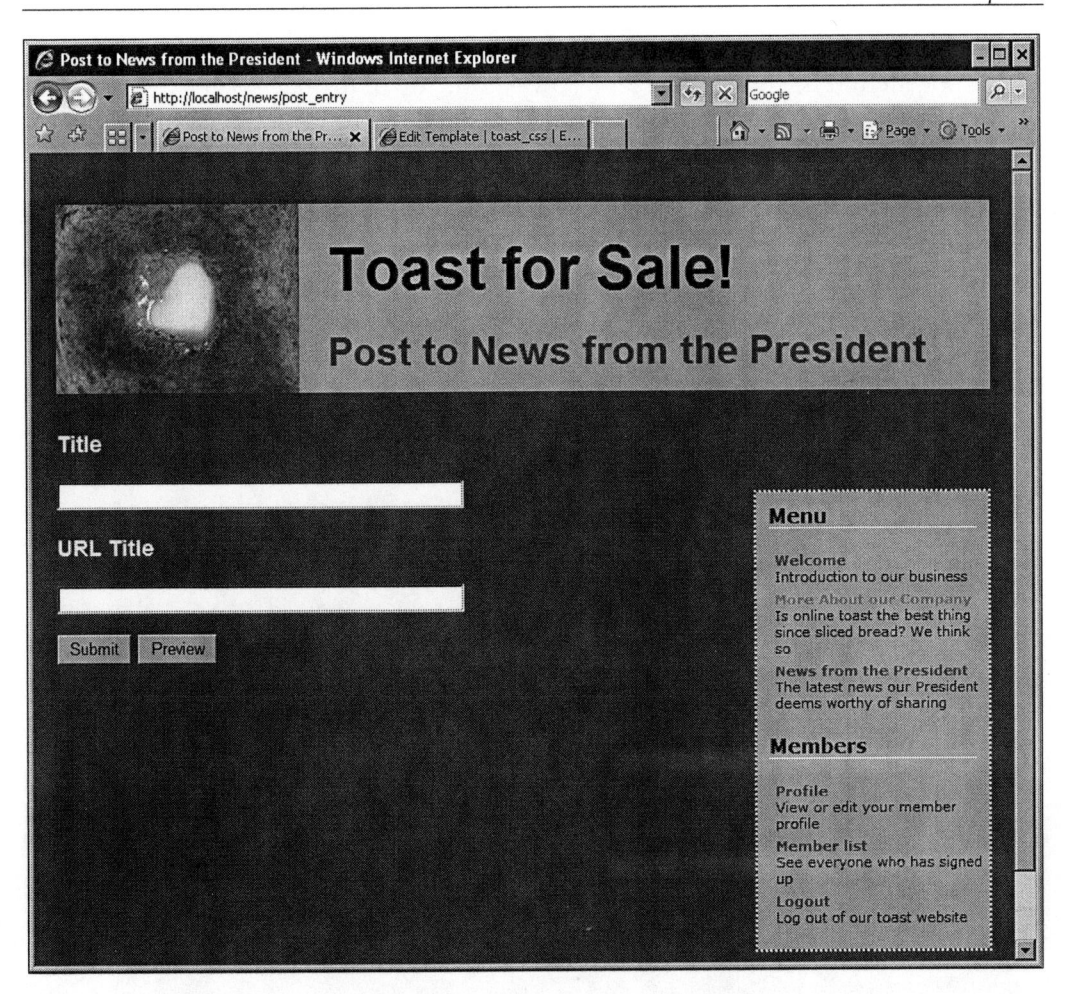

5. To get the Preview button to work, add the following code between the `<div id="content">` and the `<h3>{title}</h3>` tags.

```
<div id="content">
  {preview}
    <h3>{title}</h3>
    <div class="contentinner">
      {display_custom_fields}
    </div>
  {/preview}
  <h3>Title</h3>
```

6. Now, when we type in an example title and click **Preview** instead of **Submit**, we should be shown the blank entry at the top of the page. The page that is displayed when selecting **Preview** is defined by the `preview` parameter in the `exp:weblog:entry_form` tag.

7. Next, we should add the main fields onto the page so that we can type in the content of our news entry. As fields can be customized and there can be any number of fields of different types, the Stand-Alone Entry Form code accounts for all the types simultaneously. The tag {custom_fields} means that for each custom field the code will display. The code that does actually display depends on the field type (for example, textarea, textinput, date field, and so on). Although we know that our Toast News weblog contains only textarea fields, we are going to include code for all the field types so that if we want to make a change down the road, the change will not break our Stand-Alone Entry Form. Add the following code after the URL Title, and before the Submit/Preview buttons.

```
<h3>URL Title</h3>
<input type="text" name="url_title" id='url_title' value="{url_title}" maxlength="75" size="50" />
{custom_fields}
  <h3>{if required}* {/if}{field_label}</h3>
  {field_instructions}
  {if textarea}
    <textarea id="{field_name}" name="{field_name}"
    dir="{text_direction}" cols="65" rows="{rows}"
    onclick="setFieldName(this.name)">{field_data}</textarea>
  {/if}
  {if textinput}
    <input type="text" dir="{text_direction}" id="{field_name}"
    name="{field_name}" value="{field_data}" maxlength="
    {maxlength}" size="50" onclick="setFieldName(this.name)" />
  {/if}
  {if pulldown}
    <select id="{field_name}" name="{field_name}">
      {options}<option value="{option_value}"{selected}>
                    {option_name}</option>{/options}
    </select>
  {/if}
  {if date}
    <input type="text" id="{field_name}" name="{field_name}"
    value="{field_data}" maxlength="{maxlength}" size="50"
                    onclick="setFieldName(this.name)" />
  {/if}
  {if relationship}
    <select id="{field_name}" name="{field_name}">
      {options}<option value="{option_value}"
      {selected}>{option_name}</option>{/options}
    </select>
  {/if}
{/custom_fields}
```

Members

```
<br /><br />
<input type="submit" name="submit" value="Submit" />
<input type="submit" name="preview" value="Preview" />
```

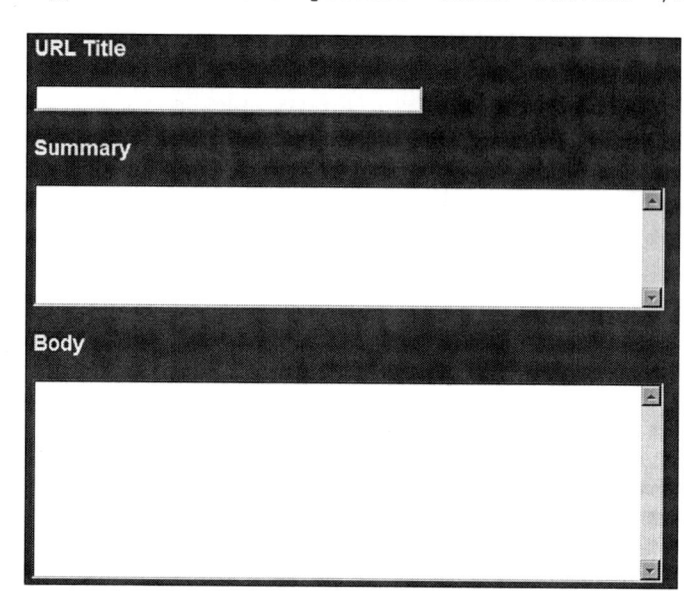

[Screenshot showing form fields: URL Title (text input), Summary (textarea), Body (textarea)]

8. Next, we are going to add some of the other options. Rather than putting them onto our main page, we are going to add them to our sidebar. Add the following code after the `{embed={my_site_wide_templates}/.menu}` line. Note that when we view the page, not all the options will necessarily appear. It depends on the options set up in the weblog preferences.

```
{embed={my_site_wide_templates}/.menu}
<h4>Other Options</h4>
 {status_menu}
   <p><b>Status</b><br />
     <select name="status">
       {select_options}
     </select>
   </p>
 {/status_menu}
 <p><b>Date</b><br />
 <input type="text" name="entry_date" value="{entry_date}"
                        maxlength="23" size="25" /></p>
 <p><b>Expiration Date</b><br />
 <input type="text" name="expiration_date" value=
 "{expiration_date}" maxlength="23" size="25" /></p>
 <p><b>Comment Expiration Date</b><br />
 <input type="text" name="comment_expiration_date"
 value="{comment_expiration_date}" maxlength="23"
                            size="25" /></p>
```

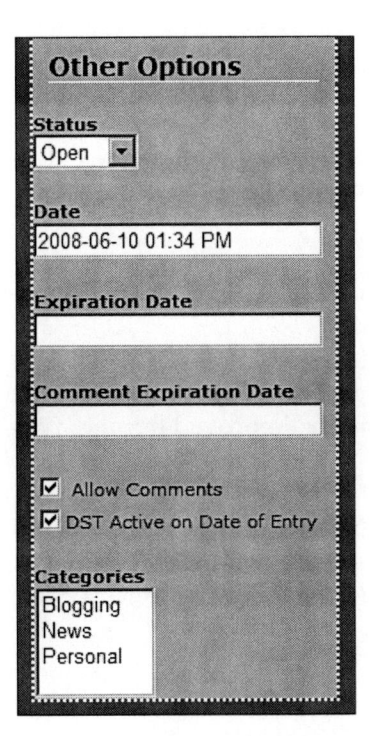

```
        <input type="checkbox" name="allow_comments" value="y"
                    {allow_comments} /> Allow Comments<br />
        <input type='checkbox' name='dst_enabled' value='y'
              {dst_enabled} />DST Active on Date of Entry
      {category_menu}
        <p><b>Categories</b><br />
          <select name="category[]" size="4" multiple="multiple">
            {select_options}
          </select>
        </p>
      {/category_menu}
    </div>
  {/exp:weblog:entry_form}
</body>
```

9. Our final adjustment will be to add the HTML buttons and the File Upload and Smiley options to the page. We will put these after the URL Title and before our custom fields in the code.

```
<h3>URL Title</h3>
<input type="text" name="url_title" id='url_title' value="{url_title}" maxlength="75" size="50" />
<br /><br />
{formatting_buttons}
```

Members

```
<p class="footnote"><a href="{upload_url}" onclick="window.open
(this.href, '_blank', 'width=400,height=600');return false;
"onkeypress="this.onclick()">File Upload</a> | <a href=
"{smileys_url}" onclick="window.open(this.href, '_blank',
'width=600,height=440');return false;"onkeypress=
            "this.onclick()">Smileys</a></p>
{custom_fields}
```

Our Stand-Alone Entry Form is now fully functional. Don't be afraid to try posting some entries via this form to get a feel for how it works.

Modify the CSS for Our Stand-Alone Entry Form

We now have the Stand-Alone Entry Form working, but as with any section of our website, the layout can always be improved through CSS.

1. First, edit the `toast/toast_css` template.

2. We will add CSS to define the `<h3>` style within the content `div`. This code will reduce the white space and make it clearer which heading refers to which input box. Add the following to our CSS file:

   ```
   #content h3{
     color: #F0E68C;
     font-family: Arial, Helvetica, sans-serif;
     font-weight: bold;
     margin-bottom: 0px;
   }
   ```

> When making adjustments to pre-existing styles, always be aware that the adjustments may have unintended consequences on pages you are not actively developing. To avoid this, always check your entire site thoroughly after making changes in CSS.

3. Next, we can add some code from ExpressionEngine to better define our HTML buttons as buttons. Paste the following code into the bottom of our stylesheet:

```
/*
    Formatting Buttons
---------------------------------------------------- */
.buttonMode {
  background-color: transparent;
  color: #73769D;
  font-family: Verdana, Geneva, Tahoma, Trebuchet MS, Arial, Sans-
                                                          serif;
  font-size: 10px;
  white-space: nowrap;
}
.htmlButtonOutter, .htmlButtonOutterL {
  background-color: #f6f6f6;
  border-bottom: #333 1px solid;
  border-right: #333 1px solid;
  border-top: #333 1px solid;
  padding: 0;
}
.htmlButtonOutterL {
  border-left: #333 1px solid;
}
.htmlButtonInner {
  background-color: transparent;
  border-bottom: #ccc 1px solid;
  border-left: #fff 1px solid;
  border-right: #ccc 1px solid;
  border-top: #fff 1px solid;
  padding: 0 3px 0 3px;
  text-align: center;
}
.htmlButtonOff {
  font-family: Verdana, Arial, Trebuchet MS, Tahoma, Sans-serif;
  font-size: 11px;
  font-weight: bold;
  padding: 1px 2px 2px 2px;
  white-space: nowrap;
}
.htmlButtonOff a:link {
  color: #000;
  text-decoration: none;
  white-space: nowrap;
}
```

```css
.htmlButtonOff a:visited {
  text-decoration: none;
}
.htmlButtonOff a:active {
  color: #999;
  text-decoration: none;
}
.htmlButtonOff a:hover {
  color: #999;
  text-decoration: none;
}
.htmlButtonOn {
  background: #f6f6f6;
  font-family: Verdana, Arial, Trebuchet MS, Tahoma, Sans-serif;
  font-size: 11px;
  font-weight: bold;
  padding: 1px 2px 2px 2px;
  white-space: nowrap;
}
.htmlButtonOn a:link {
  color: #990000;
  text-decoration: none;
  white-space: nowrap;
}
.htmlButtonOn a:visited {
  text-decoration: none;
}
.htmlButtonOn a:active {
  color: #999;
  text-decoration: none;
}
.htmlButtonOn a:hover {
  color: #999;
  text-decoration: none;
}
.htmlButtonA {
  font-family: Lucida Grande, Verdana, Geneva, Sans-serif;
  font-size: 11px;
  font-weight: bold;
  padding: 2px 3px 3px 3px;
  white-space: nowrap;
}
```

```css
.htmlButtonB {
  background: #E1E3EC;
  font-family: Lucida Grande, Verdana, Geneva, Sans-serif;
    font-size: 11px;
  font-weight: bold;
  padding: 2px 3px 3px 3px;
  white-space: nowrap;
}
.htmlButtonA a:link {
  color: #000;
  font-weight: bold;
  text-decoration: none;
  white-space: nowrap;
}
.htmlButtonA a:visited {
  text-decoration: none;
}
.htmlButtonA a:active {
  color: #999;
  text-decoration: none;
}
.htmlButtonA a:hover {
  color: #999;
  text-decoration: none;
}
.htmlButtonB a:link {
  color: #990000;
  font-weight: bold;
  text-decoration: none;
  white-space: nowrap;
}
.htmlButtonB a:visited {
  text-decoration: none;
}
.htmlButtonB a:active {
  color: #999;
  text-decoration: none;
}
.htmlButtonB a:hover {
  color: #999;
  text-decoration: none;
}
```

Members

> This code is taken directly from the ExpressionEngine website at `http://expressionengine.com/docs/modules/weblog/entry_form_css.txt`. It styles HTML that is defined within the `{formatting_buttons}` tag (we cannot see the HTML styles in our template, but when we view source we can see they are there).

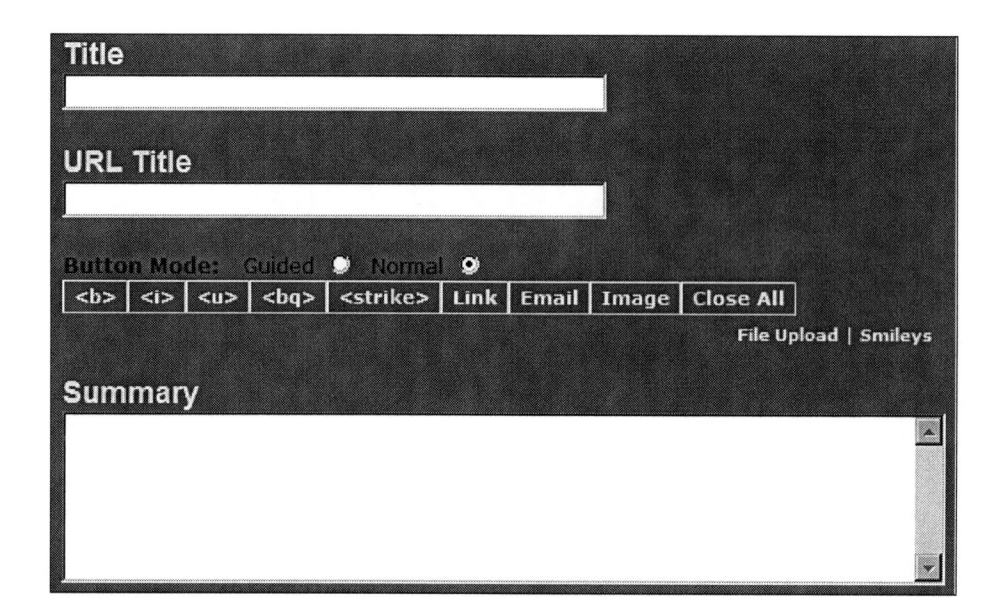

Our Stand-Alone Entry Form is complete!

The Mailing List Module

ExpressionEngine comes with a mailing list module pre-installed. It is a very straight-forward module that allows you to quickly and easily send emails to visitors of your site or to specific member groups. You can have as many mailing lists as you want.

If you are using a `localhost` environment such as XAMPP or MAMP, testing the functionality of a mailing list will be difficult because you may not get any of the emails.

Creating a Mailing List

ExpressionEngine comes with a mailing list ready to go, called `default`. However, we will walk through how to create our own mailing list, where we will announce new toast products as they become available.

1. To create another mailing list, select **Modules** from the main control panel menu, and then select the **Mailing List** module from the links on the left-hand side.

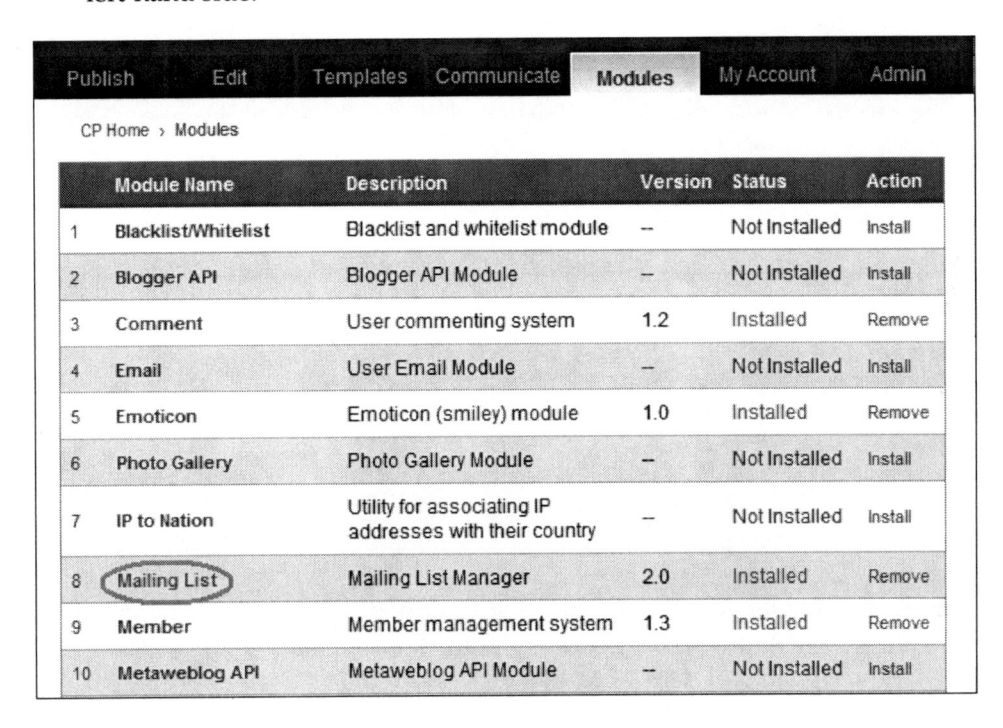

	Module Name	Description	Version	Status	Action
1	Blacklist/Whitelist	Blacklist and whitelist module	--	Not Installed	Install
2	Blogger API	Blogger API Module	--	Not Installed	Install
3	Comment	User commenting system	1.2	Installed	Remove
4	Email	User Email Module	--	Not Installed	Install
5	Emoticon	Emoticon (smiley) module	1.0	Installed	Remove
6	Photo Gallery	Photo Gallery Module	--	Not Installed	Install
7	IP to Nation	Utility for associating IP addresses with their country	--	Not Installed	Install
8	Mailing List	Mailing List Manager	2.0	Installed	Remove
9	Member	Member management system	1.3	Installed	Remove
10	Metaweblog API	Metaweblog API Module	--	Not Installed	Install

2. In the top-right of the screen, select **Create New Mailing List**.

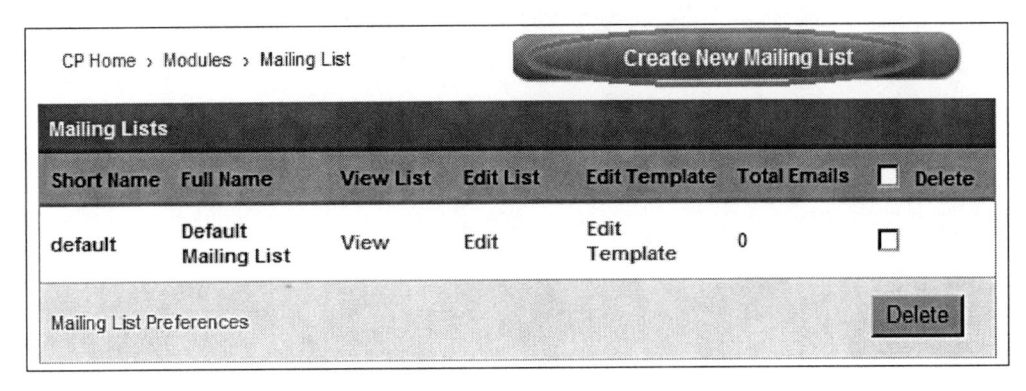

Short Name	Full Name	View List	Edit List	Edit Template	Total Emails	Delete
default	Default Mailing List	View	Edit	Edit Template	0	☐

3. We are going to use a **Short Name** of **newproducts** and a **Full Name** of **New Products**. The short name is used in our templates so that ExpressionEngine knows which mailing list a member is signing up for.

4. We will be returned to the **Mailing List** module screen. If we want, we can customize the email template by clicking on **Edit Template**. By default, each email has a footer with the unsubscribe URL (a required part of every email). However, we could also add a header or use the `{if html_email}` conditional statement to create a professional looking HTML email that the `{message_text}` is embedded in.

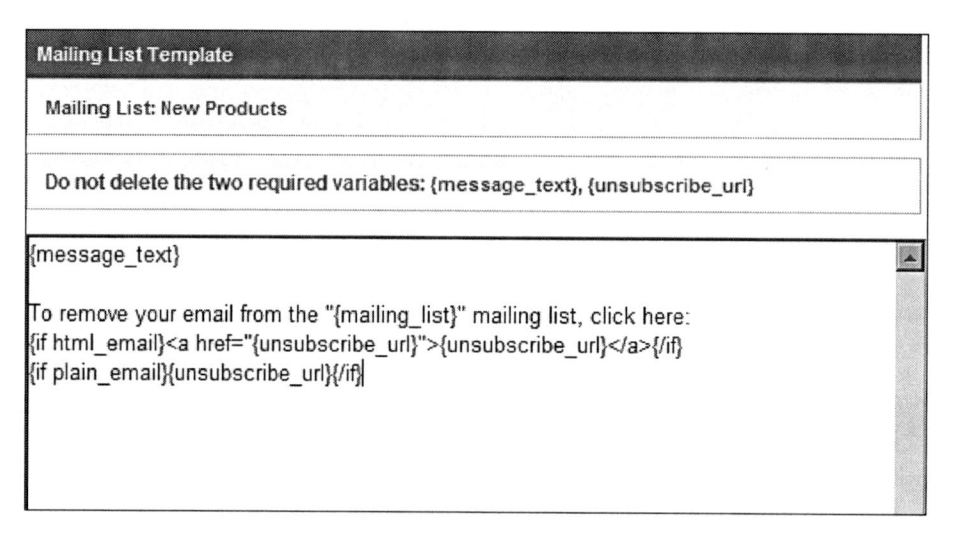

```
Mailing List Template

Mailing List: New Products

Do not delete the two required variables: {message_text}, {unsubscribe_url}

{message_text}

To remove your email from the "{mailing_list}" mailing list, click here:
{if html_email}<a href="{unsubscribe_url}">{unsubscribe_url}</a>{/if}
{if plain_email}{unsubscribe_url}{/if}
```

Also on the mailing list screen, we can batch subscribe or unsubscribe people (for example, if you were transferring over a mailing list from another application).

Allow Members to Register for a Mailing List

To allow visitors to sign themselves up to the mailing list, we are going to add an option to our menu bar.

1. Edit the `toast/.menu` template.
2. Add the following code to the bottom of the template. Notice that in the `exp:mailinglist:form` tag, we have a parameter `list` that we use to determine which mailing list the member will be signed up for.

   ```
   <h4>New Products Mailing List</h4>
   <p>
   Enter your email address to be notified right away when new toast
                                      products are available:<br />
   {exp:mailinglist:form list="newproducts"}
   <input type="text" name="email" value="{email}" /><br /><br />
   <input type="submit" value="submit" />
   {/exp:mailinglist:form}
   </p>
   ```

3. Now visit any page with a menu to see and sign up for your mailing list.

Note that any new visitors who sign up will receive an email with a link they must click on before they are actually signed up. The mailing list is strictly an opt-in feature, with an opt-out option at the end of every email.

Members

Sending Emails

The **Communicate** tab in the ExpressionEngine control panel is where we go to send emails to our members. We can send emails to one or more mailing lists, or to specific member groups. We can send either plain text emails or HTML emails (with plain text).

ExpressionEngine has many tools to help prevent you sending unwanted bulk emails. Visitors must opt into mailing lists and can opt-out at any time. Members can also set their preferences to not receive emails from the site administrators. Although these options can be overridden, many countries have laws governing the sending of commercial emails that you must abide by.

Exercises

1. Logged in as Editor Phil, try editing an existing page of our conventional website (for example, to correct a spelling mistake or reword a paragraph).
2. Try creating a new member group that can only be used to modify templates. Members of this group should not be able to post or modify any weblog entries. Further, they should not be able to modify any templates in the `site` template group (which was part of the installation of ExpressionEngine).
3. Now we have a Promotions page that is essentially for members only; let's make the menu link to this page also visible to members only.
4. Add a menu item to our Stand-Alone Entry page, but this time make it only visible to members logged in as Super Admin or as an Editor. Then try publishing a new weblog entry using the Stand-Alone Entry page.
5. Set up a new mailing list that will allow visitors to sign up for a monthly newsletter.

Summary

In this chapter:

- We went through the process a new member would go through to register for our site.
- We looked through the out of the box functionality that is available to members using our site.
- We set up a new Editors member group and walked through the various ways we could either restrict or open up the permissions for that member group.
- We logged in to the control panel as a member of our Editors member group and were able to see how different it was to the control panel we have been used to.
- We walked through how to use conditional statements to create member-only areas of our site. We can create member-only pages or text on a page that only members of a certain member group can see, or we can make entire templates only accessible to certain member groups.

- We saw how to use Stand-Alone Entry Forms to replicate the functionality of the Publish page within our own site.
- We briefly overviewed the member communication options, including setting up and managing mailing lists that members can sign up for.

In our next chapter, we will look at creating a multi-purpose events calendar that would be an asset to any website.

7
Creating a Calendar

Many organizations have events, and a very visual way of keeping people up-to-date with events is to have an events calendar. Having a calendar not only lets people easily find out what they need to know about a certain event, but can often give visitors information they didn't know they needed to know (such as another event they would enjoy).

In this chapter:

- We are going to use the native functionality of ExpressionEngine to build a simple events calendar that anyone can use.
- We will post new events to our calendar using the Publish page of ExpressionEngine.
- We are going to display an overview of upcoming events underneath the calendar.
- We will allow events to be clickable so that interested visitors can get more information than will fit in a calendar cell.

Our toast calendar will provide information on upcoming community events that our Toast for Sale! staff is participating in.

Create an Events Calendar Weblog

As with every other task we undertake in ExpressionEngine, our first step is to create a new weblog. We will create the weblog, define custom fields, and then post some entries to the weblog.

Creating a Calendar

Create the Weblog

By now, we are fairly familiar with the process of creating a weblog.

1. Log into the control panel at `http://localhost/admin.php` or `http://www.example.com/admin.php`. Select **Admin | Weblog Administration | Weblog Management**.

2. Select **Create a New Weblog**. Call the new weblog **Toast Calendar** with a **Short Name** of **toastcalendar**. Select **Yes** to **Edit Group Preferences**.

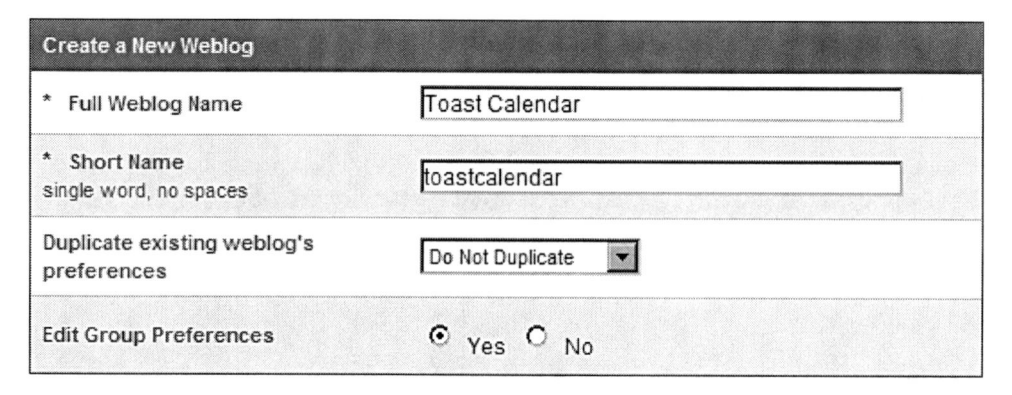

3. Select the **Default Category Group**, the **Default Status Group**, and the **Default Field Group** (we will return here once we have defined a custom field group, but it is a good habit to assign these when creating a weblog in case you forget later).

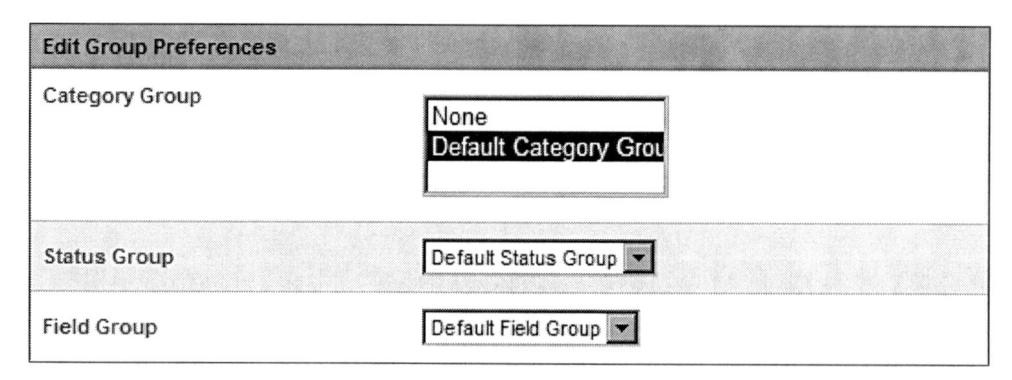

[204]

4. Finally, select **No** to **Create New Templates For this Weblog** and then click **Submit**.

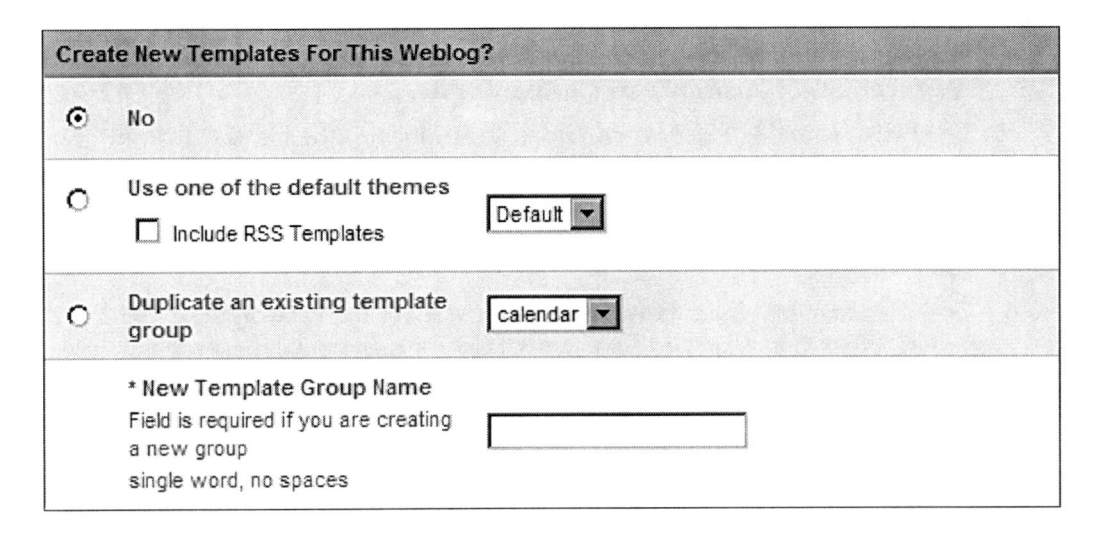

Create Custom Fields for Our Calendar

Now that our weblog is created, let us create the custom fields.

1. Select **Admin | Weblog Administration | Custom Weblog Fields**.
2. Select **Create a New Weblog Field Group** and call the field group **toastcalendar**. Click **Submit**.

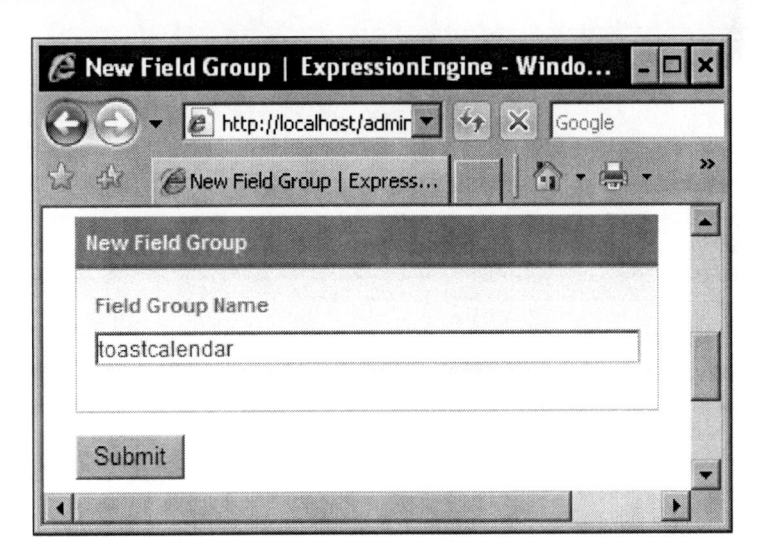

Creating a Calendar

3. Now select to **Add/Edit Custom Fields** for the **toastcalendar** field group.
4. As always with ExpressionEngine, we can choose custom fields that match our application. Our toastcalendar needs to be flexible, so we are going to keep our custom fields generic. Our first field is going to be for the location of the event. Select **Create a New Custom Field**.
5. The **Field Name** will be **toastcalendar_location**, and the **Field Label** will be **Location**. We will use a **Field Type** of **Text Input** (with a **Maxlength** of **128**) and we will also **Hide Formatting Menu** and choose a **Default Text Formatting** of **None**. The field will not be required but will be searchable. Click **Submit**.
6. Continue to create the following custom fields for the **toastcalendar** field group. We will have a field for a description of the event, a field for the time of the event, and a field for the URL if applicable. For the URL field, set the **Maxlength** to **999** so that we do not later find that we cannot fit what we need to in this field.

Field Name	Field Label	Field Type	Text Formatting	Formatting Menu
toastcalendar_time	Time	Text Input	None	Hide
toastcalendar_description	Description	Textarea	Auto 	Display
toastcalendar_URL	URL	Text Input	None	Hide

Field Group: toastcalendar

Field Label	Field Name	Field Type	
20 Location	toastcalendar_location	Text Input	Delete
21 Time	toastcalendar_time	Text Input	Delete
22 Description	toastcalendar_description	Textarea	Delete
23 URL	toastcalendar_URL	Text Input	Delete

By now we should have four custom fields in our toastcalendar field group. For the date of the calendar events, we haven't defined a custom field. This is because we will use the date of the entry to determine on what day to display the event.

Associate the Custom Field Group with the Calendar

Next, we are going to associate the field group with the toastcalendar weblog.

1. Select **Admin | Weblog Administration | Weblog Management**. Now select **Edit Groups** for the **Toast Calendar** weblog.
2. Change the **Field Group** to toastcalendar. Click **Update**.

Our weblog is now set up and is ready for us to use.

Post Example Events to Our Calendar

Our final step in creating the weblog is to post some example events so that as we create the calendar on our website, we have events to look at. Our first event is going to mark Thanksgiving Day on our calendar.

1. Select **Publish**, and select the **Toast Calendar** weblog.
2. Type in a **Title**, such as **Thanksgiving Day**. As this is a holiday rather than an actual event, we are going to leave all the other fields blank. However, before hitting Submit, select the **Date** tab at the top of the screen.

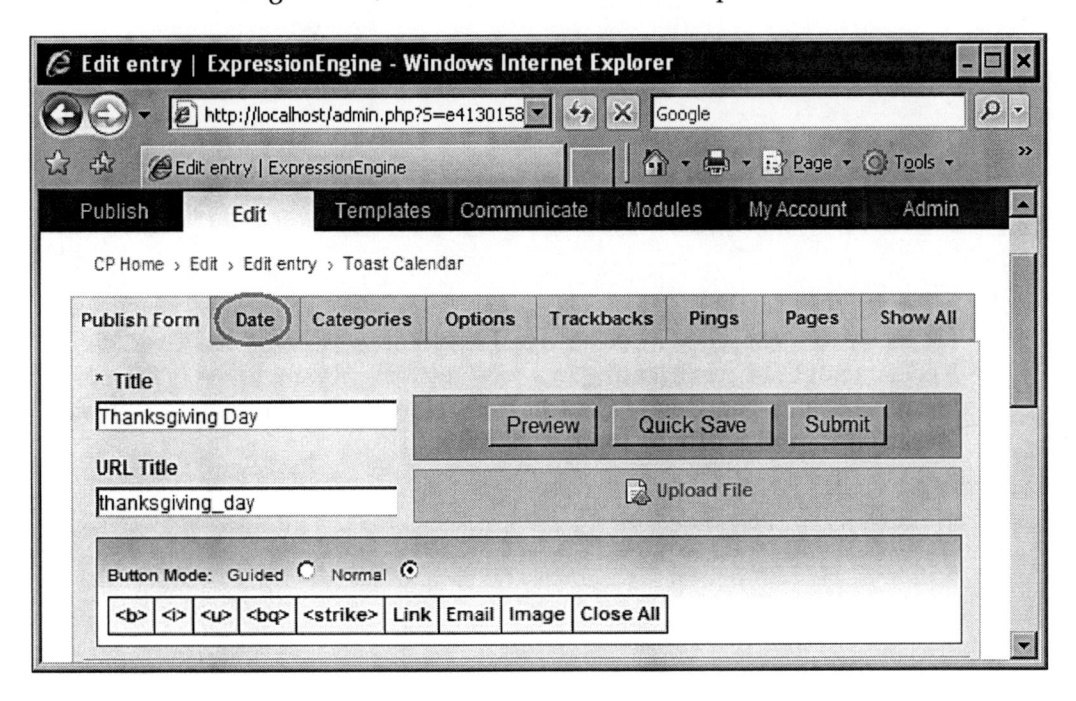

Creating a Calendar

3. We can see three calendars. The left-hand calendar controls which date our entry will appear on. Select the day of Thanksgiving on the calendar (the last Thursday in November in the United States, the second Monday in October in Canada).

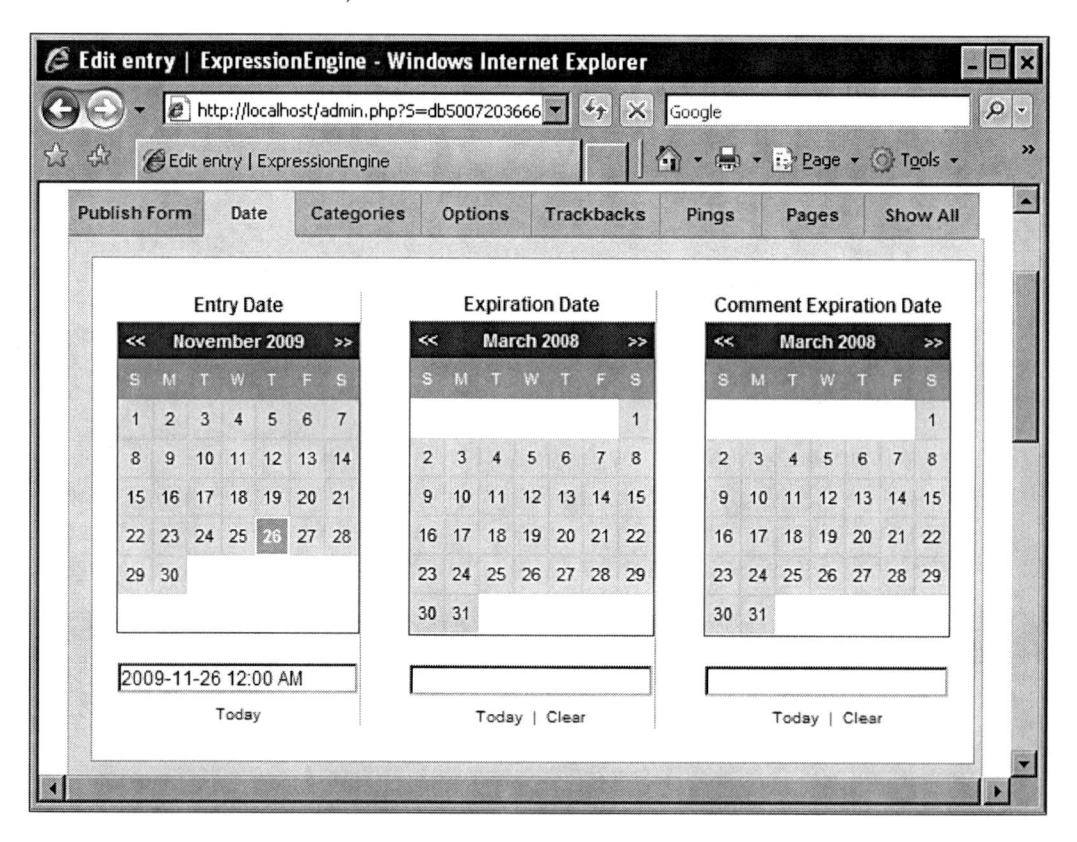

4. Click **Submit**.
5. Let us create a couple of more entries. For our second event, the Toast for Sale! site might be participating in a food festival, so we will use a **Title** of **Food Festival**, a **Location** of **Central Park, New York City**, a **Time**, a short **Description**, and a **URL** to another website.

[208]

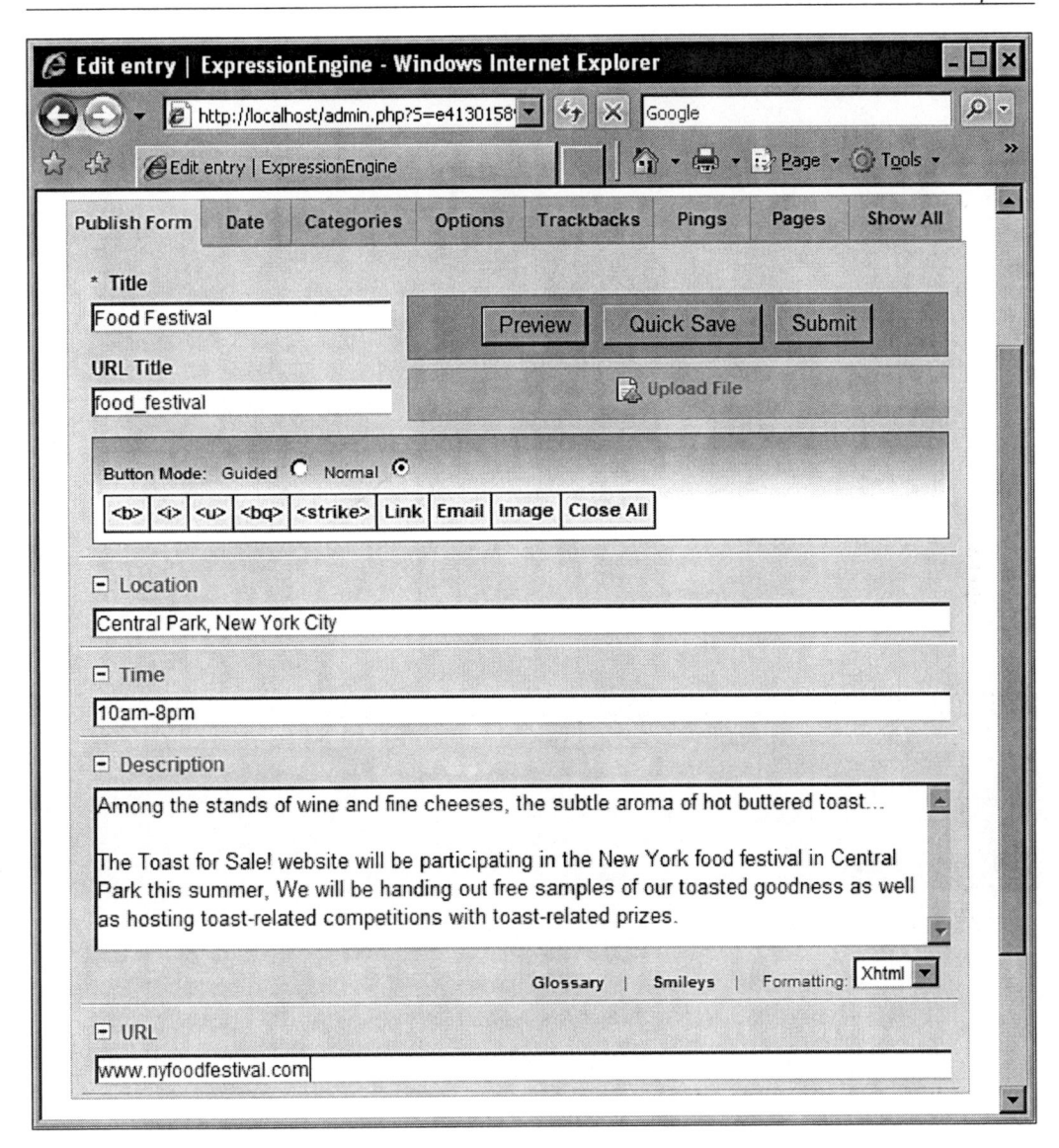

Chapter 7

| Publish Form | Date | Categories | Options | Trackbacks | Pings | Pages | Show All |

* Title

Food Festival

URL Title

food_festival

[Preview] [Quick Save] [Submit]

[Upload File]

Button Mode: Guided ○ Normal ⊙

| <b> | <i> | <u> | <bq> | <strike> | Link | Email | Image | Close All |

☐ Location

Central Park, New York City

☐ Time

10am-8pm

☐ Description

Among the stands of wine and fine cheeses, the subtle aroma of hot buttered toast...

The Toast for Sale! website will be participating in the New York food festival in Central Park this summer, We will be handing out free samples of our toasted goodness as well as hosting toast-related competitions with toast-related prizes.

Glossary | Smileys | Formatting: Xhtml

☐ URL

www.nyfoodfestival.com

Creating a Calendar

6. Click the **Date** tab and select a date. For simplicity, we are going to choose a date in the same month as our Thanksgiving Day entry.

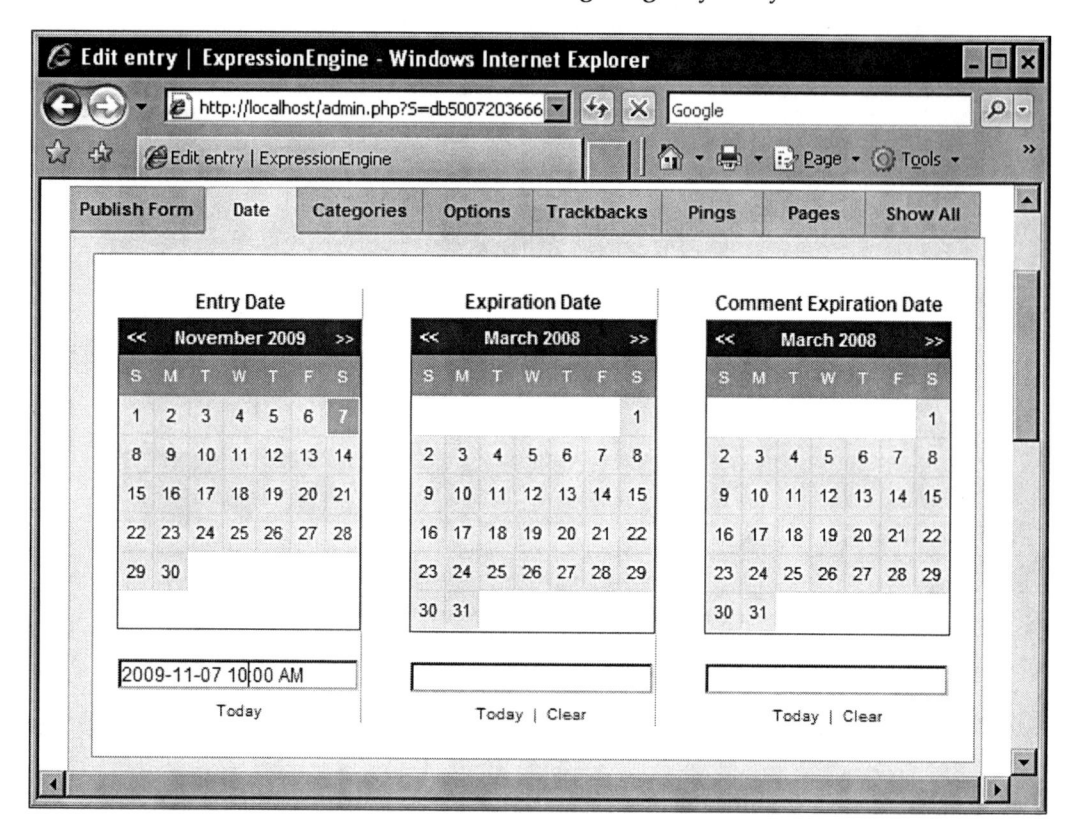

7. Our final event will be to mark the start of our online toast holiday sale. To demonstrate multiple events on the same day, this will also be scheduled on Thanksgiving Day. Write the entry, schedule the event for Thanksgiving (the last Thursday in November or second Monday in October), and then click **Submit**.

[210]

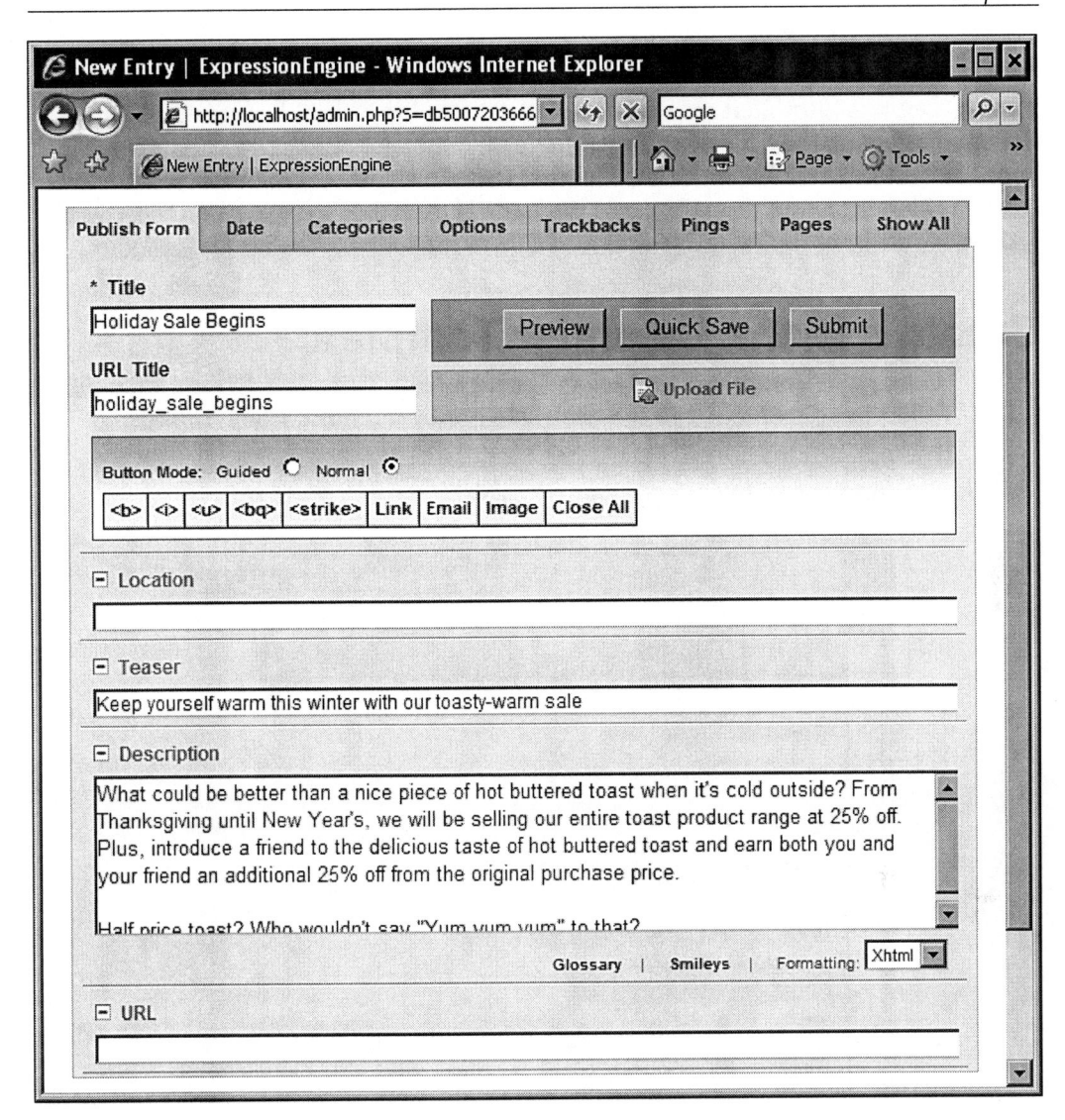

Now we have the weblog with example entries; let us create the calendar template.

Create the Calendar Template

Throughout this tutorial, it may be useful to refer to the official ExpressionEngine documentation on the **Calendar Tag** at `http://expressionengine.com/docs/modules/weblog/calendar.html`. The first steps in creating a calendar will be to create a calendar template group, add the basic HTML that we use on all our pages, build the outline of the calendar, and add CSS to make the calendar look good.

Create a Blank Calendar Template

1. First, go to **Templates** and select **Create a New Template Group**. We will, rather imaginatively, call this template group **calendar**. Click **Submit**.

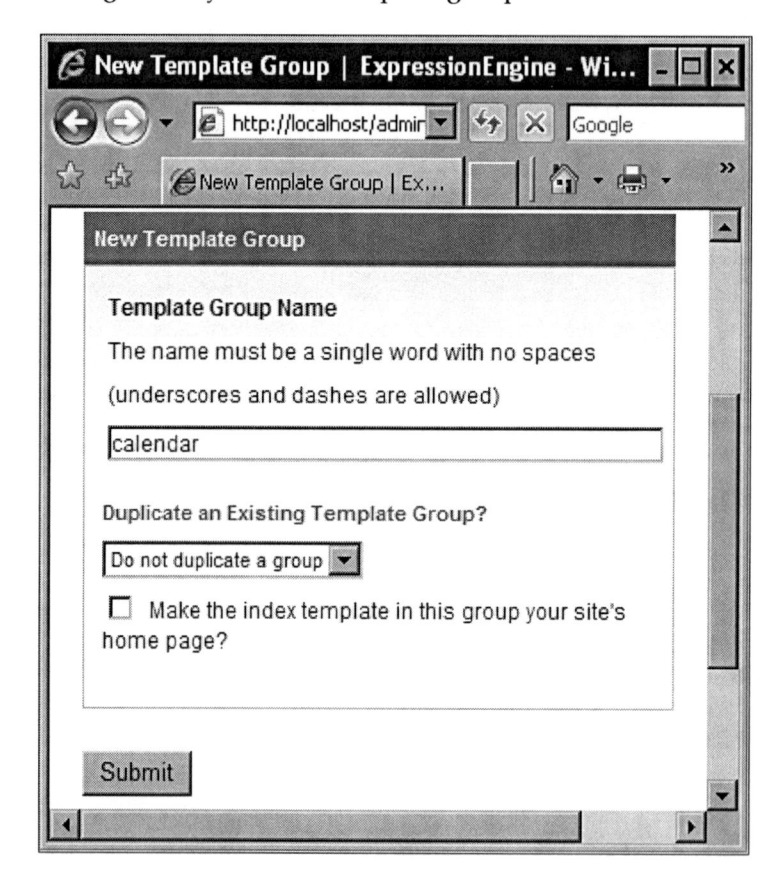

2. Edit the `calendar/index` template and add the following code, which is an outline of the HTML on all our pages except with no content. Note also that the variables at the top have been changed to reflect the `toastcalendar` weblog and the `calendar` template group.

```
{assign_variable:my_weblog="toastcalendar"}
{assign_variable:my_template_group="calendar"}
{assign_variable:my_site_wide_templates="toast"}
<!DOCTYPE html PUBLIC "-//W3C//DTD XHTML 1.0 Strict//EN"
"http://www.w3.org/TR/xhtml1/DTD/xhtml1-strict.dtd">
<html xmlns="http://www.w3.org/1999/xhtml">
  <head>
    <title>Toast for Sale: Calendar of Toast</title>
    <link rel='stylesheet' type='text/css' media='all'
    href='{path={my_site_wide_templates}/toast_css}' />
    <style type='text/css' media='screen'>@import "{path=
        {my_site_wide_templates}/toast_css}";</style>
    <meta http-equiv="content-type" content="text/html;
                                    charset=UTF-8" />
  </head>
  <body>
    <div id="header">
      <h1>Toast for Sale!</h1>
      <h2>Calendar of Toast</h2>
    </div>
    <div id="content">
    </div>
    <div id="menu">
      {embed={my_site_wide_templates}/.menu}
    </div>
  </body>
</html>
```

We now have a blank template (viewable at `http://localhost/calendar` or `http://www.example.com/calendar`) that we can use for our calendar.

Create a Blank Calendar

The next step is to create a blank calendar—it will not display our events just yet. This code is adapted from the ExpressionEngine documentation.

1. The first piece of code is the `exp:weblog:calendar` tag. This is a pair of tags with a number of parameters.

    ```
    <div id="content">
    ```

Creating a Calendar

```
{exp:weblog:calendar switch="calendarToday|calendarCell"
        weblog="{my_weblog}" show_future_entries="yes"}
{/exp:weblog:calendar}
</div>
```

> The `weblog` parameter specifies that we are using `{my_weblog}` for entries on this calendar (where `{my_weblog}` is a variable corresponding to `toastcalendar`).
>
> The `show_future_entries="yes"` means that we want to show future entries on our calendar. In most weblog applications (such as our Toast News weblog), if we set an entry date in the future, ExpressionEngine does not make that entry visible until that date. This makes sense for most weblog applications, but if a calendar only showed entries that have already happened, it would not be a very useful calendar.
>
> The `switch` parameter is used to switch between two different stylesheet styles (that we have not yet defined). If the day being displayed is not today, then the stylesheet style will be `calendarCell`. If the day being displayed is today, then the stylesheet style will be `calendarToday`. This allows us to shade today's date differently.

2. Next, we are going to display the calendar itself. A calendar is essentially a table and we will use the HTML `table` tag to display it. In the following code, we are defining the table properties—the width means that the calendar is as wide as the section it is in (in this case `#content`). We also name a style of `calendarBG` that we have not yet defined.

   ```
   {exp:weblog:calendar switch="calendarToday|calendarCell"
           weblog="{my_weblog}" show_future_entries="yes"}
     <table class="calendarBG" border="0" cellpadding="6"
       cellspacing="1" summary="My Calendar" width="100%">
     </table>
   {/exp:weblog:calendar}
   ```

3. Let us define our first row. A calendar has seven columns, one for each day of the week. In our header, we will use the far-left cell for a link to the previous month and the far-right cell for a link to the next month. The middle five cells will display the name of the current month being displayed.

   ```
   <table class="calendarBG" border="0" cellpadding="6"
     cellspacing="1" summary="My Calendar" width="100%">
   ```

```
    <tr class="calendarHeader">
      <th><a href="{previous_path={my_template_group}/index}">&lt;
                                                 &lt;</a></th>
      <th colspan="5">{date format="%F %Y"}</th>
      <th><a href="{next_path={my_template_group}/index}">
                                                 &gt;&gt;</a></th>
    </tr>
  </table>
```

> The previous and next path links both point to the current template (`calendar/index`), where {my_template_group} is a variable for calendar, < is HTML for the < symbol, and > is HTML for the > symbol.
>
> The format code to display the current month—%F %Y—is taken from ExpressionEngine's date formatting codes available at http://expressionengine.com/docs/templates/date_variable_formatting.html.

4. Go to `http://localhost/calendar` or `http://www.example.com/calendar` and we can see our calendar beginning to take shape. Click on the yellow arrows and we can see that the name of the month changes, as does the URL of the page.

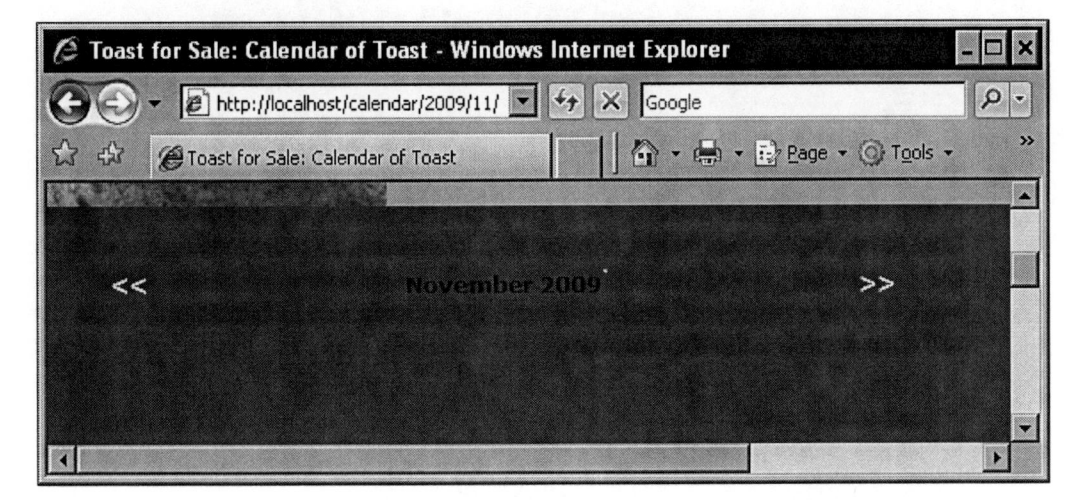

Creating a Calendar

5. The next row will display the weekdays. The code `{lang:weekday_abrev}` refers to the one letter weekdays. We could also use `_long` or `_short` instead of `_abrev` to either spell out the entire weekday or the first few letters of the weekday. This must be wrapped in a `{calendar_heading}` variable pair.

   ```
       </tr>
       <tr>
         {calendar_heading}
           <td class="calendarDayHeading">{lang:weekday_abrev}</td>
         {/calendar_heading}
       </tr>
   </table>
   ```

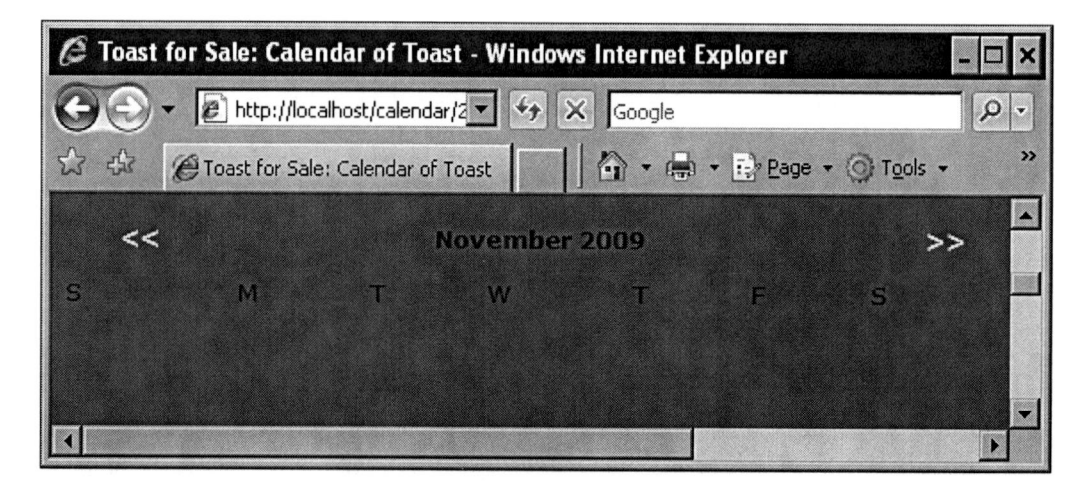

   ![Toast for Sale: Calendar of Toast - Windows Internet Explorer showing November 2009 calendar header with weekday abbreviations S M T W T F S]

6. The next row will display the actual dates. There is no way to know how many rows might be needed for a given month (February might only require four rows; September might require six). Therefore, ExpressionEngine uses the `{calendar_rows}` variable pair to apply to each row. Each row starts with the `<tr>` command and ends with the closing `</tr>` command. Each cell then contains the day number.

   ```
       </tr>
       {calendar_rows}
         {row_start}<tr>{/row_start}
   ```

[216]

```
      <td class='{switch}'>{day_number}</td>
    {row_end}</tr>{/row_end}
  {/calendar_rows}
</table>
```

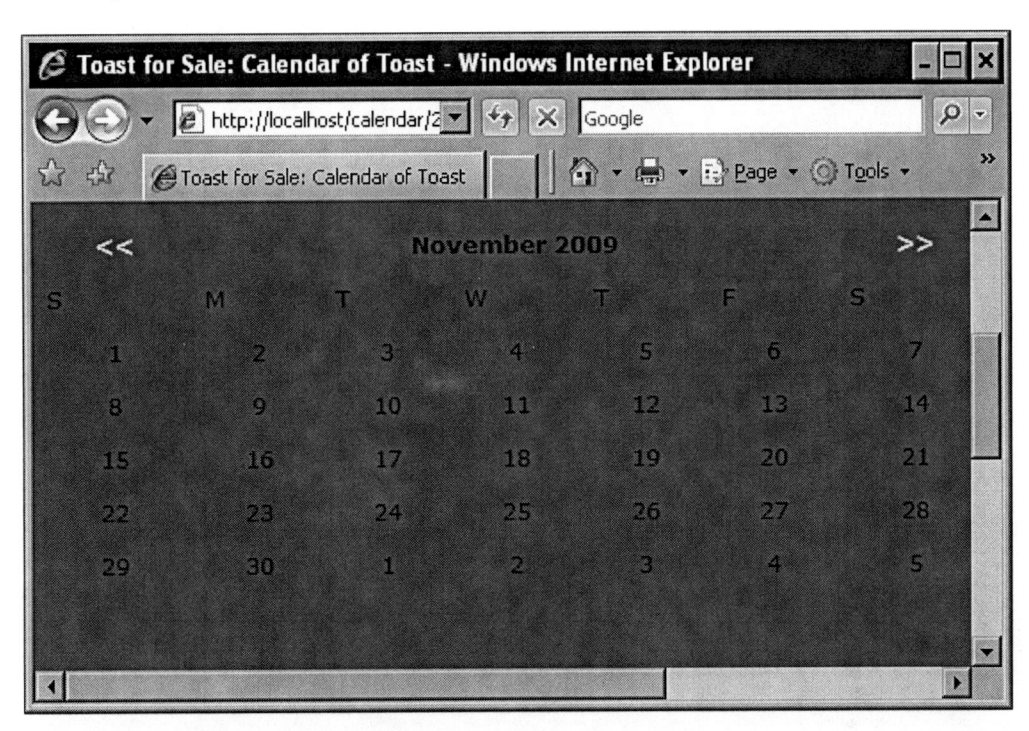

[Screenshot: Toast for Sale: Calendar of Toast - Windows Internet Explorer, showing November 2009 calendar]

7. For each calendar date there are three possibilities: there may be events for that date; there may not be events for that date; or the date may be for a prior or following month (that is, a blank date). We will want to handle each of these situations differently, although right now we will simply display the date for each. Adding the following conditional statements to our code will set us up to be able to distinguish between the three possibilities. Notice that for our blank date, we use a different class that will allow us to style it differently in our stylesheet. For simplicity, I have reproduced the entire calendar code so far:

```
<div id="content">
  {exp:weblog:calendar switch="calendarToday|calendarCell"
          weblog="{my_weblog}" show_future_entries="yes"}
    <table class="calendarBG" border="0" cellpadding="6"
      cellspacing="1" summary="My Calendar" width="100%">
      <tr class="calendarHeader">
        <th><a href="{previous_path={my_template_group}/index}">
```

```
                            &lt;&lt;</a></th>
            <th colspan="5">{date format="%F %Y"}</th>
            <th><a href="{next_path={my_template_group}/index}">
                                    &gt;&gt;</a></th>
         </tr>
         <tr>
           {calendar_heading}
              <td class="calendarDayHeading">{lang:weekday_abrev}</td>
           {/calendar_heading}
         </tr>
         {calendar_rows }
            {row_start}<tr>{/row_start}
            {if entries}
               <td class='{switch}'>{day_number}</td>
            {/if}
            {if not_entries}
               <td class='{switch}'>{day_number}</td>
            {/if}
            {if blank}
               <td class='calendarBlank'>{day_number}</td>
            {/if}
            {row_end}</tr>{/row_end}
         {/calendar_rows}
      </table>
   {/exp:weblog:calendar}
</div>
```

We now have the beginnings of a calendar, but it is looking a little basic. Before we start displaying our events on this calendar, we will use CSS to make the calendar look a little more calendar-like.

Formatting the Calendar with CSS

Rather than adding our calendar styles to our main `toast/toast_css` stylesheet, we are going to create a separate stylesheet that will contain just our calendar styles. We do this because the calendar styles are only needed on our calendar page. Much of this code is adapted from the suggested stylesheet in the ExpressionEngine documentation (http://expressionengine.com/docs/modules/weblog/calendar_css.txt), but has been formatted to better suit our toast website.

Create the Calendar CSS Template

First, we will create the template for our calendar CSS, and then we will point the `calendar/index` template to this new template.

1. Still in the calendar template group, select **New Template**. Call the new template `calendar_css`, and choose a **Template Type** of **CSS Stylesheet**. Click **Submit**.

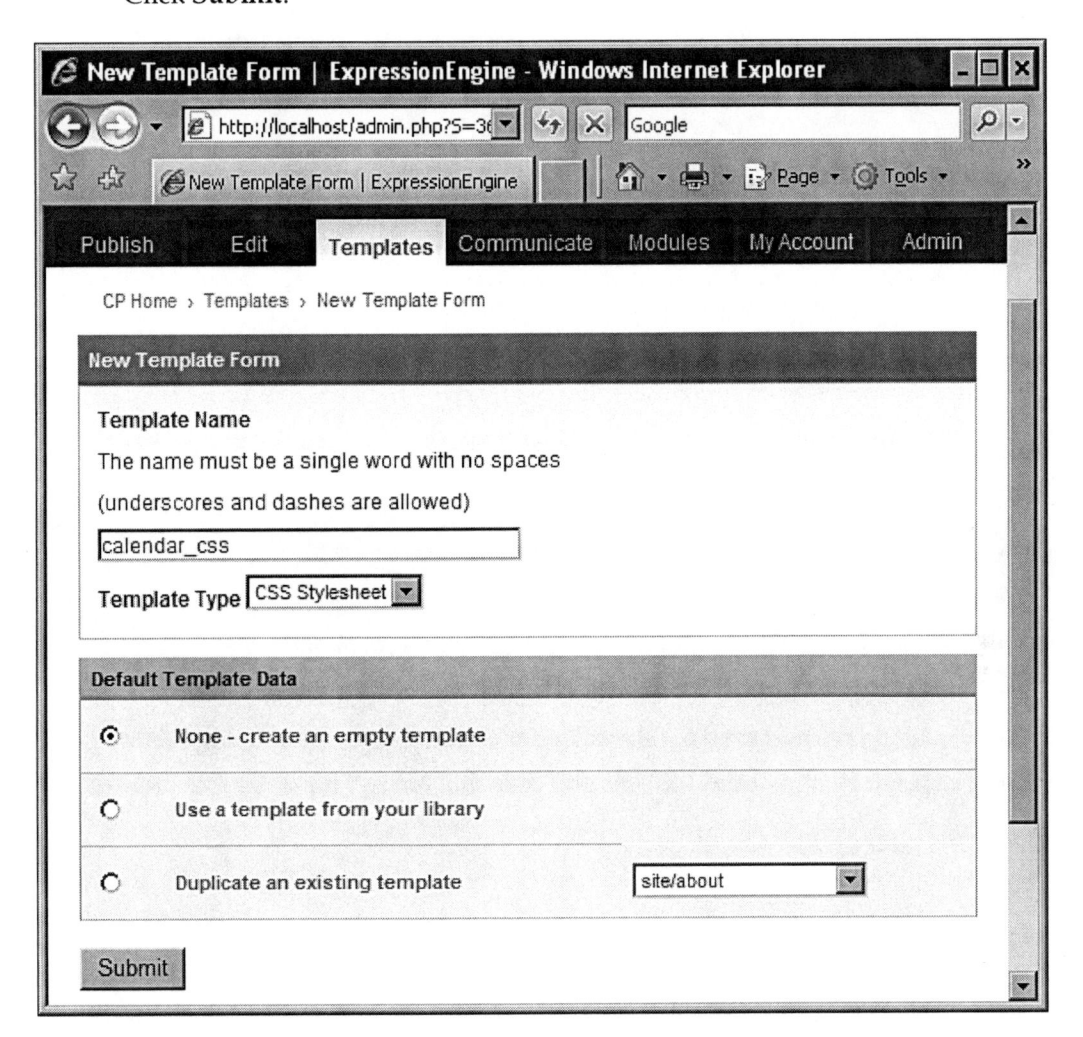

Creating a Calendar

2. The first line in our new template will be to import the main `toast/toast_css` template (otherwise all our formatting so far will be lost).

   ```
   @import url({site_url}toast/toast_css);
   ```

3. The next step is to point our existing `calendar/index` template to use this new template instead of our `toast/toast_css` template. To do this, edit the following lines:

   ```
   <link rel='stylesheet' type='text/css' media='all' href=
           '{path={my_site_wide_templates}/toast_css}' />
   <style type='text/css' media='screen'>@import "{path=
           {my_site_wide_templates}/toast_css}";</style>
   ```

   ...to read like the following:

   ```
   <link rel='stylesheet' type='text/css' media='all' href=
           '{path={my_template_group}/calendar_css}' />
   <style type='text/css' media='screen'>@import "{path=
           {my_template_group}/calendar_css}";</style>
   ```

Now let us add some styles to our CSS.

Add Styles to Our Calendar CSS

In our calendar code so far, we defined several styles:

- `calendarBG`, used to format the overall table
- `calendarHeader`, used to format the month heading
- `calendarDayHeading`, used to format the weekday headings
- `calendarCell`, used for the calendar cells except for today's date
- `calendarToday`, used for the calendar cell that represents today's date
- `calendarBlank`, used for calendar cells that are not for dates this month

Let us start styling these styles:

1. Open the template `calendar/calendar_css` for editing.
2. Add the following code to the template. We are starting with the `calendarBG` format, which applies to our entire calendar table. We are going to use this style to set the background color of the calendar to be black—onto which we will build light-colored cells.

   ```
   @import url({site_url}toast/toast_css);
   
   .calendarBG{
     background-color: #000;
   }
   ```

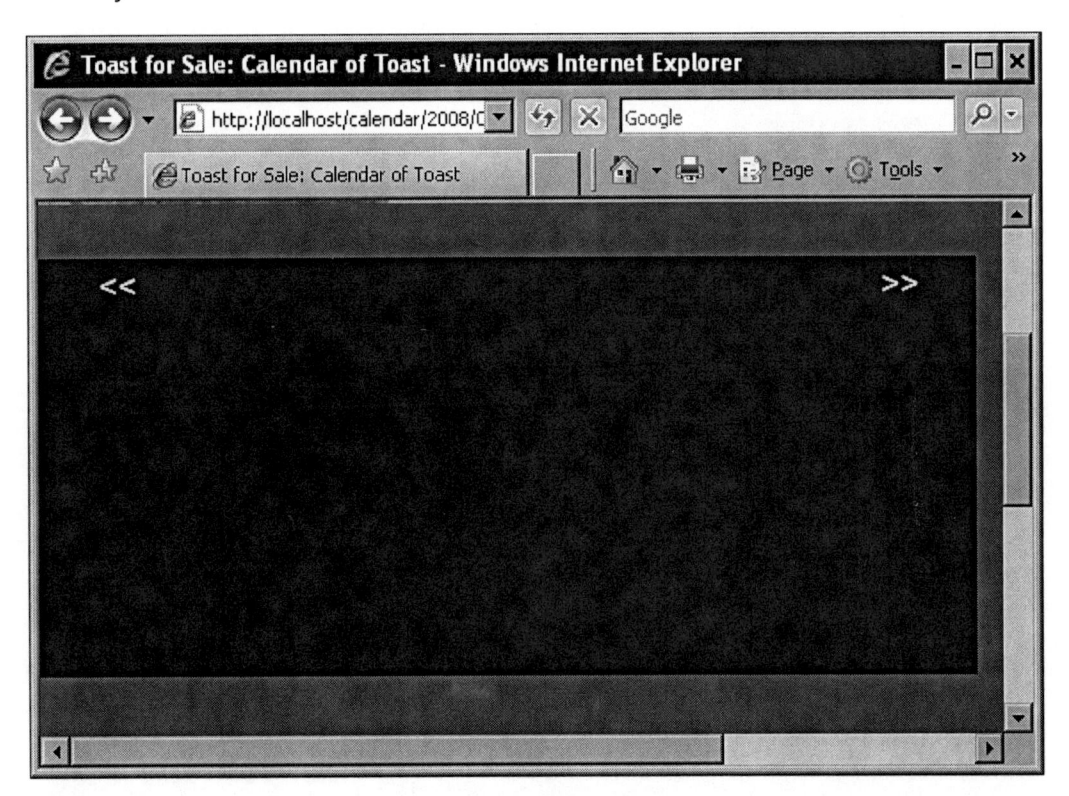

Creating a Calendar

3. Next up is the `calendarHeader`, which applies to the entire first row of the calendar. We are going to make the text white, bold, and centered, and we are going to color the links yellow. Add the following to the bottom of our stylesheet:

```
.calendarHeader{
  font-weight: bold;
  color: #fff;
  text-align: center;
  background-color: #000;
}
.calendarHeader a{
  color: #F0E68C;
}
.calendarHeader a:visited{
  color: #F0E68C;
}
```

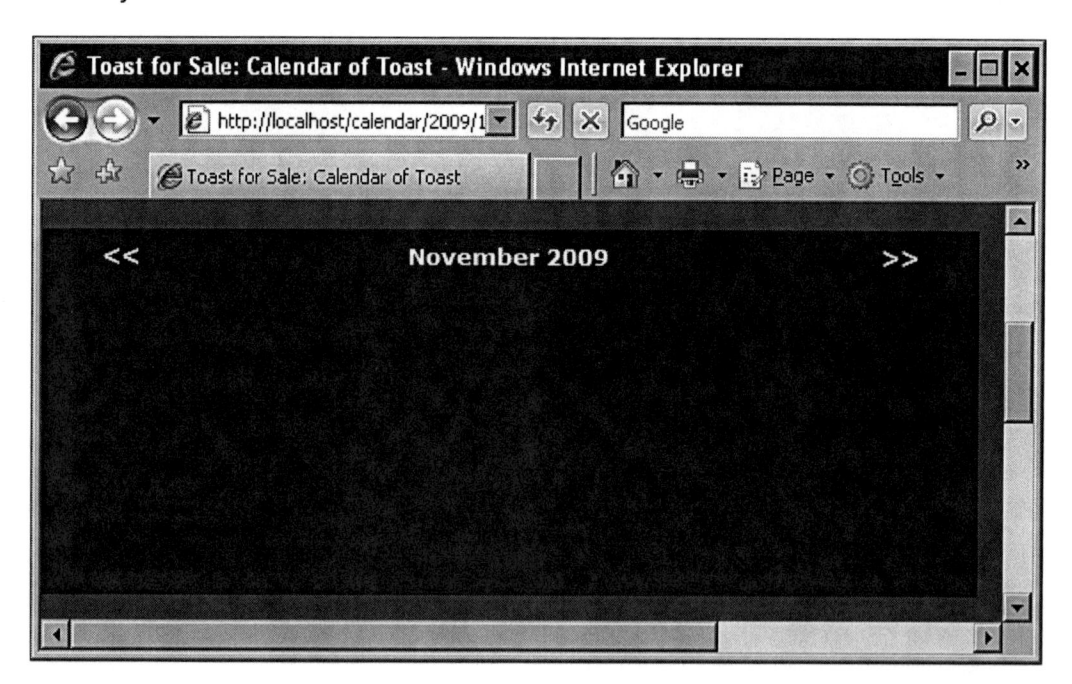

4. Next, we will format the weekday headings. In this case, we are going to make them bold and white. We will position them in the center of their cell, and we will make the background color of the cells a dark brown color. Add the following code to the bottom of our stylesheet:

```
.calendarDayHeading{
  font-weight: bold;
  font-size: 11px;
  color: #fff;
  background-color: #663300;
  text-align: center;
  vertical-align: middle;
}
```

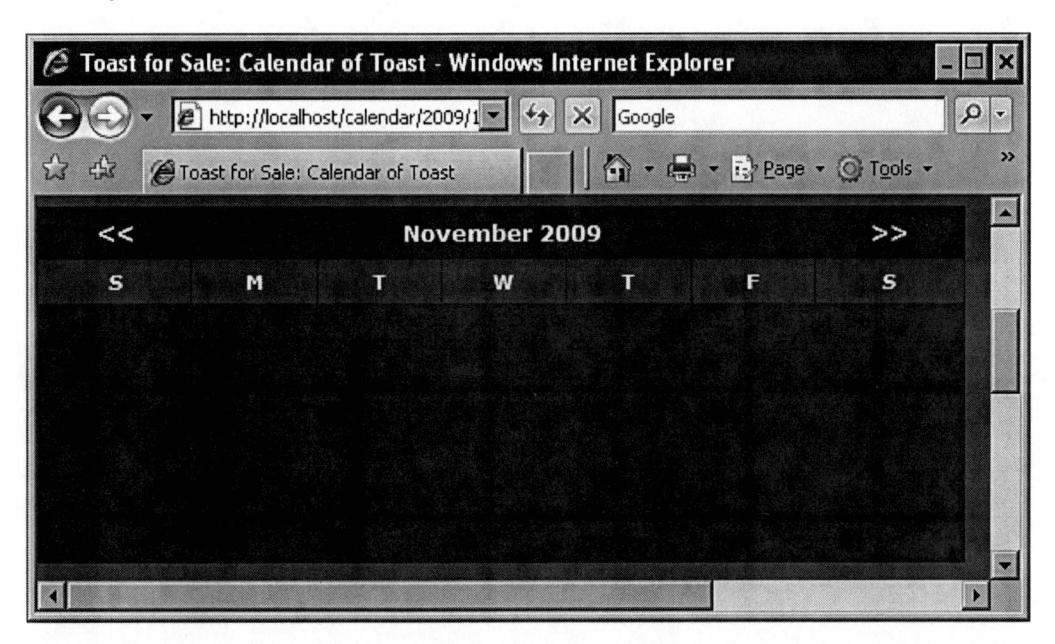

5. Next, we are going to format the cells of the month (`calendarCell`). This style will only apply to the dates that are in this month and that are not today. We will position the date in the top-left of the cell. The cells will have a white background and a grey (#666) font color. We will also set a fixed width for our cells—otherwise as events are added to our calendar, some columns will expand and other columns will shrink. Add the following code to the stylesheet:

Creating a Calendar

```
.calendarCell{
  font-weight: bold;
  font-size: 11px;
  text-decoration: none;
  text-align: left;
  vertical-align: top;
  color: #666;
  background-color: #fff;
  width: 60px;
  height: 60px;
}
```

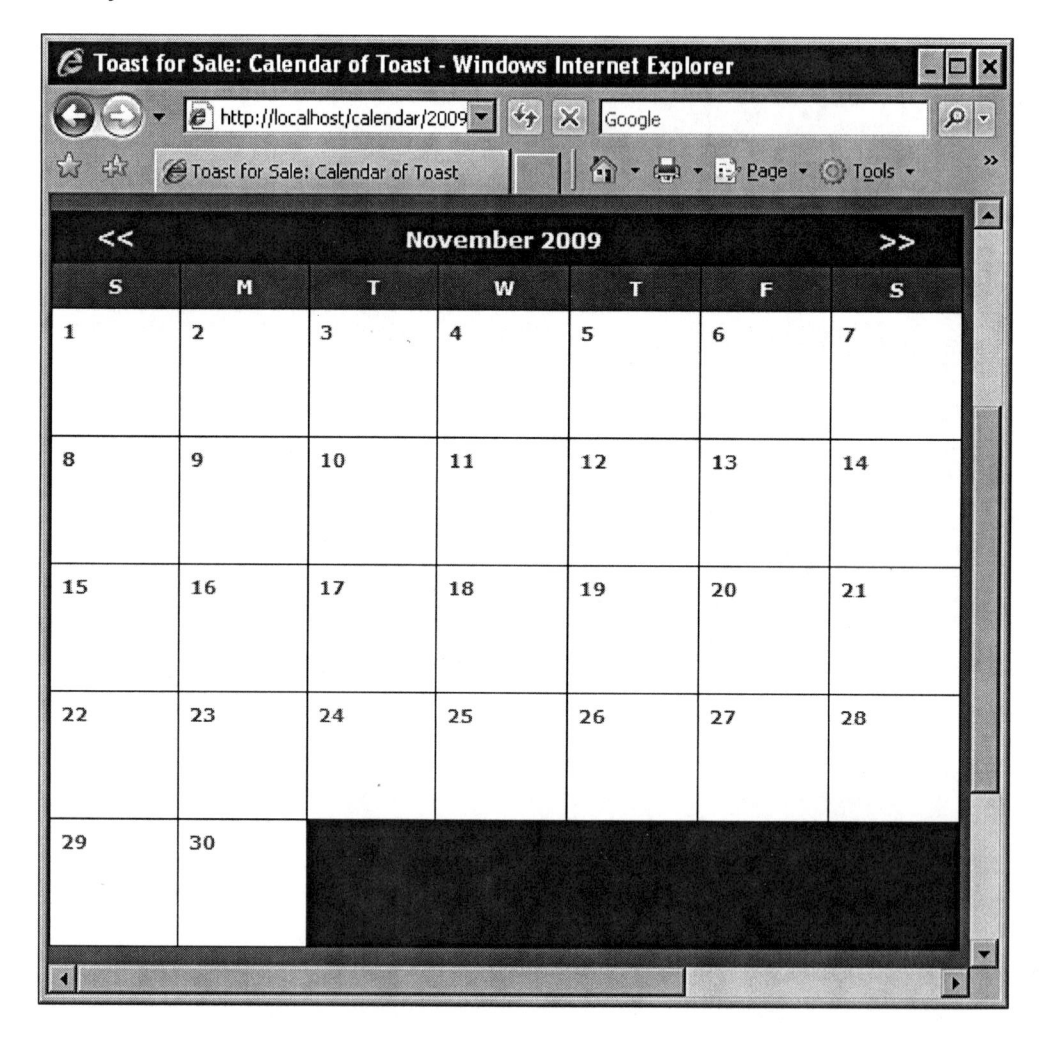

6. Although our calendar is looking much more complete, there are still two cell types that are blacked out—today's date, and the dates that are not in the current month. For today's date, we are going to use exactly the same style as any other date, but we will change the background color to be light grey instead of white and the font color to be black instead of dark grey. Add the following code to accomplish this:

```css
.calendarToday{
   font-weight: bold;
   font-size: 11px;
   text-decoration: none;
   text-align: left;
   vertical-align: top;
   color: #000;
   background-color: #ccc;
   width: 60px;
   height: 60px;
}
```

7. The final piece of code is to style the dates that are not in the current month. Right now, these cells are blacked out, and naturally, we could leave these cells like that. However, we are going to color them as a light shade of green and make the dates visible.

```css
.calendarBlank{
   font-weight: bold;
   font-size: 11px;
   text-decoration: none;
   text-align: left;
   vertical-align: top;
   color: #666;
   background-color: #9db7a7;
   width: 60px;
   height: 60px;
}
```

Creating a Calendar

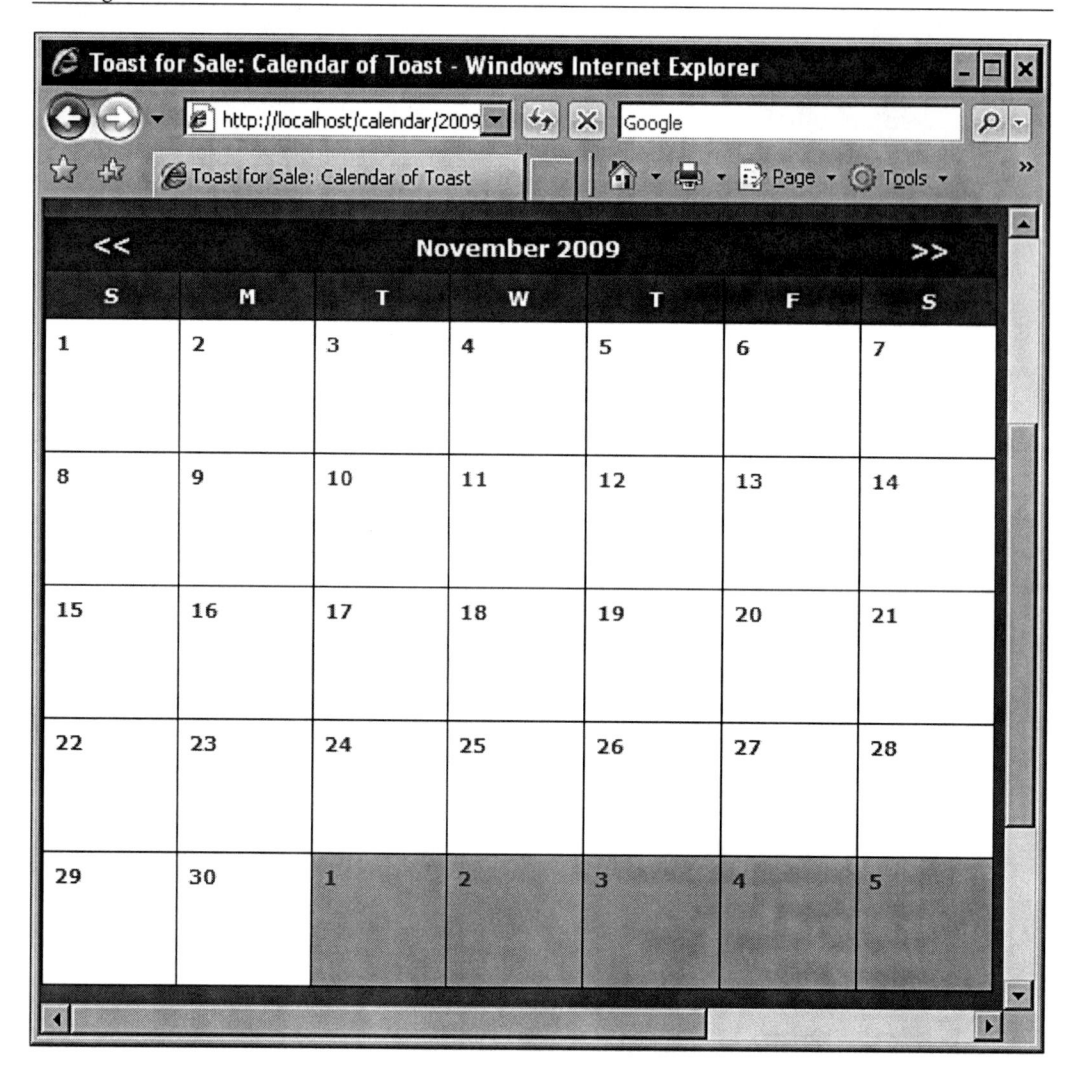

We now have a pretty but blank calendar. It is, of course, encouraged to change the styles as it suits your site—fonts, colors, and the side of the box where the dates appear, are all easily configurable within the CSS.

Next, we will want to start displaying events on our calendar. However, before we do that, we are going to add a separate weblog tag underneath the calendar to display the detail of our calendar events.

Create a Separate Template for Our Calendar Events

The calendar is a very nice visual tool, but each cell is only large enough to display a few words describing each event. Typically with an event calendar, these words would then be linked so when you click on them, more detail on the specific event (the description) appears. Many calendars will use JavaScript or pop-up windows to display the detail of an event, and while we could do that here, we are going to keep it simple and create an entirely separate template. This template will be much more like the weblogs we set up in the previous chapters, so we will not spend too much time on this.

1. Create a new template in the calendar template group called **event**. The **Template Type** will be **webpage**. Create an empty template. This template will be visible at http://localhost/calendar/event or http://www.example.com/calendar/event.

2. First, let us type in or copy the basic page structure that we have been using for all of our pages. Notice that we have changed the `<title>` of the page, as well as the `<h2>` heading. If we copy this basic structure from our calendar/index template, we would also want to point our CSS file back to the toast_css template as we are not displaying the calendar on this page. Finally, make sure the variables at the top are correct.

```
{assign_variable:my_weblog="toastcalendar"}
{assign_variable:my_template_group="calendar"}
{assign_variable:my_site_wide_templates="toast"}
<!DOCTYPE html PUBLIC "-//W3C//DTD XHTML 1.0 Strict//EN"
"http://www.w3.org/TR/xhtml1/DTD/xhtml1-strict.dtd">
<html xmlns="http://www.w3.org/1999/xhtml">
  <head>
    <title>Toast for Sale: Calendar Event</title>
    <link rel='stylesheet' type='text/css' media='all' href='
          {path={my_site_wide_templates}/toast_css}' />
    <style type='text/css' media='screen'>@import "{path={my_
          site_wide_templates}/toast_css}";</style>
    <meta http-equiv="content-type" content="text/html;
                                    charset=UTF-8" />
  </head>
```

Creating a Calendar

```
<body>
  <div id="header">
    <h1>Toast for Sale!</h1>
    <h2>Toasty Event</h2>
  </div>
  <div id="content">
  </div>
  <div id="menu">
    {embed={my_site_wide_templates}/.menu}
  </div>
</body>
</html>
```

3. Now we are going to add the `{exp:weblog:entries}` tag that will display our entry. Notice that we have to have `show_future_entries="yes"` in the same way as our calendar, otherwise entries after today's date will not display and all that visitors will see is a blank page. We have the `title` of the entry with the `date` of the entry underneath it, then a `contentinner` box with the `location`, `description`, and `URL`.

```
<div id="content">
  {exp:weblog:entries weblog="{my_weblog}"
              show_future_entries="yes"}
    <h3>{title}<br /><i>{if toastcalendar_time}
    {toastcalendar_time} on {/if}{entry_date
              format="%F %j%S %Y"}</i></h3>
    <div class="contentinner">
      {if toastcalendar_location}
        <b>{toastcalendar_location}</b><br />
      {/if}
      {if toastcalendar_description}
        {toastcalendar_description}<br /><br />
      {/if}
      {if toastcalendar_URL}
        {toastcalendar_URL}<br />
      {/if}
    </div>
  {/exp:weblog:entries}
</div>
```

4. To see what this looks like so far, we can go to the URL of a specific entry (for example, `http://localhost/calendar/event/food_festival` or `http://www.example.com/calendar/event/food_festival`).

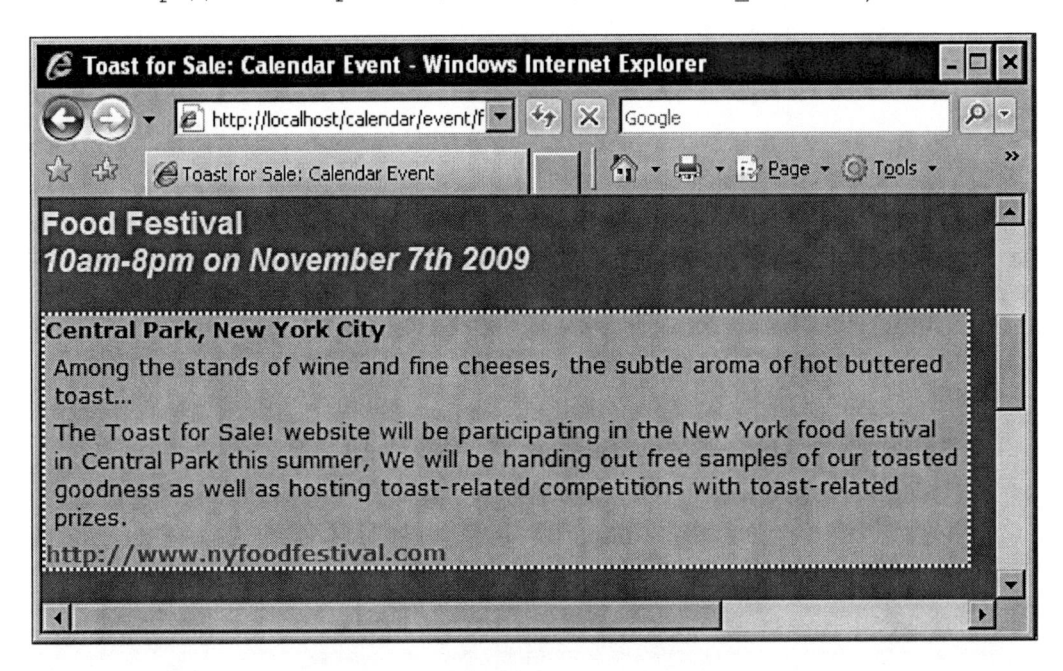

![Screenshot of browser showing Food Festival event page with details: 10am-8pm on November 7th 2009, Central Park, New York City, describing the Toast for Sale! website's participation in the New York food festival.]

5. If we do go to `http://localhost/calendar/event` or `http://www.example.com/calendar/event`, all our events are rendered. With only three entries this is not so bad. This would not work as well if our calendar starts to have lot more entries, it would turn into a gigantic page starting with events far off into the future and ending with events from a long time ago. We could make an effort to make this page more user-friendly, but rather than doing that, we will use the same code we used in other weblogs to redirect to our calendar page. Add the highlighted code:

```
<div id="content">
  {exp:weblog:entries weblog="{my_weblog}" show_future_entries=
                      "yes" require_entry="yes" limit="1"}
    {if no_results}
      {redirect="{my_template_group}/index"}
    {/if}
    <h3>{title}<br /><i>{entry_date format="%F %j%S %Y"}</i></h3>
```

Creating a Calendar

6. Now when we visit `http://localhost/calendar/event` or `http://www.example.com/calendar/event`, we are returned back to the calendar.

Now we have completed this separate weblog to show more information on our calendar entries. Let us start displaying the entries on our calendar, with hyperlinks to this weblog.

Displaying Events on Our Calendar

Displaying events on our calendar involves two parts. First, we need to add code to our `calendar/index` template so that events display on the date that they are scheduled for. Then we need to add styles to our `calendar/calendar_css` template so that the events we are displaying fit in the style of our calendar. First, let's display the events.

1. Edit the template `calendar/index`.
2. The first change we are going to make will be in between the {if entries} tags. Currently, we only display the day number, as follows:

   ```
   {if entries}
     <td class='{switch}'>{day_number}</td>
   {/if}
   ```

   Change the preceding code to the following:

   ```
   {if entries}
     <td class='{switch}'>
       {day_number}
       {entries}
         <div class="calendarEvent"><a href="{title_permalink=
            {my_template_group}/event}">{title}</a></div>
       {/entries}
     </td>
   {/if}
   ```

What we've added is a variable pair called {entries}. As one date can contain multiple events, this variable pair applies to each entry. Inside the {entries} variable pair, we have put the title of the entry, and hyperlinked it to the `calendar/event` weblog that we created in the previous section. We have created a new style, `calendarEvent`, which we will soon use to style the event on the calendar.

The net result: on the calendar, only the title of the entry is shown. When a visitor clicks on the event, they are whisked away to our other weblog that has plenty more information.

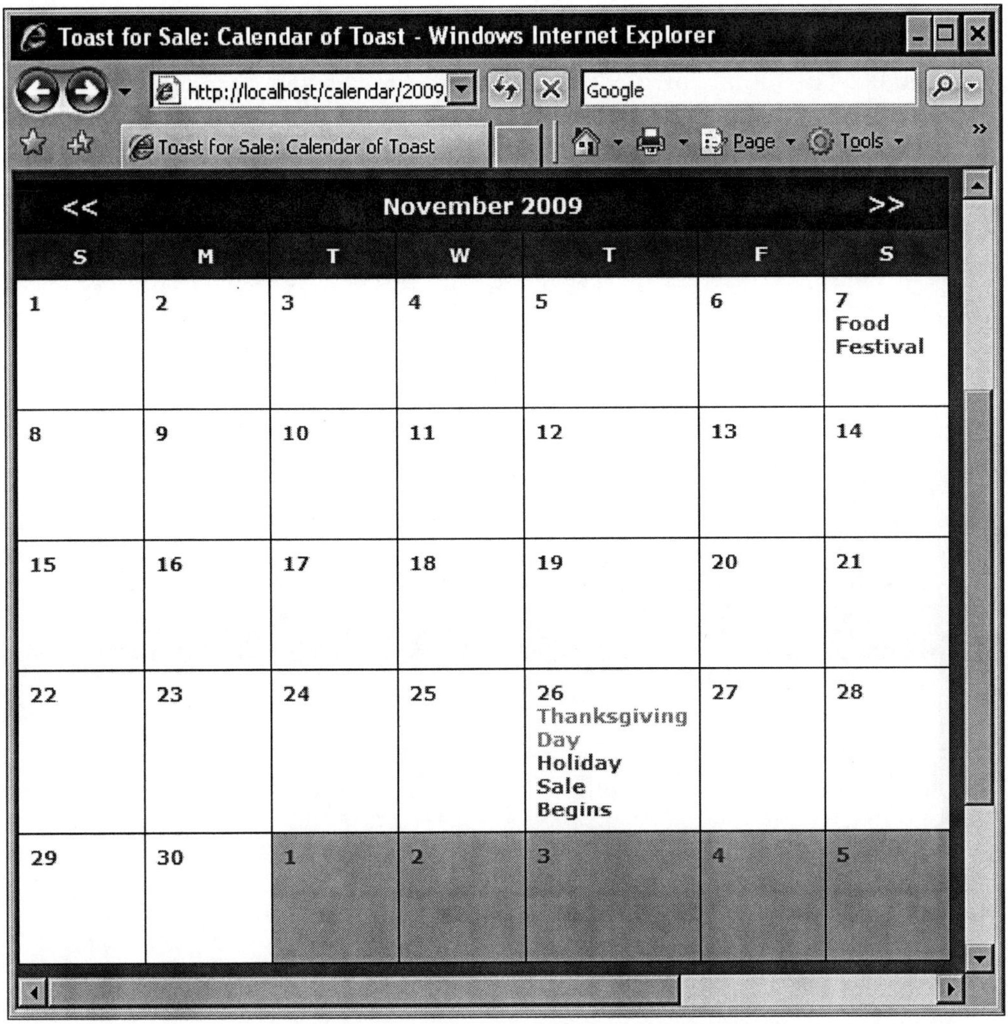

3. Go to your calendar and navigate to a month that has events. Click on one of the events to verify that we are successfully brought back to the `calendar/event` weblog.

Believe it or not, that is all we need to do to get events to display on our calendar. However, right now our events don't blend in very well to the calendar, so we are going to style them.

Creating a Calendar

Styling the Events on Our Calendar

In the last section, we created a new style called `calendarEvent`. We will now add some definition as to what we want the `calendarEvent` to look like on our calendar.

1. Open the `calendar/calendar_css` template for editing.
2. First, let us shrink down our font a little so that it better fits in the cells (an alternative that may be preferable is to not have a side menu for this page and making the calendar bigger). We will also use the Arial font as it is a very clear font to read. Add the following code to the bottom of the stylesheet template:

   ```
   .calendarEvent a
   {
       font-family: Arial, Trebuchet MS, Tahoma, Verdana, Sans-serif;
       font-size: 10px;
       text-decoration: none;
   }
   ```

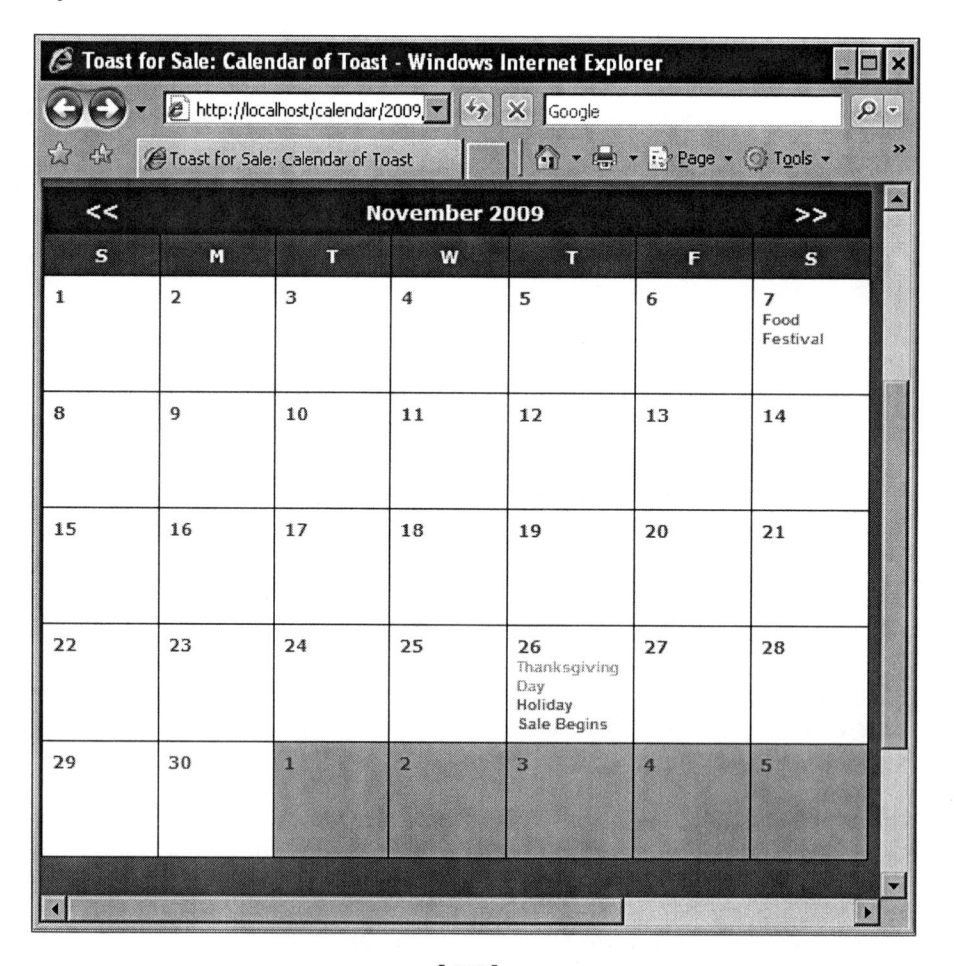

3. Next, we are going to change the colors of our links. As every event on our calendar will be clickable, we are going to make all the links black. Add the following two lines:

```
.calendarEvent a
{
    font-family: Arial, Trebuchet MS, Tahoma, Verdana, Sans-serif;
    font-size: 10px;
    text-decoration: none;
    color: #000;
    background-color: #fff;
}
```

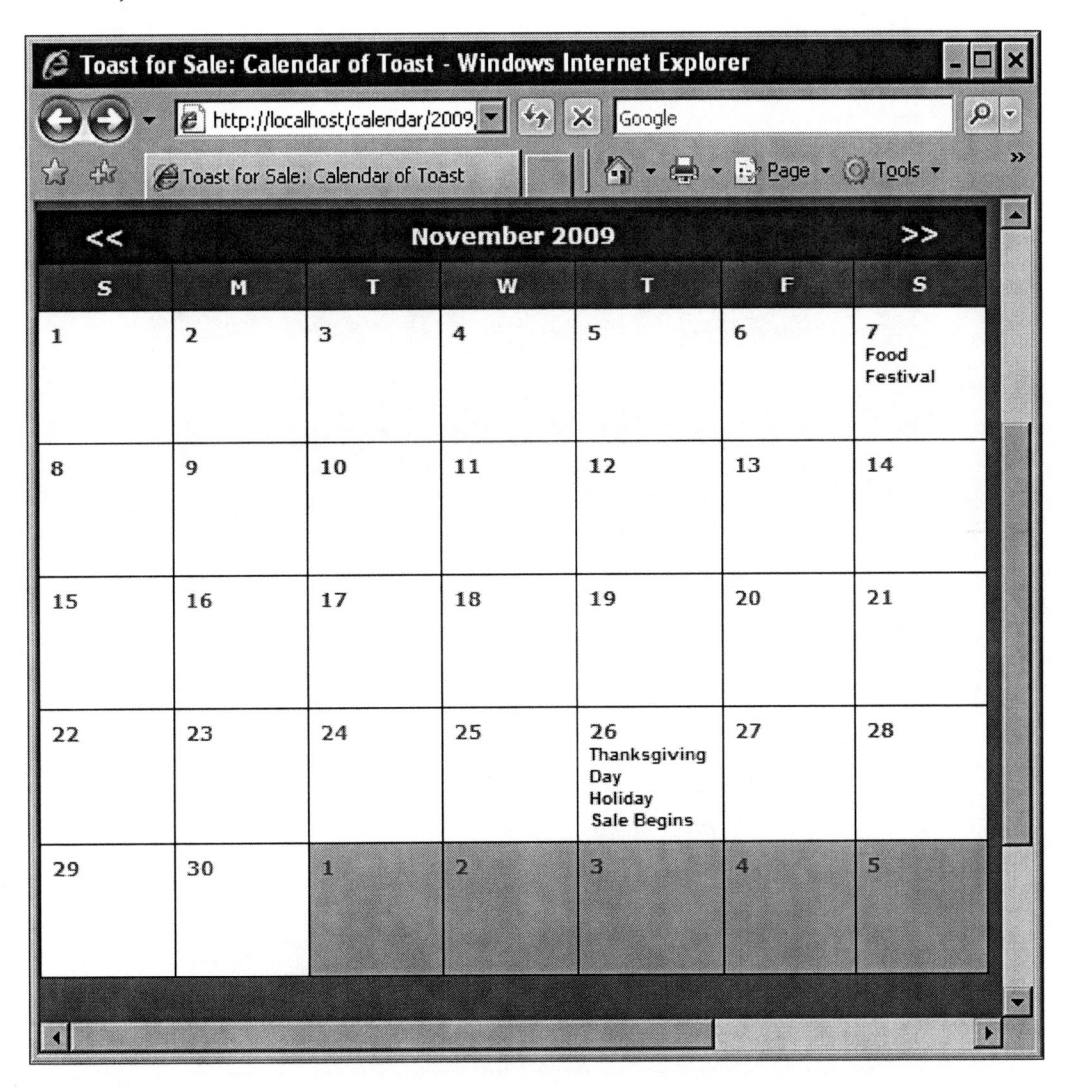

Creating a Calendar

4. Notice that on the 26th we have two events that almost appear to run together. We are now going to separate events a bit more, putting a grey line (border-bottom) underneath each event and adding some padding underneath each event. Finally, we are going to use the `display: block` command to create clickable white space around the words. Right now, people have to click on the words themselves to be taken to the next page. Add the bolded lines as follows:

```
.calendarEvent a
{
  font-family: Arial, Trebuchet MS, Tahoma, Verdana, Sans-serif;
  font-size: 10px;
  text-decoration: none;
  color: #000;
  background-color: #fff;
  border-bottom: 1px solid #666;
  vertical-align: top;
  text-align: left;
  margin: 0px;
  padding-bottom: 5px;
  display: block;
}
```

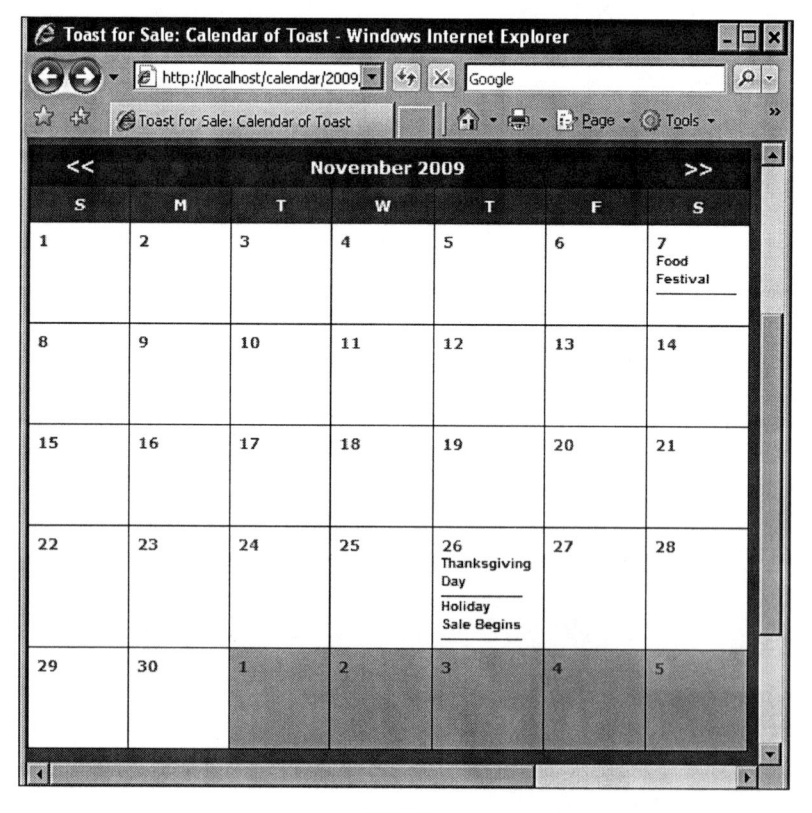

Chapter 7

5. Our final piece is to define a different style when the mouse is hovered over one of these events. We are simply going to change the background of the event to be a light grey—this should indicate that the event is clickable, and which event the users are clicking on. Add the following to the bottom of our stylesheet:

   ```
   .calendarEvent a:hover
   {
      background-color: #ccc;
   }
   ```

We are now done with the basics of creating an events calendar. There is a lot of room for customization, especially when it comes to colors, fonts, formatting, and so forth. Go ahead and experiment and have fun doing so!

Displaying Upcoming Events Underneath Our Calendar

Our calendar is great for telling people what events are going to happen on what days. However, we are going to add some text underneath the calendar to say what events are coming up. So, no matter what month is actually being displayed, the next five events from today are always going to display underneath.

1. To do this, we need to edit the `calendar/index` weblog one more time.

2. The code we are going to use is, in many ways, identical to the code we used in the `calendar/event` weblog. The main differences are that we are going to limit the number of entries to five, sort them in chronological order (ascending), and use a parameter called `dynamic="off"`. We have used this before, and it essentially decouples the weblog from the URL. Typically, ExpressionEngine uses the URL of the page to determine what entries to display. With `dynamic="off"`, if today is April, the first five entries would display no matter what calendar month we were viewing. Finally, the start_on parameter ensures that the first five entries from today's date are displayed rather than the first 5 entries since the beginning of time.

3. Finally, rather than redirecting to the calendar if there are no upcoming events, we are simply going to say that there are no upcoming events. Add the following after the closing calendar tag:

```
{exp:weblog:entries weblog="{my_weblog}" limit="5" require_
entry="yes" show_future_entries="yes" sort="asc" dynamic="off"
       start_on="{current_time format='%Y-%m-%d %g:%i %A'}"}
  {if no_results}
    <h3>No Upcoming Events</h3>
  {/if}
  <h3>{title}<br /><i>{if toastcalendar_time}{toastcalendar
    _time} on {/if}{entry_date format="%F %j%S %Y"}</i></h3>
  <div class="contentinner">
    {if toastcalendar_location}
      <b>{toastcalendar_location}</b><br />
    {/if}
    {if toastcalendar_description}
      {toastcalendar_description}<br /><br />
    {/if}
    {if toastcalendar_URL}
      {toastcalendar_URL}<br />
    {/if}
  </div>
```

```
    {/exp:weblog:entries}
</div>
<div id="menu">
```

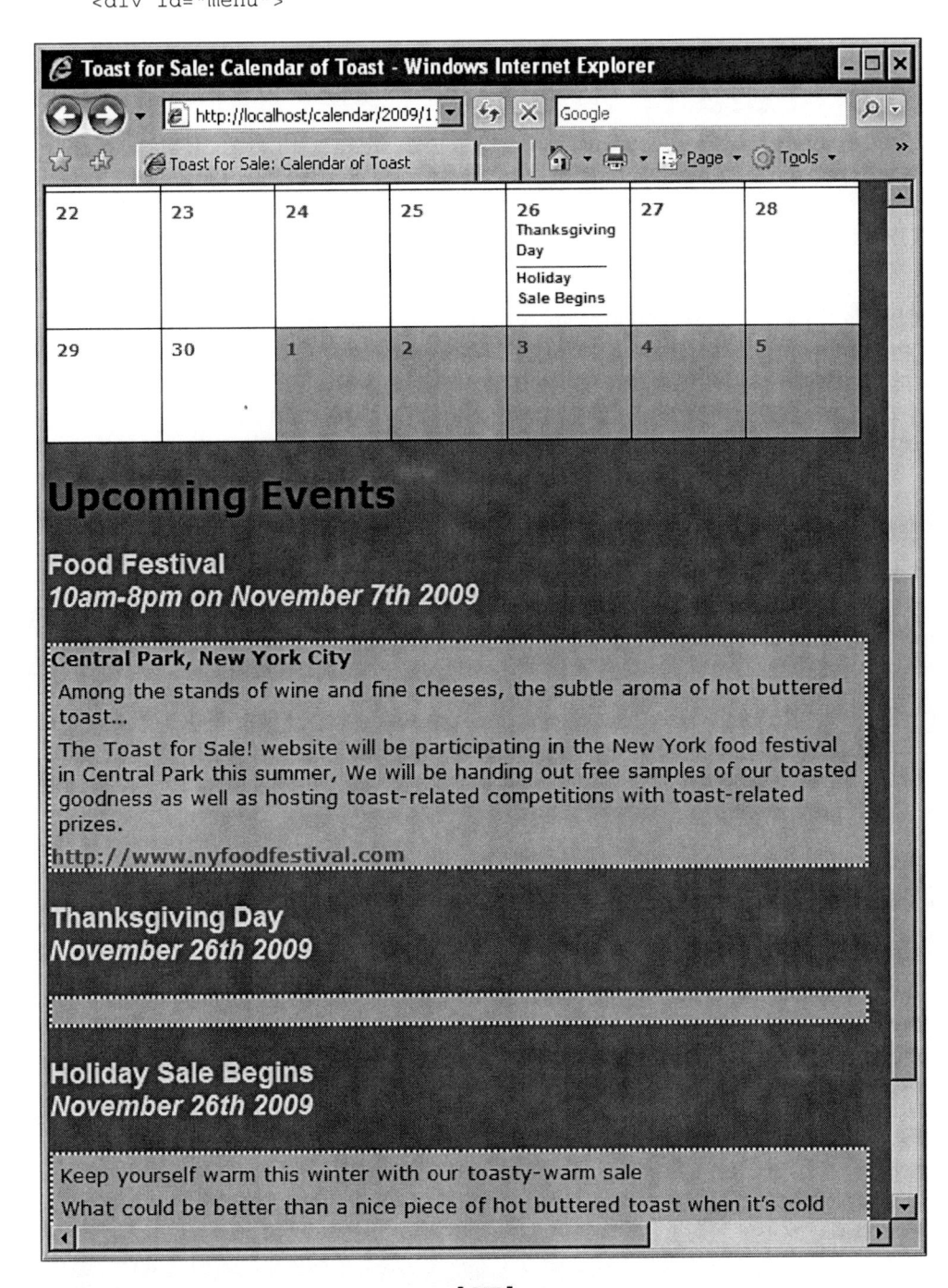

Toast for Sale: Calendar of Toast - Windows Internet Explorer

http://localhost/calendar/2009/1

| 22 | 23 | 24 | 25 | 26 Thanksgiving Day Holiday Sale Begins | 27 | 28 |
| 29 | 30 | 1 | 2 | 3 | 4 | 5 |

Upcoming Events

Food Festival
10am-8pm on November 7th 2009

Central Park, New York City

Among the stands of wine and fine cheeses, the subtle aroma of hot buttered toast...

The Toast for Sale! website will be participating in the New York food festival in Central Park this summer, We will be handing out free samples of our toasted goodness as well as hosting toast-related competitions with toast-related prizes.

http://www.nyfoodfestival.com

Thanksgiving Day
November 26th 2009

Holiday Sale Begins
November 26th 2009

Keep yourself warm this winter with our toasty-warm sale
What could be better than a nice piece of hot buttered toast when it's cold

[237]

We have now created an interactive, very visual, and very usable events calendar. To add events we post to a weblog, just like we are used to doing for every other aspect of our ExpressionEngine site.

Going Further with Our Calendar

There are a couple of tasks that we may want to achieve with a calendar that have not yet been outlined in this chapter. The first would be handling different kinds of events such as recurring events or events that stretch over a number of days. The second is displaying information in addition to the title on the actual calendar (for example, the time, or the location).

Neither of these are available options with the ExpressionEngine calendar that you get out of the box, but with a little bit of tweaking they are not hard to achieve. We are not going to walk through, step-by-step, how to accomplish these tasks because they require third-party plug-ins or more advanced code than this book can cover. Here are some pointers that should help get these features off the ground.

Handling Different Event Types

To handle different event types, check out the 3rd party plugin Repeet, available at http://lincolnite.com/ee/repeet/. Repeet uses a custom field where we can enter the repeat interval for the weblog entry (for example, daily, every x days, weekly, monthly, every Tuesday and Thursday, every 4th Thursday).

In order to get this to work, you must create the custom field yourself (according to their specifications) and what you type into the custom field must match a certain format. The weblog entry will then repeat for the given interval from the start date of the entry to the expiration date of the entry.

Displaying Fields Other Than the Title on Our Calendar

By default, the ExpressionEngine calendar does not allow us to display fields from our weblog, other than the title field. This is because our calendar weblog is based on customized fields, and there is no way for ExpressionEngine to know what field names may apply for our calendar.

There are plenty of reasons why we may want to display more than the title on our calendar. If we are using the calendar to book meeting rooms, we may want to indicate the meeting room that is being booked or the time the meeting room is booked for.

Alternatively, we may wish to use categories to style different events in different ways (for example, events that are holidays are not clickable or are colored differently). We could also use categories to allow us to filter our calendar (for example, only show events for a certain department or of a certain type).

To accomplish this, we need to use the {exp:weblog:entries} tag within the {exp:weblog:calendar} tag. For example, in the calendar/index template, put the following code between the {if entries} and {/if} variable pair:

```
{if entries}
   <td class='{switch}'>{day_number}
     {exp:weblog:entries weblog="{my_weblog}" year="{segment_2}"
     month="{segment_3}" day="{day_number}" limit="5" orderby=
            "toastcalendar_time" show_future_entries="yes"}
       <div class="calendarEvent">
         <a href="{title_permalink={my_template_group}/event}">
           {toastcalendar_time}<br />
           {title}<br />
           <i>{toastcalendar_location}</i>
         </a>
       </div>
     {/exp:weblog:entries}
   </td>
{/if}
```

Here, instead of using the {entries} tag like we did in the main part of this chapter, we are using the {exp:weblog:entries} tag that we have used for most of our weblogs so far. This gives us access to all our custom fields, categories, and so on that we may wish to use.

Creating a Calendar

> If you find events missing from your calendar using this method, it may be because that the weblog entry has a time of *shortly after midnight*. As we use a custom field to display the time of the event, change the weblog entry time so that it is after 1AM.

How does the `{exp:weblog:entries}` tag know what to display on any given calendar date? It uses three parameters to limit what displays in each calendar cell:

- `year="{segment_2}"`
- `month="{segment_3}"`
- `day="{day_number}"`

The `{day_number}` is the same variable that we are using to display the day number in each calendar cell. The use of this variable in our `weblog:entries` tag means that the only entries which are returned must fall on this day number.

From Chapter 5, we may remember that `{segment_2}` and `{segment_3}` are referring to parts of the URL. With a URL like `http://localhost/calendar/2009/11` or `http://www.example.com/calendar/2009/11`, `segment_2` is `2009` and `segment_3` is the 11, so we are essentially restricting entries to this year and month. If the website has an extra preceding segment than the one our URL has (for example, `http://localhost/calendar/index/2009/11`), then the segment numbers would need modification to match.

Although this method works fairly well, there is a downside to relying on the URL to know what calendar month/year to display entries from. Normally, when using the URL `http://localhost/calendar`, events for the current month are displayed. When using the code described here, there is no month/year in the URL, and so no events are displayed—the visitor is presented with a blank events calendar even when there are events.

To workaround this, instead of linking to `http://localhost/calendar` or `http://www.example.com/calendar` in the menus and other locations, link to:

```
{path=calendar/index/<?php echo date("Y",time()); ?>/<?php echo date("m",time()); ?>}
```

This uses embedded PHP code to calculate the current month and year and insert that onto the end of the URL. PHP code must be enabled in the template (where this code appears) for the PHP to be parsed correctly. This can be done under the **Preferences** option in each template group.

Exercises

1. Currently, our calendar displays the days of the week using single letters (for example, M, T, W). Modify this so that the first three letters of each weekday are displayed (for example, Mon, Tue, Wed).
2. Investigate the **Repeet** plug-in and see whether it could be of any use to you in your site.
3. Try following the section on displaying fields other than the title on the events calendar. Once it is working correctly, experiment with a new drop-down custom field to mark an entry as **editors-only**, then use a conditional statement in your `calendar/index` to only display calendar events that are marked as editor-only (if the current member group of the person logged in is that of an editor or Super Admin). Post a new entry (for example, an editors-only promotion day) and verify that when not logged in, the event does not appear, but when logged in as an editor or Super Admin, the entry is visible. Finally, try giving editor-only events an orange background so that they stand out for editors.

Summary

In this chapter:

- We created a calendar weblog with custom fields appropriate to how we wanted to use our calendar
- We went through the process to display a blank calendar on our website, including styling the calendar to fit our website's overall look and feel
- We added events to our calendar and also styled those events
- We created a separate `calendar/event` template to display more details about any one event, and we made the events on the calendar hyperlink to this template
- We discussed how to take advantage of more advanced calendar features, such as repeating entries or displaying more than the title of an event on the calendar

The calendar functionality in ExpressionEngine can be daunting for beginners. There is a lot of code to render the calendar, but once mastered, the ExpressionEngine calendar is very flexible in terms of what we can display on the calendar, how it is displayed, and how it all works together.

Because events are posted using the same weblog posting tools that all other features of ExpressionEngine use, it is very intuitive to learn. We can take advantage of custom fields to make our calendar events meet our needs, and we can also take advantage of member privileges to allow different people the ability to post, edit, and remove entries from the calendar. Finally, we can take advantage of conditional statements to make our calendar work differently for different members, different categories, or different events.

In our next chapter, we will look at creating a photo gallery using the power of ExpressionEngine.

8
Creating a Photo Gallery

ExpressionEngine comes with a built-in photo gallery module included as part of the purchase fee. With the prevalence of digital cameras, having a place to upload and share photos on your website is a great feature of ExpressionEngine. In this chapter we will:

- Install the photo gallery module
- Design our photo gallery to fit in with the design of the rest of our site
- Make it easy to upload new photos, add comments and descriptions, and otherwise create a very functional gallery

On our website, we can have multiple photo galleries independent of each other (the photos are in a different folder; the gallery has a different URL) or we can have one gallery for all your photos, using categories to distinguish groups of related photos.

For the purposes of this tutorial we are going to create only one photo gallery, but if desired the same principals can be followed again to create multiple galleries.

To keep our photo gallery visually interesting, we will be straying just slightly from our toast website theme, and will not be using our photo gallery to display slices of toast.

Let's get started!

Install the Photo Gallery Module

The photo gallery in ExpressionEngine is considered a separate module, even though it is included with every personal or commercial ExpressionEngine license. Installing it is therefore very simple:

1. Log into the control panel using `http://localhost/admin.php` or `http://www.example.com/admin.php`, and select **Modules** from the top of the screen.

2. About a quarter of the way down the page, we can see the **Photo Gallery** module. In the far-right column is a link to install it. Click **Install**.

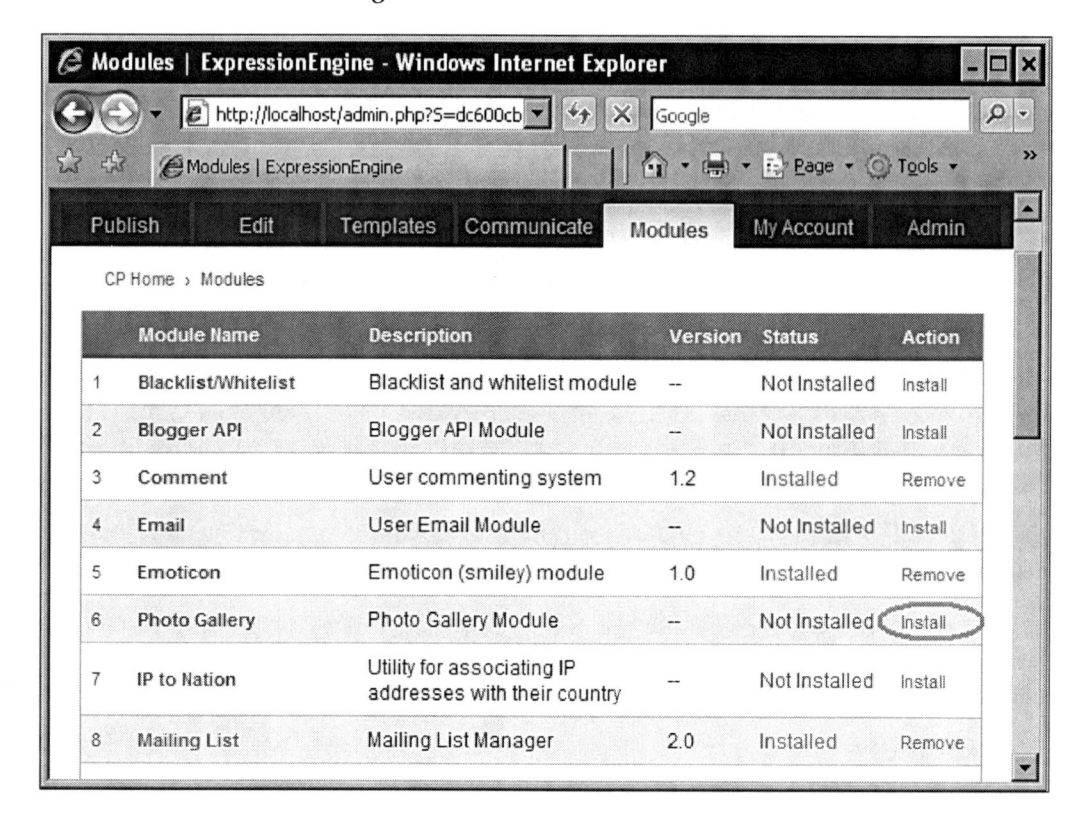

We will see a message at the top of the screen indicating that the photo gallery module was installed. That's it!

Setting Up Our Photo Gallery

Now that we have installed the photo gallery module, we need to define some basic settings and then create categories that we can use to organize our photos.

Define the Basic Settings

1. Still in the **Modules** tab, the photo gallery module should now have become a clickable link. Click on the **Photo Gallery**.

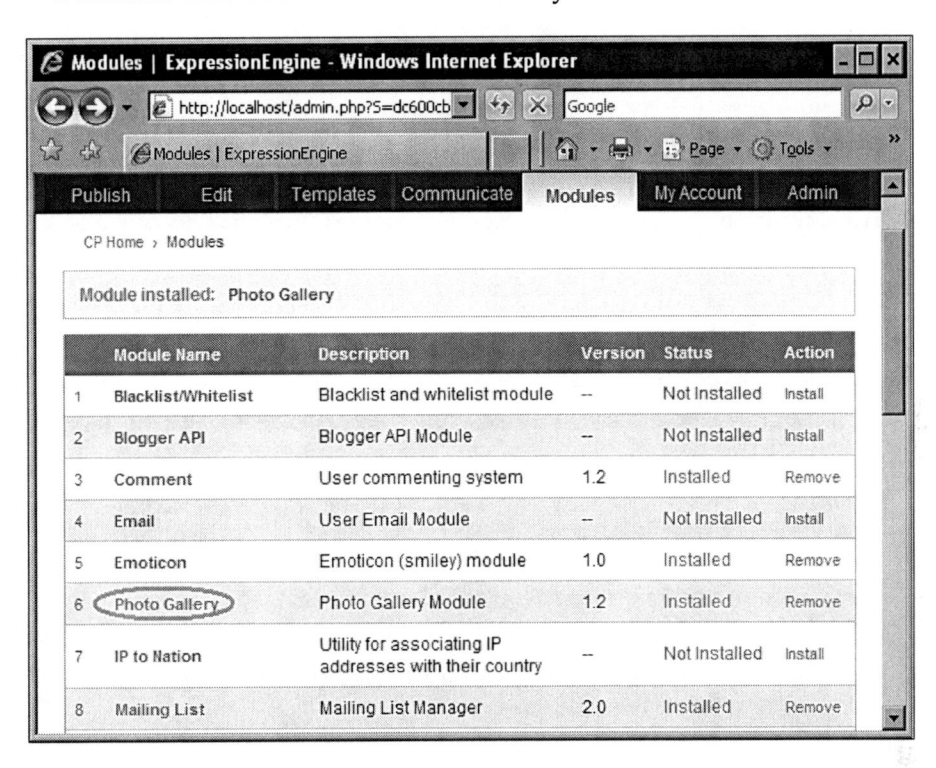

2. We are presented with a message that says **There are no image galleries**. Select to **Create a New Gallery**.

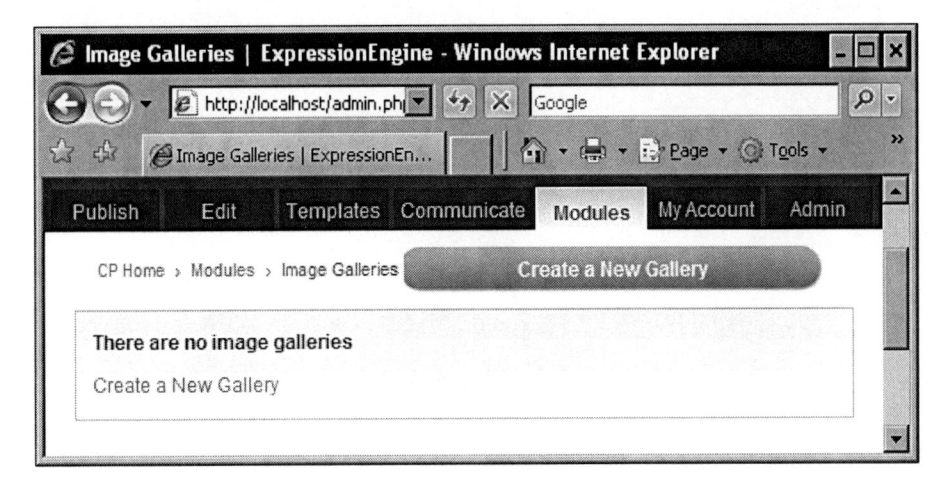

3. We are now prompted for our **Image Folder Name**. For our photo galleries, we are going to create a folder for our photos inside the images folder that should already exist. Navigate to `C:\xampp\htdocs\images` (or `/Applications/MAMP/htdocs/images` if using MAMP on a Mac) or to the images folder on your web server, and create a new folder called `photos`.

4. Inside that folder, we are going to create a specific subfolder for our toast gallery images. (This will keep our tutorial photos separate from any other galleries we may wish to create). Call the new folder `toast`.

5. If doing this on a web server, set the permissions of the `toast` folder to `777` (read, write, and execute for owner, group, and public). This will allow everyone to upload images to this folder.

6. Back in ExpressionEngine, type in the name of the folder we just created (**toast**) and hit **Submit**.

New Photo Gallery - Step One

Image Folder Name

Before creating a new photo gallery you must create a folder on your server for your images. A good location is inside your "images" folder, but feel free to place it anywhere you want.

Once you have created the folder, please set the file permissions to 777.

Server Path to Image Directory

If you are not sure how to determine your server path, enter only the name of the folder and we will try to determine the path for you

> toast

[Submit]

7. We are now prompted to name our template gallery. We will use the imaginative name of **toastgallery** so that it is distinguishable from any other galleries we may create in the future. This name is what will be used as the default URL to the gallery and will be used as the template group name for our gallery templates. Hit **Submit**.

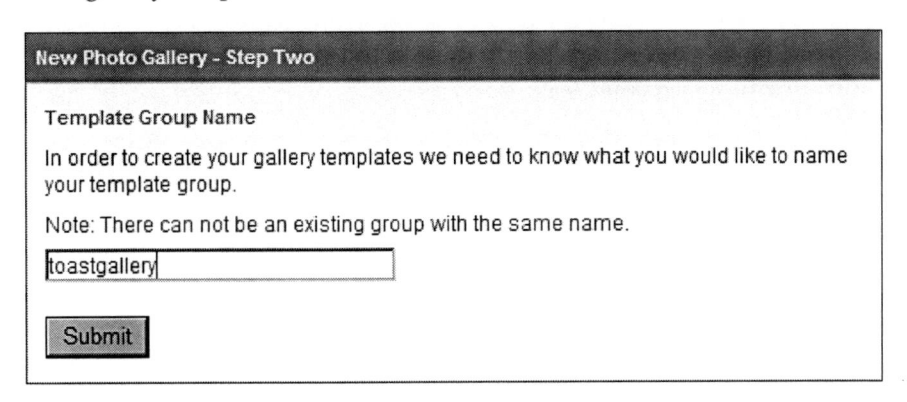

8. We are now prompted to update the preferences for our new gallery. Expand the **General Configuration** option and define a **Photo Gallery Name** and **Short Name**. We are going to use **Toast Photos** as a **Photo Gallery Name** and **toastphotos** as a **Short Name**. The short name is what will be used in our templates to reference this photo gallery.

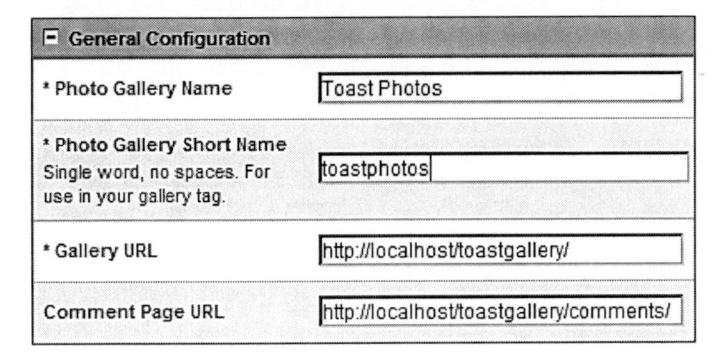

Creating a Photo Gallery

9. Next, expand the **Image Paths** section. Here the **Image Folder Name** should be the same name as the folder we created earlier (in our case **toast**). For XAMPP users, the **Server Path to Image Directory** is going to be `C:/xampp/htdocs/images/photos/toast`, and the **Full URL to Image Directory** is going to be `http://localhost/images/photos/toast`. For MAMP users on a Mac or when using a web server, these paths are going to be different depending on your setup. Verify these settings for correctness, making adjustments as necessary.

Image Paths	
* Image Folder Name	toast
* Server Path to Image Directory Can be relative or absolute server path.	C:/xampp/htdocs/images/photos/toast/
* Full URL to Image Directory	http://localhost/images/photos/toast/

10. Whenever we upload an image into the image gallery, ExpressionEngine creates three copies of the image—a medium-sized and a thumbnail-sized version of the image, in addition to the original image. The thumbnail image is fairly small, so we are going to double the size of the thumbnail image. Expand the **Thumbnail Resizing Preferences** section, and instead of a **Thumbnail Width** of **100**, choose a width of **200**. Check the box (the one outside of the text box) and the height should update to **150**.

Thumbnail Resizing Preferences				
Thumbnail Width x Height	200	150	☑	Constrain proportions
Medium Sized Image Width x Height	400	300	☑	Constrain proportions
Maintain Aspect Ratio If a thumbnail can not be scaled proportionally to your desired width and height, the values will be adjusted as close as possible while maintaining the original proportions.	Yes ⊙ No ○			
Thumbnail Quality	75			
Medium Sized Image Quality	90			

11. Hit **Submit** to save the settings so far. We will review the rest of the settings later.

We have now created our first gallery. However, before we can start uploading photos, we need to create some categories.

Create Categories

For the purposes of our toast website, we are going to create categories based on the seasons: spring, summer, autumn, and winter. We are going to have separate subfolders for each of the categories; these are created automatically when we create the categories.

1. To do this, first select **Categories** from the new menu that has appeared across the top of the screen. We will see a message that says **No categories exist**. Select **Add a New Category**.

2. We are going to use a **Category Name** of **Spring** and a **Description** that describes the category—we will later display this description on our site. We are going to create a **Category Folder** of **spring**. Leave the **Category Parent** as **None**, and hit **Submit**.

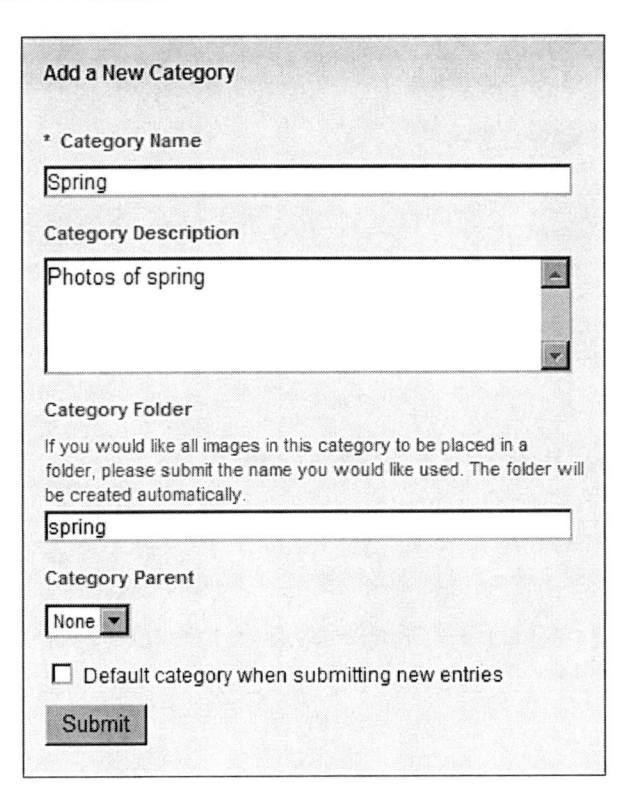

3. Select **Add a New Category**, and continue to add three more categories: summer, autumn, and winter in the same way.

ID	Order	Category	Files	Edit	Delete
3	⬆⬇	Autumn	0	Edit	Delete
1	⬆⬇	Spring	0	Edit	Delete
2	⬆⬇	Summer	0	Edit	Delete
4	⬆⬇	Winter	0	Edit	Delete

4. After we are done with creating all the categories, use the up and down arrows to order the categories correctly. In our case, we need to move **Autumn** down so that it appears after **Summer**.

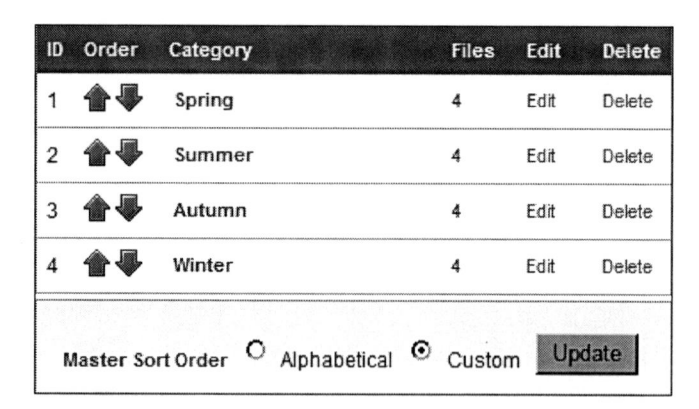

ID	Order	Category	Files	Edit	Delete
1	⬆⬇	Spring	4	Edit	Delete
2	⬆⬇	Summer	4	Edit	Delete
3	⬆⬇	Autumn	4	Edit	Delete
4	⬆⬇	Winter	4	Edit	Delete

Master Sort Order ○ Alphabetical ⊙ Custom [Update]

We now have the beginnings of a photo gallery. Next, we will upload our first photos so that we can see how the gallery works.

Upload Our First Photos

To upload a photo to a photo gallery is pretty straightforward. The example photos we are working with can be downloaded from the Packtpub support page at `http://www.packtpub.com/files/code/3797_Graphics.zip`.

1. To upload a photo, select **New Entry** from the menu within the photo gallery module.

2. For the **File Name**, click the **Browse...** button and browse to the photo **spring1.jpg**. We are going to give this an **Entry Title** of **Spring Flower**. For **Date**, we could either leave it as a default or enter the date that the photo was taken on. We are going to use a date of **2006-04-22**. Click on the calendar icon to expand the view to include a calendar that can be easily navigated.

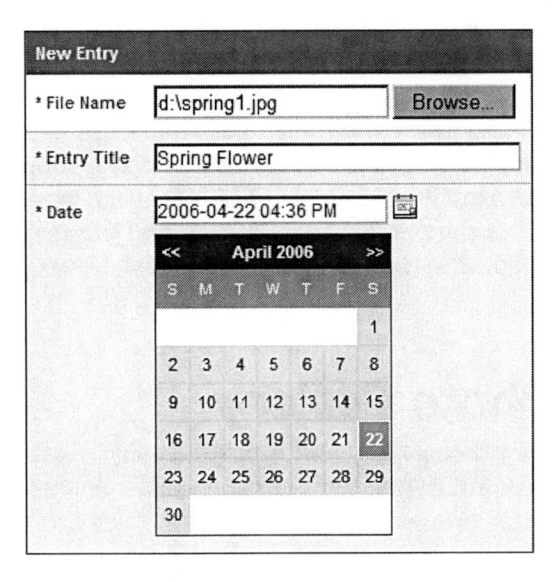

3. We are going to use a **Category** of **Spring** and a **Status** of **Open**. Leave the box checked to **Allow Comments**, and write a **Caption** that describes the photo. The **Views** allows us to indicate how many times this image has been viewed—in this case we are going to leave it at **0**. Hit **Submit New Entry** when everything is done.

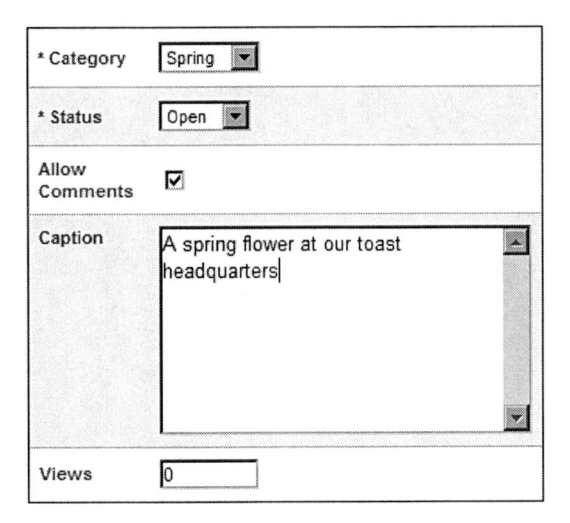

4. We are presented with a message that reads **Your file has been successfully submitted**, and the image now appears underneath the entry information.

> In the folder where our image is uploaded, three versions of the same image are made. There is the original file (`spring1.jpg`), a thumbnail of the original file (`spring1_thumb.jpg`), and a medium-sized version of the original file (`spring1_medium.jpg`).

5. Now, click on **New Entry** and repeat the same steps to upload the rest of the photos, using appropriate categories and descriptions that describe the photos. There are four example photos for each season (for example, `winter1.jpg`, `winter2.jpg`, `winter3.jpg`, and `winter4.jpg`). Having a few example photos in each category will better demonstrate how the photo gallery works.

View Our Photo Gallery

Now we've created our photo gallery and uploaded some photos. We have not yet done any customization, but ExpressionEngine creates a default photo gallery right out of the box.

1. Visit `http://localhost/toastgallery` (or `http://www.example.com/toastgallery`), or click the link **Visit Gallery** at the top-right of the Gallery module menu. We are brought to a category navigation screen where we can select which category we wish to view. At the bottom of the screen are two selections of photos: one set of four random images and one set of the last four images uploaded.

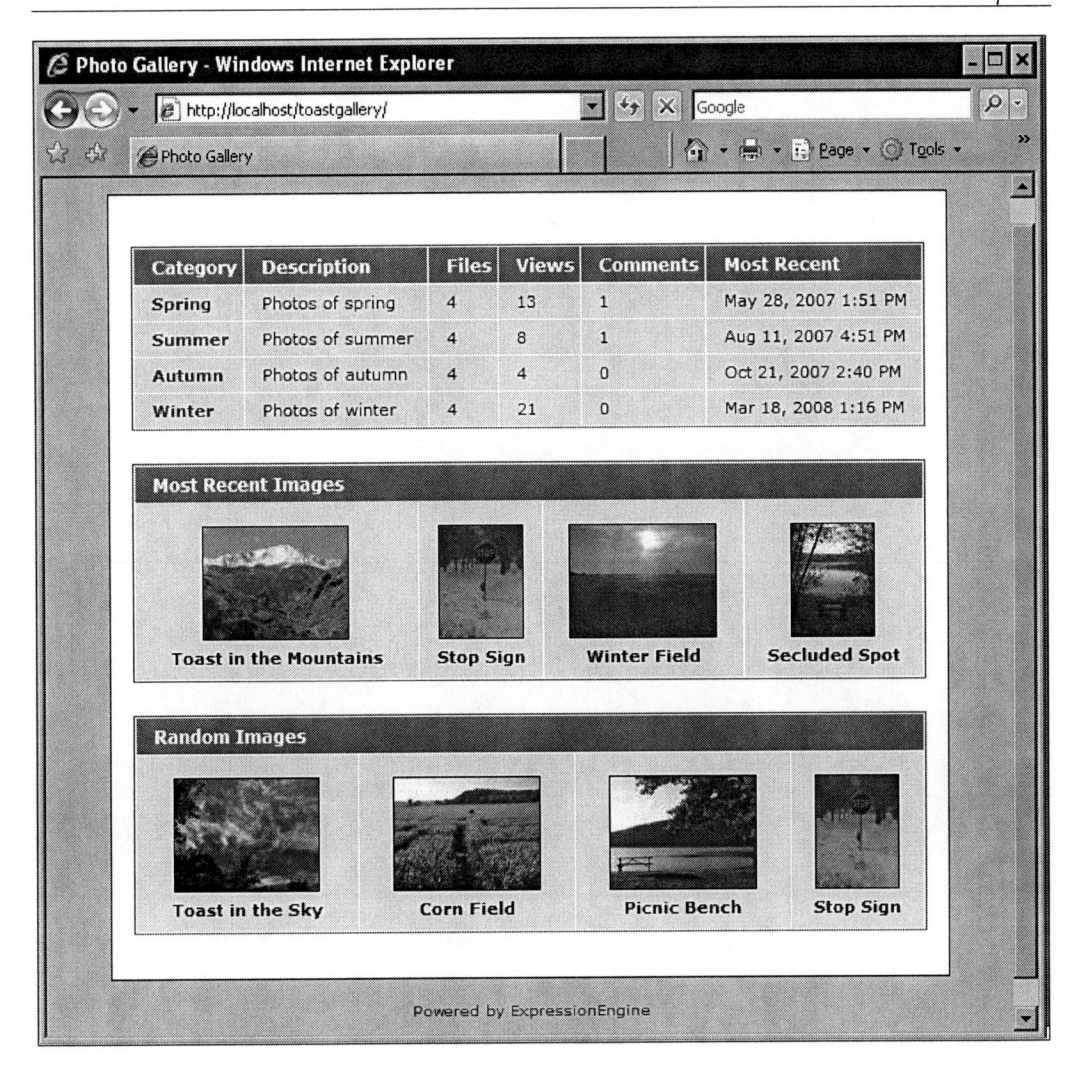

Category	Description	Files	Views	Comments	Most Recent
Spring	Photos of spring	4	13	1	May 28, 2007 1:51 PM
Summer	Photos of summer	4	8	1	Aug 11, 2007 4:51 PM
Autumn	Photos of autumn	4	4	0	Oct 21, 2007 2:40 PM
Winter	Photos of winter	4	21	0	Mar 18, 2008 1:16 PM

Most Recent Images

Toast in the Mountains   Stop Sign   Winter Field   Secluded Spot

Random Images

Toast in the Sky   Corn Field   Picnic Bench   Stop Sign

Powered by ExpressionEngine

2. Click on one of the photos at the bottom and a new tab or window is opened with a medium-sized version of the image.

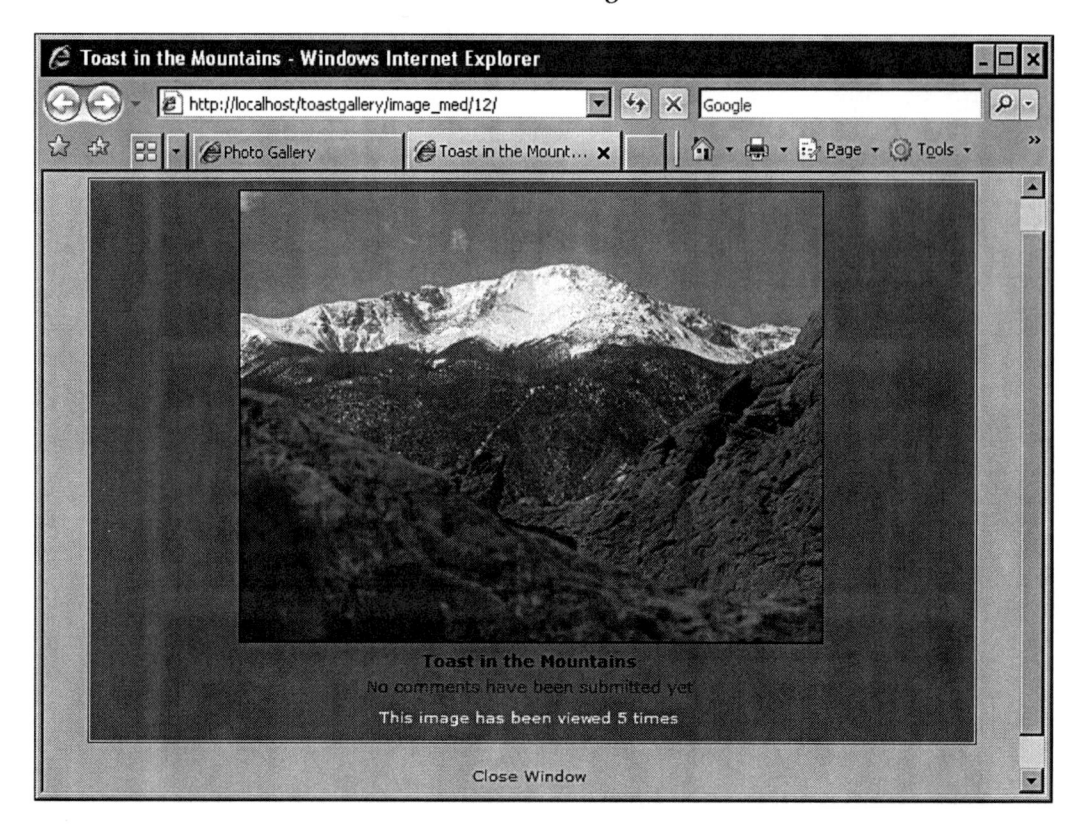

3. Select **Close Window**. Now select one of the categories (for example, **Summer**) by clicking on the category name in the left-hand column of the table. The next page that loads shows all the images in the category. At the top-left are the breadcrumbs that will allow you to return to the previous page, and at the top-right is a drop-down menu to jump to any other category.

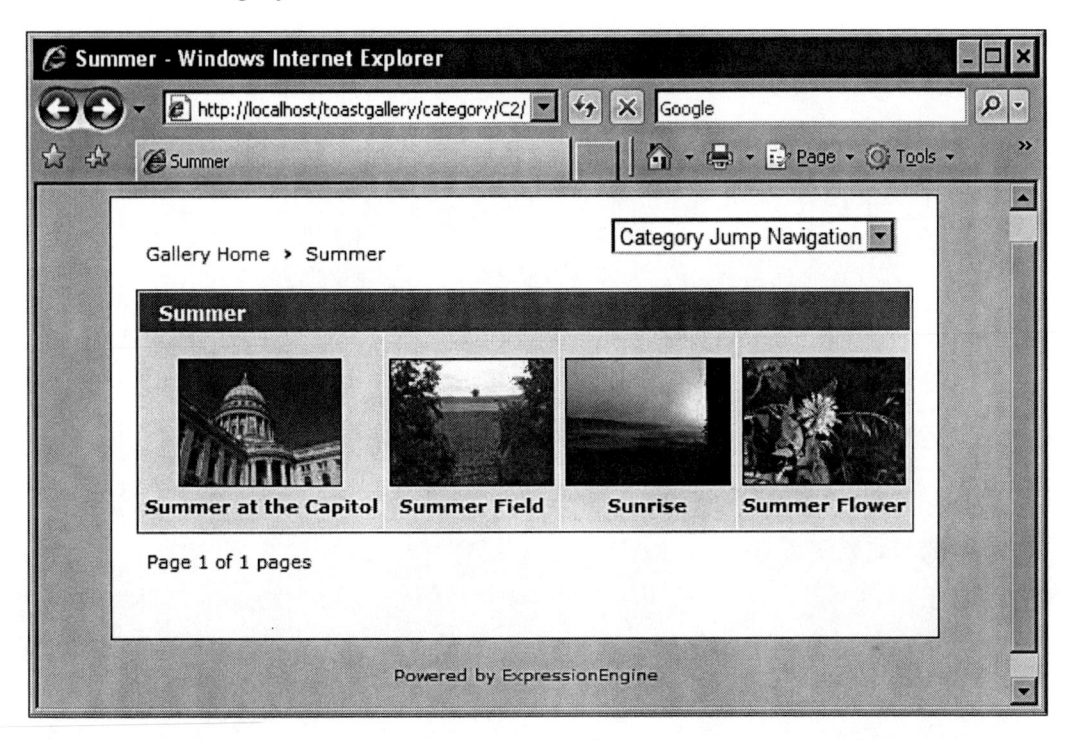

Creating a Photo Gallery

4. Click on one of the images and a new screen is displayed showing the full-sized image. At the top-left are the breadcrumbs, allowing us to jump back to either the main gallery page or the category page. At the top right, we can go to the next image or the previous image directly. Underneath the image, we can see how many times the image has been viewed, and underneath the blue box is the image description that we gave when we uploaded the image.

5. Click on the sentence **No comments have been submitted yet** and a new window opens where we can submit comments, similar to the comments on our weblog entries.

This all looks very exciting. However, the image gallery looks nothing like our existing website design. Let us change that now.

Changing the Design of Our Photo Gallery

As with everything in ExpressionEngine, what we are seeing when we visit our photo gallery is powered by templates. The only difference is that these templates were auto-generated when we created the photo gallery, whereas in the previous chapters we were the ones creating the templates from scratch.

This does make it more complicated to fit the gallery into our existing website design. To make it easier, rather than trying to retrofit the automatically generated templates to the outline of our other pages, we will create new templates starting from our normal page outline and gradually add in the gallery features from the auto-generated templates.

Create the Single-Entry Page Layout

The single-entry page is where an individual photograph is displayed, along with the caption and any comments. In the auto-generated templates, there are two single-entry pages: `http://localhost/toastgallery/image_med` (or `http://www.example.com/toastgallery/image_med`) and `http://localhost/toastgallery/image_full`. One displays medium-sized images and the other displays full-sized images.

For our gallery, we are going to create only one single-entry page. This page will have a medium-sized version of our image, along with the caption and any comments. There will be links to the next and the previous photograph in the category. If a visitor wishes to see the full-sized original image (which could often be larger than our site design will accommodate), we will make the medium-sized image clickable and it will open the image file directly.

Create Our Template Outline

The first step will be to create new templates. The auto-generated templates were created in the `toastgallery` template group. We will continue to work in this template group, but will not use the existing templates. (Later we can either delete or rename these templates so that they cannot be accidentally discovered by visitors.)

1. In the ExpressionEngine control panel, click on **Templates**. Then select the **toastgallery** template group and **New Template**. Create a new template called **photo**. Leave the **Template Type** as **Web Page** and the **Default Template Data** as **None**. Click **Submit**.

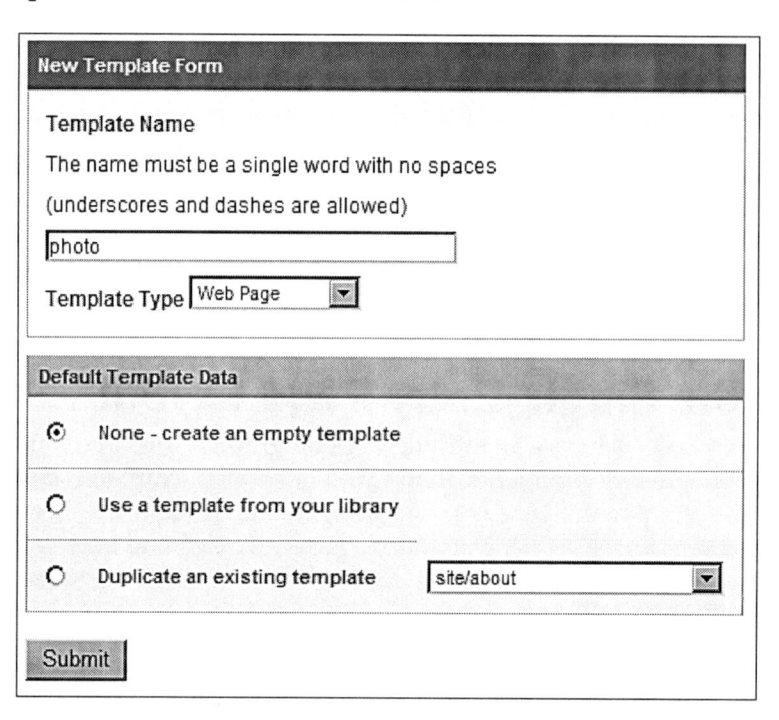

2. Open the `toastgallery/photo` template and type the following (adapted from our `calendar/index` template). We have changed the variables to reflect the photo gallery, but otherwise the page will be a blank version of other pages on our website.

```
{assign_variable:gallery_name="toastphotos"}
{assign_variable:my_template_group="toastgallery"}
{assign_variable:my_site_wide_templates="toast"}

<!DOCTYPE html PUBLIC "-//W3C//DTD XHTML 1.0 Strict//EN"
"http://www.w3.org/TR/xhtml1/DTD/xhtml1-strict.dtd">
<html xmlns="http://www.w3.org/1999/xhtml">
  <head>
    <title>Toast for Sale: Toast Gallery</title>
    <link rel='stylesheet' type='text/css' media='all' href=
         '{path={my_site_wide_templates}/toast_css}' />
```

```
        <style type='text/css' media='screen'>@import "{path=
            {my_site_wide_templates}/toast_css}";</style>
        <meta http-equiv="content-type" content="text/html;
                                            charset=UTF-8" />
  </head>
  <body>
    <div id="header">
      <h1>Toast for Sale!</h1>
    </div>
    <div id="content">
    </div>
    <div id="menu">
      {embed={my_site_wide_templates}/.menu}
    </div>
  </body>
</html>
```

3. To view our progress, we will need to get the ID number of a specific photo. If you browse to `http://localhost/toastgallery` (or `http://www.example.com/toastgallery`) and drill-down into an actual image, part of the URL will be either `image_med` or `image_full` (for example, `http://localhost/toastgallery/image_med/38`, where 38 is the image ID). Replace the word `image_med` or `image_full` with `photo` and we should see our existing template (for example, `http://localhost/toastgallery/photo/38` or `http://www.example.com/toastgallery/photo/38`).

Create the Headings in Our Template

Now that we have created the outline of our template, let us put in headings that pertain to the actual image we are using. This will be our introduction to the `exp:gallery:entries` tag that we will be using throughout our photo gallery templates to power our photo gallery.

1. Next, add the following line after our `h1` heading to create a subheading. We want the subheading to be the title of the photograph being displayed, so we use the `exp:gallery:entries` tag to accomplish this. This tag looks at the photo ID in the URL of the page to determine which photograph we are viewing, and then provides access to a range of variables about that photo (such as the title, the caption, the number of views). At this time, we are only interested in the title of the image.

   > Note also that `log_views` is set to `off`. ExpressionEngine keeps track of how many times an image has been viewed, so we can see how popular different images are. This tracking is done through the `exp:gallery:entries` tag. Each time an image is called through this tag, ExpressionEngine increments the counter. However as this line is not displaying the image itself (it displays only the title of the image), we do not want to increment the number of views, so we set the `log_views` to be `off`.

   ```
   <div id="header">
     <h1>Toast for Sale!</h1>
     <h2>{exp:gallery:entries gallery="{gallery_name}" log_views=
                     "off"}{title}{/exp:gallery:entries}</h2>
   </div>
   ```

2. We will use the same technique in the title of the page, except this time we will display both the title of the image and the category that the image falls under (for example, Summer - Sunrise).

   ```
   <head>
     <title>Toast for Sale: Toast Gallery - {exp:gallery:entries
       gallery="{gallery_name}" log_views="off"}{category} - {title}
                            {/exp:gallery:entries}</title>
   ```

```
<link rel='stylesheet' type='text/css' media='all' href=
       '{path={my_site_wide_templates}/toast_css}' />
```

[Screenshot: Browser window showing "Toast for Sale! A Bridge in the Mist" banner]

3. Next, using the same technique, we are going to create an h3 subheading on the page that will show the category and the image name. Add the following code inside the `<div id="content">` section:

```
<div id="content">
  <h3>Toast Gallery <b>&#8250;</b> {exp:gallery:entries
  gallery="{gallery_name}" limit="1" log_views="off"}{category}
   <b>&#8250;</b> {title}{/exp:gallery:entries}</h3>
</div>
```

[Screenshot: Toast Gallery › Spring › A Bridge in the Mist]

Display Our Photograph

Now that we have our headings reflecting the image we are viewing, the logical next step is to also display the image.

1. After the h3 heading, add the following code. Once again we are using the exp:gallery:entries tag to call the image, though this time we are not using log_views="off" because we do want to count this as viewing the image. We use a couple of variables in our image tag: {medium_url} corresponds to the URL of the medium-sized photo, which is what we display on this page. The tag {image_url} corresponds to the original-sized photo, which we link to directly rather than trying to fit onto this page.

Creating a Photo Gallery

```
<div id="content">
  <h3>Toast Gallery <b>&#8250;</b> {exp:gallery:entries
  gallery="{gallery_name}" limit="1" log_views="off"}{category}
   <b>&#8250;</b> {title}{/exp:gallery:entries}</h3>
  {exp:gallery:entries gallery="{gallery_name}"}
    <div align="center">
      <a href="{image_url}"><img src="{medium_url}" border="0"
                                  title="{title}" /></a>
    </div>
  {/exp:gallery:entries}
</div>
```

2. If we view the template in a browser (be sure the URL ends with a photo ID), we will see something akin to the following. Clicking on the image opens the original image directly.

3. Next, underneath the image we will add the previous and next links. This will allow a visitor to navigate through all the pictures in a given category, without having to constantly return to a page of thumbnails in order to select the next photo. We will use the `footnote` style that we defined when we were first designing our site to display the links. The codes `&#8249;` and `&#8250;` are the codes that used to render the arrows, and ` ` is the code for a space. ExpressionEngine automatically calculates the next image in a category when we use the `exp:gallery:next_entry` and `exp:gallery:prev_entry` tags in combination with hyperlinks that specify which template to use to display the next or previous entry (in our case the `toastgallery/photo` template).

```
<div align="center">
  <a href="{image_url}"><img src="{medium_url}" border="0"
                                         title="{title}" /></a>
  <br />
    <span font-weight="bold" class="footnote">{exp:gallery:
    prev_entry gallery="{gallery_name}"}<a
    href="{path=toastgallery/photo}">&#8249; Previous Image</a>
      {/exp:gallery:prev_entry}{exp:gallery:next_entry
    gallery="{gallery_name}"}  <a
    href="{path=toastgallery/photo}">Next Image &#8250;</a>{/exp:
    gallery:next_entry}</span>
</div>
```

Display Information About Our Photograph

Now that we have a page that shows the name of the photograph, the photograph itself, and allows us to circle through all our photographs, we still might have other information to display about our photo. In our case, we are going to display the photograph caption (which is where we can include a longer description of the photograph), as well as the number of times the photograph has been viewed.

Creating a Photo Gallery

All of this can be accomplished through the use of standard ExpressionEngine tags within the `exp:gallery:entries` tag. Full documentation of what is available can be found at `http://expressionengine.com/docs/modules/gallery/variables.html`.

1. Underneath our photograph, we are going to use a `contentinner` box (a style that we have defined and used on other pages of our site) to place the caption. Add the following code underneath the `<div align="center">` code.

   ```
   <span font-weight="bold" class="footnote">{exp:gallery:
   prev_entry gallery="{gallery_name}"}<a
   href="{path=toastgallery/photo}">&#8249; Previous Image</
   a>  {/exp:gallery:prev_entry}{exp:gallery:next_entry
   gallery="{gallery_name}"}  <a
   href="{path=toastgallery/photo}">Next Image &#8250;</a>{/exp:
   gallery:next_entry}</span>
   </div>
   <br />
   <div class="contentinner">
     {caption}
   </div>
   {/exp:gallery:entries}
   ```

2. Next, we will display the number of times that the image has been viewed. Given that this information is largely irrelevant to the enjoyment of the image, we will use the `footnote` style for this. We use the conditional statement `{if views == 1}` so that the word 'time' is correctly pluralized.

   ```
   <div class="contentinner">
     {caption}
   </div>
   <p class="footnote">This image has been viewed {views} {if views
   == 1}time{/if}{if views != 1}times{/if}. Click on the image to
                                           view the full-size.</p>
   {/exp:gallery:entries}
   ```

[264]

Display Comments on Our Photograph

In the default ExpressionEngine templates, comments were on a separate page from where the image was housed. For our purposes, we are going to display comments underneath the image. The `exp:gallery:comments` tag is used to accept and display comments about our image, and more information can be found at http://expressionengine.com/docs/modules/gallery/comments.html.

1. Add the following code after the caption code and before the closing `exp:gallery:entries` tag in the last example. We use the `total_comments` tag to determine whether there are any comments. If there are none, we simply say that in another `contentinner` box. If there are comments, we display them in a `contentinner` box.

   ```
   <p class="footnote">This image has been viewed {views} {if views
   == 1}time{/if}{if views != 1}times{/if}. Click on the image to
                                              view the full-size.</p>
   {if allow_comments}
     <h3>Comments ({total_comments})</h3>
     {if total_comments==0}
       <div class="contentinner">
         No comments have been submitted yet
       </div>
     {/if}
     {if total_comments > 0}
       {exp:gallery:comments}
         <div class="contentinner">
           {comment}
         </div>
         <p class="footnote">Posted by {name} on {comment_date
         format='%m/%d'} at {comment_date format='%h:%i %A'}</p>
       {/exp:gallery:comments}
     {/if}
   {/if}
   {/exp:gallery:entries}
   ```

> This image has been viewed 28 times. Click on the image to view the full-size.
>
> **Comments (0)**
>
> No comments have been submitted yet

[265]

Creating a Photo Gallery

2. We also want to add a form so that comments can be accepted. This code is very similar to the code we used in Chapter 5 when we were building our product showcase. Be careful to place this code in between the correct tags:

```
        <p class="footnote">Posted by {name} on {comment_date
        format='%m/%d'} at {comment_date format='%h:%i %A'}</p>
      {/exp:gallery:comments}
    {/if}
    <h3>Add Your Comment</h3>
    {exp:gallery:comment_form preview="toastgallery/photo"}
      {if logged_out}
        <p>
          Name:<br />
          <input type="text" name="name" value="{name}" size="50"
                                                                    />
        </p>
        <p>
          Email:<br />
          <input type="text" name="email" value="{email}"
                                                    size="50" />
        </p>
      {/if}
      <p>
        <textarea name="comment" cols="50"
            rows="12">{comment}</textarea>
      </p>
      {if logged_out}
        <p><input type="checkbox" name="save_info" value="yes"
            {save_info} /> Remember my personal information</p>
      {/if}
      <p><input type="checkbox" name="notify_me" value="yes"
          {notify_me} /> Notify me of follow-up comments?</p>
      {if captcha}
        <p>Submit the word you see below:</p>
        <p>
          {captcha}
          <br />
          <input type="text" name="captcha" value="" size="20"
                      maxlength="20" style="width:140px;" />
        </p>
      {/if}
```

```
            <input type="submit" name="submit" value="Submit" />
            <input type="submit" name="preview" value="Preview" />
        {/exp:gallery:comment_form}
      {/if}
    {/exp:gallery:entries}
```

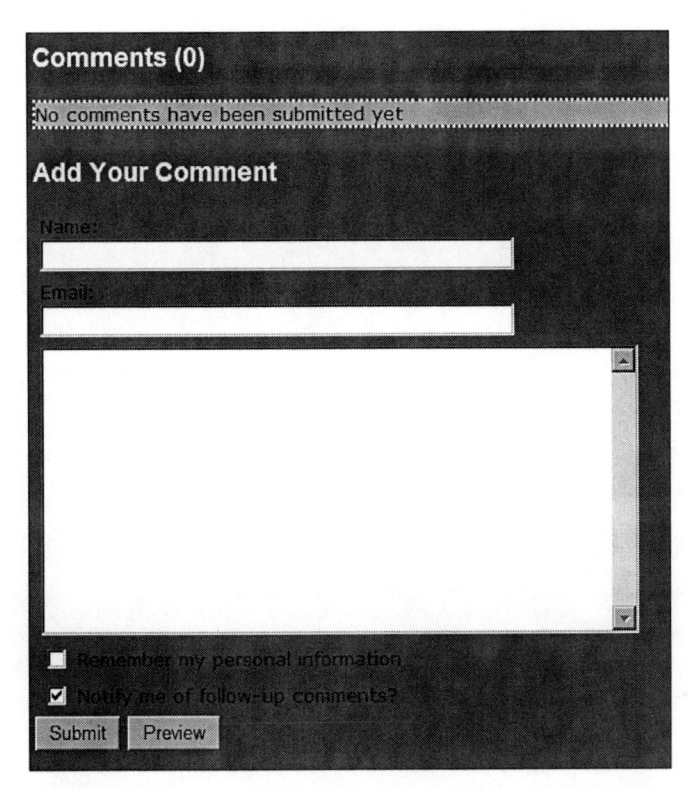

3. Finally, before we can submit any comments, we need to add a small piece of code that will allow us to preview a comment on the page before it is submitted. Add this code between the exp:gallery:comments and the exp:gallery:comment_form tags. This will not have any appreciable difference on the page until we use the **Preview** button.

```
        <p class="footnote">Posted by {name} on {comment_date
        format='%m/%d'} at {comment_date format='%h:%i %A'}</p>
      {/exp:gallery:comments}
    {/if}
    {exp:gallery:comment_preview}
      {if comment}
        <h3>Preview Comment</h3>
        <div class="contentinner">
          {comment}
```

[267]

```
      </div>
    {/if}
{/exp:gallery:comment_preview}
<h3>Add Your Comment</h3>
```

4. Now go to a photo and try submitting a comment. Before hitting the **Submit** button, try hitting the **Preview** button to see a preview of the comment first. The following screenshot shows an example of one comment that has already been submitted and another comment that is being previewed.

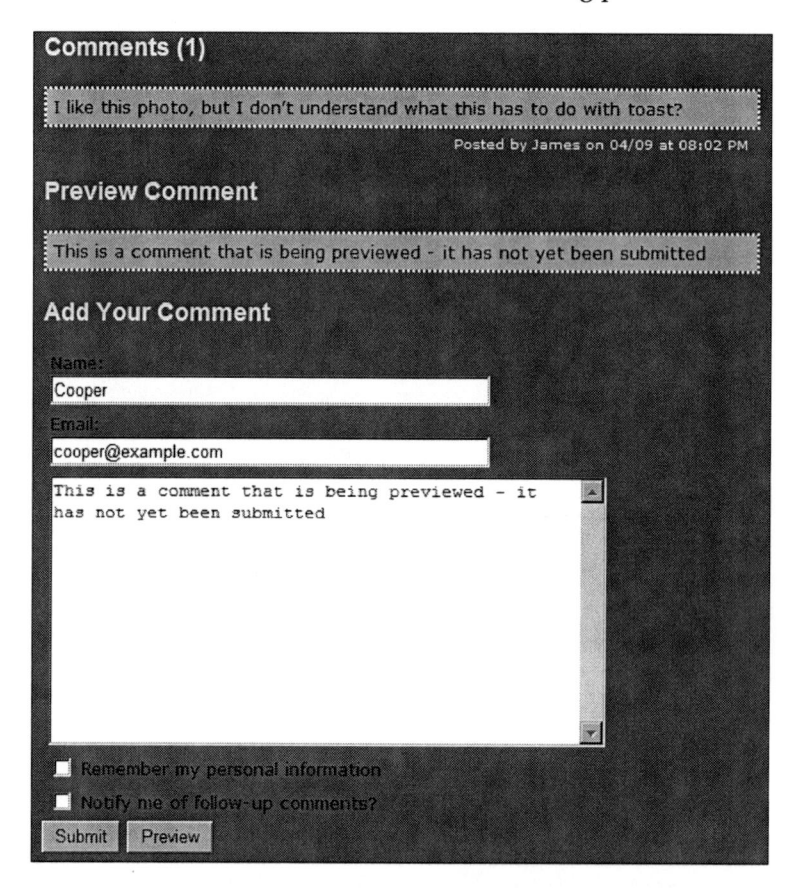

5. One final touch to this template before we are all done. Our main h3 heading at the top of the page looks like a breadcrumb, but it does not have hyperlinks. Let us add hyperlinks to this heading—the hyperlinks will not work right away because we have yet created the templates.

```
<div id="content">
  <h3><a href="{path=toastgallery}">Toast Gallery</a> 
  <b>&#8250;</b> {exp:gallery:entries gallery="{gallery
```

```
_name}" limit="1" log_views="off"}<a href="{category_
path=toastgallery/browse}">{category}</a> <b>
&#8250;</b> {title}{/exp:gallery:entries}
                                            </h3>
{exp:gallery:entries gallery="{gallery_name}"}
```

We are now done with creating our single-entry page. Now we will create our category browsing page where visitors can browse all the photos in a category and select the photo that they wish to see.

Create the Category Page Layout

The category navigation page needs to attractively display a series of photos so that our visitors can quickly browse to the photos they are most interested in. A visitor browsing our photo gallery may spend a lot of time on this page.

We are going to take the same approach in redesigning this page as we just did in the last example. Rather than trying to modify the auto-generated templates, we are going to create a new template with an outline of our design, and then add in the gallery components.

1. In the ExpressionEngine control panel, click on **Templates**. Then select the **toastgallery** template group and **New Template**. Create a new template called **browse**. Leave the **Template Type** as **Web Page** and the **Default Template Data** as **None**. Click **Submit**.

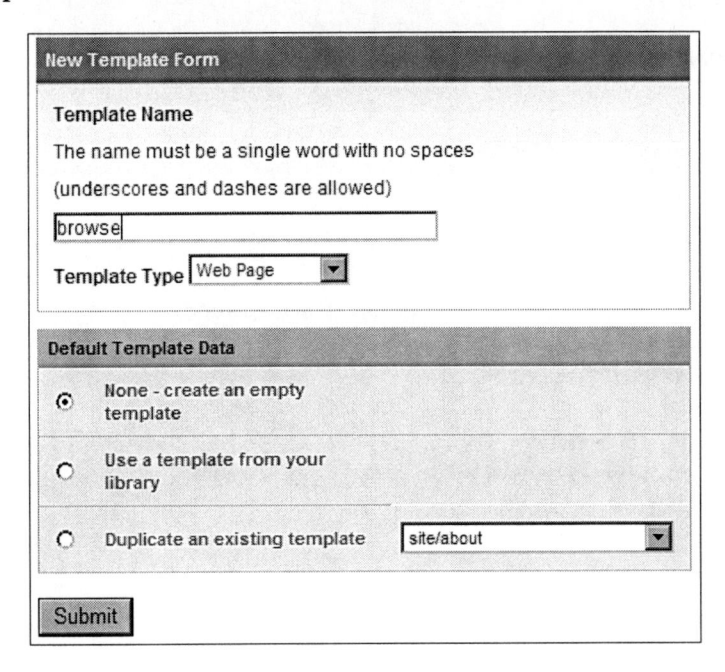

2. Open the `toastgallery/browse` template and type in the following code. This is very similar to our starting template for the single-entry page, but instead of using the `exp:gallery:entries` to retrieve the image name based on the URL, we use the `exp:gallery:category_name` tag to retrieve the category name, also based on the URL. Typically, a URL would be http://localhost/toastgallery/browse/C1 (or http://www.example.com/toastgallery/browse/C1), where C1 indicates the category. If someone chooses to visit http://localhost/toastgallery/browse without the category identifier, all the photos are displayed. Therefore, the `segment_3` logic is used to check for a missing `segment_3` (the C1 part of the URL) and display a different heading in that instance.

```
{assign_variable:gallery_name="toastphotos"}
{assign_variable:my_template_group="toastgallery"}
{assign_variable:my_site_wide_templates="toast"}
<!DOCTYPE html PUBLIC "-//W3C//DTD XHTML 1.0 Strict//EN"
"http://www.w3.org/TR/xhtml1/DTD/xhtml1-strict.dtd">
<html xmlns="http://www.w3.org/1999/xhtml">
  <head>
    <title>Toast for Sale: Toast Gallery{exp:gallery:
    category_name} - {category}{/exp:gallery:
                    category_name}</title>
    <link rel='stylesheet' type='text/css' media='all'
    href='{path={my_site_wide_templates}/toast_css}' />
    <style type='text/css' media='screen'>@import"{path=
        {my_site_wide_templates}/toast_css}";</style>
    <meta http-equiv="content-type" content="text/html;
                    charset=UTF-8" />
  </head>
  <body>
    <div id="header">
      <h1>Toast for Sale!</h1>
      {exp:gallery:category_name}<h2>{category}</h2>{/exp:gallery:
                                            category_name}
      {if segment_3 == ""}<h2>All Photos</h2>{/if}
    </div>
    <div id="content">
    </div>
    <div id="menu">
      {embed={my_site_wide_templates}/.menu}
    </div>
  </body>
</html>
```

3. Go to a category page directly (for example, `http://localhost/toastgallery/category/C1/` or `http://www.example.com/toastgallery/category/C1`), or by clicking on the category breadcrumb on the single-entry page. Notice how the page title and the page heading both reflect the category name.

> The Photo Gallery module, unlike the main weblog module in ExpressionEngine, does not support using category names in the URLs—the category ID (for example, C1) must be used instead.

4. Next, we are going to create a subheading on the page that will act as a breadcrumb, allowing the visitor to click to go back to the main navigation page. Add the following code inside the `<div id="content">` section:

```
<div id="content">
  <h3><a href="{path=toastgallery}">Toast Gallery</a>{exp:gallery:
  category_name} <b>&#8250;</b> {category}
              {/exp:gallery:category_name}</h3>
</div>
```

Creating a Photo Gallery

5. Now let us display the photos. We are going to display the photos inside our `contentinner` style. this will put a light tan box around our photo collection. We will then use the `exp:gallery:entries` tag to display our photos, just like we did for the single-entry page. ExpressionEngine determines that we want to display the photos of a specific category automatically from the URL of the page. As different categories have different numbers of photos, the `columns="2"` and `rows="3"` parameters indicate how many photos should be displayed per page and how they should be laid out. We don't have much space across our page, so we are limiting ourselves to two photos across.

   The code we are using to display the table is very similar to the code we saw when building the calendar in the previous chapter. We have a table, with each row containing a certain number of photos. As the number of rows could vary, we use the `{entries}` and `{row}` tag to loop through each row of photos. The `{row_start}`, `{row}`, and `{row_end}` define what we want each row to contain. In our case, we are saying that we want each row of photos to start with `<tr>`, have cells with the image and the corresponding image title, and then end in `</tr>`.

```
<div id="content">
  <h3><a href="{path=toastgallery}">Toast Gallery</a>{exp:gallery:
  category_name} <b>&#8250;</b> {c ategory}
              {/exp:gallery:category_name}</h3>
{exp:gallery:entries gallery="{gallery_name}"  orderby="date"
        sort="desc" columns="2" rows="3" log_views="off"}
    <div class="contentinner">
      <table cellpadding="6" cellspacing="1" border="0"
                                             width="99%">
        {entries}
          {row_start}<tr>{/row_start}
          {row}
            <td>
              <a href="{id_path=toastgallery/photo}"><img
              src="{thumb_url}" border="0" title="{title}" /></a>
              <br />
              <div>{title}</div>
            </td>
          {/row}
```

[272]

```
            {row_end}</tr>{/row_end}
         {/entries}
       </table>
     </div>
   {/exp:gallery:entries}
</div>
```

[Screenshot: Toast Gallery › Spring — showing four photos labeled "Waterfall", "A Bridge in the Mist", "Another Spring Flower", and "Spring Flower"]

6. We have defined three rows and two columns of photos, allowing six photos per page. What happens if a category has more than six photos per page? We need to spread out the photos over multiple pages, and provide links so that the visitor can move between the pages easily. In fact, ExpressionEngine automatically spreads the photos across multiple pages, so all we need to do is add ExpressionEngine tags to provide the links. To do this, let us use the `footnote` style. Add the following code after the table but before our closing `exp:gallery:entries` tag:

```
      </table>
    </div>
    {paginate}
      <div class="footnote">
        <span>Page {current_page} of {total_pages} pages</span>
        <br />
        {pagination_links}
      </div>
    {/paginate}
  {/exp:gallery:entries}
</div>
```

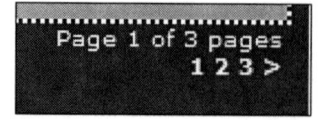

> If there are less than six photos in a single category, the links to other pages will not be visible. However, there will still be a message saying **Page 1 of 1 pages**. An alternative to pagination is to allow more photos per page—by expanding either the number of rows or the number of columns. To make this work with our site design, we would need to shrink the size of each individual thumbnail.

7. As a final step to make browsing our galleries as easy as possible, we are going to include the drop-down box that allows visitors to switch between categories without going back to the main category menu. Add the following code after the `div class="contentinner"` but before the `table` tag. This code uses the `exp:gallery:category_list` tag to display a list of every category we have. This list is then combined into a HTML drop-down box, complete with hyperlinks.

```
<div class="contentinner">
  <form>
    <select name="URL" onChange="window.location=this.options
                                 [this.selectedIndex].value">
      <option value=" ">Category Jump Navigation</option>
      {exp:gallery:category_list gallery="{gallery_name}"}
```

```
        <option value="{category_path=toastgallery/browse}
                                ">{category_name}</option>
    {/exp:gallery:category_list}
  </select>
</form>
    <table class="tableBorder" cellpadding="6" cellspacing="1"
                                    border="0" width="99%">
```

We now have both our single-entry page and our category navigation page redesigned. Now all we need to do is redesign our main index page so that it is more consistent with our overall site design.

Create the Main Index Page

The index page is the main jumping off point for visitors to our photo gallery. They are presented with a list of categories to choose from. In the original design, the categories are listed in a table, and underneath are eight random images. Also in the table next to each category were statistics regarding number of images, number of comments, number of views, and last file upload.

These statistics are going to be fairly meaningless to the average visitor trying to choose a category. So rather than doing this, we are going to display our categories as a list, and display a sample of photos from each category.

Unlike the previous two templates that we could create from scratch, we are going to modify the existing `index` template.

Backup the Existing Index Template

First, as we are modifying a template that was auto-generated, let us back up the existing gallery index template.

1. In the ExpressionEngine control panel, click on **Templates**. Then select the `toastgallery` template group, and select to edit the `index` template of that group (click on the name `index`).

2. Select all the text in the main white box where we type our template code. Expand the **Template Notes** section and do a cut-and-paste. Cut all the code from the main template and paste it into the notes section.

> The Template Notes section is a scratch-pad where we can write anything we want about the template, and it is saved with the template. What we put in the notes section does not appear anywhere else on our site.

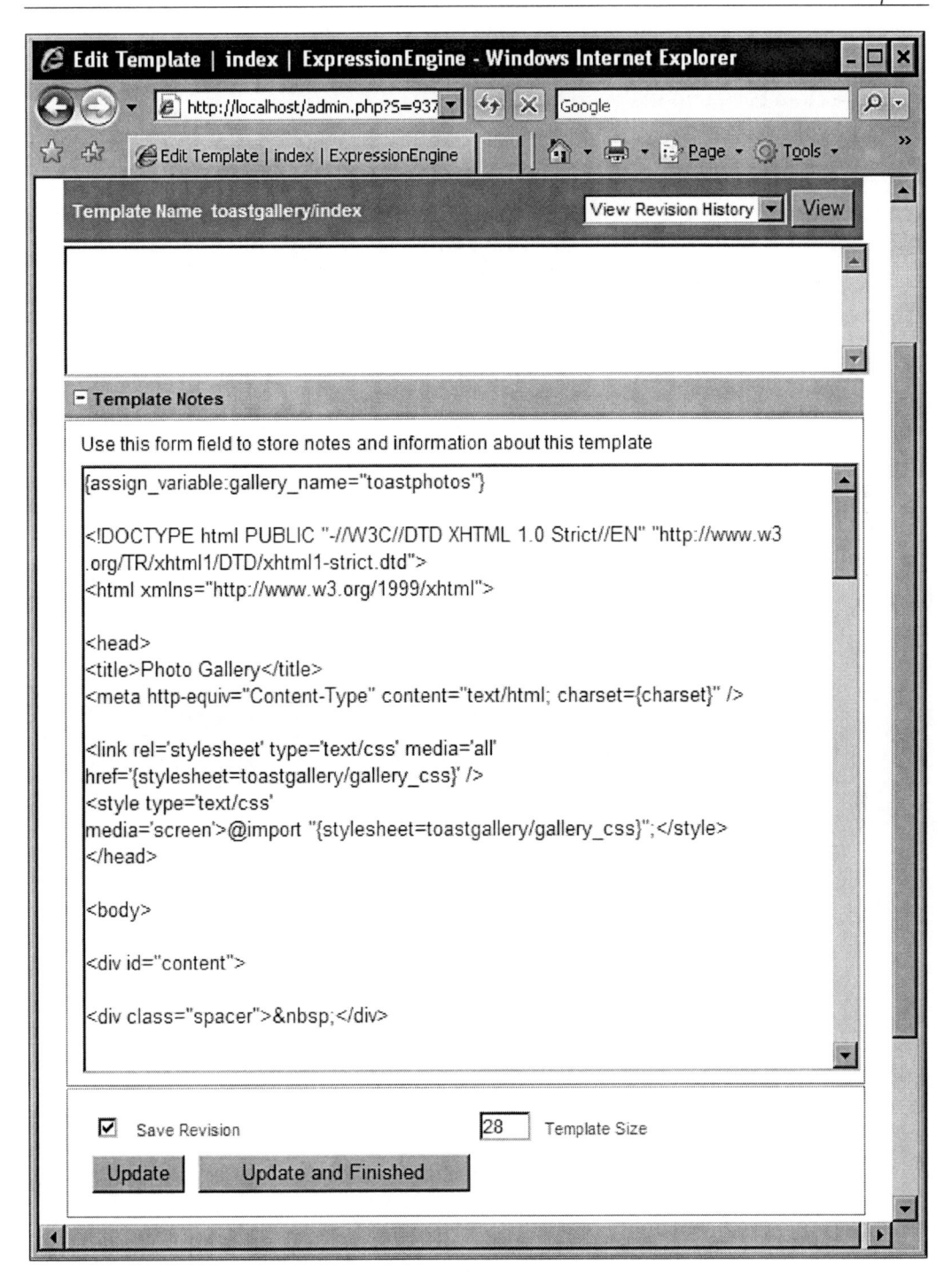

Template Name toastgallery/index

Template Notes

Use this form field to store notes and information about this template

```
{assign_variable:gallery_name="toastphotos"}

<!DOCTYPE html PUBLIC "-//W3C//DTD XHTML 1.0 Strict//EN" "http://www.w3.org/TR/xhtml1/DTD/xhtml1-strict.dtd">
<html xmlns="http://www.w3.org/1999/xhtml">

<head>
<title>Photo Gallery</title>
<meta http-equiv="Content-Type" content="text/html; charset={charset}" />

<link rel='stylesheet' type='text/css' media='all' href='{stylesheet=toastgallery/gallery_css}' />
<style type='text/css' media='screen'>@import "{stylesheet=toastgallery/gallery_css}";</style>
</head>

<body>

<div id="content">

<div class="spacer"> </div>
```

☑ Save Revision   28   Template Size

[Update]   [Update and Finished]

3. Now hit **Update**. The template should now appear blank, but if we need access to what it used to look like, we can always copy the Template Notes section back into the main template.

Create the Main Page for Our Photo Gallery

Now let's change our template so that we are displaying a list of the categories along with their descriptions, which are hyperlinked to the corresponding category page.

1. Still in the `index` template of the `toastgallery` template group, type the following. This will place our normal header and our normal menu on the page, but nothing else.

```
{assign_variable:gallery_name="toastphotos"}
{assign_variable:my_template_group="toastgallery"}
{assign_variable:my_site_wide_templates="toast"}
<!DOCTYPE html PUBLIC "-//W3C//DTD XHTML 1.0 Strict//EN"
"http://www.w3.org/TR/xhtml1/DTD/xhtml1-strict.dtd">
<html xmlns="http://www.w3.org/1999/xhtml">
  <head>
    <title>Toast for Sale: Toast Gallery</title>
    <link rel='stylesheet' type='text/css' media='all'
    href='{path={my_site_wide_templates}/toast_css}' />
    <style type='text/css' media='screen'>@import"{path=
        {my_site_wide_templates}/toast_css}";</style>
    <meta http-equiv="content-type" content="text/html;
                                    charset=UTF-8" />
  </head>
  <body>
    <div id="header">
      <h1>Toast for Sale!</h1>
      <h2>Toast Gallery</h2>
    </div>
    <div id="content">
    </div>
    <div id="menu">
      {embed={my_site_wide_templates}/.menu}
    </div>
  </body>
</html>
```

2. Next, we will display a list of the categories that we have. We are going to display the list in a table, with each category name in the h3 heading style. The code we are using is very similar to the code in the browse template. We have a table, with each row representing a different category. As the number of categories could vary, we use the {category_row} and {row} tag to loop through each category we defined, and display the category heading (using the {category} tag). Type in the following code:

Creating a Photo Gallery

```
<div id="content">
  {exp:gallery:categories gallery="{gallery_name}"}
    <table cellspacing="50">
      {category_row}
        {row}
          <tr>
            <td>
              <h3>{category}</h3>
            </td>
          </tr>
        {/row}
      {/category_row}
    </table>
  {/exp:gallery:categories}
</div>
```

Spring

Photos of spring

Summer

Photos of summer

Autumn

Photos of autumn

Winter

Photos of winter

3. Next up, let us make these category headings hyperlinks so that when we click on them we are taken to the relevant category page. Change the following line to add the highlighted code. Note that `toastgallery` may need to be changed to the name of the photo gallery your site is using.

```
<td>
  <h3><a href="{category_path=toastgallery/browse}" title="Jump to
                                    {category}">{category}</a></h3>
</td>
```

4. Now let us add a description underneath the category name. We will use the {category_description} tag to grab the description that was created when we created our categories. Add the following code:

```
<td>
   <h3><a href="{category_path=toastgallery/browse}" title="Jump to {category}">{category}</a></h3>
   <br />
   <i>{category_description}</i>
</td>
```

5. Now we are going to add the photo to the right of each category. We are going to display a random photo from each category, so the page looks different at each visit. We are going to use the thumbnail version of the image by using the code `src="{thumb_url}"`. The image is hyperlinked to the category page in the same way that our h3 heading was in the last example. Add the following code:

```
<tr>
   <td>
      <h3><a href="{category_path=toastgallery/browse}" title="Jump to {category}">{category}</a></h3>
      <br />
      <i>{category_description}</i>
   </td>
   <td>
      {exp:gallery:entries gallery="{gallery_name}" orderby="random" category="{category_id}" log_views="off"}
         <a href="{category_path=toastgallery/browse}"><img src="{thumb_url}" alt="{title}" title="{title}" border="0" /></a>
```

[281]

Creating a Photo Gallery

```
    {/exp:gallery:entries}
  </td>
</tr>
```

> This code is a little unusual within the `exp:gallery:categories` tag. Typically, we cannot display images inside this tag—only information about the category (such as the description, number of files and number of views). The `exp:gallery:entries` tag is the tag used to display images in a photo gallery. By embedding it within the `categories` tag with the parameter `category="{category_id}"`, we allow photos to be displayed but restrict the photos to the corresponding category. Without this parameter, we could display photos, but the photos would be from any category.

We have now completed the main navigation page for our photo gallery, and with that, our photo gallery is complete. We've integrated the pages into our site's existing look and feel, and changed each page so that we use less templates but each template has more functionality.

Next, we will discuss some of the fancier features of the ExpressionEngine photo gallery.

In the meantime, many of the default `toastgallery` templates are not being used (`category`, `comments`, `comment_preview`, `gallery_css`, `image_full`, `image_med`, and `smileys`). In most of these cases, we replicated the functionality of these templates inside the three templates we do use, for example, we do not have separate templates for comments because they are built into our single-entry page. After thoroughly testing our photo gallery to be sure it is working in the way we need it to, it is safe to delete these excess templates.

Advanced Photo Gallery Features

Now that we have gone through the process of creating a photo gallery, uploading images and creating the corresponding templates, it is a good time to discuss some of the more advanced features of the ExpressionEngine photo gallery module.

Batch Uploads

As anyone with a digital camera can attest, sometimes we might have quite a number of images to upload at any one time. In this case, rather than uploading each image one at a time as we did earlier in the chapter, we can take advantage of a batch upload. Essentially, we FTP all our photos into a folder on our web server, and then process them altogether.

In order to take advantage of this feature, we must first define the preferences.

1. In the ExpressionEngine control panel, select **Modules**, then the **Photo Gallery** module and the **toastgallery** photo gallery. Then select **Preferences** from the menu and expand the **Batch Processing Preferences**.

2. Define a batch processing folder and the corresponding server path and URL to that folder. For our purposes, we are going to create the following folder in XAMPP: `C:\xampp\htdocs\images\photos\toast\batch` (this path will be different depending on the web server or if you are using MAMP for the Mac). Hit **Update**.

Batch Processing Preferences	
Batch Processing Folder	C:\xampp\htdocs\images\photos\toast\batch
Server Path to Batch Folder	C:/xampp/htdocs/images/photos/toast/batch/
Full URL to Batch Directory	http://localhost/images/photos/toast/batch/

Creating a Photo Gallery

3. Next, upload some images into the batch folder via FTP.
4. Select **Batch Entries** from the top photo gallery menu. Now, rather than having to browse to each image on your computer, the image is already loaded and a default entry title is suggested. Make any necessary changes or additions to the fields and hit **Submit This Entry** to quickly submit the new image.

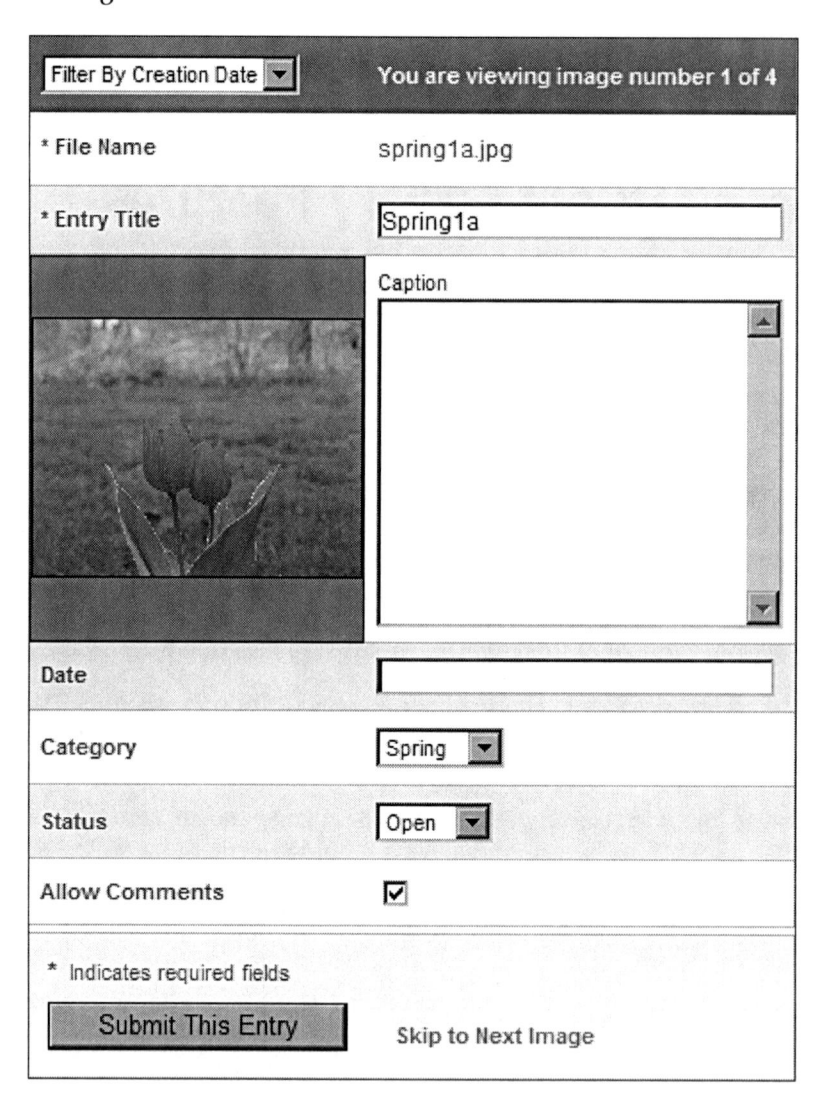

Image Editing

Another feature of ExpressionEngine is the ability to edit photos after they have been uploaded. Photos can be cropped, resized, and rotated after uploading.

1. Select **Toolbox** from the photo gallery menu, select the photo to be edited from the drop-down box, and then select a tool.

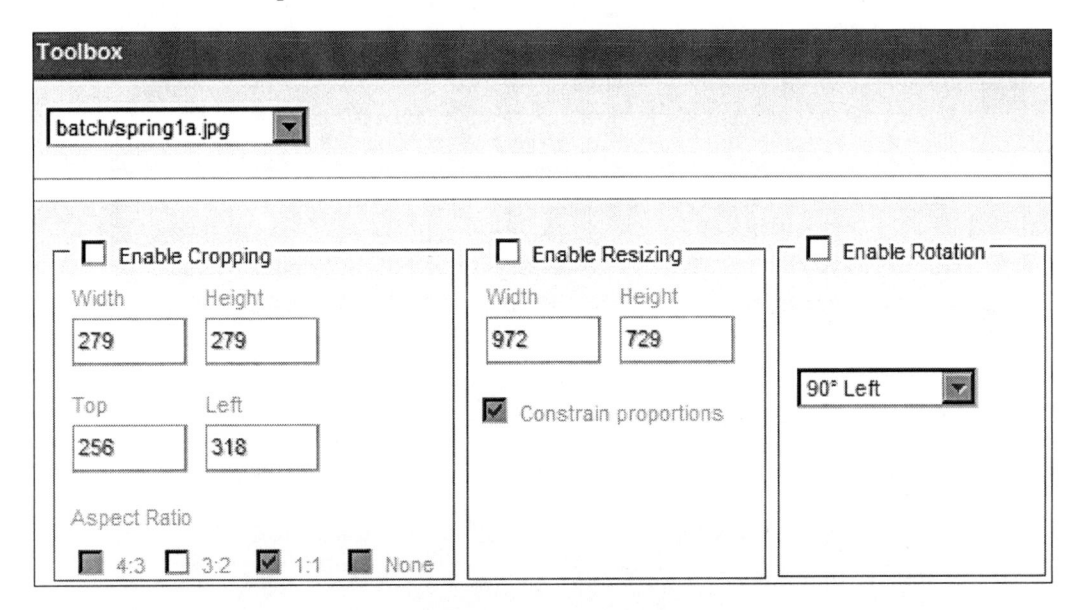

2. If, for example, we wanted to crop an image, we would first select the **Enable Cropping** option. We then drag the rectangle over the picture until the part of the picture we want is framed. (Use the shift key to resize the rectangle).

3. Once the rectangle is placed, underneath the image there are a few options. We can overwrite the original image or change the name to create a copy. We can choose an image quality (where **100** is no loss in quality), and we can decide to update the thumbnails or not. Once these options have been selected, hit **Modify the Image** to create the updates.

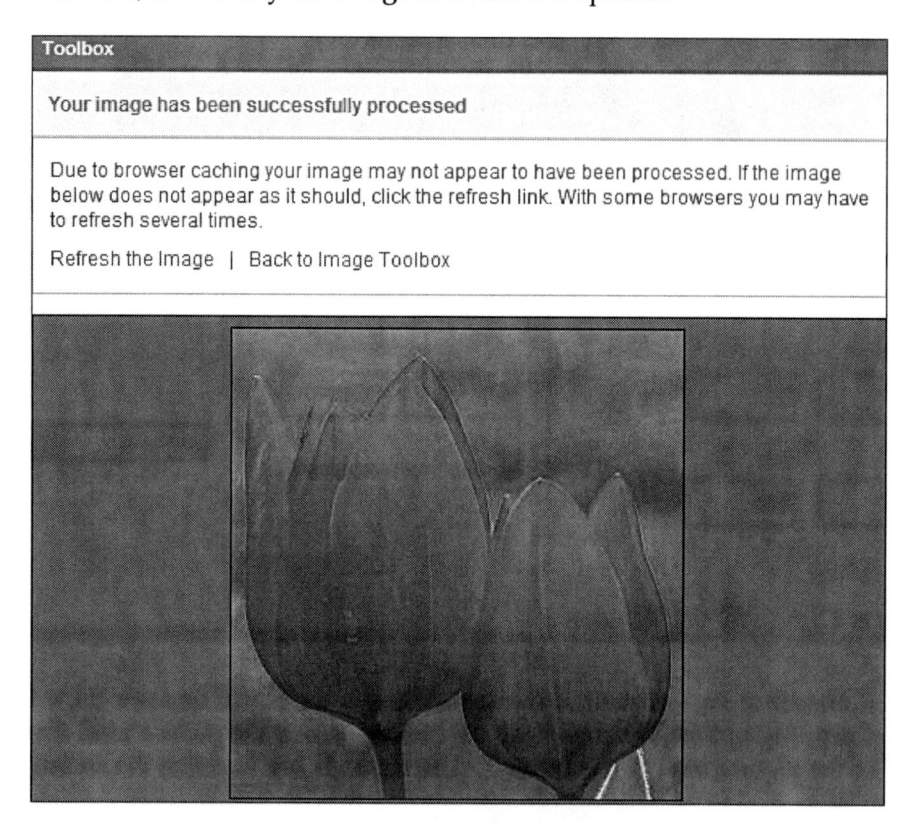

Put a Watermark on Our Images

The ExpressionEngine photo gallery comes with a built-in feature that automatically puts a watermark on each of our images to discourage others from copying and/or stealing them. We can have either an image-based or a text-based watermark—either way we can completely control how the watermark looks. As an example, we are going to use a text-based watermark that places the words 'Toast For Sale!' over each of our images.

> Please note that watermarks are only applied to new images being uploaded—we cannot apply a watermark to existing images as the watermark is actually made part of the image when the image is uploaded.

Chapter 8

1. The first step in defining a watermark is to set up the preferences. Select **Preferences** from the photo gallery menu and then select **Watermarking Preferences**.
2. Select **Text Version** and a set of previously hidden options will appear. For the most part, we are going to accept the defaults (for example, font color, font size, and so on). However, we are going to place the watermark in the middle-center of our images, and we are going to **Apply Watermark to Medium Sized Images**. We will use **Watermark Text** of **Toast for Sale**.

Watermarking Preferences	
Enable Watermarking	○ Disabled ● Text Version ○ Graphic Version
Watermark Alignment	Middle ▼ Center ▼
Padding	10 ▼
Horizontal Offset	0
Vertical Offset	0
Apply Watermark to Thumbnails	Yes ○ No ●
Apply Watermark to Medium Sized Images	Yes ● No ○
Watermark Text	Toast for Sale
Use True Type Font	Yes ● No ○
Font	Texb ▼
Font Size	16
Text Color	#ffff00
Enable Dropshadow	Yes ● No ○
Dropshadow Distance	1 ▼
Dropshadow Color	#999999
Server Path to Test Image The button below allows you to test your watermark preferences without leaving this page. In order to do so you must set the server path to a test image.	./themes/cp_global_images/watermark_test.jpg

[287]

Creating a Photo Gallery

3. If desired, we can use the option to test our watermark settings to see how our watermark looks. After doing this, hit **Update**. Now any new photos that are uploaded will have this watermark embedded into the image.

Custom Fields

Another useful feature with the ExpressionEngine photo gallery is custom fields. Although ExpressionEngine captures some data for each photo that is made available through the `exp:gallery:entries` tag (for example, the title, the caption, the number of views), there may be something specific you wish to capture about each image in your photo gallery beyond what ExpressionEngine offers.

In order to accomplish this, the photo gallery module has built-in custom fields that can be defined in any way we wish. For example, if we wanted to capture the location of a photo, or who is in the photo, or what camera the photo was taken with, or what camera settings were used, we can set up a custom field, capture that data when our photos are uploaded, and display that data on our single-entry page.

1. In the Photo Gallery preferences, select **Custom Entry Field Preferences**, and select to **Enable Custom Field one**. For this example, we will use a custom **Field Name** of **Location** with a text formatting of **Auto
. The **Field Type will be **Text Input**.

[288]

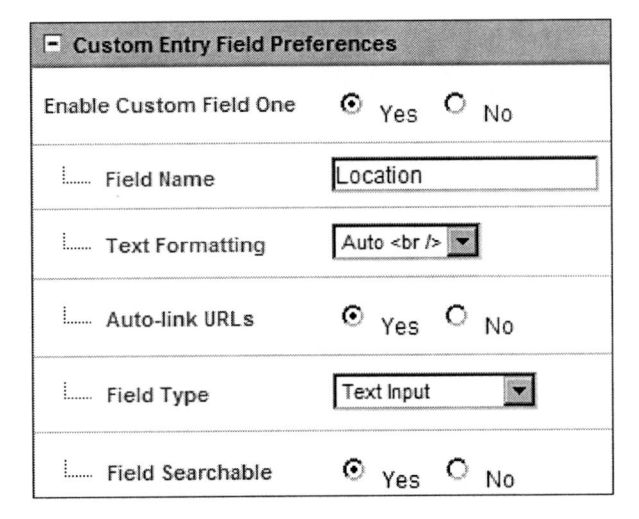

2. Now, select **View Entries** from the photo gallery module menu, and drill-down to the photo level. We can see that the new field has now been added to the form. Fill in the **Location** where the photo was taken, in this case **Colorado Springs, CO**.

3. Before this new field will appear on our website, we have to edit our template. Edit the `h3` heading in the `toastgallery/photo` template to include the location after the title of the photo. Notice how the custom field is still called {custom_field_one} and not {location}.

   ```
   <h3><a href="{path=toastgallery}">Toast
   Gallery</a> <b>&#8250;</b> {exp:gallery:entries
   gallery="{gallery_name}" limit="1" log_views="off"}<a
   href="{category_path=toastgallery/browse}">{category}</
   a> <b>&#8250;</b> {title} ({custom_field_one}){/exp:
   gallery:entries}</h3>
   ```

4. Now view a photo that we know has a location defined. we should see the location after the title of the photo, as in the following screenshot.

Creating a Photo Gallery without the Photo Gallery Module

With all the flexibility that is built into the photo gallery module, it can be tempting to think that we have to use the photo gallery module in order to create a photo gallery in ExpressionEngine. Not so!

Some ExpressionEngine users choose to use the default weblog module to build a photo gallery (the same module we used to create our product showcase). The main argument for doing this is flexibility. Whereas the photo gallery has six custom fields, the weblog module offers many more, and you can take advantage of all the advanced features available in the weblog module (related entries, custom entry statuses, standalone entry forms, more granular membership control).

Finally, in the photo gallery module URLs are not quite as user-friendly (photos and categories have numbers whereas in the weblog module it is possible to use category URL titles in links, rather than the category ID number).

However, choosing not to use the photo gallery module means many of the advanced features of the photo gallery module, such as watermarking, batch uploads, and image editing are not available. You may also find yourself spending a lot of time trying to accomplish a task (such as a thumbnail gallery) that the photo gallery module handles automatically.

Exercises

1. In this chapter, we did not discuss subcategories and how to distinguish between categories and subcategories on our thumbnail browse page. Create some subcategories and upload photos to them, then using the ExpressionEngine documentation at `http://expressionengine.com/docs/modules/gallery/index.html` as your guide, see if you can distinguish between categories and subcategories on your site.

2. ExpressionEngine tracks the number of times an image is viewed through the `exp:gallery:entries` tag. Using a conditional statement, indicate on the `browse` template which photos are **hot** photos, based on either the number of views or the number of comments.

Summary

In this chapter:

- We installed the photo gallery module, set some initial preferences, and uploaded photos.
- We reviewed the out of the box configuration for the photo gallery.
- We created our own templates for a photo gallery that better integrated into our existing site design than the default templates. We created a single-entry page where one photo was showcased, as well as a category browsing page where all the photos in a category could be reviewed. We also created a main index page to give visitors a taste of the photos in each gallery.
- We reviewed all the more advanced features of the photo gallery module, such as watermarking and built-in image editing.
- We discussed the pros and cons of using the photo gallery module versus the weblog module when building a photo gallery.

The photo gallery module is a feature-rich, well-built module that comes free with the personal and commercial versions of ExpressionEngine. It balances ease-of-use against flexibility, allowing even a beginner to quickly create a photo gallery and start uploading photos, but allowing a more experienced user to design a photo gallery that is unique to them.

This wraps up most of our step-by-step approach to ExpressionEngine. In the next chapter, we will be discussing some of the more advanced features of ExpressionEngine that can take a site from looking good to great.

9
Other Modules and Functionality

So far, this book has taken a step-by-step approach to implementing the most popular modules in ExpressionEngine. Many of the same basic skills have been used time and again—creating a new weblog, setting up custom fields, configuring our preferences, and posting entries to the new weblog. We have also covered using templates to merge a normal HTML and CSS page with ExpressionEngine tags that control what is displayed and which member groups can see it.

Breaking away from a step-by-step approach, this chapter looks at a general overview of modules and functionality that go beyond what we have discussed this far. Not all these features are appropriate for every site, and many of them can be used in different ways for different sites.

We will discuss how to:

- Find new modules and plug-ins
- Create a discussion forum
- Use Simple Commerce to integrate PayPal into ExpressionEngine in order to sell goods
- Start a wiki

We will also look at how to:

- Add search functionality to our site
- Use status groups to create workflows
- Use categories to organize our entries

- Use related entries in a weblog
- Back up our site and restore it
- Upgrade ExpressionEngine when new versions and builds are released

The goal of this chapter is to spark your imagination and encourage you to take advantage of online resources (including the official ExpressionEngine documentation at http://www.expressionengine.com/docs/) to achieve what you need to achieve on your website.

ExpressionEngine Add-Ons

Although not open-source software, ExpressionEngine has many ways in which both EllisLab and members of the ExpressionEngine community can add to or extend the functionality of ExpressionEngine.

Finding and Managing Add-Ons

ExpressionEngine can be customized through modules, plug-ins, and extensions. Add-ons can be developed either by EllisLab (first-party license) or by third parties. Add-ons can be browsed and downloaded at http://expressionengine.com/downloads/addons/.

Modules

ExpressionEngine itself is modular—a module is a feature that stands on its own. One of the benefits of a modular design is that we can pick and choose modules that are of interest to us, and ignore modules that are not. Already in this book we have used several modules (the weblog module, the member module, the comment module, and the photo gallery module). Many of the available modules come pre-installed or ready to install. Modules vary in size and scope.

> Documentation for pre-installed modules can be found at
> http://expressionengine.com/docs/#modules_docs.

Modules are controlled through the Modules tab in the control panel. (Select **Modules** from the main menu). Here, we can install or remove modules, and for some modules (such as the photo gallery) we can enter the configuration screens.

Plug-Ins

Plug-ins are less involved than modules, and so there are a lot more of them. A module has to store data in the ExpressionEngine database (such as our photos or our weblog entries) whereas as a plug-in does not store data in the database (though it may still query the database). A plug-in typically works by creating a new tag that can then be added to templates.

Plug-ins are managed using the Plugin Manager—go to **Admin | Utilities** and select **Plugin Manager** from the main list.

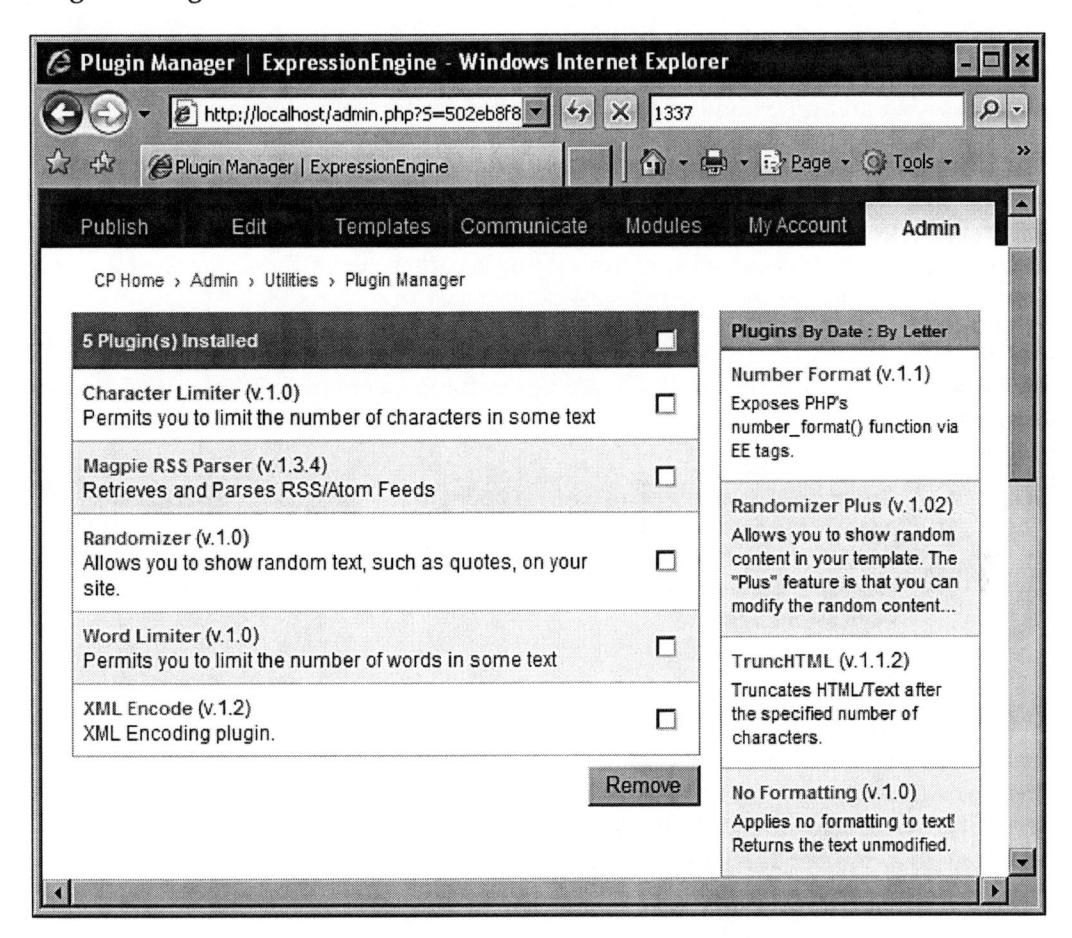

Plug-ins that are already installed are on the left-hand side. Clicking on the title of an installed plug-in will give you instructions on how to use it. A list of available plug-ins is on the right-hand side and can also be browsed at http://expressionengine.com/downloads/addons/category/plugins/.

Extensions

Extensions are a third type of add-on that modifies how ExpressionEngine itself works, for example by changing the Control Panel in some way. Extensions can be found at http://expressionengine.com/downloads/addons/category/extensions/ and are managed through the Extensions Manager (**Admin | Utilities | Extensions Manager**).

The Discussion Forum

The Discussion Forum is a module that can be purchased at the ExpressionEngine Store (https://secure.expressionengine.com/, or select **Buy Now!** from the main ExpressionEngine home page). It requires ExpressionEngine to run.

The Discussion Forum module uses **Forum Boards** to distinguish between unrelated forums. Each forum board has its own preferences and settings, including separate URLs. **Forums** are where visitors can post questions or new discussion threads (called **topics**). Forums can be split into multiple **categories** or there can be one generic category for all the forums.

For example, a forum board for an organization to exchange computer tips and tricks might have categories for software tips and hardware tips. Within the software category, it might have forums for Excel, Word, PowerPoint, and Outlook

> An excellent example of an ExpressionEngine forum board is the forums page on the ExpressionEngine site (http://expressionengine.com/forums). Here, we can not only see how a very active forum is managed, but we can also exchange help and advice on all aspects of ExpressionEngine.

Setting up the Discussion Forum

To install, follow the instructions at http://expressionengine.com/docs/modules/forum/forum_installation.html. The installation is very straightforward: upload files to the web server, set the permissions of key folders, and then go to the **Modules** page inside the control panel and click **Install** (next to the discussion forum).

After installation, the settings for the discussion forum can be found by clicking on **Discussion Forum** in the **Modules** page of the control panel. The only settings that have to be established now are the **General Settings** to set up the first forum board.

General Settings	
Forum Board Label	Computer Tips & Tricks
Forum Board Short Name single word, no spaces	tips
Forum URL	http://localhost/forums/
Forum Triggering Word When this word is encountered in your URL it will display your forum. The word you choose cannot be the name of an existing template group.	forums
Enable Forum Board	Yes ⦿ No ○

Each new discussion forum board contains one category, **Forums**, that contains one forum, **My Forum.** New categories can be created, and new forums within categories can also be created. Each category and forum can have their own permissions and preferences.

Permissions define which member groups can do what in a forum—whether they can post new forum entries, reply to existing forum posts, or whether they can even see the forum.

Preferences define how a particular forum works. Are moderators emailed when there is a new topic or a reply to an existing topic? How many topics display on each page? How many posts display on each page? How long can a posting be? What order do posts display in?

Other Modules and Functionality

It is recommended to define the **Default Permissions** and **Default Preferences** before creating all the categories and forums. This is because the default permissions and preferences apply to all *new* categories and forums. However, to change permissions and preferences for *existing* categories and forums, each forum must be updated individually. On the plus side, this provides enormous flexibility in allowing different settings for each forum. On the down side, it makes it a little more time-consuming to change settings.

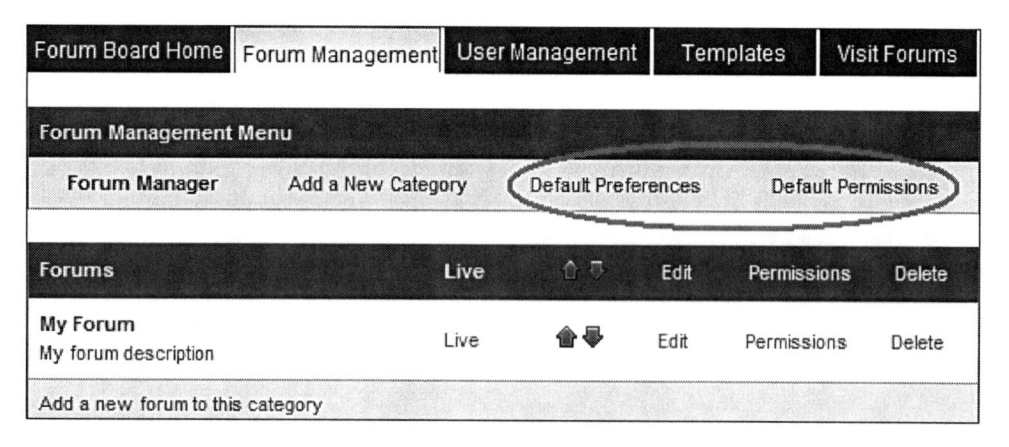

Setting up Users

From the Discussion Forum module, select **User Management** from the main menu. Here, we can define the administrators and moderators of the forum. A **moderator** is assigned on a per-forum basis—each forum can have a different moderator or can share the same moderator. Each moderator can have different permissions, or indeed the same moderator can have different permissions in different forums if desired.

[298]

Chapter 9

An **administrator** applies to the entire forum board—they can essentially do everything that a moderator can do, including banning other users.

The **Member Ranks** section allows us to define custom titles that members can earn based on the number of posts they make.

Forum Board Home	Forum Management	User Management	Templates	Visit Forums

User Management Menu

Administrators	Moderators	**Member Ranks**

Rank Title	Min Posts	Stars	Edit	Delete
Newbie	0	▪	Edit	Delete
Jr. Member	30	▪▪	Edit	Delete
Member	50	▪▪▪	Edit	Delete
Sr. Member	100	▪▪▪▪	Edit	Delete

Add a New Member Rank

Rank Title	
Min Posts	
Stars	

submit

[299]

Other Modules and Functionality

What Does the Discussion Forum Do?

The default URL for the forum board is `http://localhost/forum/` (or `http://www.example.com/forum/`) although we can change this during installation. On the forum board, the forums in each category are separated from each other. In the following screenshot, we have a **General** category with one forum and a **Software** category with more than one forum.

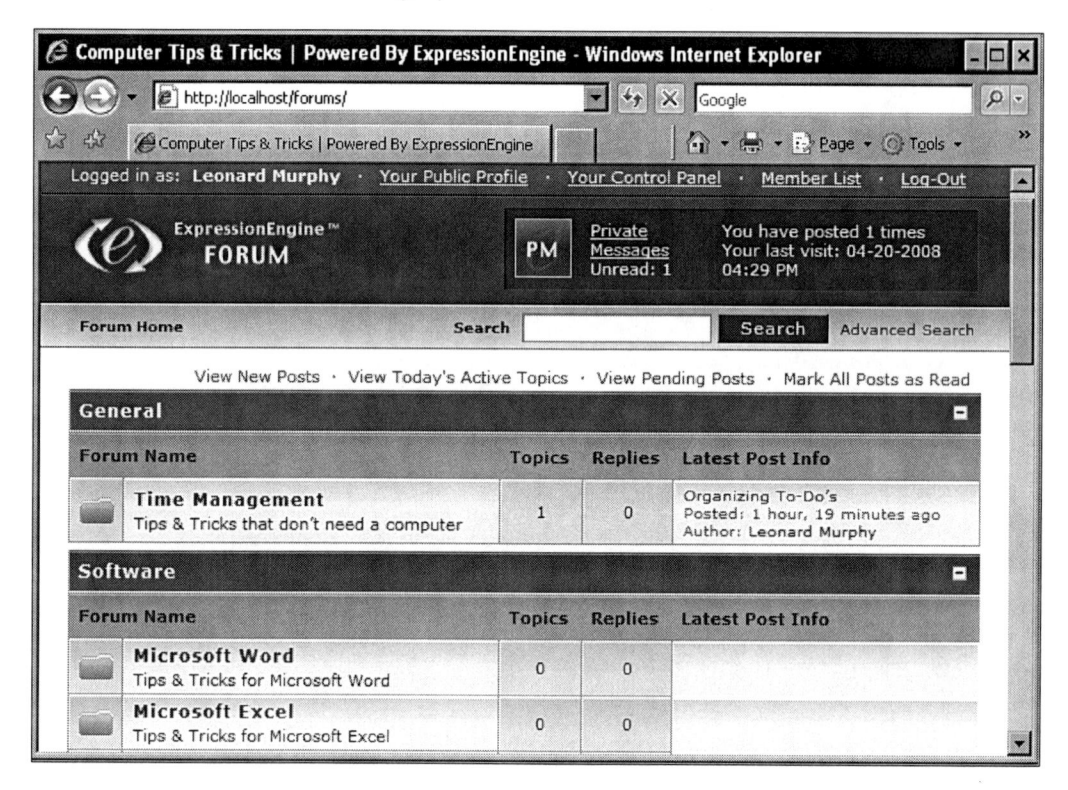

Visitors can select a forum they wish to visit and either post a new topic (if they are logged in) or read an existing topic.

Within a topic, members can reply to posts. Moderators, administrators, and Super Admins can also edit other people's posts, move posts to a different forum (for example, if they were incorrectly categorized), and other administrative tasks.

Another feature of the discussion forum is the ability to change the theme. The discussion forum comes with several themes ready-to-go. At the bottom of each page, underneath the legend, is a drop-down box where visitors can change the theme of the discussion forum.

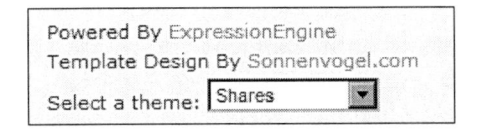

The theme can also be changed in the Discussion Forum module pages. Select **Forum Management**, then **Default Preferences**. The default theme is defined under **Theme Preferences**.

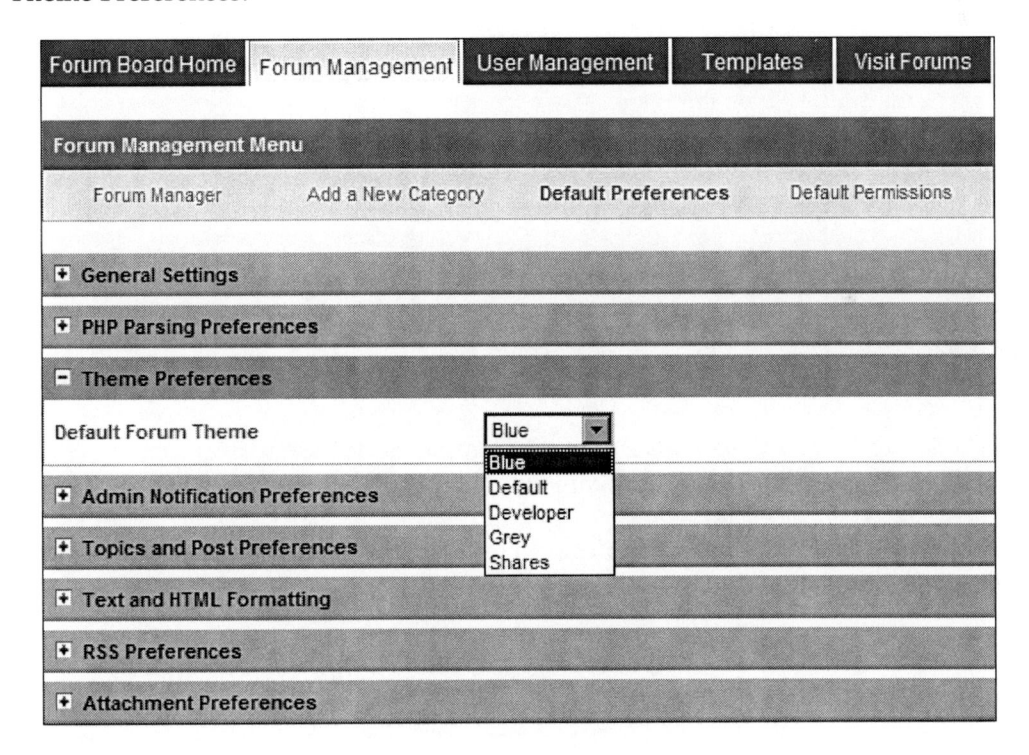

Customizing the Discussion Forum

Like the photo gallery module, the Discussion Forum module comes pre-configured so that it will work right out of the box. This makes it very easy to get up and running.

Other Modules and Functionality

However, unlike the photo gallery, the design is not contained in normal templates but is done as a theme. This means there is a very steep learning curve when trying to match the forums to your own site design. Further, having customized themes makes updates to the Discussion Forum module more complicated—any changes to the default themes in an update have to be reflected in the customized themes.

The first step is to choose a theme to start with and modify it. The developer theme is a good starting point as it is stripped down specifically to make it easier to create new themes.

Next, we should take a backup of the theme we are going to modify, in case we ruin it. Do this in the `themes\forum_themes` folder (`C:\xampp\htdocs\themes\forum_themes` if you are running XAMPP, `/Applications/MAMP/htdocs/themes/forum_themes/` if running MAMP on a Mac). We will name our copy `toast`.

In the Discussion Forum module, select **Templates,** and then select the template we just created (in our case, **Toast**).

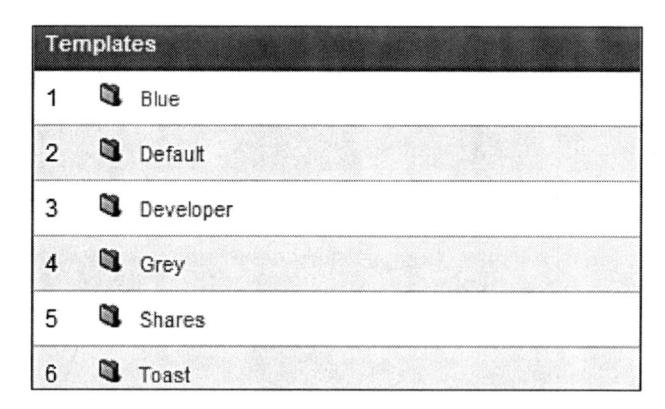

Templates		
1		Blue
2		Default
3		Developer
4		Grey
5		Shares
6		Toast

A list of template headings will appear. The templates are essentially structured by page. For example, the main index page (that appears when we go to `http://localhost/forums/` or `http://www.example.com/forums/`) can be found by clicking on **Index Page Templates** and then selecting the **Forum Main Index Page** template.

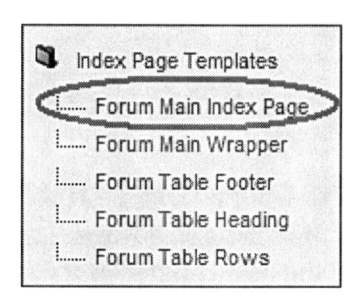

- Index Page Templates
  - Forum Main Index Page
  - Forum Main Wrapper
  - Forum Table Footer
  - Forum Table Heading
  - Forum Table Rows

This template then includes all the templates that make up the index page, including the HTML header and footer and each component that appears on the page.

```
{include:html_header}
{include:top_bar}
{include:page_header}
{include:page_subheader}
<div id="content">
{if logged_in}
    [Code Omitted for Brevity]
{/if}
{include:recent_posts}
{include:main_forum_list}
{include:visitor_stats}
{include:forum_legend}
</div>
{include:html_footer}
```

There are a number of page templates, all ending in page, such as the **Topic Page**, the **Thread Page**, the **Announcements Page**, the **Edit Avatar Page**, and so on.

The best place to start when customizing the discussion forum is by taking a single page (such as the **Forum Main Index Page**), navigating to that page, and viewing the source code. It is then possible to establish where adjustments need to be made, and then to find the corresponding sub-template. It is a very slow process.

> The normal ExpressionEngine tags do not work in the discussion forum theme templates, so adjustments may need to be made. For example, if the right-hand menu bar retrieves data from a weblog, this would need to be changed so that the data is hard-coded or not included at all. Any links made via the {path} variable would need to be altered, so they include the actual path. Any code embedded in sub-templates (for example, toast/.menu) would need to be placed in the main template.

Customizing a Discussion Forum for Our Toast Website

To customize the discussion forum so that the pages have the header and menu that the rest of our toast site has, the rough steps are:

- Adjust the **Global Templates | HTML Header** to include our normal stylesheet (using a direct link rather than the path tag). Also add our normal `<div id="header">` section which puts our logo at the top of the page.

Other Modules and Functionality

- Adjust the **CSS Templates | CSS Stylesheet** to remove CSS styles that conflict with styles from our main stylesheet (for example, `body` and `footer`).
- Adjust the **Global Templates | HTML Footer** to include our normal sidebar menu, immediately before the `</body>` tag. Remember to use direct links rather than the `path` tag.
- Adjust the **CSS Templates | CSS Stylesheet** if there are colors or fonts that need modification.
- Consider moving items that are by default in the **Global Templates | Page Header** template, so that they appear in the side bar instead.
- Review every template page to be sure that it has the correct look and feel.

Each of these steps is fraught with difficulties. Working with the source code of the final page will help to determine when a component is in the wrong `<div>` element (or when there is a missing closing tag, for example), and when the CSS needs to be adjusted.

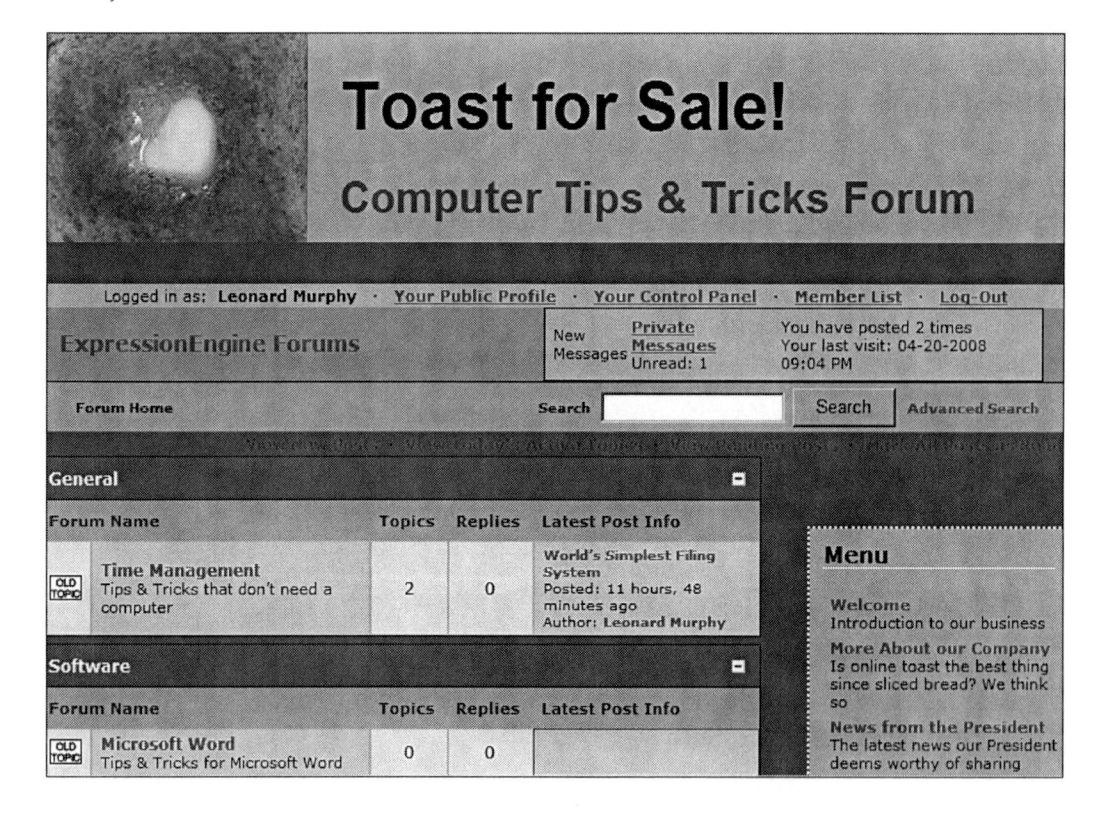

[304]

The Simple Commerce Module

The Simple Commerce module is included with ExpressionEngine (Personal and Commercial versions). It is not a fully-fledged commerce module, but does allow us to create a simple store where purchases can be made through PayPal. All payment information is transferred directly between the visitor and PayPal—at no point does our website or ExpressionEngine handles the payment information.

Essentially, we create a weblog (or adapt an existing weblog) that will showcase our items for sale. The module associates a price with each item, supports payments through Paypal, and supports automatic emails.

> The ExpressionEngine website includes a showcase that features examples of websites that have successfully implemented a module, including this one. Visit http://expressionengine.com/showcase/websites and choose the **Simple Commerce** category to see how other sites are using this module.

Setting Up the Simple Commerce Module

Simple Commerce is included in ExpressionEngine automatically, so we do not need to download any files. To install, simply log into the control panel, select **Modules** from the main menu, scroll down to **Simple Commerce**, and select **Install**. After installation, the Simple Commerce line will turn into a link that we can use to configure the module.

In order to use Simple Commerce effectively, we must register at the PayPal website (http://www.paypal.com/) for a Premier or Business PayPal account. When logged into PayPal, select **Profile** (under **My Account** on the menu). Select **Instant Payment Notification Preferences** (under **Selling Preferences** on the menu) and click **Edit**.

We are prompted for the **Notification URL**, which is provided by ExpressionEngine when we first log into the Simple Commerce module.

> PayPal integration will only work with real website addresses (for example, http://www.example.com), and not with localhost addresses (http://localhost/) used by XAMPP and MAMP.

Other Modules and Functionality

Inside the Simple Commerce module, there are some settings we must define, including our PayPal account. After doing so, hit **Submit**.

> We are also prompted as to whether we wish to encrypt PayPal buttons and links. This requires that our website has OpenSSL support, and that we use public and private keys. See `http://expressionengine.com/docs/modules/simple_commerce/sc_encrypted_payments.html` for more information on how to do this.

We also need to have a weblog setup with products that we can sell. Chapter 5 walked through how to do this on our toast website.

Once you have a weblog with items to sell, go back to the Simple Commerce settings page (**Modules | Simple Commerce**) and select **Add Item**.

Simple Commerce			
Store Items	Add Item	Edit Items	Export Items
Store Purchases	Add Purchase	Edit Purchases	Export Purchases
Store Emails	Add Email Template	Edit Email Templates	--

Put a check mark next to each weblog entry we wish to sell, and then click **Submit** at the bottom of the page to add Items. For each item, we can then enter the regular price and the sales price.

If we have defined email templates, we can choose which email the customer and the administrator receives. (for example, the customer might get a simple thank you email whereas the administrator might need to know where to ship the item to).

> We have to define each email template ourselves (click on **Add Email Template** from the Simple Commerce main page). If no email templates are yet defined, we can edit the item later to add the email templates.

Finally, if we wish, we can change the member group of the person who has made the purchase. This might be useful if, for example, we were selling the site membership. By having areas of our site restricted to a certain member group (for example, Paid Member), we can then automatically give new members access using this module.

> Although Simple Commerce can be used to charge for initial site membership, it requires some manual work (or SQL setup) to handle member renewals.

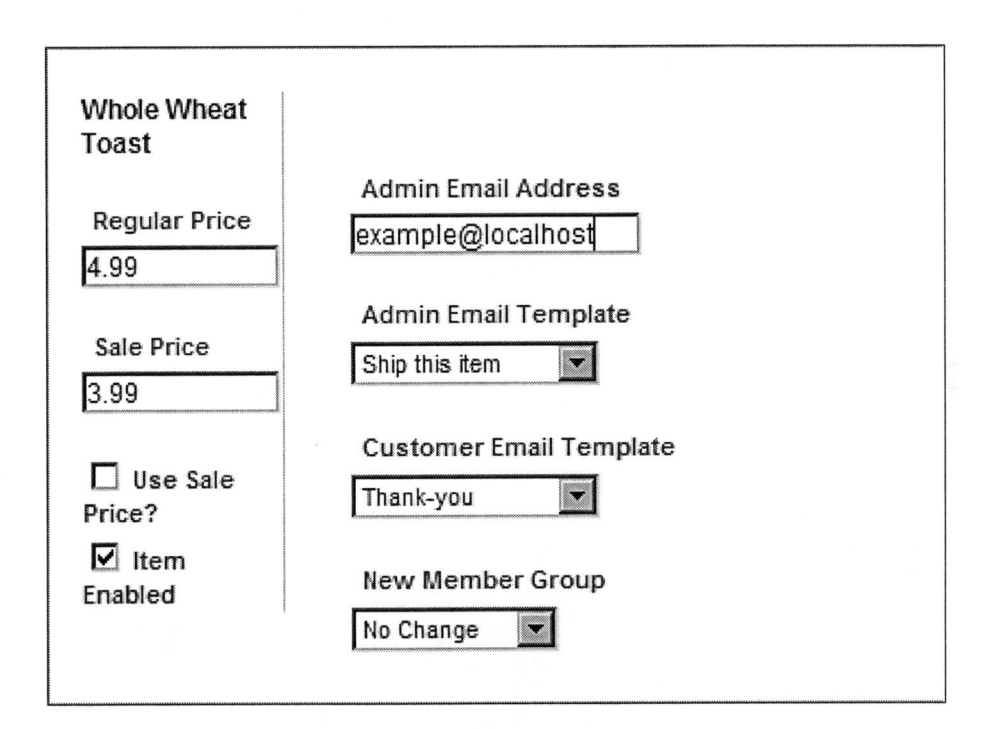

[Screenshot showing Whole Wheat Toast item settings: Regular Price 4.99, Sale Price 3.99, Use Sale Price? unchecked, Item Enabled checked, Admin Email Address example@localhost, Admin Email Template "Ship this item", Customer Email Template "Thank-you", New Member Group "No Change"]

Customizing Simple Commerce for Our Toast Website

The beauty of the Simple Commerce module is that it integrates directly into the existing weblog module. The display of the items for sale can be handled using everything we already know about weblogs and templates.

We have to make one edit to our existing template in order to place the price and shopping cart links on our website (Buy Now, Add to Cart, View Cart). This is outlined in the documentation: `http://expressionengine.com/docs/modules/simple_commerce/sc_purchase.html`.

Other Modules and Functionality

In our `products/index` template, the following code will add the price to each product that is for sale and will add links to purchase the items. Note that each item in the `products` weblog must also be added to Simple Commerce.

```
{exp:weblog:entries weblog="{my_weblog}" limit="1"}
  {exp:simple_commerce:purchase entry_id="{entry_id}"
              success="{my_template_group}/success"
              cancel="{my_template_group}/index"}
    <h3>{title} - only ${if item_use_sale=="y"}{item_sale_
         price}{if:else}{item_regular_price}{/if}</h3>
    <div class="contentinner">
      <div class="innerbox">
        <img src="{toastproducts_photo}" alt="{title}" />
        {toastproducts_description}
      </div>
    </div>
    <h3>Nutritional Information</h3>
    <div class="contentinner">
      <p><strong>Calories per Serving: </strong>{toastproducts
                                              _calories}</p>
      <p><strong>Total Fat: </strong>{toastproducts_fat}</p>
      <p><strong>Sodium: </strong>{toastproducts_sodium}</p>
      <p><strong>Total Carbohydrate: </strong>{toastproducts
                                              _carbs}</p>
      <p><strong>Dietary Fiber: </strong>{toastproducts_fiber}</p>
      <p><strong>Sugars: </strong>{toastproducts_sugars}</p>
      <p><strong>Protein: </strong>{toastproducts_protein}</p>
    </div>
    <p class="footnote"><a href="{buy_now_url}" onclick="window.open
       (this.href);return false;">Buy Now</a> | <a href="{add_to_cart
       _url}" onclick="window.open(this.href);return false;">Add
                to Cart</a> | <a href="{view_cart_url}" onclick="
                     window.open(this.href);return false;">View
                         Cart</a> | <a href="{site_url}{my_
                            template_group}" title="Back
                               to Products">Go back to
                                  all products</a></p>
  {/exp:simple_commerce:purchase}
{/exp:weblog:entries}
```

The `exp:simple_commerce:purchase` associates the weblog entry with the data in Simple Commerce (for example, the price). It also defines the templates to display once a successful purchase has been made, or if a person cancels his order. In our case, we display the `products/success` template (that we would have to create).

In the title, we use a conditional to display either the regular price or the sales price, depending on whether the item is marked as being on sale inside the Simple Commerce module.

In the footnote, we add the shopping cart links.

Whole Wheat Toast - only $4.99

Surveys suggest most people do not get enough whole grain foods in their diet; this is a healthy but tasty way of achieving that goal.

Our toasted whole wheat sandwich bread consists of a single slice of heart-healthy whole wheat sandwich bread, lightly toasted with one tablespoon of salted butter spread on top. For best taste, eat shortly after opening.

Nutritional Information

Calories per Serving: 176
Total Fat: 12g
Sodium: 227mg
Total Carbohydrate: 13g
Dietary Fiber: 2g
Sugars: 1g
Protein: 4g

Buy Now | Add to Cart | View Cart | Go back to all products

Testing the Simple Commerce Module

If we wanted to test that the Simple Commerce module is working without actually taking live payments via PayPal, PayPal supports a development account that can be used to make mock purchases.

The instructions to set up a PayPal developer account and to point ExpressionEngine links to the developer account rather than the live account are located at `http://expressionengine.com/docs/modules/simple_commerce/sc_debug_mode.html`.

Essentially, we sign up for a developer account at `https://developer.paypal.com/`, and create a fictitious PayPal user, complete with fictitious account numbers and credit card information. We then edit the `mod.simple_commerce.php` file in our `system/modules/simple_commerce` folder to set debug mode to `TRUE`.

We can then go through our site, purchasing items using the fictitious PayPal user information to see how it works. Once we are done with testing, we would need to change the debug mode back to point to the live PayPal.

The Wiki Module

A wiki is an area of the website where visitors themselves can edit the content or create new content. One of the most famous wiki's on the web is Wikipedia (`http://www.wikipedia.org/`)—an online encyclopedia that anyone can contribute content to.

At first glance, it can be difficult to see the use for a wiki. However, if we think about it as a collection of documents that can be shared among a group of people of any size, and updated in real time by the same group of people that actually use the content, the business advantages start to become clearer.

Want to hash out a project with a group of people remotely? Rather than creating a word processing document, sending it to five people, and then manually merging the changes, we can create a base plan in a wiki, and have everyone working on the same document.

If this book were a wiki, it could be updated in real time. If a reader finds an error, they could make the correction and it would be immediately shared with all the other readers. If the capabilities of ExpressionEngine changed, a reader could update (or add) a chapter in near real-time, or at least far faster than it would take to publish another edition. The collective knowledge of many people with many different areas of expertise could be combined.

> There is in fact an ExpressionEngine wiki, located at `http://expressionengine.com/wiki/`.

By combining the capabilities of a wiki and the membership capabilities of ExpressionEngine, we have the potential to create a collaborative environment.

The Wiki module is included with ExpressionEngine (Personal and Commercial versions). It is a very easy way to set up a wiki on our website.

Setting up the Wiki

The Wiki module is included in ExpressionEngine automatically, so we do not need to download any files. To install, log into the control panel, select **Modules** from the main menu, scroll down to Wiki, and select **Install**. After installation, the Wiki line will turn into a link that we can use to configure the module.

Going into the Wiki module, there is already a wiki setup by default, called EE Wiki. Click on it to customize the settings.

The full name is visible on our site, and the short name is only used in templates. We are going to rename ours to **Toast Wiki** and **toastwiki**. The **Text Formatting** and **HTML Formatting** can also be defined. If we trust the users of our wiki, and wish to enable file uploads, we can specify where files are uploaded to.

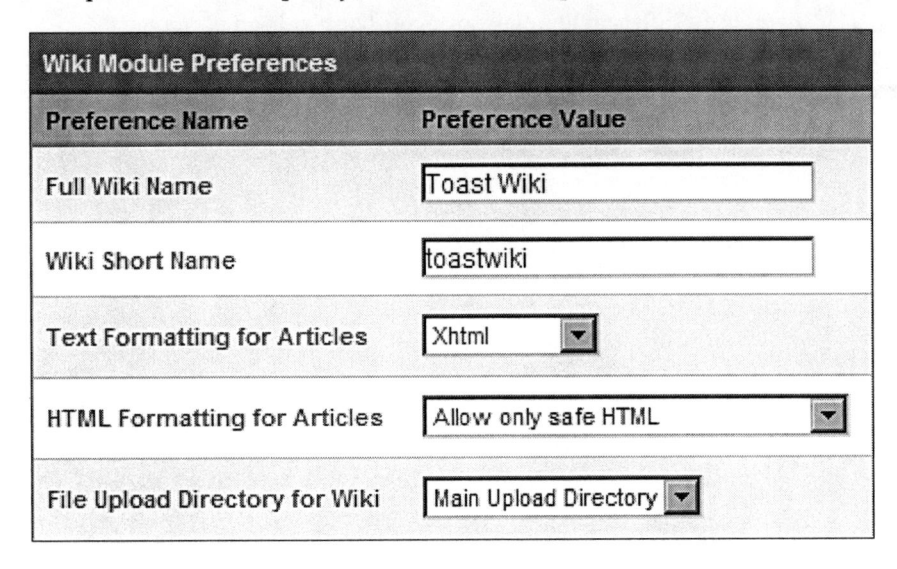

Wiki Module Preferences	
Preference Name	Preference Value
Full Wiki Name	Toast Wiki
Wiki Short Name	toastwiki
Text Formatting for Articles	Xhtml
HTML Formatting for Articles	Allow only safe HTML
File Upload Directory for Wiki	Main Upload Directory

Other Modules and Functionality

> Different file upload directories can be specified on the **File Upload Preferences** page. Select **Admin | Weblog Administration | File Upload Preferences**.

Next, we choose who can administer the wiki and who can use it. Users can add and edit content; administrators can delete content, mark an article as locked (no one can edit it), or mark an article as moderated (meaning users can edit it but an administrator must approve the change before it happens). Hit **Update** when done.

> A namespace allows us to group articles. The main advantage to using a namespace rather than a category is to set different permissions for different users. For example, we may want members of the Project1 member group to be able to add/edit content to the Project1 namespace but not the Project2 namespace.

The final step in creating a wiki is to create a template with the `exp:wiki` tag. For example, create a new template group called `wiki`, and in the `index` template, type:

```
{exp:wiki base_path="wiki/index" wiki="toastwiki" theme="default"}
```

We do not need to wrap this code in any other HTML or ExpressionEngine tags. This line will create the entire wiki.

> If you use a different template group or template name, change the `base_path` parameter accordingly. The `wiki` parameter should be the short name of the wiki. The theme can be either `default` or `azure`.

Now view this template in a browser (http://localhost/wiki or http://www.example.com/wiki).

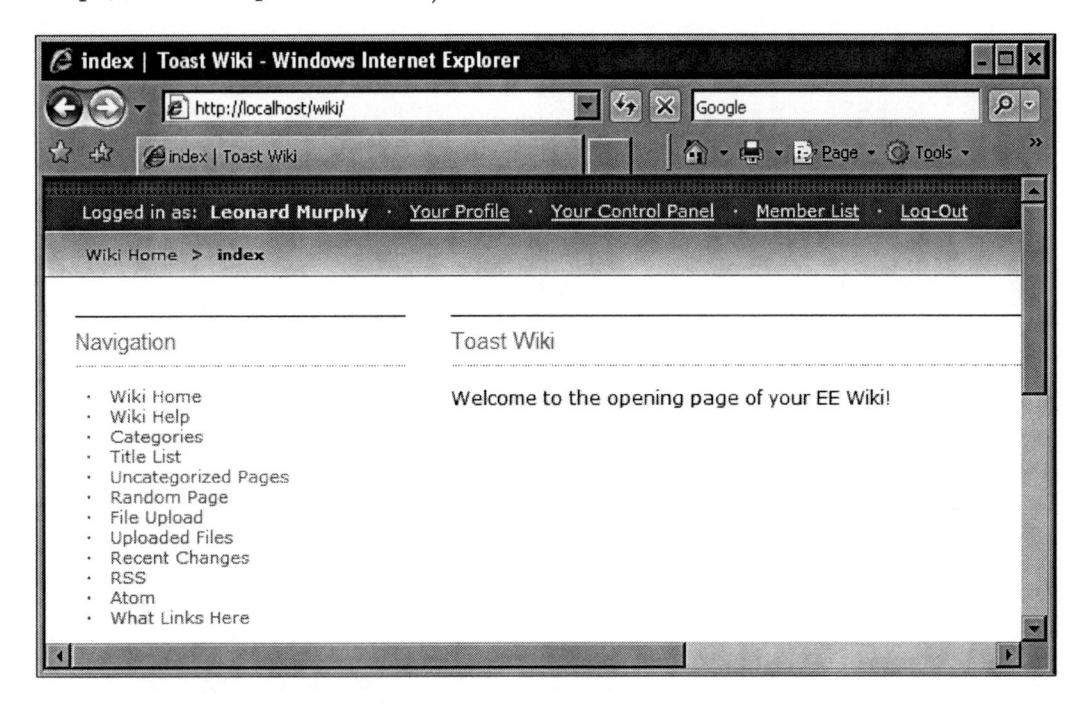

How Does the Wiki Work?

Let us create a wiki for a generic group project. On the first page of the wiki, click **Edit** (at the top-right) to edit the page.

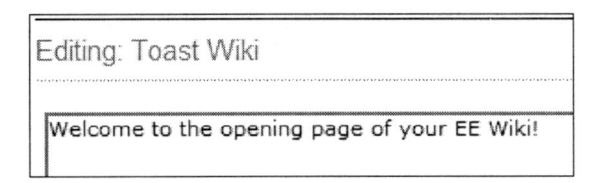

We can type in whatever text we wish. To create a link to a new article, enclose the article in double square brackets. For example,

```
Welcome to our project home page. Our project wiki is split into 4
areas:
[[Project Objectives]] defines the objectives of this project
[[Issues]] describes all issues that need to be addressed
[[Decisions Made]] describes decisions that have been made
Our project status [[Meeting Notes]] are available for all to read.
```

Other Modules and Functionality

In the notes section, we can write a brief description of the change we made. (This will show in the history log). Then hit **Submit**.

> Toast Wiki
>
> Welcome to our project home page. Our project wiki is split into 4 areas:
>
> Project Objectives defines the objectives of this project
> Issues describes all issues that need to be addressed
> Decisions Made describes decisions that have been made
>
> Our project status Meeting Notes are available for all to read.

We can now click any of the links in blue to be brought to the new article and create more pages with more text. More than one page can link to the same article. For example, if we wish to reference an article on an issue in the meeting notes or in the decisions made, we can easily do so.

> Remember that a wiki is a multi-user environment. The intent is not to have one person create all the content, but for it to be a collaborative effort. So, for example, if one person creates a new article for the weekly meeting notes, another person can go in and add a topic that was discussed that the first person forgot to mention. Or, as an example, anyone can update an article on an issue with the latest status of that issue.

The ExpressionEngine wiki also supports the use of categories. Use the following code anywhere in an article to assign the article to a `Meeting Notes` category.

    [[Category:Meeting Notes]]

> 7th January
>
> Category:Meeting Notes
>
> The main focus of this meeting was Issue 12.
>
> Although we could avoid fixing Issue 12, our stakeholder wasn't in favour.
>
> The meeting lasted a very long time and was very boring. No resolution was agreed upon.
>
> Also discussed Issue 11 which was resolved earlier this week.
>
> Categories:
>
> - Meeting Notes

We can assign one article to multiple categories. We can also assign articles to subcategories using the following format:

```
[[Category:Meeting Notes:January]]
```

We can also use standard HTML tags to bold, italicize, or underline the content we want to.

However, the wiki is not just a place to store plain-text articles. If enabled, images, diagrams, and documents can be uploaded by users and linked to or embedded in one or more articles using the **File Upload** and **Uploaded Files** link on the main menu.

Customizing the Wiki

Like other modules, the wiki comes pre-configured so that it works right out of the box. This makes it very easy to get up and running. However, the design is not contained in normal templates but is done as a theme, which makes it more difficult to fit into our existing website design.

Editing the theme for the wiki is much easier than editing the theme for the discussion forum module, as the theme is stored in a single file. This makes it far easier to identify the relationship between different pieces of code and therefore integrate our code within it. However, familiarity with HTML and CSS is a must.

The theme is a file located in `themes/wiki_themes` on our webserver (or `C:\xampp\htdocs\themes\wiki_themes` or `/Applications/MAMP/htdocs/themes/wiki_themes/`). The first step before making modifications is to copy an existing theme folder (for example, the `default` theme) and call it something else (for example, `toast`). This way, if we irreversibly screw up, we can always return to our starting point.

Next, inside the new toast folder is a PHP file. Rename this to `toast.php` for consistency. It is this file where all the code that makes up the wiki theme is stored. There are comments to make it clear where different sections start and end, but essentially this is what needs modification in order to make our wiki fit in with the rest of our site.

> Full documentation for modifying the wiki theme can be found at http://expressionengine.com/docs/modules/wiki/wiki_templates.html.

Other Modules and Functionality

The basic steps are:

- Adjust the HTML `<head>` section to include our normal stylesheet (using a direct link), and adjust the CSS to remove or edit CSS styles that conflict with styles from our main stylesheet (for example, the way links and headings are formatted). It may be best to combine both stylesheets into one. There will be a lot of work with the CSS to merge the two stylesheets in a way that makes the finished theme look good.

- At the start of the `<body>` section, include our normal `<div id="header">` section to put our logo at the top of the page.

- Add our normal sidebar menu immediately before the `</body>` tag. Incorporate the items from the wiki top and left menu into our normal menu using `<ul>`, `<li>`, and `<div>` tags.

- Place the main content inside a `<div id="content">` tag and (optionally) use the `footnote` class for the **View**, **Edit**, and **History** links.

- Use the `<div class="contentinner">` wrapper to put the `{article}` inside the pale `contentinner` box. Do the same for the Categories information and the text that says **This Article Does Not Exist Yet**.

- Change the `Template - Edit` section so that the edit form is integrated into our site design. View all the pages that visitors can get to while browsing the wiki to verify that they are all rendering correctly.

These are only broad guidelines as to what will be necessary. A good understanding of the HTML in the theme will be essential to determine if an unwanted effect is due to conflicting CSS styles or HTML element pairs that do not match up (for example, too many or not enough closing tags).

Wiki Home > index

View - Edit - History

Welcome to our project home page. Our project wiki is split into 4 areas:
Project Objectives defines the objectives of this project
Issues describes all issues that need to be addressed
Decisions Made describes decisions that have been made
Our project status **Meeting Notes** are available for all to read.

More ExpressionEngine Features

Throughout this book, we have touched on many different aspects of ExpressionEngine in our goal to build a functional website. However, there are many aspects that we did not touch on, but that are still important to be aware of. This section will introduce these features, describe how to implement them, and explain how they can be used.

Adding Search Functionality to Our Site

ExpressionEngine comes with a pre-built search tool that will allow visitors to search our site. Although technically a module, the search functionality comes pre-installed (including a `search` template group) and does not have any special setup.

> If, for any reason, the `search` template group no longer exists, the source code for the templates can be downloaded from http://expressionengine.com/templates/.

How to Add Search Box to Our Site

To add a search box to our menu bar, open the `toast/.menu` template, and add the following code at the end of the template:

```
{exp:search:simple_form search_in="everywhere"}
  <h4>Search</h4>
  <p align="center">
    <input type="text" name="keywords" size="18" maxlength="100" />
    <br />
    <a href="{path=search/index}">Advanced Search</a>
  </p>
  <p align="center"><input type="submit" value="Submit" /></p>
{/exp:search:simple_form}
```

This will result in a small **Search** box that visitors on any page can use to search the website.

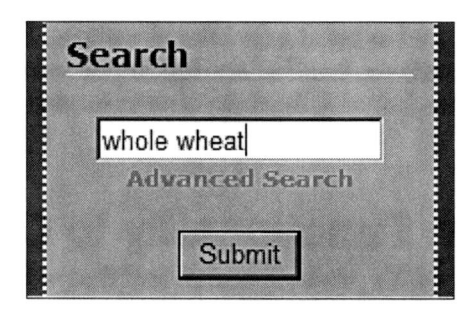

Clicking on the **Advanced Search** button will bring up the `search/index` template where visitors can choose more options.

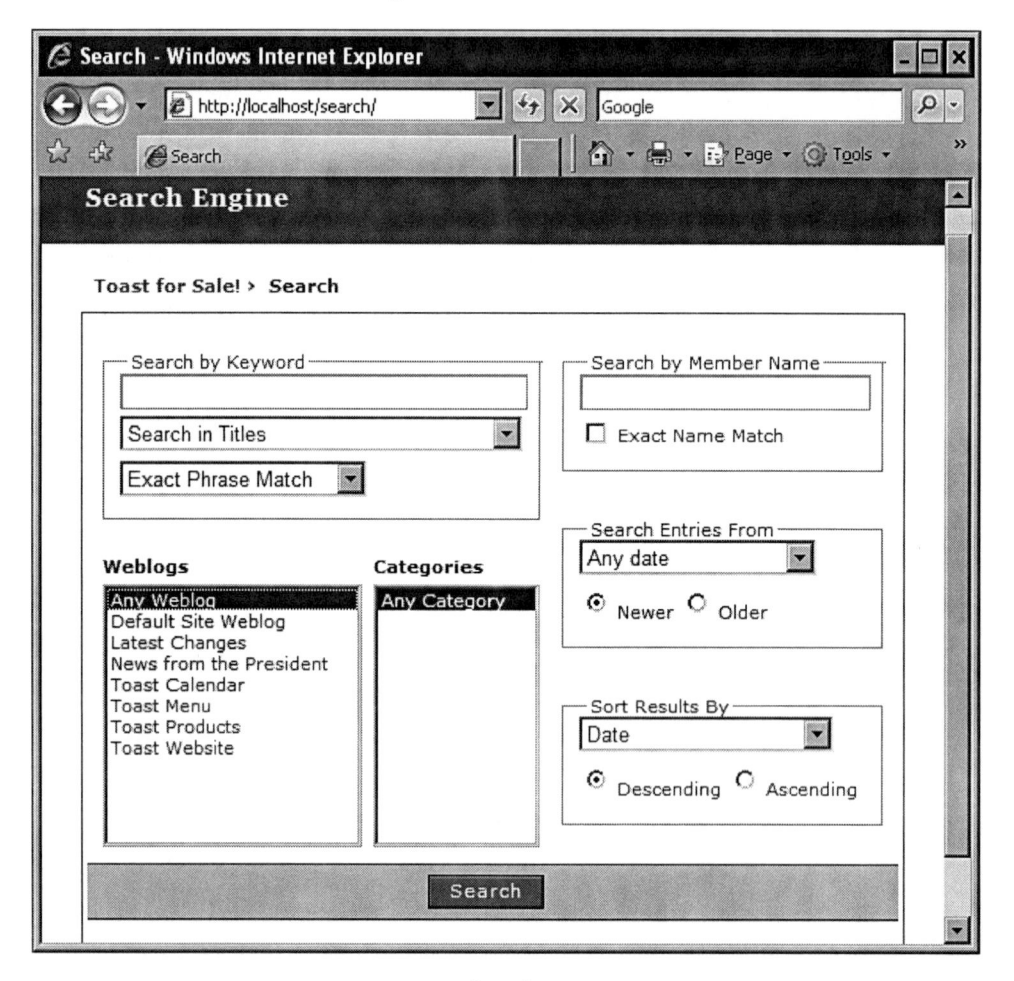

Finally, after the search is performed, the results are displayed using the `search/results` template.

Title	Excerpt	Author	Date	Total Comments	Recent Comment
Whole Wheat Toast	A slice of paradise, our whole wheat sandwich bread is toasted to perfection. With a dollop of butter, you can reach your recommended daily serving of heart-healthy whole grains without compromising on taste.	Leonard Murphy	01/21/08	2	02/17/08

When we first created the custom fields for each of our weblogs, we were able to define if a field was searchable or not. This is helpful in keeping search results relevant. The one way we could use this is to create a custom field dedicated for search terms that people might use when looking for the specific entry. These search terms never display on any page and are not part of the excerpt, but may help to make searching more reliable.

The field that is used for the excerpt when displaying results is located in the **Weblog Preferences**, under **Administrative Preferences**. As each weblog can have different custom fields, this is defined on a per-weblog basis.

> Note that the search functionality only searches weblogs. The discussion forum module and the wiki module both have separate search functions. The photo gallery module does not currently include a search tool.

Customizing the Search Functionality

On the advanced search page (`http://localhost/search` or `http://www.example.com/search`), it is apparent that visitors can search every weblog in our ExpressionEngine installation—even the weblogs that we do not use or would not want to be searched.

We can start customizing the search functionality by restricting the weblogs (or categories) that may be searched. This is done by opening the `search/index` template and editing the `exp:search:advanced` tag.

Other Modules and Functionality

For example, to exclude the `Default Site Weblog` and the `Toast Calendar` from our search results, we can use the following parameter (note the use of the | to list multiple weblogs):

```
{exp:search:advanced_form result_page="search/results" cat_style="nested" weblog="not default_site|not toastcalendar"}
```

For more options using the `exp:search:advanced` tag, including whether to include or exclude specific categories, statuses, future-dated and expired entries, visit the official ExpressionEngine documentation page at `http://expressionengine.com/docs/modules/search/advanced.html`.

The search templates are also much easier to customize than themed modules (such as the discussion forum or wiki module). The templates already exist, so the best way to approach this is to start with an empty toast site page, and then add the main pieces of code from the search templates.

In the following screenshot, the CSS for the form was left as-is from the ExpressionEngine default template. However, the entire form was placed inside a Toast Website page, complete with header and side menu.

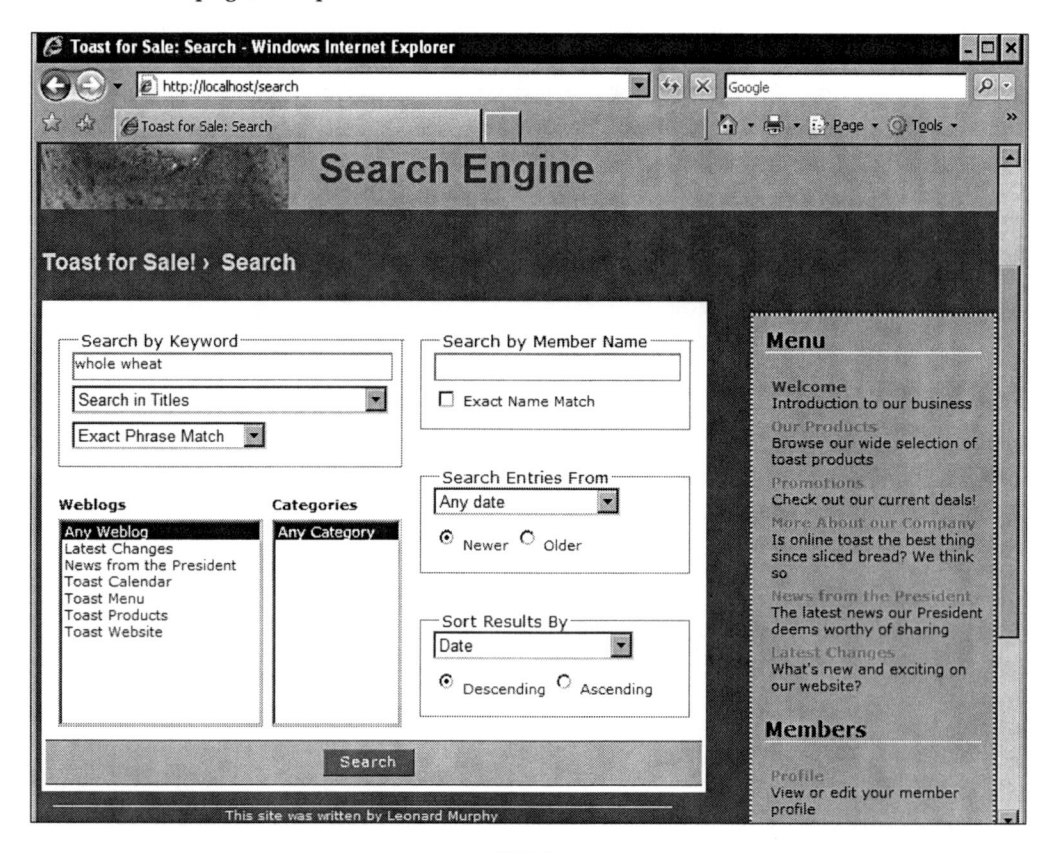

Using Status Groups in Our Weblogs

So far, we have used status groups very sparingly. A status group is essentially a way to mark the status of an entry. The **Default Status Group** (that comes with ExpressionEngine) contains two statuses: Open and Closed. A post marked as **Open** is visible to anyone visiting the template; a **Closed** entry is not visible to visitors (unless we specifically mark them as visible).

However, status groups can be combined with member groups to create a workflow. For example, say we have two groups of people. Writers create the content for our website, and editors review the content before it is published. To achieve this, we can create a writer member group, and allow members to publish to our weblog, but restrict them to only publishing entries with a custom status of **Needs Review**.

Weblog posts with a status of **Needs Review** will not, by default, appear on our main website, but we could create a template that only the editor member group can access, which shows all the postings with a **Needs Review** status. Editors could then log into the control panel, and after any edits have been made, can change the custom status to **Open**, thus making the article visible to everyone.

This system could be iterated through many times with as many custom statuses and member groups as needed, depending on the business. Perhaps an article goes through several stages of review—by editors, the legal department, and the marketing department—before it appears on the website. It is easy to do.

Another option (if an article needs to go back and forth multiple times between two groups of people before it can be published) is to create a custom field in our weblog that does not display on the main site, to be used to store notes about the post (for example, what needs to be changed).

Other Modules and Functionality

Create a Custom Status Group

To create a status group or add to the Default Status Group, go to **Admin | Weblog Administration | Custom Entry Statuses**. Once in a status group, we can create a new status on the right-hand side, and define which member groups can assign weblog posts to this status group. Then hit **Submit**.

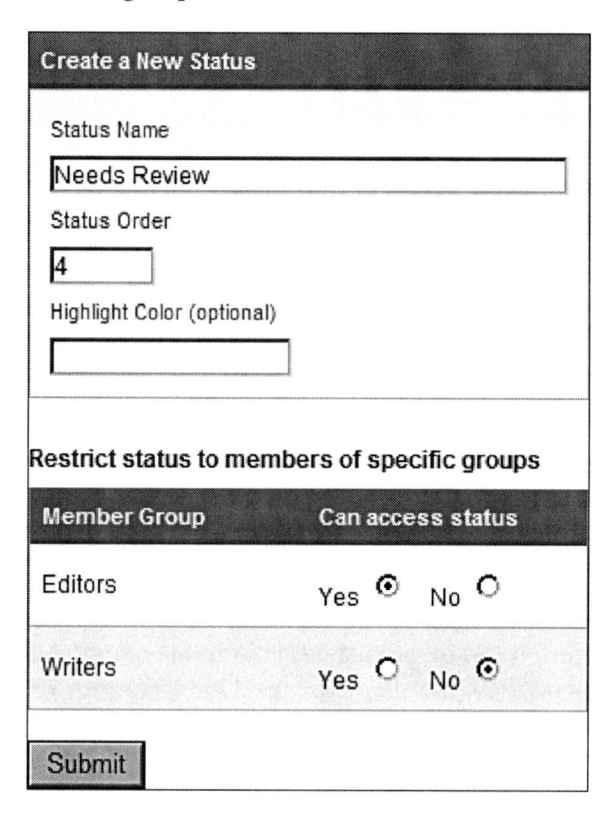

We can then go into the existing Open status by clicking on **Edit** and restrict this status to **Editors** only.

Now, if we log in as a writer and go to edit an existing weblog post, we can only set the **Status** to **Needs Review** or **Closed**. We cannot, as a writer, set the weblog to be open.

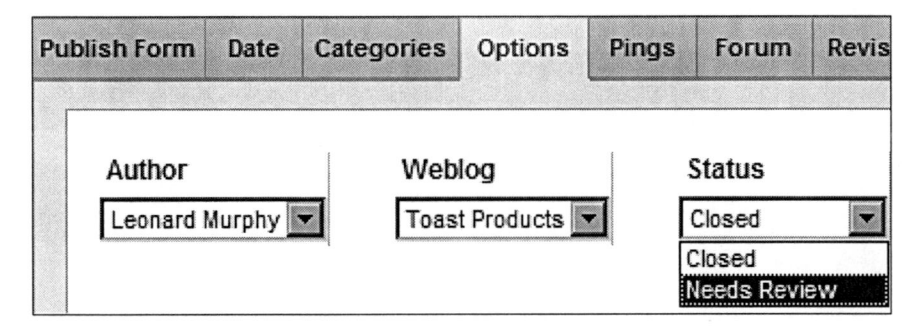

Display a Queue of Entries That Have a Certain Status

To create a queue of entries that needs review from editors, we can create a template and use the `exp:weblog:entries` tag to display the weblog entries, just like we normally would. However, we will use the parameter `status="Needs Review"` to ensure that only entries with a status of `Needs Review` are displayed.

```
{exp:weblog:entries weblog="{my_weblog}" dynamic="off" sort="asc"
status="Needs Review"}
```

> If we are using the above tag to display open or closed entries, it is important to use only lowercase letters (`status="open"` or `status="closed"`).

Other Modules and Functionality

We can then restrict this template to a certain member group. On the main **Template** page, select **Access** next to the template in question. We are then brought to a screen where we can restrict the template to only the editor member group, redirecting everyone else to our `toast/404` template.

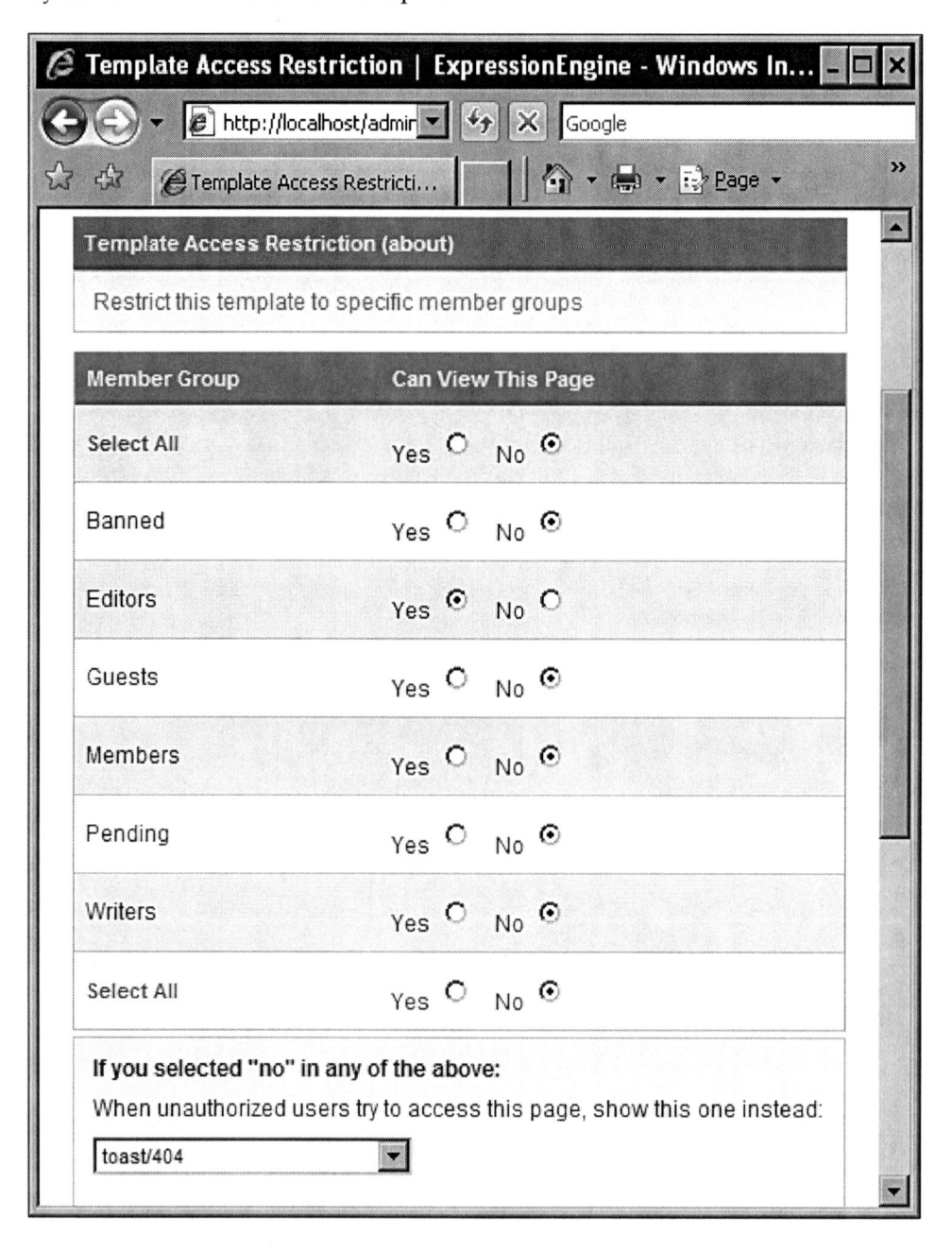

Member Group	Can View This Page
Select All	Yes ○ No ⦿
Banned	Yes ○ No ⦿
Editors	Yes ⦿ No ○
Guests	Yes ○ No ⦿
Members	Yes ○ No ⦿
Pending	Yes ○ No ⦿
Writers	Yes ○ No ⦿
Select All	Yes ○ No ⦿

If you selected "no" in any of the above:
When unauthorized users try to access this page, show this one instead:
`toast/404`

Using Categories to Create Our Site Structure

So far, our toast website hasn't been called for the use of categories because it is so small. However, as the number of toast products that our site sells expands, categories become a great way to organize the information.

As with custom fields and custom status groups, categories can be entirely customized and then associated with a particular weblog. So, for example, we might have one set of categories for our `toastproducts` weblog and another set of categories entirely for our `toastnews` weblog.

Alternatively, you can use the same category group for multiple weblogs. If you have a themed website, the chances are that your different weblogs still fall into the same category structure. By sharing a category structure, it can make it easier for you.

It is also possible to assign multiple category groups to the same weblog. This may be useful in a situation where there are two (or more) logical groupings for the same weblog but the two groupings are not, in themselves, related. For example, calendar events may be categorized based on where they are and what kind of event it is. By creating one category group for location (Central Park, Brooklyn, Manhattan) and another category group for event type (food show, art fair, wedding exhibitions), and assigning both groups to the `toastcalendar` weblog, we can categorize events by both where they are and what kind of event they are, and then allow our visitors to browse our events using either category group.

Creating Our Category Groups

To create custom categories, go to **Admin | Weblog Administration | Category Management**. Here, we can create a new category group and then create the categories to go inside.

Other Modules and Functionality

Each category can have a name (that can display on the website), a URL title (that is used in the address), a description, and an image. In addition, categories can also be nested.

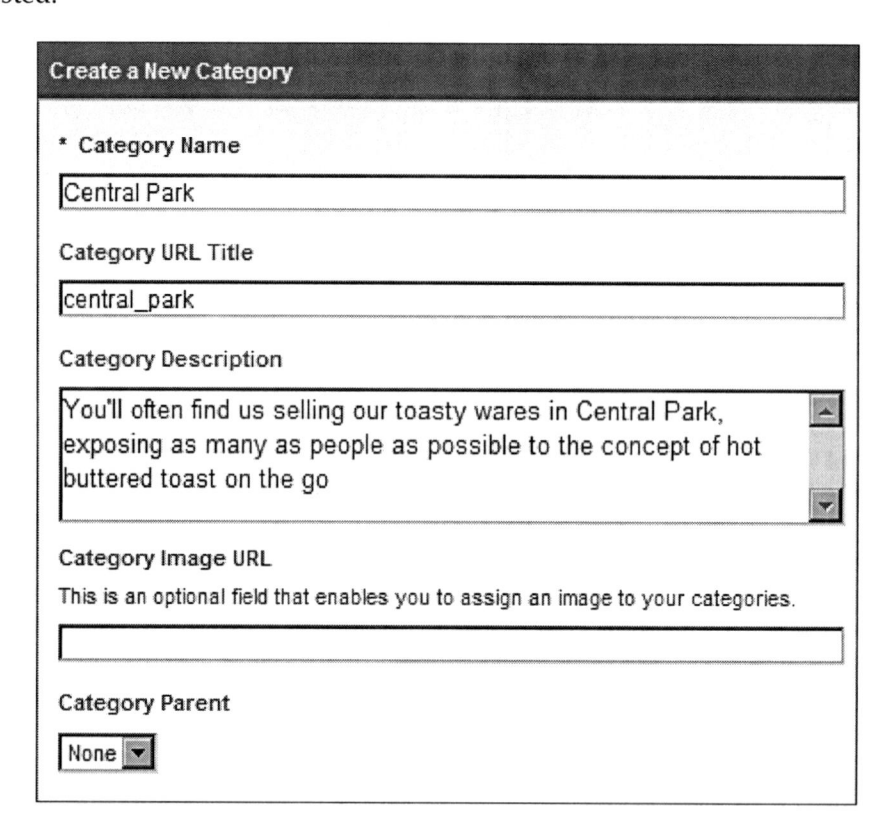

Categories themselves can have custom fields associated with them. For example, if we were building a category structure for the location of our calendar events, we may create custom fields to store the best way to get to each of the locations.

We can do this by selecting **Manage Custom Fields** from the main **Category Groups** screen. The custom fields are set up very similarly to weblog or photo gallery custom fields.

Category groups then have to be assigned to a weblog. To assign a weblog go to **Admin | Weblog Administration | Weblog Management**, and then select **Edit Groups** to choose a different (or multiple) category group.

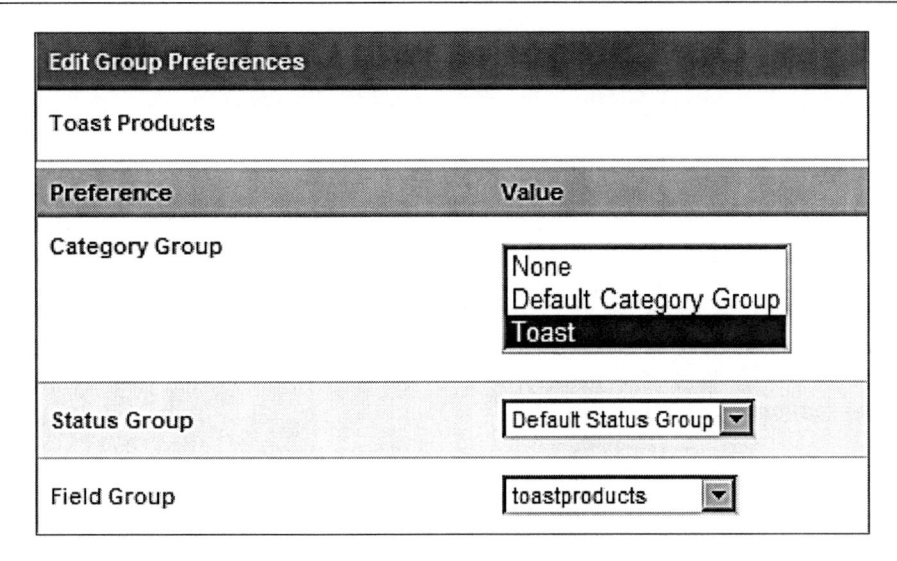

Edit Group Preferences	
Toast Products	
Preference	**Value**
Category Group	None / Default Category Group / **Toast**
Status Group	Default Status Group
Field Group	toastproducts

Any posts under that weblog can then be assigned a category or multiple categories in our category group.

Next, we should set ExpressionEngine to use category names rather than ID numbers in the URL. By default, ExpressionEngine will reference a category using the unintuitive category ID (for example, `http://localhost/products/C4` or `http://www.example.com/products/C4`). We can set this differently by going to **Admin | Weblog Administration | Global Weblog Preferences**, and setting **Use Category URL Titles in Links?** to **Yes**.

Global Weblog Preferences	
Use Category URL Titles In Links? This preference determines whether the category ID number or the category URL Title is used in category-related links.	Yes ● No ○
Category URL Indicator If you set the above preference to "yes" you must choose a reserved word. This word will be used in the URL to indicate to the weblog display engine that you are showing a category. Note: whatever word you chose CAN NOT be the name of a template group or a template.	category

Other Modules and Functionality

Displaying Our Categories with Our Entries

Let us say that our events calendar has grown, and we have created a category group for our `toastcalendar` weblog and categorized our events both by location and by type.

Currently, our `calendar/event` template is organized so that it only displays one entry and redirects to the main `calendar/index` template if an entry is not found.

The first task is to display the categories that an entry belongs to. We can do this using the `{categories}` variable pair that is part of the `exp:weblog:entries` tag. This variable pair, when used inside the `exp:weblog:entries` tag, displays all the categories that an entry belongs to.

```
        {if toastcalendar_URL}
          {toastcalendar_URL}<br />
        {/if}
      </div>
      <div class="footnote">{categories backspace="2"}<a href="
      {path={my_template_group}/event}">{category_name}</a> | {
                                                /categories}</div>
{/exp:weblog:entries}
```

> When using this variable pair, everything between the `{categories}` opening tag and the `{/categories}` closing tag is repeated. As we don't know how many categories an entry might be assigned to, the backspace parameter is used to say that, for the last repetition, do not include the last two characters (in this case the | symbol that we are using to separate our categories).
>
> Full documentation for the categories variable pair can be found at http://expressionengine.com/docs/modules/weblog/variable_pairs.html#var_categories.

Food Festival
10am-8pm on November 7th 2009

Central Park, New York City
Among the stands of wine and fine cheeses, the subtle aroma of hot buttered toast...

The Toast for Sale! website will be participating in the New York Food Festival in Central Park this fall. We will be handing out free samples of our toasted goodness as well as hosting toast-related competitions with toast-related prizes.

http://www.example.com

Central Park | Food Show

Creating Our Category Browsing Page

In our `calendar/event` template, we currently have the `require_entry` parameter set to `yes`, the `limit` parameter set to `1`, and we use the `{if no_results}` tag to redirect people back to the `calendar/index` template if they are not browsing an actual event. None of this will work with our category pages, which will also use the `calendar/event` template.

To get around this, we can use a conditional statement such as `{if segment_3=="category"}` to determine whether we are on a multiple-entry category browsing page or a single-entry weblog page. All category browsing pages have a URL with the word category in it. For example, `http://localhost/calendar/event/category/food_show` or `http://www.example.com/calendar/event/category/food_show` will display all the entries in the `food_show` category (unless in the **Global Weblog Preferences** you chose a different word instead of category for your URLs).

Here is an example of how the `calendar/event` template might be structured:

```
<body>
  {if segment_3!="category"}
    <div id="header">
      <h1>Toast for Sale!</h1>
      <h2>Toasty Event</h2>
    </div>
    <div id="content">
      [Existing code omitted for space]
    </div>
  {/if}
  {if segment_3=="category"}
    <div id="header">
      <h1>Toast for Sale!</h1>
      <h2>Category Listing</h2>
    </div>
    <div id="content">
      {exp:weblog:entries weblog="{my_weblog}"
                show_future_entries="yes"}
        <h3>{title}<br /><i>{if toastcalendar_time}
          {toastcalendar_time} on {/if}{entry_date
                    format="%F %j%S %Y"}</i></h3>
        <div class="contentinner">
          {if toastcalendar_location}
            <b>{toastcalendar_location}</b><br />
          {/if}
          {if toastcalendar_description}
```

Other Modules and Functionality

```
            {toastcalendar_description}<br /><br />
          {/if}
          {if toastcalendar_URL}
            {toastcalendar_URL}<br />
          {/if}
        </div>
        <div class="footnote">{categories backspace="2"}<a href="
          {path={my_template_group}/event}">{category_name}</a> |
                                           {/categories}</div>
      {/exp:weblog:entries}
    </div>
  {/if}
```

Now, when you click on one of the category links underneath the weblog entry, you are shown all `toastcalendar` weblog entries that fall into the same category.

Finally, if desired, we can add the `exp:weblog:category_heading` tag to the h2 heading, where it currently says `Category Listing`, and instead displays the category title.

```
<h2>{exp:weblog:category_heading weblog="{my_weblog}"}Category:
         {category_name}{/exp:weblog:category_heading}</h2>
```

Display All Our Categories

To display all the categories in a list (for example, in our sidebar), we can use the `exp:weblog:categories` tag:

```
<h4>Events by Location</h4>
  {exp:weblog:categories weblog="toastcalendar" show_future
                    _entries="yes" category_group="2"}
    <a href="{path=calendar/event}">{category_name}</a>
  {/exp:weblog:categories}
<h4>Events by Type</h4>
  {exp:weblog:categories weblog="toastcalendar" show_future
                    _entries="yes" category_group="3"}
    <a href="{path=calendar/event}">{category_name}</a>
  {/exp:weblog:categories}
```

> Notice how the `category_group` parameter is used to distinguish between the two different category groups assigned to this weblog. The category group number can be found in the left-hand column on the **Admin | Weblog Administration | Category Management** screen.
>
> The main difference between the `exp:weblog:categories` tag and the `exp:weblog:category_heading` tag is that the `categories` tag will display information about every category in the category group, regardless of what page we are on, making it ideal for our sidebar. The `category_heading` tag only displays information for the current category being displayed, and only works on a category specific page.
>
> Full documentation for the `categories` tag can be found at http://expressionengine.com/docs/modules/weblog/categories.html.

Events by Location

Brooklyn
Central Park
Manhattan

Events by Type

Art Fair
Food Show
Wedding Exhibitions

Using Related Entries

Whereas categories allow us to show which entries are related to which other entries (by virtue of them sharing the same category), the Related Entries feature allows us to actually include the content of one weblog entry in another weblog entry.

The first clue that related entries may be the way to go is when you find yourself reusing the same information in multiple posts. If you simply want to indicate that two entries are related to each other (but not actually display one entry inside the other entry), then categories are a better bet.

Other Modules and Functionality

Let us say that we have a toastpromotions weblog, which our toast company uses to promote various deals. Different toast products go on sale at different times and on our promotions page, we want to display a little bit of information about the toast on sale.

We could build in a custom field, `toastpromotions_product`, which we could use to describe the toast product. However, it will be tedious to fill in every time, and we already have a fantastic description of the product on the products page. The Related Entries feature allows us to display the {summary} field (or any field we want) from the toastproducts weblog. No matter which product goes on promotion next, we can simply select from a drop-down list of all products the product that is on offer, and the template will automatically display the {summary} for that product.

Buy 1 Whole Wheat Toast Slice, Get Another Free

Buy one whole wheat slice of toast and get a 2nd slice absolutely free. Offer valid until 12/15.

More About Whole Wheat Toast

A slice of paradise, our whole wheat sandwich bread is toasted to perfection. With a dollop of butter, you can reach your recommended daily serving of heart-healthy whole grains without compromising on taste.

Terms and Conditions

Only one free slice of toast per customer per month. Free slice of toast to be consumed only by original purchaser - we reserve the right to deny free slices of toast to anyone we suspect of reverse engineering or otherwise attempting to steal our toasting technology.

Creating a Related Entry

> A toastpromotions weblog was not created as part of our toast site, but can be easily created. It is simply a weblog like our toastnews weblog that has three custom fields: `toastpromotions_summary`, `toastpromotions_product`, and `toastpromotions_tc`.

To create a related entry, we first create a new custom field for the relationship (or assign an existing custom field). This field must be in the parent weblog (the weblog that will display the data from the other weblog). In this case, the toastpromotions weblog will display the data from the toastproducts weblog, so we edit the toastpromotions weblog custom fields.

For this **Field Type**, select **Relationship**. This will allow us to choose the weblog that we wish to relate to (in our case, the Toast Products weblog), and how we can sort the options.

> Note that we can also relate weblog entries to gallery entries, allowing us to display photos we upload to the photo gallery module within weblogs.

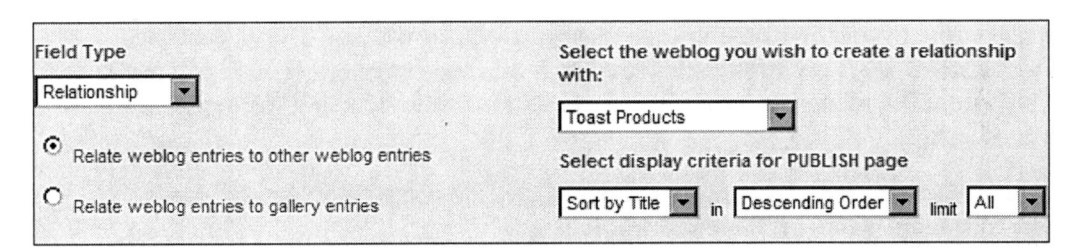

Now, when we go to post a new entry to our toastpromotions weblog, we get a drop-down box of all the entries in our toastproducts weblog.

Now, all we have to do is edit the template that displays our toastpromotions weblog, so that it now shows fields from the toastproducts weblog. To demonstrate, this is an except from the promotions/index template (that was not created as part of this book):

```
{exp:weblog:entries weblog="{my_weblog}" limit="1"}
  <h3>{title}</h3>
  {if toastpromotions_summary}
    <div class="contentinner">{toastpromotions_summary}</div>
```

```
      {/if}
      {related_entries id="toastpromotions_product"}
        <h3>More About {title}</h3>
        <div class="contentinner">{toastproducts_summary}</div>
      {/related_entries}
      {if toastpromotions_tc}
        <h3>Terms and Conditions</h3>
        <div class="contentinner">{toastpromotions_tc}</div>
      {/if}
    {/exp:weblog:entries}
```

The `related_entries` tag has an id that is the field name of the **Relationship** field we created. Notice how within the `related_entries` tag, we are using tags like `{title}` and `{toastproducts_summary}`, even though these are fields from the toastproducts weblog instead of the toastpromotions weblog. This is because the `related_entries` tag acts like the `exp:weblog:entries` tag—we can use any fields from the related entry in this entry without actually using the `exp:weblog:entries` tag.

In this example, the toastpromotions weblog is the parent weblog and the toastproducts weblog is the child weblog.

For more information on Related Entries, including relating gallery entries to weblogs, please visit http://expressionengine.com/docs/modules/weblog/related_entries.html.

Reverse Related Entries

We can also show reverse relationships if we want to display the promotional information on the toastproducts weblog page. Note that each child weblog entry may be associated with multiple parent weblog entries, so sometimes this may not be desirable.

The template code on the `products/index` template to show reversed entries is as follows:

```
{reverse_related_entries}
  <div class="contentinner">{promotionsummary}</div>
{/reverse_related_entries}
```

Once again, we are able to use the {promotionsummary} and other custom fields of the toastpromotions weblog in the toastproducts template.

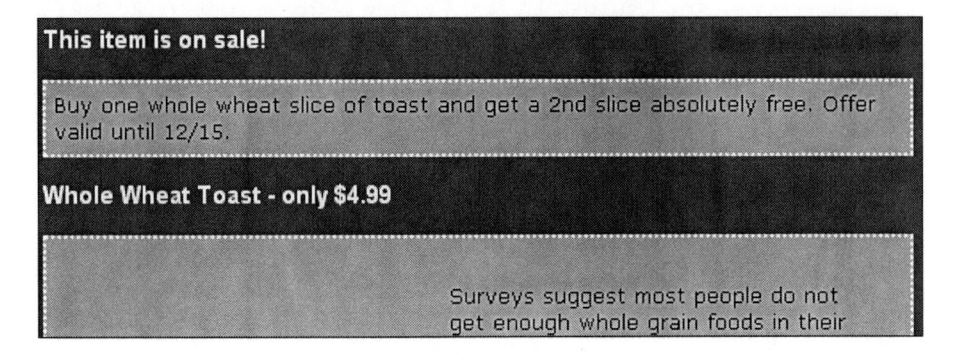

This item is on sale!

Buy one whole wheat slice of toast and get a 2nd slice absolutely free. Offer valid until 12/15.

Whole Wheat Toast - only $4.99

Surveys suggest most people do not get enough whole grain foods in their

For more information on Reverse Related Entries, please visit http://expressionengine.com/docs/modules/weblog/reverse_related_entries.html.

Backups and Restores

ExpressionEngine is a database-driven application and so to back it up we need to back up both the individual files that we upload to our web server and the database itself.

To Backup an ExpressionEngine-Powered Site

To back up ExpressionEngine, you need a tool such as phpMyAdmin. If your website is hosted by a website hosting provider, contact them and ask if phpMyAdmin or another tool is installed that will allow you to do MySQL database backups. If necessary, phpMyAdmin can be downloaded from http://www.phpmyadmin.net/.

1. The first step to doing a backup is to clear all the unnecessary data from the database (such as cached templates). To do this, go into the control panel, and select **Admin | Utilities | Clear Cached Data**. Select to clear **All caches**, and hit **Submit**.

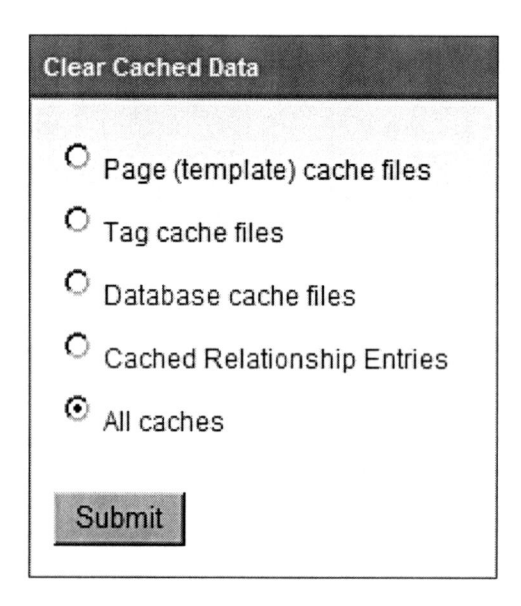

2. When using XAMPP or MAMP, phpMyAdmin is installed by default. Visit http://localhost/phpmyadmin/ or http://localhost/MAMP/ to access the phpMyAdmin control panel.

Chapter 9

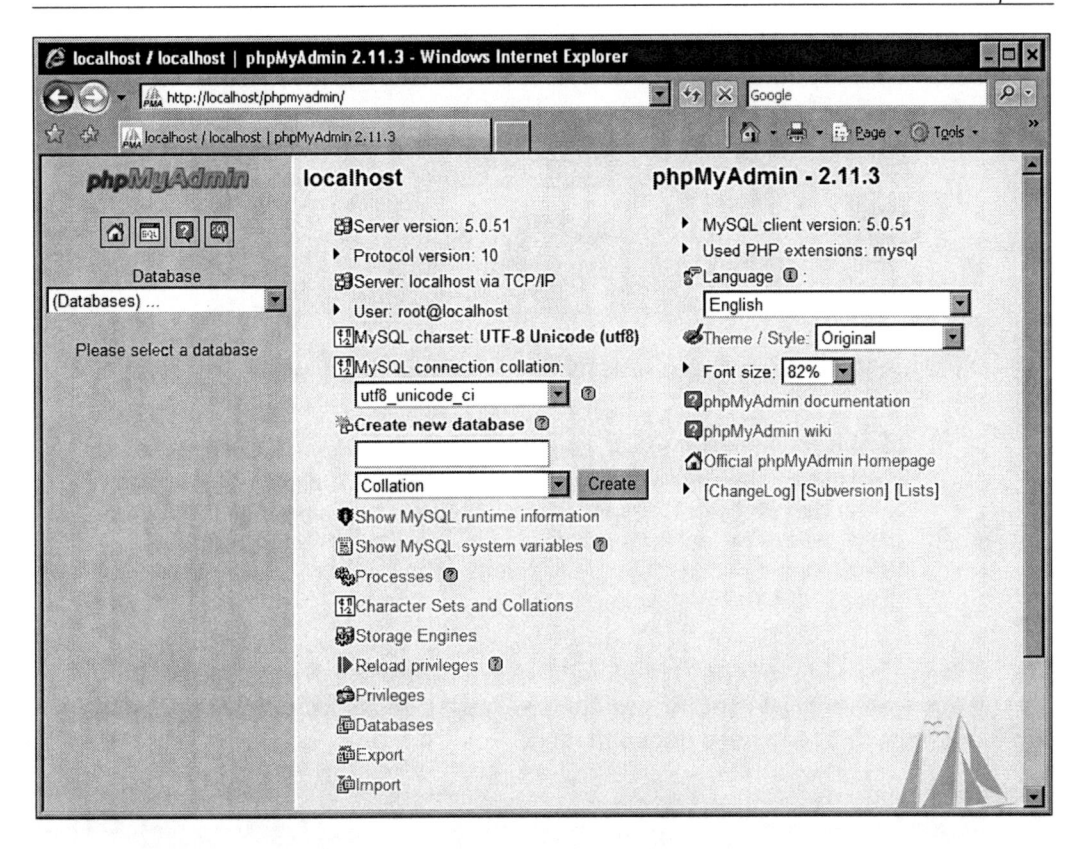

3. From the drop-down list on the left-hand side, select the ExpressionEngine database. We are then brought to a screen that shows all the ExpressionEngine tables on the left-hand side.
4. In the main window, select **Export** from the top menu.
5. On the export page, at the top of the left column, verify that all the tables are selected.

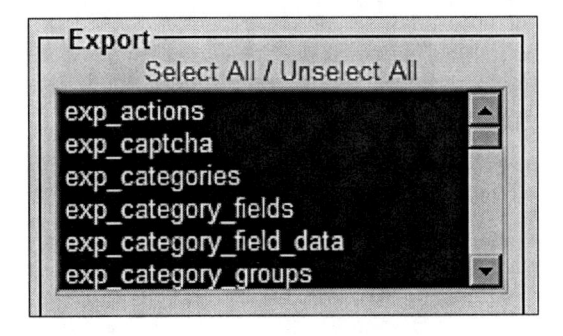

6. All the options on the right-hand side can be left as their default. At the bottom, check the box **Save as file**. Select a **Compression** method of either "**zipped**" or "**gzipped**", and then select **Go**.

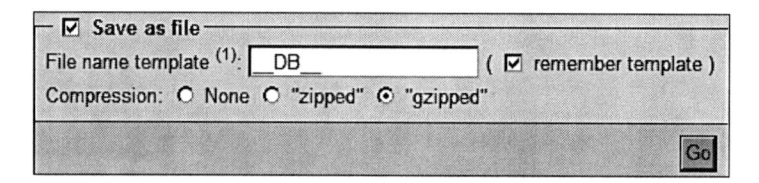

7. We are then prompted to save the file; save it to a safe place.

> Note that while phpMyAdmin is sufficient for smaller databases, the backup may time out when backing up very large databases. One option to work around this is to split out the database backup so that not all the tables are backed up into a single file. Another option is to look at the command line MySQL code or a utility such as My SQL Dumper (http://www.mysqldumper.de/en/).

In addition to backing up our MySQL database, it is also prudent to backup all the files on our web server, including any themes, language packs, modules, plug-ins, and extensions that may have been installed.

To Restore an ExpressionEngine-Powered Site

First, make sure that all the files on the web server have been restored and/or are intact.

To restore a backed up database file, go back into phpMyAdmin, and select the ExpressionEngine database on the left-hand side.

If restoring over the top of an existing ExpressionEngine installation, we first have to delete the existing ExpressionEngine database. Before doing this, be *very* sure that the database is well backed up or that losing the database will not be a problem.

Select **Drop** from the menu in the top window. A message will appear saying **You are about to DESTROY a complete database!**. Select **OK**. This will delete everything in your ExpressionEngine database.

Next, go back to the home page (click on the home icon on the left-hand side), and create a new ExpressionEngine database, using the same name as the database we just deleted.

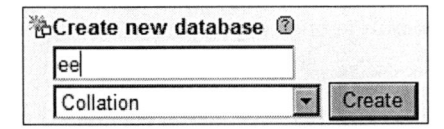

Then, in the empty database, select **Import** from the menu in the top window, and browse to the location where the database backup was saved.

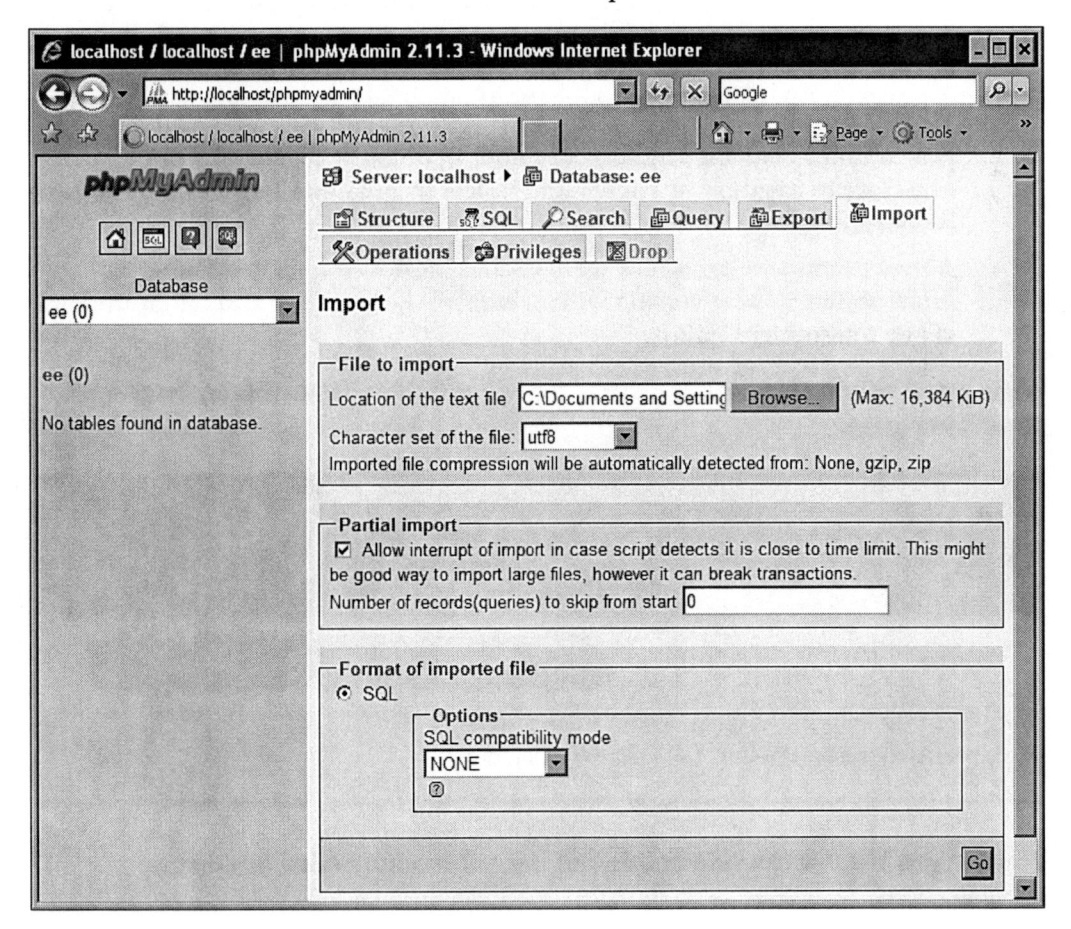

Leave all the other options as is and select **Go**.

Upgrading ExpressionEngine

EllisLab is always busy on a new version of ExpressionEngine. These versions are often packed full of new features as well as bug fixes. A purchase of ExpressionEngine includes one year of free updates, with the option of renewing each year for a nominal fee.

> Occasionally, EllisLab will put a price on a new feature (such as the discussion forum). However, the prices are generally very fair, and reflect the cost of development and support. Doing this also keeps the cost of ExpressionEngine itself lower for users who have no interest in the new feature.

There are two types of releases that ExpressionEngine will go through:

- A new **build** contains bug fixes or minor updates. It is generally not necessary to upgrade to a new build unless it contains a bug fix that you have been waiting for.
- A new **version** contains new features and improvements to existing functionality. A new version will include all the bug fixes and minor updates of any intermittent builds.

When a new version is released, ExpressionEngine will indicate this on the control panel home page.

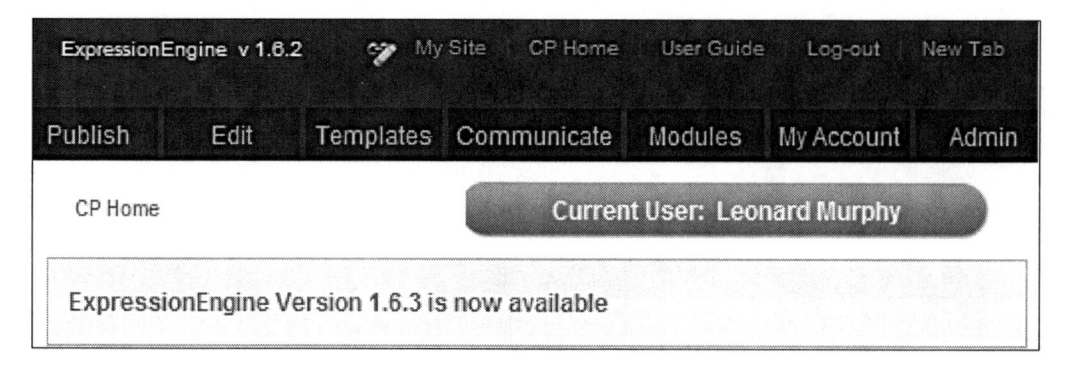

When upgrading, we can skip builds, but it is not recommended to skip too many versions.

The instructions for updating to the latest build can be found at
`http://expressionengine.com/docs/installation/update_build.html`.

The instructions for updating to the latest version can be found at
`http://expressionengine.com/docs/installation/update.html`. Note
that the instructions remain the same from one version to the next:

- Perform a backup of the database and key ExpressionEngine files (`path.php` and `system/config.php`), as well as any themes, extensions, language packs, modules, or plug-ins that have been installed.
- Download the latest version from the ExpressionEngine download area and upload key folders from the system directory to the web server (bearing in mind that we renamed the `system` directory when ExpressionEngine was installed).
- Set the file permissions for certain ExpressionEngine files and folders (`system/config.php`, `system/config.php.bak`, and `system/cache`).
- Point a browser to `system/update.php` (for example, `http://localhost/system/update.php` or `http://www.example.com/system/update.php`) to perform the update to each new version.

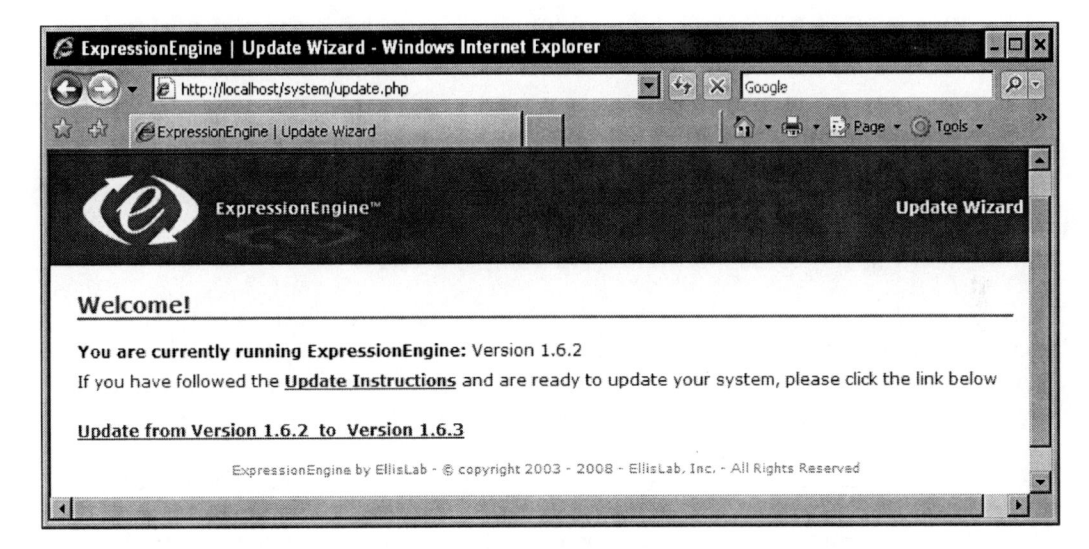

![ExpressionEngine Update Wizard screenshot showing Welcome page with current version 1.6.2 and link to update from Version 1.6.2 to Version 1.6.3]

- Delete the `system/update.php` file and `system/updates` folder from the web server.
- Follow the **Version Specific Notes** for any versions between the version you are updating to and the version you are updating from.

The **Version Specific Notes** will contain details on any changes that need to be made above and beyond the normal upgrade changes just listed. For example, if additional files need to be uploaded, or if a new setting in the control panel needs to be defined, the **Version Specific Notes** is where we find that out.

Occasionally, there may also be changes to themes or language packs that require us to reflect the changes in our own themes (if we are not using the default theme or English language pack).

Finally, in addition to ExpressionEngine itself, modules we install are also subject to new versions. For example, the discussion forum version update instructions can be found at `http://expressionengine.com/docs/modules/forum/forum_update.html`. The discussion forum is one place where, if we have customized the theme to fit our site design, we will have to update our theme templates manually in order to be able to take advantage of new features.

Summary

In this chapter:

- We installed, configured and customized the discussion forum, simple commerce, and wiki modules.
- We reviewed features of ExpressionEngine such as search, custom status groups, categories, and related entries.
- We reviewed how to maintain our ExpressionEngine site through backups, restores and updates.

Not everything in this chapter is going to apply to every site. When we get to this level of implementation, there is great diversity in what different sites are trying to achieve, which is difficult to account for in a single book.

Throughout this chapter, we have continually referenced the ExpressionEngine documentation at `http://expressionengine.com/docs/index.html`. It is an excellent resource for finding out how different features and tags work and all the options that they offer.

In terms of getting support to implement a specific feature, the ExpressionEngine support forums (`http://expressionengine.com/forums`) are a hot bed of activity. The chances are that no matter what you are trying to do, someone else has already asked a question about it—searching the forums can yield lots of useful information, pointers, and pitfalls.

If you are still stuck, posting a question in the forum will often yield a rapid response. The clearer the question the more on-target the response will be. The forums are populated with hundreds of people who use ExpressionEngine daily—your question is just as likely to be answered by someone who works for EllisLab (as someone who doesn't work for EllisLab, but happens to know the answer).

A
Installing XAMPP

In this appendix, we will walk through downloading, installing, and setting up the XAMPP package. XAMPP is a free package that includes an easy-to-set up web server (Apache), database server (MySQL), and server-side scripting language (PHP), all of which are requirements of ExpressionEngine. Installing XAMPP allows us to experiment with ExpressionEngine on our own computer before we change anything on a live website.

Setting up a local AMP (Apache, MySQL, PHP) environment has typically required configuring the different applications to work on their own, and then to work with each other. With XAMPP, this interplay has already been set up for you, and the system comes configured and ready to go, so we can concentrate our time on learning ExpressionEngine in a risk-free environment.

> We are installing XAMPP here as a 'development' or 'testing' environment only. We will only be using XAMPP for testing and exploring ExpressionEngine, and not as a 'production' environment for serving our website to the outside world. Setting up a production web server and a database server and securing and optimizing them is a topic beyond the scope of this text.

There is a version of the XAMPP package available for Windows, Linux, Mac OS X, and the Solaris operating system. XAMPP is free to download, and the package contains the following:

- The AMP environment of Apache, MySQL, and PHP needed to install ExpressionEngine.
- The software phpMyAdmin, the leading web-based interface to MySQL, which is needed to manage the ExpressionEngine database.

XAMPP also comes with other features such as OpenSSL and FileZilla (an FTP server) that we do not take advantage of in this book, but that you may find useful.

Installing XAMPP

The installation walk-through in this chapter only covers Windows. If you find yourself in need of further help, check out the XAMPP documentation page at `http://www.apachefriends.org/en/faq-xampp.html`.

If you are running Mac OS X, you may prefer to check out MAMP at `http://www.mamp.info/en/index.php` as an alternative to XAMPP. This application creates an AMP environment just like XAMPP, but is exclusive to the Mac OS environment. The installation and configuration may be a little different, but the end result is an `http://localhost` environment that you can use to test ExpressionEngine. If you decide to use MAMP (or already have it installed), please skip to *Setting Up the ExpressionEngine Database* at the end of this appendix.

Download XAMPP

There are multiple ways to download XAMPP. There are four different packages as well as two add-ons:

- XAMPP Basic Package
- XAMPP Development Package
- XAMPP Upgrade Package
- Perl (add-on for XAMPP)
- Tomcat (add-on for XAMPP)
- XAMPP Lite

The packages can be downloaded in multiple ways, through:

- Installer
- ZIP Archive
- Self-extracting ZIP archive

For the purposes of this appendix, we will be downloading the Installer version of the basic XAMPP package. We do not need the development package or the Perl or Tomcat add-ons. However, if you have a slower internet connection, or if you already have XAMPP installed, you may prefer to choose the Lite or the Upgrade package.

1. Visit http://www.apachefriends.org/en/xampp.html.
2. On that page, there will be a link to the XAMPP version for your particular operating system. We are going to select **XAMPP for Windows**.
3. Select the **Installer** version of **XAMPP for Windows**—it will most likely be one of the first options on the page.
4. Clicking the **Installer** link takes you to SourceForge where we can download the file. The file download should begin automatically, depending on the security features of your browser.

> If you have Internet Explorer 7, Internet Explorer may block the site from downloading files to your computer. A warning will appear in a small bar at the top of your browser screen—click on it and select **Download File**.

5. Finally, we will be prompted to save the file. Save it to your Desktop or My Documents area.

Depending on the speed of your internet connection, the file may take some time to download.

Install XAMPP

Now that we have downloaded the XAMPP file, the next step is to install it.

> If you are running the Skype VOIP application, or if you are running IIS Server, you will need to exit them before proceeding. Apache cannot start as a service if Skype or IIS is also running—though when XAMPP is not in use, you can exit XAMPP to use Skype or IIS.

1. Double-click on the file that we downloaded in order to run it.
2. Select the language you wish the installation process to use, and click **Ok**.

3. A welcome message will display. Click **Next**.
4. Next, we have to choose a place to install XAMPP. This book assumes that XAMPP is installed in `c:\xampp`. Choose a directory and select **Next**. Note that for Windows Vista, Apache Friends recommends *not* installing XAMPP into your `c:\Program Files\` folder.

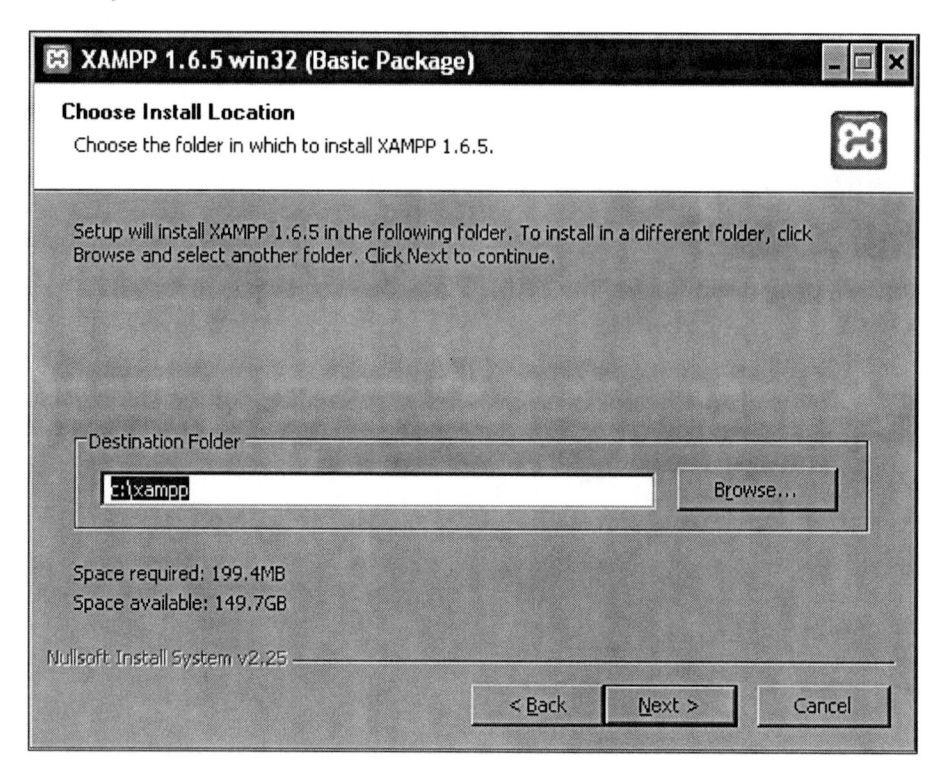

5. In the next screen, we are prompted to install Apache and MySQL as services. Doing this will save us from having to start XAMPP every time we switch on our computer (and will allow other applications you may have, such as Skype, to run simultaneously), so check those boxes (but do leave the FileZilla box unchecked). Then click **Install**.

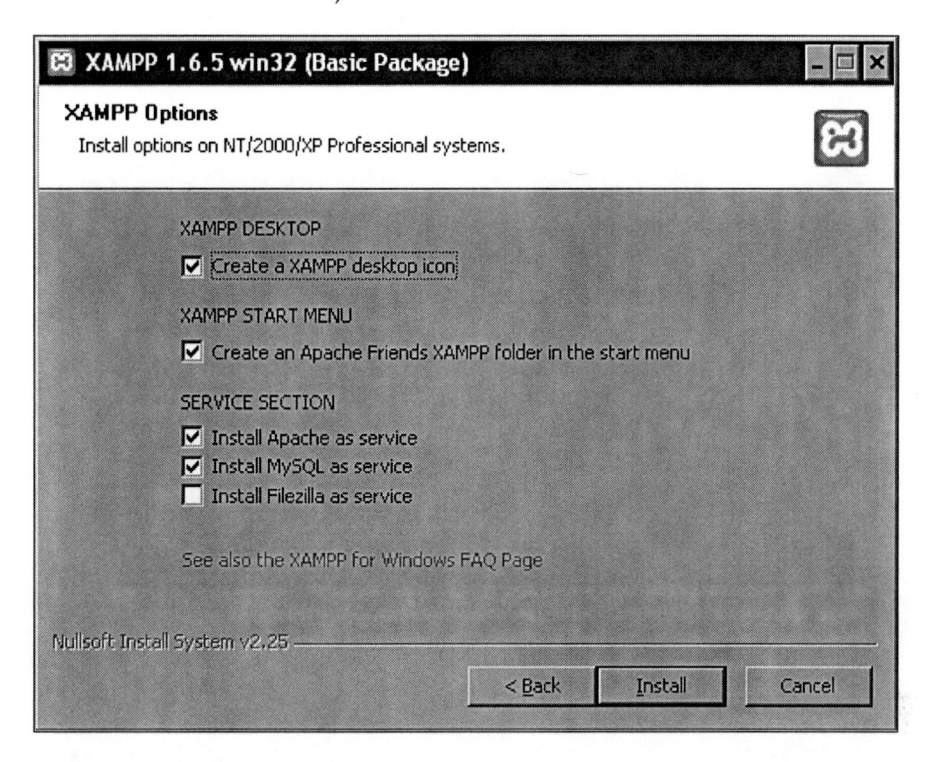

6. XAMPP will then install. At one point, a command-line window will open; do not be alarmed—this is normal! After the installation is complete, we will get a message indicating so. Click **Finish**.

7. Next, we are prompted to start the XAMPP control panel, which can also be opened by selecting **Start | All Programs | XAMPP | XAMPP Control Panel**, or by running `c:\xampp\xampp-control.exe`. Select **Yes**.

We are now done with the installation.

Using XAMPP

The XAMPP control panel is used to control and monitor the status of services that XAMPP has installed. When the control panel is running, the following icon will be visible in your system tray:

Double-clicking on this icon will bring up the **Control Panel**.

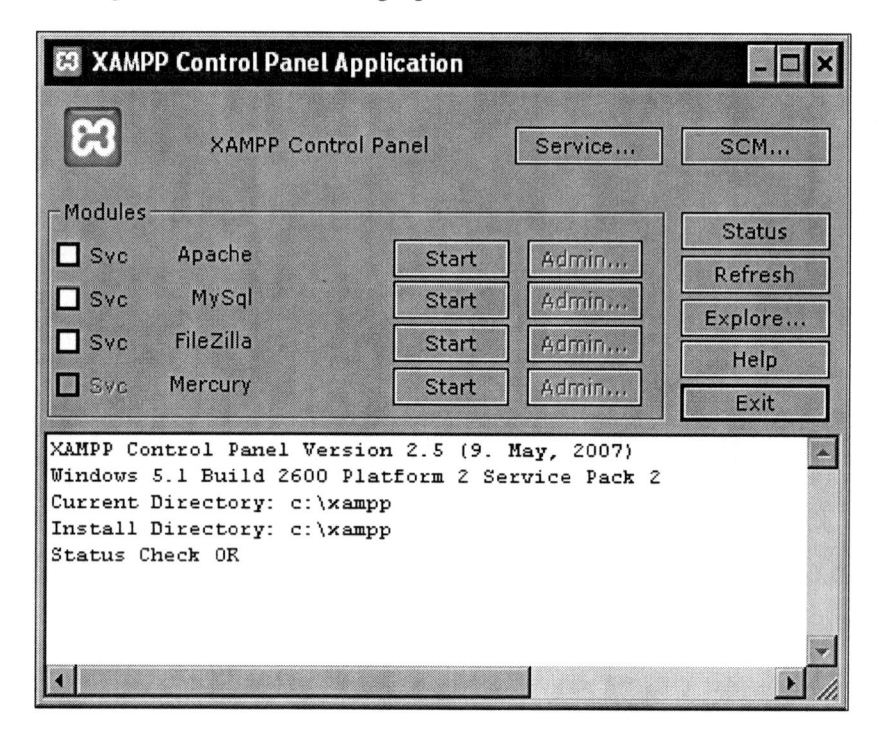

For ExpressionEngine to be able to install and run, both Apache and MySQL need to be running. If they are not, check the box marked **Svc**, and click **Start** to start them as services.

> If the Apache service will not start and stay started, verify that you have exited out of Skype and/or ISS.

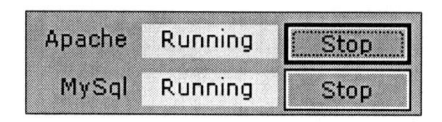

Allowing .htaccess Files to Be Used

To take advantage of some features in ExpressionEngine (such as removing the `index.php` from ExpressionEngine URLs), we need to use a `.htaccess` file, which requires the Apache module `mod_rewrite` to be enabled.

1. First, browse to `C:\xampp\apache\conf` in Windows Explorer, and open the file `httpd.conf` in a text editor.

2. Do a search for the phase `mod_rewrite` and you should find a line that reads:

    `#LoadModule rewrite_module modules/mod_rewrite.so`

3. Remove the leading # symbol, and save the file. (This uncomments the line in question).

Your `.htaccess` files should now be recognized—we will be using them in Chapter 2.

XAMPP in Action

With Apache and MySQL running, we are ready to go.

1. Open up a browser and navigate to `http://localhost/`.
2. If XAMPP is running, you should see a splash screen as follows. Select **English**.

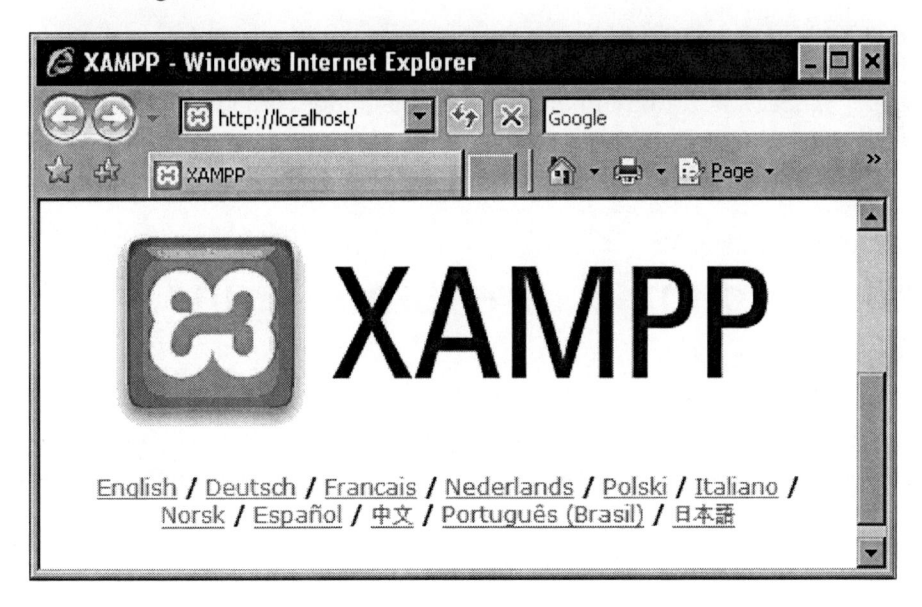

Installing XAMPP

3. We are then brought to the main XAMPP home page.

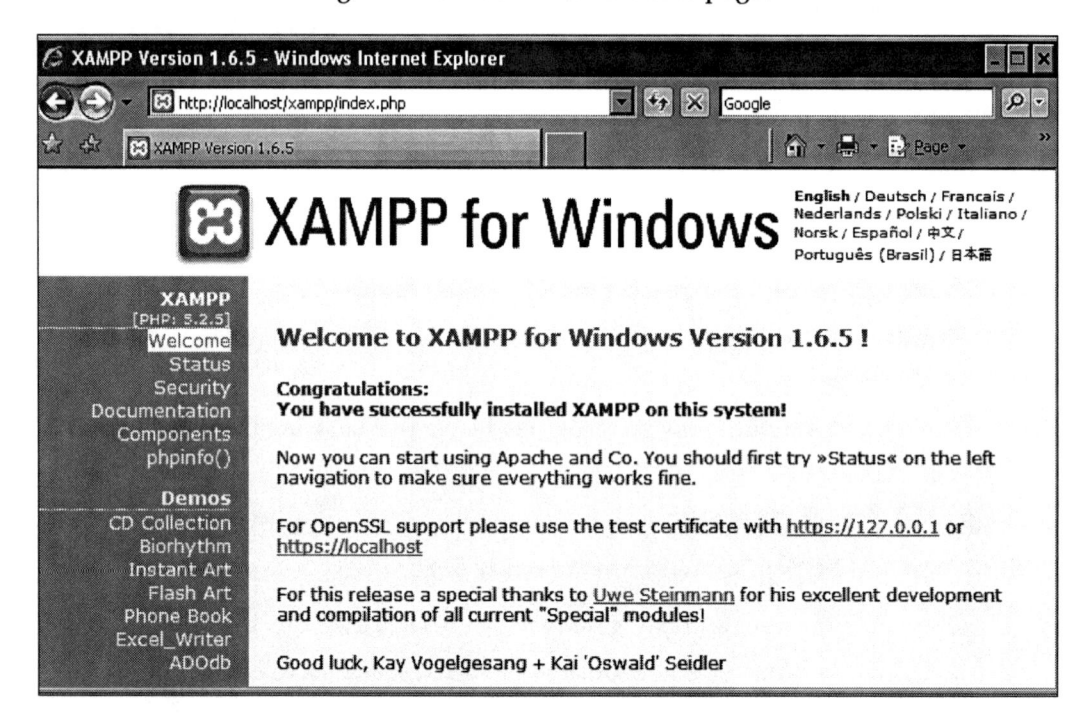

Now that XAMPP is installed, there is one important folder to note: `C:\xampp\htdocs`. This is our web server root. A file placed in this folder will be accessible via our `http://localhost/` domain. Right now, this folder contains all the files for the web page shown in the previous screenshot. we can remove or backup these files so that they do not conflict in anyway with ExpressionEngine when we install it.

Setting Up the ExpressionEngine Database

One final step before we can install ExpressionEngine is setting up a database. When using a hosting service, the host will often have set up your database for you and provided you with the database name, server address, and username and password.

1. First, navigate to phpMyAdmin (which is installed with XAMPP). Navigate to `http://localhost/phpmyadmin/`.

Appendix A

2. In the left-hand column there should be a text box that says **Create new database**. We are going to call our database **ee**. Then click **Create**.

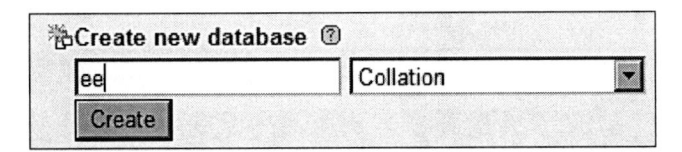

3. We are then brought to our database screen. Notice on the left-hand side that no tables have been found in the database. This is because the tables are created when ExpressionEngine is installed. For now, we are going to create an ExpressionEngine username. Select **SQL** from the top menu.

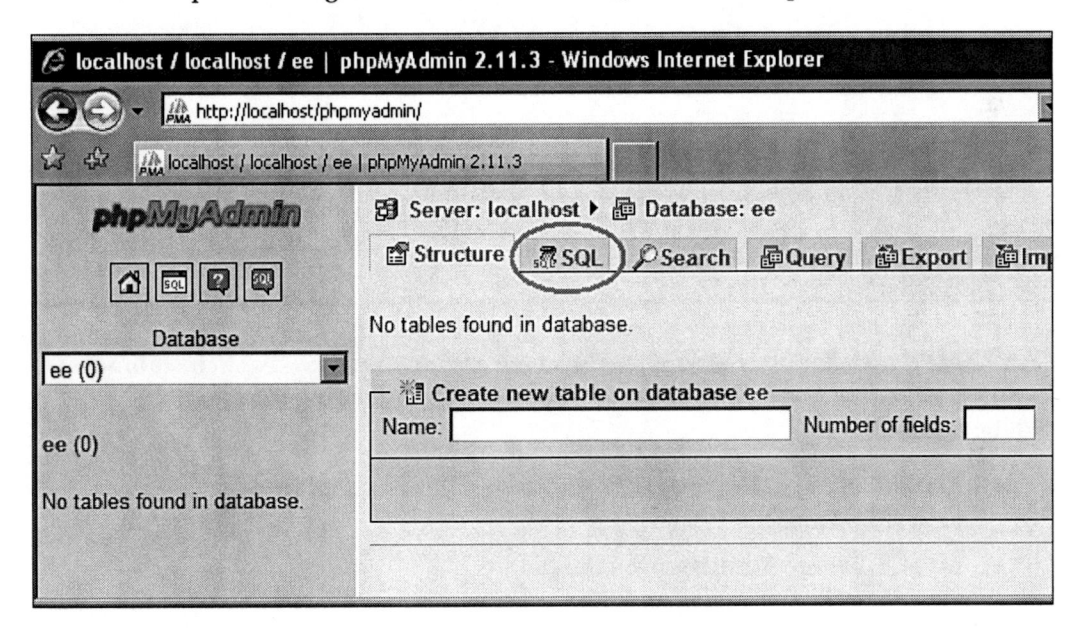

4. Next, type in the following command to create a new user called `eeuser` with a password of `password`, which has all rights to the `ee` database. Click **Go**.

```
GRANT ALL PRIVILEGES ON ee.* TO eeuser@localhost IDENTIFIED BY
                              'password' WITH GRANT OPTION
```

Installing XAMPP

5. We should then see a message **Your SQL query has been executed successfully**. If so, you can click the **Privileges** tab to verify that `eeuser` has been set up and only has access to the `ee` database.

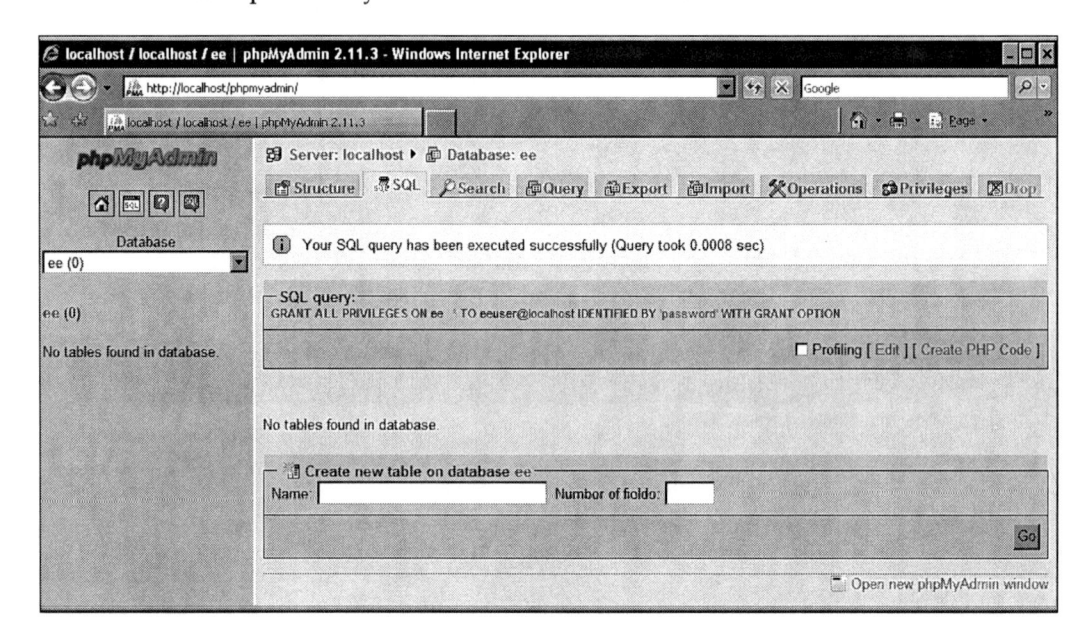

Our XAMPP installation is now set up, and we are now ready to begin installing ExpressionEngine! For the purposes of Chapter 2, the following information will be needed:

- Root of our website: `http://localhost/` (files located in `c:\xampp\htdocs\`)
- MySQL Server Address: `localhost`
- MySQL Username: `eeuser`
- MySQL Password: `password`
- MySQL Database Name: `ee`

B

Solutions to Exercises

Most of the exercises throughout this book have more than one solution. The following are the example solutions to some of the exercises in this book. Where a solution has not been provided, the instructions in the chapter can be adapted to complete the exercise.

Chapter 3

Chapter 3 described how to set up your first blog and introduced the use of CSS within Expression Engine.

Exercise 1

To post a new entry to a weblog, log into the control panel at `http://localhost/admin.php` (or `http://www.example.com/admin.php`), and select **Publish** from the menu at the top of the screen. Select the weblog you wish to post to (in this case **Toast News**), and type in the new entry. Hit **Submit** when you are done.

Solutions to Exercises

Exercise 2

To create a second weblog, follow the instructions in Chapter 3 to create a new weblog and post a starting entry to it. Then create a new template group. Copy the `index` template from the `news` template group into the new template group's `index` template and change the following line so that it points to the short name of the new weblog:

```
{exp:weblog:entries weblog="toastnews"}
```

You can also change the title of the page to reflect the different content.

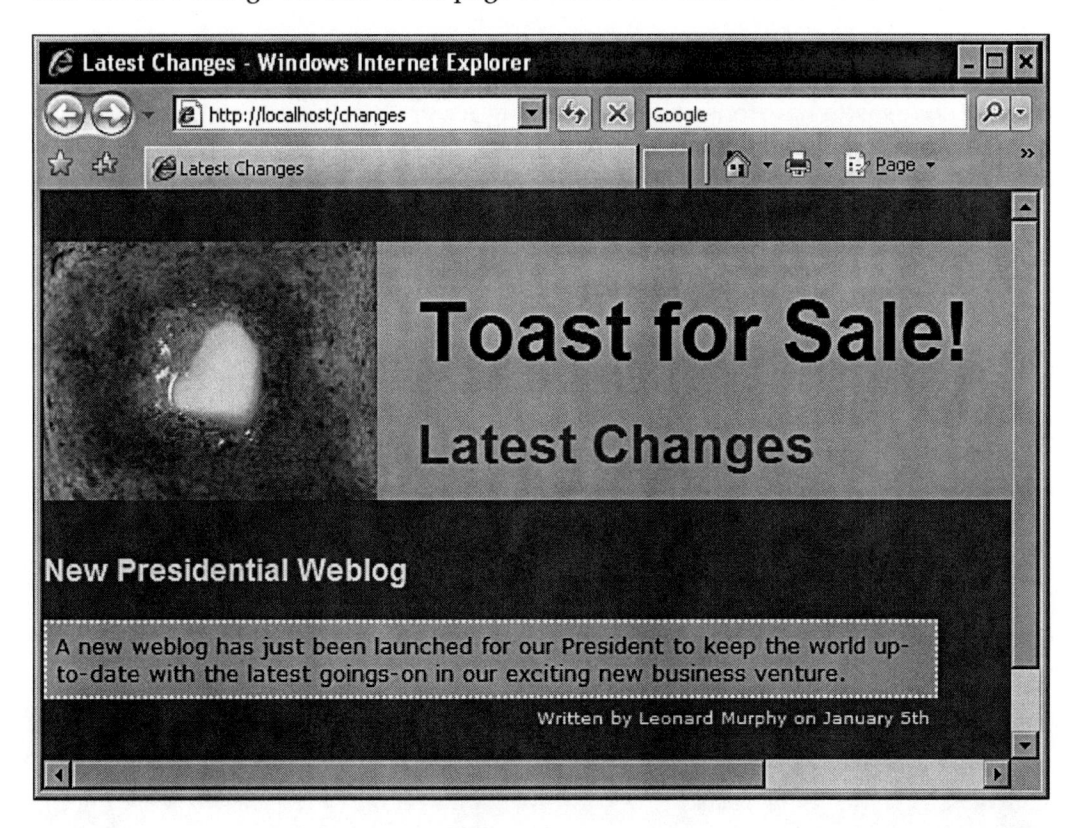

Solutions to Exercises

Exercise 3

Exercise 3 involves modifying our CSS. To change the color scheme of the templates, select some complimentary colors and then edit `toast/toast_css` to replace your original colors with new tones. In the following screenshot, the original browns have been dubiously replaced with shades of yellow:

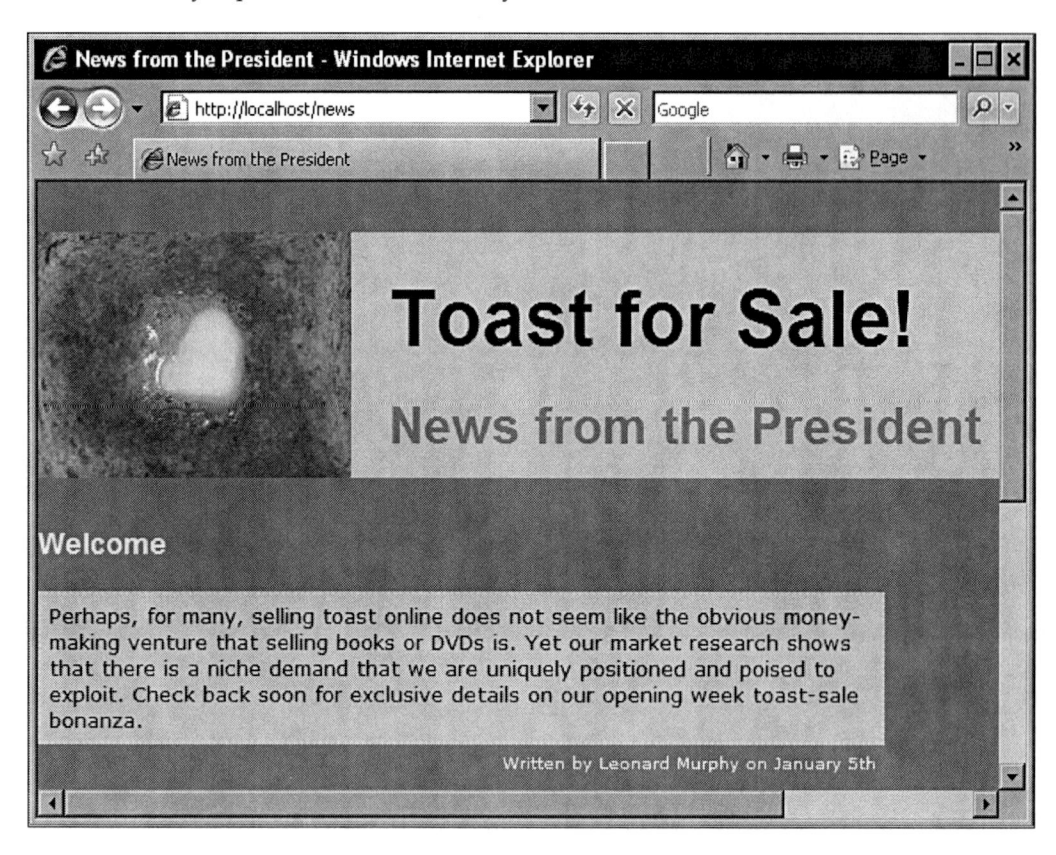

Appendix B

To move your entries so that they no longer leave space for the menu, you can change the following line in our CSS so that it reads 100%:

```
#content{
  font-size: 80%;
  width: 70%;
  float: left;
}
```

To play around with a different photo size, you will first need to copy or upload the new photo to your `images` folder.

Next, you need to change the `toast/toast_css` template. The `header` element should point to the new image, and you will need to adjust the `header` height to match the height of the new image (for example, `200px`).

Solutions to Exercises

If the image overlaps with our page headings, you will also need to adjust the `margin-left` property of your `#header h1` and `h2` elements. In the following screenshot, the `margin-left` was set to `275px` as shown next:

```
#header{
  background: url('{site_url}images/square.png ') no-repeat top left;
  background-color: #DEB887;
  height: 200px;
  margin-bottom: 30px;
}
```

Chapter 4

Chapter 4 described how to set up customized fields and create a weblog that will hold the text for a conventional website.

Exercise 1

To create a new page, you will want to **Publish** to the **Toast Website** weblog. Before you hit **Submit**, don't forget to select the **Pages** option, and choose a **Page URI** for your new posting (for example, `/promotions`). You will also likely want to add a link to the new page in the `toast/.menu` template.

Exercise 2

First, create a new weblog (for example, **toastmenu**) following the same instructions as used in the chapter to create the **toastwebsite** weblog.

Then, create the custom fields as specified. You have two options: you can either create just one set of custom fields and have each weblog item be a separate post Or you can create several copies of these custom fields in your custom field group, so you only need one weblog post for all your menu items. Either way, you will still want to set the **Default Text Formatting** to **None**, and you will want to **Hide Formatting Menu** as you are using Text Inputs. Associate the custom fields with the **toastmenu** weblog.

Then, publish the menu items to the weblog. A sample entry might be the following:

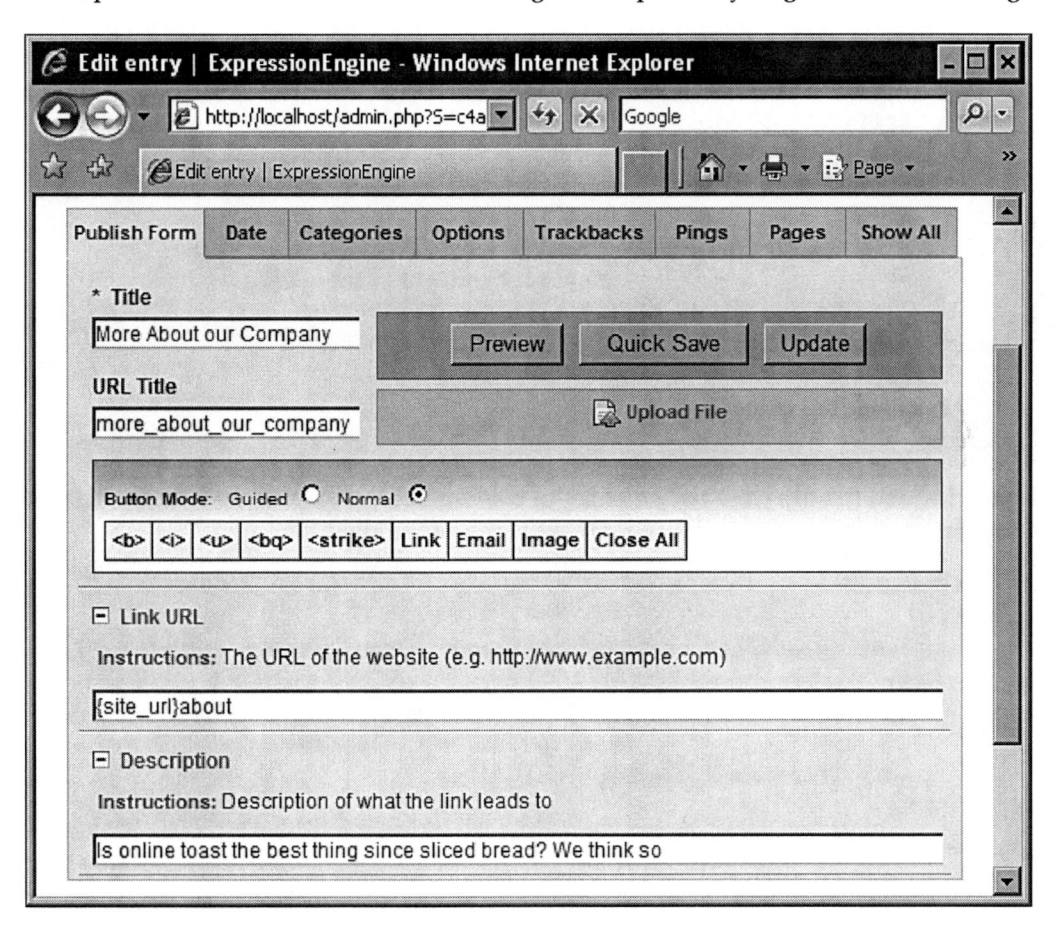

Solutions to Exercises

An example of the new menu template code appears as follows:

```
<h4>Menu</h4>
<ul>
  {exp:weblog:entries weblog="toastmenu" dynamic="off" sort="asc"}
    {if toastmenu_link1}
      <li>
        <a href="{toastmenu_link1}" title="{toastmenu_
                            description1}">{title}</a>
        <div>{toastmenu_description1}</div>
      </li>
    {/if}
    {if toastmenu_link2}
      <li>
        <a href="{toastmenu_link2}" title="{toastmenu_
                            description2}">{title}</a>
        <div>{toastmenu_description2}</div>
      </li>
    {/if}
    {if toastmenu_link3}
      <li>
        <a href="{toastmenu_link3}" title="{toastmenu_
                            description3}">{title}</a>
        <div>{toastmenu_description3}</div>
      </li>
    {/if}
  {/exp:weblog:entries}
</ul>
```

If you decided to only have only one set of custom fields and post each menu item as a separate weblog, your template code may look more like this:

```
<h4>Menu</h4>
<ul>
  {exp:weblog:entries weblog="toastmenu" dynamic="off" sort="asc"}
    <li>
      <a href="{toastmenu_link}" title="{toastmenu_
                          description}">{title}</a>
      <div>{toastmenu_description}</div>
    </li>
  {/exp:weblog:entries}
</ul>
```

Note that by default a weblog displays the items with the newest items on top. This can be manipulated by adjusting the dates of the entries. First, in the just shown template, we have set the weblog tag to display entries as oldest first (`sort="asc"`).

You can then change the date of our menu item entries so that our first menu item is on the 1st of last January, the 2nd menu item on the 2nd of January, and so on.

Exercise 3

An example footer CSS might be as follows:

```css
#footer{
  width: 65%;
  text-align: center;
  margin: 10px;
  border-top: 1px solid #F0E68C;
  font-size: 65%;
  color: #F0E68C;
  float: left;
}
```

Clearly, it can be styled in many ways. The only key part is the `float: left;` and `width: 65%`, which force the footer underneath the body of the page, rather than next to the menu.

Exercise 4

An example styling of a top menu might be as follows:

```css
#topmenu{
  background: #DEB887;
  text-align: center;
  font-size: 75%;
}
#topmenu ul li{
  display:inline;
  margin-top: 5px;
  margin-right: 5px;
}
#topmenu a{
  color: red;
  text-decoration: none;
```

Solutions to Exercises

```
    font-weight: bold;
}
#topmenu a:hover{
  border-top: 1px solid #FFEFD5;
  border-bottom: 1px solid #FFEFD5;
}
#topmenu a:visited{
  color: #A52A2A;
}
```

Clearly it can be styled in many ways.

Chapter 5

Chapter 5 described how to set up an advanced weblog with customized fields, multiple-and single-entry pages, and comments.

Exercise 2 and 3

To complete this exercise, modify the `index` template of the `news` template group to be more like the `products` template group. Follow the same instructions as in the chapter. Example changes are:

Appendix B

- The variables at the top of the page should be updated to point to the toastnews weblog and the news template group.
- The title and headings of the page should reference News from the President.
- The fields should be changed from our custom field group to the default {summary}, {body}, and {extended} that our News from the President weblog uses.
- The wording of links should reference news instead of products.

Example code with changes highlighted follows:

```
{assign_variable:my_weblog="toastnews"}
{assign_variable:my_template_group="news"}
{assign_variable:my_site_wide_templates="toast"}
<!DOCTYPE html PUBLIC "-//W3C//DTD XHTML 1.0 Strict//EN"
"http://www.w3.org/TR/xhtml1/DTD/xhtml1-strict.dtd">
<html xmlns="http://www.w3.org/1999/xhtml">
  <head>
    {if segment_2}
      <title>Toast for Sale: {exp:weblog:entries weblog="{my_weblog}"
      limit="1" disable="categories|custom_fields|member_data|
      pagination|trackbacks"}{title}{/exp:weblog:entries}</title>
    {if:else}
      <title>News from the President</title>
    {/if}
    <link rel='stylesheet' type='text/css' media='all' href='{path=
                        {my_site_wide_templates}/toast_css}' />
    <style type='text/css' media='screen'>@import site_wide_
                        templates}/toast_css}";</style>
    <meta http-equiv="content-type" content="text/html; charset=UTF-
                                                              8" />
  </head>
  <body>
    <div id="header">
      <h1>Toast for Sale!</h1>
      {if segment_2}
        {exp:weblog:entries weblog="{my_weblog}" limit="1" disable="
        categories|custom_fields|member_data|pagination|trackbacks"}
          <h2>{title}</h2>
        {/exp:weblog:entries}
      {if:else}
        <h2>News from the President</h2>
      {/if}
```

[363]

Solutions to Exercises

```
        </div>
        <div id="content">
          {if segment_2}
            {exp:weblog:entries weblog="{my_weblog}" limit="1"
                                            require_entry="yes"}
              {if no_results}
                {redirect="404"}
              {/if}
              <h3>{title}</h3>
              <div class="contentinner">
                {body}
                {extended}
              </div>
              <p class="footnote">Written by {author} on {entry_date
                                          format="%F %j%S"}</p>
              <p class="footnote"><a href="{site_url}{my_template_group}"
                      title="Back to News">Go back to all news...</a></p>
            {/exp:weblog:entries}
            <h3>Comments</h3>
{exp:comment:preview}
            <div class="contentinner">
              {comment}
            </div>
            <p class="footnote">Being Previewed by {name} on {comment
            _date format='%m/%d'} at {comment_date format='%h:%i
                                                        %A'}</p>
{/exp:comment:preview}
            {exp:comment:entries}
              {if comments}
                <div class="contentinner">
                  {comment}
                </div>
                <p class="footnote">Posted by {name} on {comment_date
                format='%m/%d'} at {comment_date format='%h:%i %A'}</p>
              {/if}
            {/exp:comment:entries}
            <h3>Post a Comment</h3>
            {exp:comment:form preview="{my_template_group}/index"}
              {if logged_out}
                <p>
                  Name:<br />
                  <input type="text" name="name" value="{name}" size="50"
                                                                    />
                </p>
                <p>
```

```
                    Email:<br />
                    <input type="text" name="email" value="{email}"
                                                    size="50" />
                </p>
            {/if}
            <p>
                <textarea name="comment" cols="50"
                    rows="12">{comment}</textarea>
            </p>
            {if logged_out}
                <p><input type="checkbox" name="save_info" value="yes"
                    {save_info} /> Remember my personal information</p>
            {/if}
            <p><input type="checkbox" name="notify_me" value="yes"
                {notify_me} /> Notify me of follow-up comments?</p>
            {if captcha}
                <p>Submit the word you see below:</p>
                <p>
                    {captcha}
                    <br />
                    <input type="text" name="captcha" value="" size="20"
                                maxlength="20" style="width:140px;" />
                </p>
            {/if}
            <input type="submit" name="submit" value="Submit" />
            <input type="submit" name="preview" value="Preview" />
        {/exp:comment:form}
    {/if}
    {if segment_2==''}
        {exp:weblog:entries weblog="{my_weblog}"}
            <h3><a href="{title_permalink="{my_template_
                            group}"}">{title}</a></h3>
            <div class="contentinner">
                {summary}
            </div>
            <p class="footnote"><a href="{title_permalink="{my_
                    template_group}"}">Read more...</a></p>
        {/exp:weblog:entries}
    {/if}
    </div>
    <div id="menu">
        {embed={my_site_wide_templates}/.menu}
    </div>
  </body>
</html>
```

Solutions to Exercises

Exercise 4

To set the amount of time to show a comment, go to **Admin | Weblog Administration | Weblog Management**. Select the **Toast News** weblog and click **Edit Preferences**. Select **Comment Posting Preferences** and change the **Comment Expiration** field to **30**.

Exercise 5

To edit the Publish page preferences, go to **Admin | Weblog Administration | Weblog Management**. Select the **Toast News** weblog, and click **Edit Preferences**. Select **Publish Page Customization**. Some options that may be unnecessary for the Toast News weblog include:

- Trackback Form
- Author Menu
- Status Menu
- Date Fields
- Option Buttons
- Ping Buttons
- Category Menu
- Pages Submission Fields
- Show All Tab

Experiment with each option and then return to the **Publish** page to see what the difference is.

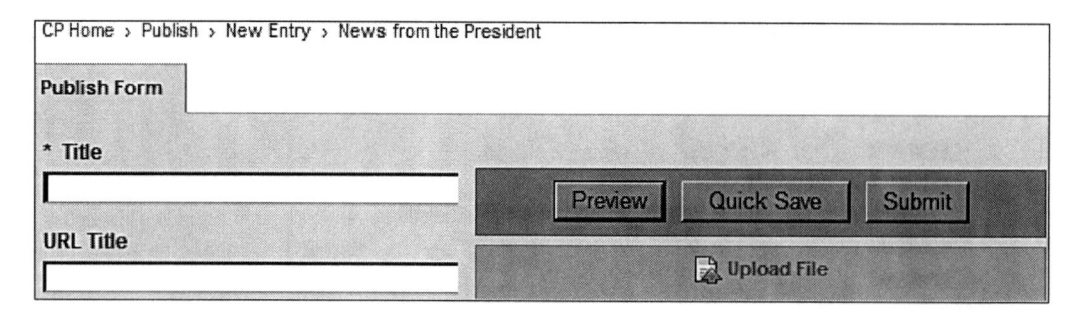

Chapter 6

Chapter 6 introduced members and member groups.

Exercise 1

To edit an existing page as Editor Phil, first log into the control panel as `editorphil`. From the menu, select **Edit** and click on the entry to be edited. If there are lots of weblog entries, filter them by weblog so that you only see a few entries. Select the entry, make the update, and click **Update**.

Exercise 2

To create a template group that can only modify templates, go to **Admin | Members and Groups | Member Groups** and select **Create New Member Group**. The new group will need control panel access (under **Control Panel Access**) and will need to be able to access the TEMPLATES area (under **Control Panel Area Access**). Under **Template Editing Privileges**, you can decide which templates can be edited and which cannot. Register and assign a new member to this group, then log in and verify that it works as expected.

Solutions to Exercises

Exercise 3

To create a menu item that only members can see, you need to edit the `.menu` template. If each menu item is listed out separately, then add the following code around the menu item:

```
{if logged_in}
  <li>
    <a href="{site_url}promotions" title="Promotions">Promotions</a>
    <div>Check our our current deals!</div>
  </li>
{/if}
```

Alternatively, if you are using a weblog to manage our menu content (as suggested in an exercise at the end of Chapter 4), then add the following code to the `toast/.menu` template. This is a little more complex, but essentially says that if the member is logged out and the `url_title` of the `toastmenu` entry is `promotions`, then do not display it (all other menu items will display). If the member is logged in, then display the menu item no matter what the `url_title` is.

```
{if (logged_out AND url_title!="promotions") OR logged_in}
  <li>
    <a href="{toastmenu_link}" title="{toastmenu_
                      description}">{title}</a>
    <div>{toastmenu_description}</div>
  </li>
{/if}
```

Chapter 7

Chapter 7 introduced the calendar functionality in ExpressionEngine.

Exercise 1

To display the days of the week in our calendar using single letters, you need to edit the code in between our `calendar_heading` tags in our `calendar/index` template to read as follows:

```
{calendar_heading}
  <td class="calendarDayHeading">{lang:weekday_short}</td>
{/calendar_heading}
```

Exercise 2

See Chapter 9 for more information on plug-ins. To install a plug-in, download the files and place the plug-in file (begins with `pi`) in the `system/plugins` directory and the language file in the `system/language` directory. Follow the instructions as outlined at `http://lincolnite.com/ee/repeet`.

Exercise 3

After following the section in the chapter, go to the **toastcalendar** custom field group and create the additional custom field; call it `editorsonly`. Use a type of **Drop-down List** with two options: **Yes** and **No**.

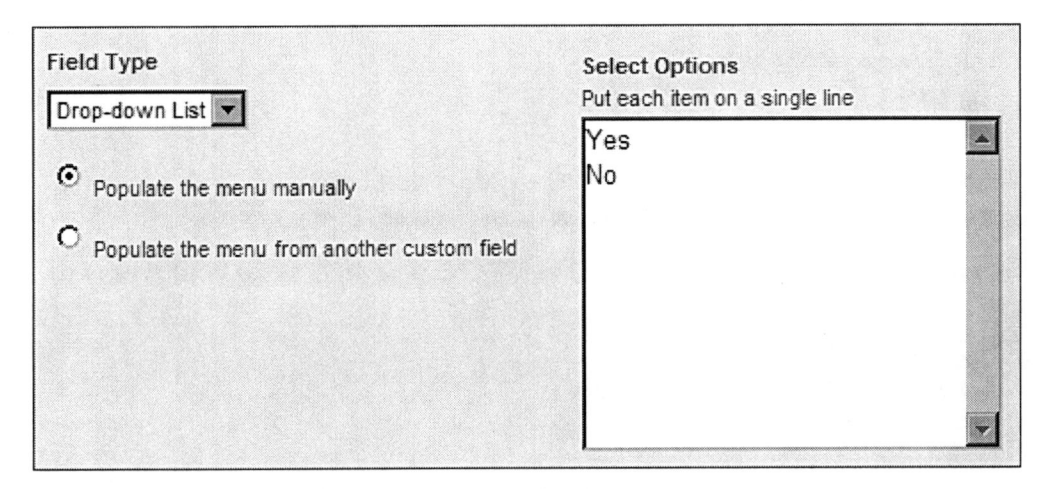

Next, edit the `toastcalendar` weblog entries so that the current entries are marked as `No` and then post the new entry to mark the Editors-only promotion day.

Next, add the following code inside the `{if entries}` tag on the `calendar/index` page. Notice how the indentation makes it easier to tell which if statement the `if: else` command applies to.

```
{if entries}
   <td class='{switch}'>{day_number}
     {exp:weblog:entries weblog="{my_weblog}" year="{segment_2}"
     month="{segment_3}" day="{day_number}" limit="5" orderby=
            "toastcalendartime" show_future_entries="yes"}
       {if editorsonly=="Yes"}
         {if member_group=='1' OR member_group=='6'}
           <div class="calendarEvent">
             <a href="{title_permalink=calendar/event}">
               {toastcalendartime}<br />
```

Solutions to Exercises

```
                {title}<br />
                <i>{toastcalendarlocation}</i>
              </a>
            </div>
        {/if}
      {if:else}
          <div class="calendarEvent">
            <a href="{title_permalink=calendar/event}">
              {toastcalendartime}<br />
              {title}<br />
              <i>{toastcalendarlocation}</i>
            </a>
          </div>
        {/if}
      {/exp:weblog:entries}
    </td>
{/if}
```

Visit the calendar page, both logged in as an editor and logged out, and verify that the menu item only appears when logged in as a Super Admin or editor.

To create an orange border, add the following CSS class style to the bottom of your `calendar/calendar_css` template:

```
.orange{
  border-left: 1px solid orange;
  border-right: 1px solid orange;
}
```

Next, change the following piece of code to use this new class:

```
{if editorsonly=="Yes"}
  {if member_group=='1' OR member_group=='6'}
    <div class="calendarEvent orange">
```

Now when you visit the calendar as an editor, the extra **Editors Only** item appears with an orange border.

<<			November 2009			>>
Sun	Mon	Tue	Wed	Thu	Fri	Sat
1	2	3	4	5	6	7 10am-8pm Food Festival Central Park, New York City
8	9	10	11	12	13	14
15	16	17	18	19	20	21
22	23	24	25 All day Editors Only Promotion Day All locations	26 Thanksgiving Day Holiday Sale Begins	27	28
29	30	1	2	3	4	5

Solutions to Exercises

Chapter 8

Chapter 8 introduced the photo gallery module.

Exercise 1

Before we can display subcategories, we first need to create a subcategory, and assign a photo to it. For the purposes of this solution, we are going to create a subcategory of **Winter**, called **Snow**. Next, upload a new photo into this subcategory, or change the category of an existing photo.

There are two ways to display subcategories in our photo gallery: subcategory markers and subcategory rows. This solution demonstrates the marker method.

Edit the following code in the `toastgallery/index` template to place a subcategory marker before a subcategory:

```
<td>
  <h3>{subcat_marker}*{/subcat_marker} <a href="{category_
  path=toastgallery/browse}" title="Jump to {category}">
                                  {category}</a></h3>
  <br />
  <i>{category_description}</i>
</td>
```

The {subcat_marker} will indent the title of each subcategory and place an * symbol before each subcategory. Instead of an *, we could also have used an image.

[372]

Exercise 2

To indicate if an image is ***hot***, edit the `toastgallery/browse` template as follows:

```
<td>
   <a href="{id_path=toastgallery/photo}"><img src="{thumb_url}"
                                 border="0" title="{title}" /></a>
   <br />
   <div>{if views>10}*hot* {/if}{title}</div>
</td>
```

Then visit a photo in the photo gallery, and verify that the ***hot*** symbol appears after the appropriate number of views. (Note that we could have also used an image instead of the words).

Index

Symbols

404 page error
  behavior, altering 138
  defining 94-97

A

advanced features, photo gallery
  batch uploads 283, 284
  custom fields 288-290
  photos, editing 285
  watermark, adding on photos 286-288
advanced weblog
  creating 107, 108
  features 107
  fields, customizing 109-113
advanced weblog, creating
  exercise 144
  solutions 362-366
AMP
  about 343
  setting up 343
Apache, MySQL, PHP. *See* **AMP**

B

banned member group 163

C

calendar
  custom fields, associating 207
  custom fields, creating 205, 206
  events, displaying 230, 231
  events, styling 232-235
  examples, posting 207-211
  exercise 241
  need for 203
  separate template, creating 227-229
  solutions 368-370
  tasks 238
  upcoming events, displaying 236, 238
  weblog, creating 204
calendar CSS template
  creating 219, 220
  styles, adding 220-226
calendar template
  blank calendar, creating 213-218
  blank calendar template, creating 212, 213
  calendar, formatting with CSS 218
  calendar CSS template, creating 219
  creating 212
captcha 9
categories, using to create site structure
  category browsing page, creating 329, 330
  category groups, creating 325-327
  category groups, displaying 328
  displaying 330
comment
  about 125
  form, creating 131-134
  moderating, in control panel 135
  previewing 136
  spam, preventing 126-130
content management system
  ExpressionEngine 7
  need for 7
  static and dynamic website, differentiating 8
control panel, ExpressionEngine
  bulletin board 35
  communicate tab 36

CP home 34
main menu bar 35
modules tab 36
my account tab 36
my admin tab 36
templates link 35
conventional website
   template, creating 83-90
custom field
   creating 71
   field group, creating 72, 73

D

design, photo gallery
   category page layout, creating 269-276
   changing 257
   main index page, creating 276
   single-entry page layout, creating 257
discussion forum, ExpressionEngine add-ons
   about 296
   activity 300, 301
   themes, changing 301
   categories 296
   customizing 301-303
   customizing for website 303, 304
   forum boards used 296
   forums 296
   permissions 297
   preferences 297
   setting up 296
   users, setting up 298

E

editor member
   creating 170, 172
editor member group
   creating 163, 164
exercise
   solutions 353
ExpressionEngine
   about 8
   add-ons 294
   additional features 9, 10
   advantages 10

calendar 203
captcha 9
control panel 34
control panel, logging into 25
database, setting up 350-352
directories 18
drawbacks 10
example 33
features 317
files 18
files, downloading 16, 17
files, uploading 17-20
hosting server 16
installing 20-25
mailing list module 196
member 145
overview 7
photo gallery 243
requirements 15
templates 8, 36
upgrading 340, 342
URLs 92
user-friendly URLs, creating 16, 26
variables, using 139
weblog 44
ExpressionEngine-powered site
   backing up 335
   backing up, phpMyAdmin tool used 336
   backing up, steps 336-338
   restoring 338, 339
ExpressionEngine add-ons
   about 296
   discussion forum 296
   finding 294
   managing 294
   modules 294
   plug-ins 295
   Simple Commerce module 305
ExpressionEngine features
   categories, using to create site structure 325
   closed status 321
   open status 321
   related entries, using 331
   search functionality, adding to site 317
   status groups, using 321
extensions 296

F

field group, weblog
  Textarea 75

G

guests member group 163

H

homepage
  first draft, creating 83

I

installing
  photo gallery 244
  XAMPP 344

M

mailing list
  creating 197-199
  emails, sending 200, 201
  member registration, allowing 199, 200
main index page, creating
  existing index template, backing up 276, 278
  photo gallery main page, creating 278-283
member
  global preferences 159-162
  links, setting up for member functions 145-148
  member group 162
  member list 156
  member profile 151
  registering 149-151
member-only section, creating
  about 175, 176
  content, making visible to members 176-179
  entire template, making accessible 180
member group
  banned member group 163
  configuring 164
  creating, exercise 201
  editor member group 163
  editor phil, logging in as 172-175
  guests member group 163
  introducing 162
  members group 163
  pending member group 163
  super admins member group 162
member group, configuring
  options, outside control panel 165, 166
  options, within control panel 167-170
member group, creating
  solutions 367, 368
member group content
  changing 182-185
member list 156-158
member profile
  exploring 151-155
members group 163
moderator 298
modules 294
multiple templates
  working with 42-44

P

page
  About Us page 92
  creating 91
pending member group 163
permissions 297
photo gallery
  advanced features 283
  creating, without photo gallery module 291
  design, changing 257
  installing 244
  photos, uploading 250, 252
  setting up 244
  viewing 252-257
photo gallery, creating
  exercise 291
  solutions 372, 373
photos, photo gallery
  uploading 250, 252
plug-ins 295
posting entries
  solutions 353-357
posting entries, ExpressionEngine
  exercise 67

preferences 297
product
  publishing 113-117
  template, creating 117-122

R

related entries
  creating 333, 334
  reverse related entries 334, 335

S

SAEF
  about 185
  creating 185-191
  CSS, modifying 192-195
search functionality, adding to site
  customizing 319, 320
  search box, adding 317, 319
setting up, photo gallery
  basic settings, defining 245-247
  categories, creating 249, 250
Simple Commerce module, ExpressionEngine add-ons
  about 305
  customizing, for website 307, 309
  setting up 305, 306
  testing 310
single-entry page
  creating 123
single-entry page layout, photo gallery
  creating 257
  photo, displaying 261, 262
  photo comments, displaying 265-269
  photo information, displaying 263, 264
  template heading, creating 260, 261
  template outline, creating 257-259
status groups, using
  custom status group, creating 322
  queue of entries with status, displaying 323
super admins member group 162
Stand-Alone Entry Form. *See* SAEF

T

tag
  about 52

parameters 52
variables 52
tasks, calendar
  event types, handling 238
  fields, displaying 238-240
templates, ExpressionEngine
  about 36
  ExpressionEngine tags, using 37
  multiple templates 42
  URLs, relating to 37-41

U

upgrading, ExpressionEngine
  instructions 341
  releases 340
URLs
  customizing 92
  page module, installing 92, 93
  short URLs, defining for individual weblog entries 93, 94, 105
user-friendly URLs, ExpressionEngine
  creating 26
  index.php, hiding 27, 28
  index.php, renaming 29-31
users, discussion forum
  administrator 299
  member ranks 299
  moderator 298

V

variables
  about 139
  using 139-143

W

weblog
  comment, allowing 126
  creating 70
  exercise 103, 104
  field group, creating 72, 73
  field group, customizing 75-79
  fields, associating 79-81
  solutions 358-361
weblog, creating
  additional options 47-50

weblog, ExpressionEngine
  about 44
  creating 44, 46
  modifying 56
  tag, including in template 52
  template, pointing 51-55

weblog, modifying
  colors, defining 59-62
  creating, to a styling template 56-58
  CSS, using 56
  elements, moving around 63-67
  fonts, defining 59-62
  HTML, using 56
  linking, to a styling template 56-58

website
  menu, writing 97-102

wiki module 310

wiki module, ExpressionEngine add-ons
  about 310

customizing 315
customizing, steps 316
setting up 311, 312
working 313, 314, 315

X

XAMPP
  about 343
  contents 343
  downloading, ways 344, 345
  features 343
  installing 344
  installing, steps 345-347
  starting 349, 350
  using 348

XAMPP, using
  .htaccess files usage, allowing 349

[PACKT PUBLISHING] Thank you for buying Building Websites with ExpressionEngine 1.6

About Packt Publishing

Packt, pronounced 'packed', published its first book *"Mastering phpMyAdmin for Effective MySQL Management"* in April 2004 and subsequently continued to specialize in publishing highly focused books on specific technologies and solutions.

Our books and publications share the experiences of your fellow IT professionals in adapting and customizing today's systems, applications, and frameworks. Our solution based books give you the knowledge and power to customize the software and technologies you're using to get the job done. Packt books are more specific and less general than the IT books you have seen in the past. Our unique business model allows us to bring you more focused information, giving you more of what you need to know, and less of what you don't.

Packt is a modern, yet unique publishing company, which focuses on producing quality, cutting-edge books for communities of developers, administrators, and newbies alike. For more information, please visit our website: www.packtpub.com.

Writing for Packt

We welcome all inquiries from people who are interested in authoring. Book proposals should be sent to authors@packtpub.com. If your book idea is still at an early stage and you would like to discuss it first before writing a formal book proposal, contact us; one of our commissioning editors will get in touch with you.

We're not just looking for published authors; if you have strong technical skills but no writing experience, our experienced editors can help you develop a writing career, or simply get some additional reward for your expertise.

[PACKT PUBLISHING]

Building Powerful and Robust Websites with Drupal 6

ISBN: 978-1-847192-97-4 Paperback: 330 pages

Build your own professional blog, forum, portal or community website with Drupal 6

1. Set up, configure, and deploy Drupal 6
2. Harness Drupal's world-class Content Management System
3. Design and implement your website's look and feel
4. Easily add exciting and powerful features
5. Promote, manage, and maintain your live website

PHP Oracle Web Development: Data processing, Security, Caching, XML, Web Services, and Ajax

ISBN: 978-1-847193-63-6 Paperback: 350 pages

A practical guide to combining the power, performance, scalability, and reliability of the Oracle Database with the ease of use, short development time, and high performance of PHP

1. Program your own PHP/Oracle application
2. Move data processing inside the database
3. Distribute data processing between the web/PHP and Oracle database servers
4. Create reusable building blocks for PHP/Oracle solutions

Please check www.PacktPub.com for information on our titles

[PACKT PUBLISHING]

Building Websites with Joomla! 1.5

ISBN: 978-1-847195-30-2   Paperback: 362 pages

The best-selling Joomla! tutorial guide updated for the latest 1.5 release

1. Learn Joomla! 1.5 features
2. Install and customize Joomla! 1.5
3. Configure Joomla! administration
4. Create your own Joomla! templates
5. Extend Joomla! with new components, modules, and plug-ins

WordPress Theme Design

ISBN: 978-1-847193-09-4   Paperback: 211 pages

A complete guide to creating professional WordPress themes

1. Take control of the look and feel of your WordPress site
2. Simple, clear tutorial to creating Unique and Beautiful themes
3. Expert guidance with practical step-by-step instructions for theme design
4. Design tips, tricks, and troubleshooting ideas

Please check **www.PacktPub.com** for information on our titles

Printed in the United Kingdom by
Lightning Source UK Ltd., Milton Keynes
138838UK00001B/158/P